AF600465

NOMADIC TEXT

INDIANA SERIES IN BIBLICAL LITERATURE

Herbert Marks, *editor*

NOMADIC TEXT

A Theory of Bibilical Reception History

BRENNAN W. BREED

INDIANA UNIVERSITY PRESS
Bloomington & Indianapolis

This book is a publication of

Indiana University Press
Office of Scholarly Publishing
Herman B Wells Library 350
1320 East 10th Street
Bloomington, Indiana 47405 USA

iupress.indiana.edu

Telephone 800-842-6796
Fax 812-855-7931

♾ The paper used in this publication meets the minimum requirements of the American National Standard for Information Sciences—Permanence of Paper for Printed Library Materials, ANSI Z39.48–1992.

Manufactured in the United States of America

Library of Congress Cataloging-in-Publication Data

Breed, Brennan W.
Nomadic text : a theory of biblical reception history / Brennan W. Breed.
pages cm. — (Indiana studies in biblical literature)
Includes bibliographical references and index.
ISBN 978-0-253-01252-4 (cl : alk. paper) — ISBN 978-0-253-01262-3 (eb)
1. Bible—Criticism, interpretation, etc. 2. Bible—Hermeneutics.
3. Bible. Job—Criticism, interpretation, etc. I. Title.
BS511.3.B74 2014
220.601—dc23
2013046356

1 2 3 4 5 19 18 17 16 15 14

For Catherine

Spinoza offers philosophers a new model: the body. He proposes to establish the body as a model: "We do not know what the body can do . . ." This declaration of ignorance is a provocation. We speak of consciousness and its decrees, of the will and its effects, of the thousand ways of moving the body, of dominating the body and the passions—but *we do not even know what a body can do.* Lacking this knowledge, we engage in idle talk. As Nietzsche will say, we stand amazed before consciousness, but "the truly surprising thing is rather the body . . ."

—Gilles Deleuze, *Spinoza: Practical Philosophy*

CONTENTS

Acknowledgments ix
List of Abbreviations xi

Introduction: The Constitutive Divide of Reception History 1

1. The Miltonesque Concept of the Original Text 15

2. Living in Pottersville: An Alternate Approach to Textual Criticism 52

3. Anchor or Spandrel: The Concept of the Original Context 75

4. On Tigers and Cages: Rethinking Context 93

5. Mapping the Garden of Forking Paths: A Nomadic Reception History 116

6. Justice, Survival, Presence: Job 19:25–27 142

7. Trajectories of Job 19:25–27: The Example of Survival 163

Conclusion: Nomadology and the Future of Biblical Studies 202

Notes 207
Bibliography 247
Index 275

ACKNOWLEDGMENTS

Writing this book has been an equally joyful and terrifying process. At the outset of such a task, it would have been impossible to imagine how much help I would require in order to finish it. Now, looking back on its completion, I am struck by how difficult it is to name all those who have contributed to it along the way. Perhaps, as one does in making a sacrifice to an "unknown god," I can say "thank you" here to all those whom I have forgotten to include. Let me know I forgot to mention you, and I'll offer you a libation sometime.

First and foremost, I extend my heartfelt thanks—and, at the same time, and for many of the same reasons, my sincere apologies—to Catherine. While I was writing this book, Catherine brought home the bacon and brought our children, Frederick and Margaret Ann, into being. And she not only put up with the demands of this project: without her constant encouragement, unflagging optimism, and seemingly endless reserves of patience and energy, this would never have been possible. Catherine, I dedicate this work to you.

I am forever indebted to the constant support of my parents, Mary and Jerome Breed, whose emphasis on education and hard work in my youth—which may not have seemed to take hold at the time—has helped me to achieve my goals. Hopefully, this is proof that old dogs can learn some of those old tricks that you began trying to teach them when they were young pups even if it would have been better to have learned them years ago. Well, at least I got some of them at some point.

I thank all of the formative pedagogues that I have been fortunate enough to encounter over the years, including Beverly Gilbert, the late Stephen Innes, and Richard Drayton. At Princeton Theological Seminary, the hospitality and generosity of Patrick Miller, Dennis Olson, Jacqueline Lapsley, Chip Dobbs-Allsopp, Jeremy Hutton, and Jeremy Schipper gave me the confidence and the skills to aim for excellence in my work. And, above all, to Choon-Leong Seow. I cannot possibly begin to enunciate my gratefulness.

I thank also the many colleagues whose conversations and critiques have contributed to the shape of this book. Most of all, I am grateful for Brent Strawn, David Petersen, John Hayes, Martin Buss, William Gilders, Jacob Wright, and Joel LeMon, who have put much time and effort into sharpening my often blunt thoughts. I am also grateful for Walter Melion, Elizabeth Pastan, Herbert Kessler, and Geoffrey Bennington, who helped me to find my way in the fields of Art History and Literary Theory. Without their help, my work would be quite shallow. Any depth in this book is attributable to their influence.

I owe much to the generosity of the Woodrow Wilson Foundation, whose fellowship funded the completion of this manuscript. I hope that my work may contribute to the goal of the Newcombe Fellowship by furthering the study of ethical and religious values.

I am also very grateful to Columbia Theological Seminary, and in particular Steve Hayner and Deborah Mullen, for their hospitality, as they offered me a place in their community to finish this project. I would also like to thank my colleagues, particularly Christine Roy Yoder and Bill Brown, for their warm collegiality and endless reserves of patience.

Of course, this book would not exist were it not for the work of Dee Mortensen, Herbert Marks, and Sarah Jacobi at Indiana University Press. Thank you for your help throughout this process. And to those who have offered their comments and corrections at various points in this manuscript's trajectory, including M. J. Devaney, Scott C. Jones, Mark Brummitt, Matthew Lynch, Josey Snyder, R. C. Griffin, and Aubrey Buster: many thanks for your contributions to both style and content.

Finally, I owe an enormous debt to Carol Newsom, who believed in this project even before I did. Like one presiding over an ancient Near Eastern creation scene, Carol brought form out of a seemingly bottomless sea of scholarly chaos. I began this project with a 157-page "chapter" sans thesis statement or conclusion. It took some serious chops to know even where to begin with that mess. But her graciousness and wisdom were great enough to overcome even those formidable odds. And then some.

And as a supplemental postscript to the acknowledgments, because as he knows, there is nothing more central than an exception, perhaps no one has helped more, in terms of my intellectual development as well as the writing and editing process of this book, than C. Davis Hankins, whose name occurs now and again throughout it. We wrote together for about a year, cramped in a long, skinny office in the icy bowels of the library, sitting next to each other on the same side of a table. It was like an academic summer camp, complete with camping-quality food, camping-like physical contests, and camping-level banter. I am very glad that I do not have to say nostalgically that I wish those bygone days would return. Instead, I say: it's time to gear up for the next book, Davis. Let's go find us a long table.

LIST OF ABBREVIATIONS

AB	Anchor Bible
BBC	Blackwell Bible Commentaries
BETL	Bibliotheca ephemeridum theologicarum lovaniensium
BHS	*Biblia hebraica stuttgartensia*. Edited by Karl Elliger and Wilhelm Rudolph. Stuttgart: Deutsche Bibelgesellschaft, 1983.
BHQ	*Biblia hebraica quinta*. Edited by Adrian Schenker et al. Stuttgart: Deutsche Bibelgesellschaft, 2004–.
CIL	*Corpus inscriptionum latinarum*
CLE	*Carmina latina epigraphica*
CSCO	Corpus scriptorum christianorum orientalium. Edited by I. B. Chabot et al. Paris: Reipublicae, 1903–.
DJD	Discoveries in the Judaean Desert
GCS	Die griechische christliche Schriftsteller der ersten [drei] Jahrhunderte
HUB	Hebrew University Bible Project
ILCV	*Inscriptiones latinae christianae veteres*. Edited by Ernst Diehl. 2nd ed. Berlin: Weidmann, 1961.
JSOT	SupJournal for the Study of the Old Testament Supplement Series
KTU	*Die keilalphabetischen Texte aus Ugarit*. Edited by Manfried Dietrich, Oswald Loretz, and Joaquín Sanmartín. Neukirchen-Vluyn: Neukirchener, 1976.
LXX	Septuagint
MT	Masoretic text
NETS	New English Translation of the Septuagint
NJB	New Jerusalem Bible
NPNFSS	*A Select Library of Nicene and Post-Nicene Fathers of the Christian Church, Second Series*. 14 vols. Edited by Philip Schaff and Henry Wace. Edinburgh: Clark, 1890–1900.
NRSV	New Revised Standard Version
OG	Old Greek
OHB	Oxford Hebrew Bible Project
Pesh	Syriac Peshitta
PG	*Patrologia graeca*. 162 vols. Edited by J.-P. Migne. Paris: Garnier, 1857–86.

PL	*Patrologia latina*. 217 vols. Edited by J.-P. Migne. Paris: Garnier, 1844–64.
PO	*Patrologia orientalis*. 40 vols. Edited by François Nau and René Graffin. Paris: Librarie de Paris, Firmin-Didot, 1903–.
SamPent	Samaritan Pentateuch
SC	Sources chrétiennes. Paris, Cerf: 1943–.
STDJ	Studies on the Texts of the Judaean Desert
VTS	Supplements to Vetus Testamentum
WBC	Word Biblical Commentary

NOMADIC TEXT

INTRODUCTION

The Constitutive Divide of Reception History

> You begin by saying, that when, in my discussion with our friend Bassus, I used the Scripture which contains the prophecy of Daniel when yet a young man in the affair of Susanna, I did this as if it had escaped me that this part of the book was spurious. . . . [C]onsider whether it would not be well to remember the words, "You shall not remove the ancient landmarks which your fathers have set."
>
> —Origen

> I guess I'm supposed to say that I believe in the line that exists between the US and Canada, but for me it's an imaginary line. It's a line from someone else's imagination; it's not my imagination. It divided people like the Mohawk into Canadian Mohawks and US Mohawks. They're the same people. It divided the Blackfoot who live in Browning from the Blackfoot who live at Standoff, for example. So the line is a political line, that border line. It wasn't there before the Europeans came.
>
> —Thomas King

Introduction to the Introduction: Where to Begin?

This book begins here, as many books do, with a sketch of the contours of my general argument. I attempt to delimit its borders and situate it within the context of recent scholarship. Immediately, a problem arises: this book is concerned with the concept of borders. In particular, it challenges the ways in which borders function throughout critical biblical studies. Perhaps the best way to begin is to sketch this border problem itself.

Initially, I imagined this project as a study of the reception history of a particular passage from the biblical book of Job. But from the very start the question of where to begin the study proved troublesome. Following in the footsteps of most reception-historical studies of biblical texts, I could have opened with a chapter titled "Job in Early Jewish and Christian Interpretation," thus bypassing the problem of the border by starting after the close of the presumed original "biblical" period. Or perhaps I could have opened with a chapter titled "Job in the Septuagint," which would have implied that the proto-MT book of Job was "the real book of Job" and that questions about composition, redaction, and textual pluriformity ought to be left to biblical criticism.[1]

Yet I became uneasy with these possible approaches because the convoluted processes of biblical composition and redaction and the resulting textual and semantic pluriformity seemed to be qualitatively indistinguishable from the reception of biblical texts. That is, biblical texts seem to overrun borders as a matter of course. And, conversely, texts generally called "the reception of the book of Job," such as the Septuagint, Theodotion, the Targums and the Peshitta, seemed to actually be part of the book of Job. Or at least they functioned as the book of Job for many of its readers. Labeling these texts exclusively as receptions seems a bit misleading. Of course they are receptions, too—but so is the Masoretic text of the book of Job, as it seems the story of Job predates any written version of the tale.[2] The oldest imaginable Hebrew text of the story of Job is simultaneously a reception as well as an original.

Since biblical texts appear on both sides of the borderline between original and reception, I began to wonder about the line itself. Often, common-sense acceptance of this line functions as a natural starting point for scholarly studies in reception history. In order to keep things orderly, biblical scholars take turns volunteering for the border patrol. But many questions remain unasked. What belongs in the original text or its original context, and what gets turned away at the border? Who has the authority to draw these borders, and who minds the checkpoints? Are texts on one side of the divide truly different from texts on the other side? If so, how do we measure this difference? Though the issue of borderlines may seem marginal, borders take on quite a central role in the constitution and maintenance of any identity, including the identity of a text or a field of scholarly inquiry.

These questions encouraged me to outline a general theory of biblical reception, which is a very different sort of project than my initial proposal. The practical case study dealing with Job 19:25–27 has now shrunk to two chapters. In its current form, this book critiques the concept of the borderline that separates an "original text" or an "original context" from its "receptions" and in turn proposes a different manner of framing the practice of biblical reception history, one that, I argue, does more to clarify both text and reception.

As a result of these transformations, this project has become much more theoretical and much less practical. And yet is there anything quite as practical as knowing the point from which one should begin a task? And is there anything more theoretical than the assumed borderline between original and reception that would have provided the point of departure for my so-called practical research?

Mind the Gap?

Once a finished text leaves the pen of its author, or perhaps once a text moves beyond its original context, it enters into the world of reception history.[3] This is, at least, the foundational assumption that allows for the very study of reception history.

As James Barr claims, reception history is the "history of the effects of writings rather than [their] origins," and thus it focuses on the period "after they were composed, after they were finalized."[4] Without this separation between the original and its reception, there would be no such thing as biblical reception history. There would only be biblical criticism, which, in the words of John J. Collins, carries out the work of "placing the Bible in its historical context."[5] It is only by means of the distinction between the Bible's historical context and other historical contexts that biblical critics constitute manageable borders for their scholarly domain. Owing to its fundamental importance, however, this divide between original and reception has undergone little scrutiny within the growing field of biblical reception history.

For the sake of biblical reception history's rigor, it is imperative for biblical critics to take note of this constitutive boundary and discern its contours. For example, is the Septuagint a later reception or a version of the text itself? Is Bel and the Dragon a reception or an original text? Is the Noah story a biblical text or a later reception of the original Mesopotamian flood myth? The answers to these questions simultaneously define the fields of biblical criticism and reception history.

In many reception-historical studies, one finds the constitutive divide between textual production and reception either simply posited or merely implied. This general assumption appears quite clearly in the major reception-historical efforts underway. Perhaps most importantly, the series preface of the Blackwell Bible Commentary series, which describes itself as the first commentary series to focus primarily on reception history of biblical texts, claims that the series "is based upon the premise that how people have interpreted, and been influenced by, a sacred text like the Bible is often as interesting and historically important as what it originally meant."[6] This statement presupposes a clear distinction between the text's original meaning in its original context and its later meanings in later contexts. While the series challenges the dominance of the original text and its original meaning within biblical studies, it accepts the premise that they exist. But what allows one to separate originals from later meanings, regardless of the two categories' relative importance?[7]

The Encyclopedia of the Bible and Its Reception, another scholarly reception-historical series currently underway, defines its work in much the same way as the BBC: "The Encyclopedia of the Bible and Its Reception (EBR) pursues the twofold task of (1) comprehensively recording—and, indeed, advancing—the current knowledge of the origins and development of the Bible in its Jewish and Christian canonical forms and (2) documenting the history of the Bible's reception in Judaism and Christianity as evident in exegetical literature, theological and philosophical writings of various genres, literature, liturgy, music, the visual arts, dance, and film, as well as in Islam and other religious traditions and contemporary movements."[8] Thus, the series divides its data into two categories, namely, the context that produced and canonized the biblical texts and the readings and transformations of biblical texts within other contexts, presumably after their canonization. Likewise, Choon-Leong Seow, one of the editors of the series, calls his approach "the 'history of consequences,' using 'consequences' to connote *what comes after* (as in the history of interpretation and reception) as well as *impact* and *effects*."[9] Yet how can we tell what came after something if we do not know where that something ends?

Often scholars at home in the worlds of philosophy and literary theory also assume but do not examine this constitutive divide. For example, in her monograph exploring the literary *Nachleben,* or afterlife, of the book of Jonah, Yvonne Sherwood begins with the history of Christian interpretation of Jonah.[10] Her title, *A Biblical Text and Its Afterlives,* adumbrates the divide running underneath her work, as the biblical text is separated from its afterlives by means of the conjunction "and."

Sherwood's use of the term "Nachleben" derives from the work of Walter Benjamin and, after him, Jacques Derrida, and has caught on especially among scholars familiar with poststructuralist theory.[11] Though Benjamin and Derrida primarily use this term (and with it "Überleben," "Fortleben," and "survie") to complicate the borderline between originals and reception, this aspect of Benjamin and Derrida's thought does not seem to have complicated the borderline for many biblical scholars.[12] For example, David Gunn begins his study of the reception history of the book of Judges with a section titled "Early Christian and Jewish Interpreters," without justifying why *this* is the place to begin.[13]

Perhaps the explanatory lack derives in part from the basic, yet problematic, distinctions that created and continue to sustain the field of biblical criticism. The foundational gesture of modern biblical criticism seems to be the assertion that scholars should read the original version of biblical texts within the cultural, political, literary, theological, and semantic boundaries provided by its original context. Since assumedly unoriginal versions and meanings of the Bible have exerted such a powerful and complicated influence over the history of biblical interpretation in general, modern biblical scholars have understandably focused much of their attention on differentiating original texts and meanings from those that came later and in turn analyzing in more detail the original context and content.

This method has helped biblical scholars and sections of the public at large to understand that many of a given biblical text's most influential meanings were not likely to have existed in the ancient world. For example, the narrative of original sin would have been nearly incomprehensible to ancient Israelites; a Second Temple–period Jew read Genesis 1–3 in a very different light than Augustine.[14] What this discovery about how Genesis was understood by ancient Israelites has exposed is that texts have meant many different things throughout history, and one can attempt to recover many of these meanings—including potential meanings of biblical texts in ancient Israel. Following this discovery, many scholars have assumed that the meanings of biblical texts within the reconstructed context of ancient Israel are qualitatively different from the meanings of biblical texts within every other context, from Greco-Roman Palestine to the present. But the discovery of alternative perspectives does not necessarily presume a natural hierarchy of perspectives. Such hierarchies are never simply found. They are fabricated.

Yet most biblical scholars do not challenge the boundaries set by modern biblical studies. Scholars working in reception history generally shift the emphasis from one side of the divide—the original—to the other—the reception. This problem with boundaries can be seen in some of the most ubiquitous metaphors for biblical criticism. Luke Timothy Johnson, for example, remarks that "biblical scholars in the future will probably find the examination of the world that the New Testament creates more fruitful than the study of the world that created the New Testament."[15] In order to differentiate between the original and its reception, Johnson here uses the familiar trope of separate "worlds." Deriving from the work of Paul Ricoeur, this model of biblical criticism envisions a tripartite schema: the world behind the text, the world in the text, and the world in front of the text.[16] In this model, the "world behind the text" refers to the context of the text's production and can be addressed through the work of so-called historical criticism. The "world in the text" refers to the text itself, which can be taken up through formalist close readings and rhetorical criticism, otherwise known as synchronic or literary readings. The "world in front of the text" refers to the later contexts wherein the text was received and can be explored through the work of reception history, reader-response criticism, and other situated readings.

Terry Eagleton has used Ricoeur's model to periodize the history of modern literary theory, and it could serve as a rough guide to biblical scholarship as well, demonstrating as it does "a preoccupation with the author (Romanticism and the nineteenth century); an exclusive concern with the text (New Criticism);

and a marked shift of attention to the reader over recent years."[17] This popular schema emerges from a series of simple distinctions, or constitutive boundaries, between author, text, and reader. Such an articulation of the elements involved in biblical criticism has immediately apparent value: for example, recognizing that the modern reader inhabits a situation quite different from that presumed by the text at hand can allow for a reconceptualization of a text as it would have functioned in another context.

Yet while these distinctions allow for the coherence of much of contemporary biblical scholarship, they also distort the fields indexed by the tripartite schema. When biblical critics talk about the text itself as something distinguishable from the world in front of the text, they obscure the complicated zones—that is, the borderlines—in between these worlds. What do we look at when we look at the text itself? The *Biblia hebraica stuttgartensia,* the most commonly used critical edition of the Hebrew Bible, is a modern scholarly edition of a medieval manuscript with late antique vowels, written in an anachronistic script and surrounded by diachronous layers of paratextual symbols. How can biblical scholars talk about something so historically sedimented as if it belongs to a world all by itself (i.e., the "world of the text")? Clearly, several worlds other than the text itself, such as the Masoretic scribes and modern scholars, mediate the text and supply the conditions by which the text appears to us. So, what is the "text itself" if not a complicated mix of things behind and in front of the text?

For that matter, how will we read this text itself? First, we will have to master the rules of classical biblical Hebrew and use a dictionary. Our only access to any text itself is mediated not only by the worlds in front of the text that devised grammars and lexica but also by the worlds behind the text—such as other ancient Semitic languages—that the modern grammarians and lexicographers study in order to create the means by which to read the text (now not all by) itself. And whatever the text itself *is,* it must include just enough of the world in front of the text to let the reader in, however minimally. As for the world behind the text, we encounter it through the texts themselves and modern scholarly research, which we only know by means of previous work on the world behind the text from those already in front of it. So, what *is* the world behind the text if not for a complicated mix of things in and in front of the text?

Thus when we look closely at these constitutive boundaries, instead of three nicely delineated worlds we find infinitely regressive mutual dependencies. Yet abandoning these distinctions might result in a collapse of the modern form of biblical criticism, since it relies so heavily on the differentiation of a reader's context from the context in which the text was produced. In the absence of these distinctions, one might read whatever one likes into whatever text one happens to read, which is commonly disparaged as the practice of "eisegesis."

Though this state of affairs might delight some reader-response critics, it would by and large erase many of the fascinating and quite convincing achievements of modern biblical criticism, the most important of which is the discovery of the complicated history of the biblical text's composition and development.[18] But should not the field of biblical studies, which is rightfully proud of its commitment to the truth no matter where it leads, take an unflinching look at these problematic borderlines on which its identity depends?

Indeed, in the wake of the surprising discoveries at Qumran there has been more scrutiny of the borderline region, if not the concept of the border itself. As John Choi points out, much recent work in Pentateuchal studies attempts to locate the moment of transition wherein the Torah qua Mosaic law emerged. This moment, then, might constitute a boundary between composition and reception of the Pentateuch.[19] As Choi notes, "With regard to the Hebrew Bible, studies of reception history have generally focused on the history of interpretation of a given text within Jewish or Christian contexts. The present study, however, will take a slightly different path through a focus on the inner-biblical reception history of the Pentateuch."[20] Yet even Choi, whose work brings him close to this border, continues to define reception history as merely "the manner in which a certain text was regarded by later authors and readers. . . . Rather than examining the cultural and sociological factors that inform text composition, reception-historical studies focus on the aftermath of composition and promulgation."[21] But where is the line between the "math" and the aftermath—that is, between composition and promulgation? Do we only have receptions of the later ways in which the Pentateuch was regarded by later readers, or is it possible that the border had not yet been drawn? How would we know, in either event?

Many biblical scholars interested in both reception history and historical-critical approaches resolve this tension by positing the border as a solution to its own problem. For example, like Choi, James Kugel distinguishes between a "biblical period" and a period of "the rise of the ancient interpreters" without much discussing what would distinguish the reading of, say, Jeremiah in Daniel 9 from the reading of Habakkuk in Pesher Habakkuk.[22] Among biblical scholars interested in questions of inner-biblical interpretation, as well as scholars of literature of the late Second Temple period, one can find a sensitivity to the issue of the border between original and reception. The debate concerning the phrase "rewritten Bible" is a function of this very issue.[23] Yet aside from the "final form" provided by canonical criticism, the original text of some text critics, or the fiat authority of particular authors or readers, what are other possible definitions of the borderline?

Perhaps the difficulties with borders derive from the fact that, in general, biblical scholars working with reception history have shown mild disinterest in the details of theories of reception. A clear index of this situation may be found in remarks made by Christopher Rowland, the lead editor of the BBC series. In a paper titled "A Pragmatic Approach to *Wirkungsgeschichte,*" Rowland explains his lack of interest in methodological discussion: "The inspiration for the BBC series did not come from immersion in the theoretical literature on reception history, most of which I have not found too helpful in the task on which I have set out. Instead of beginning from a particular hermeneutical theory the series focuses on the task of exploring some of the many and various effects of biblical books."[24] While Rowland's invaluable contributions to the field of reception history are beyond question, his decision to eschew theory in favor of a "pragmatic" approach is, I think, unfortunate.

Though I agree with Rowland that current theories of reception could be more helpful, the BBC series could have been consciously used to think through, propose, and revise methodologies for reception history. If we bypass the question of theory, we then must rely on unanalyzed (and probably unhelpful) methodological assumptions. This attitude is not unique to biblical studies: as Charles Martindale laments, "Few have attempted, within classics, to theorize reception, or explore how such studies should best be pursued; indeed reception has been largely turned back into a form of positivist history, often of a rather amateurish kind."[25] "Amateurish" may be a bit harsh, but as Rachel Nicholls points out, many studies of reception history do amount to a "scrapbook of effects" that juxtapose readings emerging from contexts later than the Second Temple period.[26] In many ways, the scrapbook method reflects a lack of interest in reflecting on the practices of selecting, organizing, and comparing the various interpretations. One always employs a theory: that is, a way of organizing by means of a scheme. Even a scrapbook is a scheme, though uncritical and usually unhelpful for any purpose beyond creating the effect of sentimentality.

Yet one cannot blame this problem solely on biblical scholars—the problem seems to be much broader. Even seasoned philosophers and theorists seem confused and have hedged on the problem of the constitutive divide. For example, neither Hans-Georg Gadamer, the author of *Truth and Method* and popularizer of the term "Wirkungsgeschichte," or "history of effects," nor Hans-Robert Jauss, who is responsible for the term "Rezeptionsgeschichte," or "reception history," offer clear guidelines concerning the delineation of the original text or context.[27]

In *Truth and Method,* Gadamer does not argue against the claim that recovering the author's intention is the goal of the hermeneutical project.[28] Yet neither does he want to assert that the text itself is entirely constructed by each interpretive community.[29] On one hand, Gadamer's insistence on contemporary relevance keeps him from locating truth in the past; on the other hand, his interest in the "truth of tradition" and the "voices of the past" keep him from positing total discontinuity between the contemporary relevant meaning of the text and the past meanings of the text.[30] Thus Gadamer sits quite close to many biblical scholars, but he is in no less of a dilemma. Gadamer needs a strong border to separate contexts so that they can fuse in dialogue, but simultaneously he needs a weak border so that both texts and readers can traverse it. Gadamer confronts this dilemma only indirectly in various brief passages of *Truth and Method* and sometimes addresses it with contradictory statements.[31]

In order to maintain this tension, Gadamer proposes that in the act of reading there exist two horizons, one of the reader, and one of the "historical horizon from which the traditionary text speaks."[32] The divide between the (original) past and the present is in fact necessary to proper interpretation: "Temporal distance . . . lets the true meaning of the object emerge fully" because "the true meaning has filtered out of it all kinds of things that obscure it."[33] Gadamer argues that the task of reading involves staging a dialogue between the two horizons, thereby creating a "fusion of horizons" that in turn produces "understanding."[34] This generates a "tension . . . in the play between the traditionary text's strangeness and familiarity to us, between being a historically intended, distanciated object and belonging to a tradition. The true locus of hermeneutics is this in-between."[35] Thus Gadamer posits that reading occurs "in-between" the poles of "original context" and "reader's context"—in other words, at the borderline between original and reception.

Yet Gadamer issues a series of conflicting judgments that complicate this picture. To begin, Gadamer argues that reconstructing the original author and audience is impossible and thus worthless but then claims that there can be no clear distinction between the original audience and the succeeding audiences.[36] Are all audiences equally worthless? Why should we construct our own horizon then, and the horizon of the text, if these cannot be differentiated from the original context?

Gadamer also argues that one cannot fully objectify the past, as the subject cannot be rid of its own historicity, while simultaneously maintaining that the original text is rather like a speaking subject, thus casting hermeneutical investigation as a dialogue.[37] Yet how is one supposed to dialogue with an object that cannot be objectified enough to be separated from oneself? Moreover, the interpreter cannot treat the text as an object, because the text directly addresses her as an interlocutor.[38] Thus the interpreter waits for the "thing itself—the meaning of the text—to assert itself."[39] But how can the meaning assert itself if we cannot distance ourselves from it? Gadamer seems to desire both diametric dialectical tension and total continuity, but in the end he seems to collapse history into continuity: "Are there really two different horizons here—the horizon in which the person seeking to understand lives and the historical horizon within which he places himself? . . . [T]hey together constitute the one great horizon that moves from within and that, beyond the frontiers of the present, embraces the historical depths of our self-consciousness. Everything contained in historical consciousness is in fact embraced by a single historical horizon."[40]

Thus, there is no border between original and reception, and thus there is no reception. There is only the original context, the "context itself" of the "one great horizon." Yet Gadamer then attempts to retain the concept of a fusion of horizons, which requires an initial separation between original and reception:

> Every encounter with tradition . . . involves the experience of a tension between the text and the present. The hermeneutic task consists in not covering up this tension by attempting a naive assimilation of the two but in consciously bringing it out. This is why it is part of the hermeneutic approach to project a historical horizon that is different from the horizon of the present. Historical consciousness is aware of its own otherness and hence foregrounds the horizon of the past from its own. On the other hand, it is itself, as we are trying to show, only something superimposed upon continuing tradition, and hence it immediately recombines with what it has foregrounded itself from in order to become one with itself again in the unity of the historical horizon that it thus acquires.[41]

These remarks present a paradox. Gadamer posits a tension between the original context and the reader's context, but he also argues that this tension is "only something superimposed" on an actual underlying unity, and thus this false separation "immediately recombines" in "unity." One must ask: is the constitutive divide only ever false, a duplicitously artificial superimposition on a naturally continuous, unified plane? Or is it a natural division between two elements held in tension that can be overcome by the fusion of dialogic reading, forever eliminating the gap? Gadamer offers no particular means of resolving his own internal difference, and thus his theory claims an ultimate unity that stubbornly resists its own unification.

Hans-Robert Jauss relies on Gadamer's image of "horizons," thus setting in dialogue the "original horizon of the past" with the reader's "horizon of expectations."[42] Yet while Jauss follows Gadamer's lead in retaining the text as something other than the readers and simultaneously as "always already enveloped within the horizon of the present," he then paradoxically asserts the "objectifiable" nature of the "horizon of expectations" that constitutes a set of "literary data."[43] If historians and literary scholars can bracket their own situation and objectively reconstruct the horizon of expectations for a particular audience, then why does Jauss posit a seamless continuity of history that disallows the concept of an original meaning? And if formal elements are "objectively present" in both the audience and the work, then why must Jauss continue to assert that the past is enveloped and constituted by the present?

Perhaps the border between original and reception remains troublesome because borders are simply troublesome things. Borders separate, or clarify, or demarcate an inside from an outside: in this way, distinctions—and thus boundaries—are necessary for the possibility of thought to exist. One could not even gesture toward anything if it were not in some way distinguished from its surroundings.[44] But the distinction itself seems part neither of the thing distinguished nor its background. As C. S. Peirce puts the question:

> A drop of ink has fallen upon the paper and I have walled it round. Now every point of the area within the walls is either black or white; and no point is both black and white. That is plain. The black is, however, all in one spot or blot; it is within bounds. There is a line of demarcation between the black and the white. Now I ask about the points of this line, are they black or white? Why one more than the other? Are they (A) both black and white or (B) neither black nor white? Why A more than B, or B more than A? It is certainly true, First, that every point of the area is either black or white, Second, that no point is both black and white, Third, that the points of the boundary are no more white than black, and no more black than white. The logical conclusion from these three propositions is that the points of the boundary do not exist.[45]

The boundary, Pierce concludes, does not exist. It is neither black nor white. It is fictitious but also necessary to the existence of both the white and the black area.

So is a border a real thing, or is it purely imaginary? Does the border belong to one or both of the elements that it separates? Are borders sharp, or vague? Do they have substance or are they one dimensional? To what degree are they permeable, and at what point does permeability render a border worthless as a border? If borders create conceptual territories that allow for the very activity of thought, does the collapse of the border necessitate a collapse in thought?

As a preliminary response to these questions, I offer the epigraph to this introduction. Thomas King, an author and advocate for Native American peoples, points out that the line dividing the United States from Canada is both imaginary and real. It is imaginary because it was thought up by human beings and imposed in the form of an unnatural straight line. Yet it is quite real in the sense that it severed communities of people and imposed political, physical, and economic differences. King points out that contingent historical events led to the line separating the Blackfoot in Browning and the Blackfoot in Standoff. There were, of course, other, perhaps more fluid boundary lines that were created before the Europeans to divide the Blackfoot Confederacy from other peoples. Borderlines even run through the Blackfoot Mountains themselves, dividing the four Blackfoot nations—the Piegan, Siksika, Northern Piegan and Kainai. Borders must exist for there to be anything identifiable at all, but those same borders are always historically and logically contingent. No borderline has to be exactly where it is.

Borderlines are transient, and always open to change. They are not necessary, natural, or original. There is no objective moral hierarchy that organizes the objects divided by such lines. They were formed by quirks of history and are always in the process of being reformed, albeit sometimes at glacial paces. A glance at a political map of the world from a mere one thousand years ago is enough to see that even the most seemingly natural and necessary border lines are but emergent properties of always transforming social processes. A glance at a physical map of the world from a mere 250 million years ago—a meager amount of time in the scale of the universe—shows that even the illusion of rock solid boundaries between Asia and the Americas hides the true nature of the earth. We think we are seeing a stable identity when we look at "the Americas," but in fact we are looking at a snapshot of a changing process. Change is a central part of the identity of the earth's land mass.

In many ways, the border between an original text and its reception is similar to the imposition of a border between two modern nation-states or the production of a physical border between continents. An ocean separating two landmasses may not be a cultural construct, but nevertheless it is produced. A physical distinction emerges at a particular moment in time as a result of particular material forces. It is a construct, and as such it is historically contingent, unoriginal, and carries with it no natural moral authority. The biblical literature is itself a changing process. It was built up over a lengthy span of time and continued to develop and transform until well after any supposedly "original" period. In the form of translations, critical editions, and innovative readings, it continues to change still.

Yet if we are to study texts, then we have no choice but to make and remake these sorts of distinctions. When one chooses to read a particular form of a text in reference to a particular historical context, one chooses to draw the lines in a particular way. By choosing to read the *BHS* version of the book of Amos with reference to eighth-century BCE Israelite language, culture and history, for example, one creates a particular bounded space within which the text has a certain potential to mean. Yet part of Amos was written much later, and thus one could read it in reference to its sixth-century Judean redactors. Which context is the right one? If I am correct that biblical texts are processes, then this question is absurd. Is the current position of the Americas correct, or should they be several hundred miles to the east, as they were many years ago? Attempting to judge the long process of the composition of a biblical text is, in my opinion, similar to an attempt to judge the long process of the formation of a landmass. Both are simple material facts, and one of the various stages in their long developmental histories are not naturally better or worse, or any more original or corrupt, than any other stage.

This state of affairs requires scholars to admit the contingency of their distinctions even while boldly making them. Some distinctions are more helpful or more defensible than others, to be sure. And borders disturb elements more or less violently, such as the borderlines that displace Native American groups. We can judge borderlines by means of many different metrics. But in the end, all of them are lines that were not there before the scholars came.

With regards to biblical studies, this book argues that the phrase "the original text" actually means "the text I have chosen to study for various contingent reasons." Likewise, the phrase "the original context" is another way to say "the environment to which my study of this text will refer." Though this may smack of nihilism, it by no means discounts the reality and force of these distinctions. These boundaries may not exist in a certain sense, but they certainly do create effects. And biblical scholars can revolutionize the field by admitting that we are drawing lines. More importantly, we can draw these lines in many different ways in order to explore the potential effects that a given text may create. We must pay attention to how we draw lines, how we justify them, and what these lines do to texts, to people, and to our constructions of history. So, let us mind the gap.

Moving on from the Border

With this frame in place, recall my initial statement: once a finished text leaves the pen of its author, or perhaps once a text moves beyond its original context, it enters into the world of reception history. One of the implications of this assertion is that the original context can be at least minimally distinguished from previous contexts or later contexts, and a second implication is that there is an identifiable text that moves between these contexts.

If we are to examine the nature of this divide, we must produce a definition of what constitutes the essence of the original and supply a reasonably reliable determination of the moment at which this original essence changes into something different. We can then also discern what criteria should adjudicate the placement of the boundary. In the chapters that follow, I attempt to analyze the divide as rigorously as possible. I analyze programmatic statements from respected textual critics and higher critics that articulate the identities of the original text and the original context.

Scholars have somewhat different ways of determining the identity of the original and, in turn, the secondary. Textual critics foreground the change in physical text through acts of editing, miscopying, or other forms of physical alteration from the original as the moment of the structural divide. Some literary-minded critics may foreground a particular change in sociopolitical structures (for example, the Persian period, or the advent of hellenization, or perhaps the destruction of the Second Temple) as the boundary of the original context, since the shift would establish a different set of reading and writing practices from those in place at the time of a biblical text's composition, which would necessarily alter a general reader's understanding of a text's meaning.[46] Both the text critic and the historicist literary critic, in these examples, would understand their methodological orientations as tools designed to overcome the constitutive divide and rediscover the material or ideal elements missing in later contexts that allow for a recovery of the original. Most every biblical scholar plays both of these roles at times, since the ultimate goal of so-called lower criticism is to locate the original text among the debris of history, while the goal of so-called higher criticism is to place this original text back in its original context, thus allowing for an interpretation that is consonant with its original meaning. Most methodologies used within biblical studies—textual criticism, source criticism, redaction criticism, form, social-scientific, and so forth—are designed for these specific purposes.

As a starting point, one can schematize definitions of "the original" in biblical studies as follows:

(1) one may point to the original text, which may be differentiated from later (corrupt or otherwise altered) versions of the text;
(2) one may point to the original context, which is a reconstruction of particular elements of the social, political, ideological, linguistic, literary (and countless other) structures that were contemporaneous with the production of the text and function and that may serve as a hermeneutical key by which to decipher the potential limits of the text's original meaning, including the original author's intentions, or some roughly equivalent expression, as well as the original audience.

In what follows I take up these alternatives in turn. In the first part of the book, I analyze various definitions of the "original text" in textual criticism and then offer an alternate method of textual criticism that does not rely on the constitutive divide between original and reception. In the second part, I critique different ways of approaching the concept of the "original context," and then offer my own theory of historical contextualization. In the final part, I turn to the task of constructing my own theory of reception history and providing a sketch of my own practice.

ONE

The Miltonesque Concept of the Original Text

> Wyman's overpopulated universe is in many ways unlovely. It offends the aesthetic sense of us who have a taste for desert landscapes, but this is not the worst of it. Wyman's slum of possibles is a breeding ground for disorderly elements. . . . I feel we'd do better simply to clear Wyman's slum and be done with it.
>
> —W. V. O. Quine

> You know, I like to walk in the slums. I can breathe when I walk through the slums.
>
> —Jorge Luis Borges

Introduction: What is an Original Text?

According to many biblical scholars, biblical critics study original texts and contexts, while reception historians are responsible for studying later versions of texts and their meaning in later contexts.[1] The reception historian looks beyond the original text, while the traditional biblical scholar looks at the original text itself. Thus, in order to begin a thorough study of the later texts and contexts that constitute the field of reception history, one must know what the original is, where it begins, and where it ends.[2] Textual criticism is the field entrusted with discovering the original text of the Bible, so one might look to text critics to learn where, exactly, reception begins. However, the field of textual criticism has yet to give a definitive answer about what constitutes the original text, and in this chapter I argue that, ultimately, it never can. Yet textual criticism *can* offer the means to rethink the concept of reception history in a systematic manner.

Some recent biblical critics object to the language of origin, because the concept of the original text ignores the various source and redaction layers that one may analyze as parts of the history of a text's composition.[3] As John Barton claims, there are many origins in every biblical text, and thus there is a variety of possible original texts.[4] On the other hand, Emanuel Tov argues that the word "original" does not necessarily denote a moment of creation. Rather, Tov claims that "original" can signify a moment of "correctness" that stood at the end of a complicated history of production.[5] The object of textual criticism, according to Emanuel Tov, can thus be understood as that single text that stood at the beginning of the process of transmission. Tov adds that "those who claim that a certain reading is preferable to another actually presuppose one original text," since preference for any particular text as the right text—or even the somewhat more right text—assumes at least a moment of relative correctness that existed in the biblical text's history.[6] Preference for a particular reading over another is, in this way, tantamount to a belief in a text that at least functions as if it were an original text.

Other scholars object to the search for the original text because it sounds too similar to outmoded discussions of authorial autographs. Even B. B. Warfield hedged that there were biblical texts whose exact autographic wordings were not within "direct reach."[7] Thus, almost all textual critics use qualifiers that concede that their search cannot recover the presumably lost original manuscripts. Scholars who reject the notion of autograph entirely, since it implicitly denies a complicated and redactional composition history, distance their text-critical goal from a presumed original text by claiming to seek an archetype or hyparchetype. These terms are used to admit an epistemic humility, since only an ideal later version of the original text based on sometimes spotty data, not the original text itself, can be reconstructed.

For example, Ronald Hendel seeks what E. J. Kenny refers to as "earliest inferable textual state" of each extant edition of a given biblical text, such as the proto-MT and the proto-OG, both of which present different literary editions.[8] Hendel still holds that there was, at one point, an original text that was the basis of each subsequent edition, but the original texts are themselves on the whole unrecoverable. Thus the goal of Hendel's text-critical work is necessarily archetypes that are a "step toward the original text" but not the original text itself.[9] The concept of the original text thereby remains part of the schema, but it is rendered as an asymptotic ideal at a remove from the "actual" original, which may be approached, but never fully attained.

Despite these objections to the term "origin" on the grounds of either the diverse histories of composition of any biblical text or the necessarily limited modern scholarly abilities to locate precisely any pristine text form, the underlying concept of the original text still remains ensconced within biblical criticism. I seek to understand how textual criticism defines the separation it effects between the object of its study and the object of reception historical analysis, regardless of the particular terms used to do so. In order to focus the discussion of this chapter, I examine the work of several prominent text critics who are also in some way are responsible for major biblical text-critical projects: Emanuel Tov, Ronald Hendel, Moshe Goshen-Gottstein, and Eugene Ulrich. My hope is to critique what I see as unhelpful elements within their methodologies.

Telos and Authority

It is difficult to overstate Emanuel Tov's scholarly contributions to the field of textual criticism, as his prodigious learning and prolific output have forever enriched the biblical studies community. Tov has, among other things, served as the editor in chief of the Dead Sea Scrolls Publication Project, as an editor of the Hebrew University Bible (HUB), and as the managing editor of the HUB edition of Jeremiah. He has also written what is currently the most comprehensive and prominent introduction to textual criticism, *Textual Criticism of the Hebrew Bible*, which provides a conspicuous index of the broader field of textual criticism.[10] For this reason, I focus my critique on the conception of the original text presented in this book, though Tov has begun to question this approach in recent years.[11]

Since the discovery of the manuscript collections near Qumran, scholars have become keenly aware that the texts of the Hebrew Bible exhibited significant textual diversity several centuries before the common era.[12] Thus, various large-scale differences between the OG and the MT, for example, are not only due to translation divergences and sloppily transmitted manuscripts. Instead, it seems that the MT is a late, expanded form of several books, while the OG reflects some later versions as well as some Hebrew texts that likely indicate an earlier version of the text than the MT.[13] The manuscripts at Qumran also testify to the early existence of textual forms of biblical books that were later edited by the Samaritan community, from whence came the Samaritan Pentateuch, biblical texts written in a particularly late scribal mode, and biblical texts exhibiting variants heretofore unknown.[14] Tov labels the latter group "nonaligned" texts, since they do not agree with any previously known form of the biblical text. This hefty chunk of the biblical manuscripts found at Qumran do not form a coherent textual group but rather testify to a theoretically unlimited number of alternative text forms.[15] At least some of these variant editions date from a time before the developments that led to the proto-MT, and thus there was never a moment at which the proto-MT offered the only version of biblical texts.[16] In spite of Qumran's snapshot of irreducible textual pluriformity, however, Tov has generally argued in favor of the urtext theory of textual criticism, claiming that the proper objective of textual criticism is to locate the original text of the Bible.[17]

In light of the synchronic pluriformity discovered in the Qumran manuscripts and the diachronic diversity within each textual tradition, how might one argue that one manuscript of one textual tradition is naturally privileged as the original? Tov does so by relying on the concepts of telos and authority. Tov posits that one particular manuscript of the biblical text functioned briefly as both the telos of a long, complex process of textual production and as the origin of a long, complex history of transmission. Among the various versions that coexisted at all points in the Second Temple period, one was chosen as authoritative by a particular community at a particular point in time that, Tov claims, carries universal force.

According to Tov, textual criticism describes the "external conditions" and "procedure" of the text's transmission and evaluates the variants in order to discover which one was "most likely to have been contained in the original text," but it ignores "readings included in textual witnesses" that were produced "at an earlier stage, that of the literary growth of the biblical books."[18] At first glance, this logic seems unimpeachable: when faced with a group of medieval and ancient witnesses to an even more ancient text, the textual critic must discern the relationships between the manuscripts and evaluate which readings most closely represent the text that stands at the source of the tradition of transmission. With respect to the central task of text criticism, Tov thus consciously follows in the footsteps of Paul de Lagarde, who first proposed an overarching theory of the biblical urtext, or "original text."[19]

Tov defines the original text, the goal of his methodology, in the following manner: "At the end of the process of the composition of a biblical book stood a text which was considered authoritative (and hence also finished on the literary level), even if only by a limited group of people, and which at the same time stood at the beginning of a process of copying and textual transmission. . . . All the textual witnesses—except those that reflect an early literary stage of the book—developed from the final authoritative copy which it is the object of textual criticism to reconstruct."[20] Thus, Tov claims that the original text is both the text that began the process of transmission and the final text that was the capstone of the compositional process. This delineation of the textual process well describes modern compositional practices: an author composes a text by means of drafts and then subsequently the corrected text is published. But does this model account for the data in the case of biblical texts?

The Paradoxical Moment of Final Origin

Tov claims that the authoritative edition of each biblical text was the text that was both finished and deemed authoritative. How does one discern a point of completion from a stage along the path to completion, or even from a point of corruption?

Though he does not mention a precise date, Tov places the moment of textual originality/finality soon after the events of 70 CE: "Those who fostered [the MT] probably constituted the only organized group which survived the destruction of the Second Temple. Thus, after the first century CE a description of the transmission of the text of the Hebrew Bible actually amounts to an account of the history of M."[21] Tov claims that only one "organized group" that used biblical texts continued to exist post-70 CE and that this hegemony coincides with the relative textual stabilization of the proto-MT. But contrary to Tov's presumption, rabbinical adherents of the proto-MT were not the only organized group occupying the post-70 CE landscape. The Samaritan Pentateuch continued to be the base text for the Samaritans, and the variant editions presented by the OG became, at least for a time, the base text for Christians. The history of the transmission of the biblical text only amounts to a history of the MT if one does not mention the other forms of the text and their own authority-granting communities. Thus, Tov admits the existence of multiple literary editions of biblical texts but defines them as nonfinal and nonauthoritative. He defines the variant edition of Jeremiah presented by the proto-OG, for example, as an early literary stage, something premature that nevertheless continued to function as an authoritative text and be copied as such.

Yet Ulrich points to the telic problem underlying this argument and the entire vocabulary of "proto-MT" and "proto-OG": these two supposedly discernible groups of texts exhibit no global typological similarities and thus did not undergo any definitive recension before being admitted into various communities as sacred texts.[22] In other words, the "proto-MT" texts exhibit no common recensional traits, since some so-called proto-MT texts contain "midrashic expansions" (e.g., Jeremiah) and others are textually problematic (e.g. Samuel) relative to the versions that ended up being translated and used in the Greek Bible. Calling a text "proto-MT" only makes sense in retrospect, since these texts were not grouped together over against other editions; thus the names "proto-MT," "proto-OG" and "proto-Samaritan Pentateuch" treat an essentially contingent series of developments as if they were entirely necessary. Tov here claims that the essence of these texts, unbeknownst to the people who wrote and rewrote them, was only to be fulfilled in their future canonical actualization. In Armin Lange's words, this classificatory scheme is a "retro-projection."[23]

Moreover, Tov defines stages of the text's development that occur later than the MT as something else entirely: "Literary stages preceding the literary editions included in M are taken into consideration, but later ones are not. . . . Thus the recensionally different Hebrew texts behind various sections in G in 1 Kings (3 Reigns in G), Esther, and Daniel, in our mind all later than the edition of M, and probably reflecting late midrashic developments, need not be taken into consideration."[24] According to Tov, developments that occur before the final stage of the MT are thus considered "early literary stages" that precede the "final" form, while later alterations are considered "midrashic" and thus are in a different class from changes associated with the composition of the text itself. Again, Tov asserts a definition assuming an ontological difference—here literary versus midrashic—and then proceeds to argue for the distinction based on the definition.

Diachronic categories of "earlier" or "later" also prove difficult to sustain, since each textual form was used without interruption throughout the ancient world. For texts such as Jeremiah, which he admits paradoxically "reached a final status not just once, in M, but also previously," Tov seems to allow that the previous stage of Jeremiah reflected in the proto-OG was authoritative, at least for a particular community.[25] Yet how can OG Jeremiah be "previous" to MT Jeremiah, since both proto-OG Jeremiah and proto-MT Jeremiah coexist at Qumran, as in 4QJer[a,c,e] and 4QJer[b,d], and since later derivative editions of both continue to function as sacred scripture for different communities post-70 CE?[26] It would be more historically precise to claim that there was a multiplicity of textual forms circulating simultaneously at the earliest stages for which we have textual evidence.

Yet Tov is very clear that for him textual multiplicity does not reflect the original text: "If we had reconstructed a number of pristine texts constituting this multiplicity, we would have been laboring under a misconception, since they merely reflect a relatively late stage in the textual development of the Bible."[27] Again, Tov implicitly defines pristine texts as those texts that reflect the proto-MT. The period of time that marks the original text is not something determinate but rather is itself defined by means of exclusion: if something was written prior to the final text, it is a late stage of development. If it was written after the final text, then it is an early stage of midrash or an early corruption. Is this not circular logic?

From this paradoxical foundation, Tov distinguishes between authors-editors of the Hebrew Bible and copyists. While both categories of scribe alter the text, somewhere along the line these alterations shift from "redactions" or "literary developments" to "corruptions."[28] Yet that there was such an aporetic transition from author to copyist seems unlikely. Scribes performed both of these tasks regularly throughout the Second Temple period. More recent evidence from Qumran shows that in Second Temple Palestine "scribes and their predecessors were at work along two lines," as Ulrich claims, one being that of copying "as exactly as humanly possible," the other being that of "intentionally insert[ing] new material" at times.[29] The result of this process can be seen in the quite late harmonistic developments in 4QpaleoExod[m] as attested at Qumran, a text that was later altered further and declared authoritative by the Samaritan community.[30]

Manuscripts such as 4QpaleoExod[m] produce particularly thorny issues for any theory that presupposes an original text. Tov has wrestled with another manuscript, tentatively named 4QReworked Pentateuch, that similarly exhibits large-scale revisions, such as an expanded Song of Miriam.[31] Tov has noted the typological similarities between 4QReworked Pentateuch and 4QpaleoExod[m] and has concluded that since 4QpaleoExod^{m} should be considered an attestation of Exodus, 4QReworked Pentateuch must be reclassified as "4QPentateuch," following the arguments of Ulrich and Flint.[32]

At any given point in time along the development of any of the variously intertwined traditions of biblical text forms, there have been textual alterations that occurred prior to as well as subsequent to that point. Even outside the proto-Masoretic tradition, scribes continued to work in similar ways on either side of the presumed ontological divide: as Jeffrey Tigay has shown, the process of rewriting the Samaritan Pentateuch seems almost formally indistinguishable from the presumed compositional process of the Pentateuch in the early Second Temple period.[33] Scribes were always both copyists and authors, always changing and transmitting to various degrees.[34]

An example of the paradoxical telos in Tov's work can be found in his discussion of Jeremiah 9–10. As Tov himself has shown, Jeremiah exists in two major ancient versions, the proto-OG and the MT.[35] The proto-OG version is one-sixth shorter and contains sections that are ordered differently from those in the MT. It appears that, over time, the MT expanded and altered a text that was nearly identical to the proto-OG.

In Jeremiah 10, the MT has rearranged and added several verses to the proto-OG, as attested by 4QJer^{b,d}.[36] Proto-OG Jeremiah 10 contains, in order of the MT, verses 1–5a, 9, 5b, 11–12; it is missing what in the MT constitutes verses 6–8 and 10. What is more, in both 4QJer^{b} and the MT, verse 11 is written in Aramaic, not Hebrew. The verses present in the proto-OG have the uniform focus of deriding idol worship, while the verses absent in the proto-OG version share a different focus: namely, they "extol the Lord of Israel."[37] Verse 11, though present in both versions, seems to expand the critique of idol worship further than the rest of the proto-OG material, since it accuses the foreign gods of not cooperating in YHWH's creation of the world and declares that these foreign gods will "perish." These theological interests seem to be at odds with the rather less severe critique of idol worship in verses 1–5.

Most likely, a scribe added verse 11 in Aramaic to an early version of the text, which is preserved in the proto-OG as well as the MT. Then, the proto-MT rearranged and augmented the earlier proto-OG version. We have three distinct versions in the literary development of this text, two of which are represented by manuscript evidence. It seems relatively clear that the earliest version was both copied and altered by two successive communities, each with their own distinctive theological perspective. Presumably, the earlier groups did not think their versions were incomplete. With this history of continual production in mind, it seems strange to identify the proto-OG version as being still "in production," its scribes as still being "authors-editors" and its alterations still "compositional," but to describe minor changes made to the MT version after the addition of verses 6–8 and 10 as corruptions.

In order to argue that the proto-MT is objectively the original text, Tov constructs a paradoxical object of textual criticism, the "final/original" text, that exists only briefly in the moment at which redactors transform into copyists, additions metamorphose into corruptions, and all previous versions become something less than the true text.[38]

Yet even of his own presumed original moment of stability and authoritative hegemony, Tov concludes that it "was brief at best, but in actual fact it probably never existed, for during the same period there were also current among the people a few copies representing stages which preceded the completion of the literary composition."[39] There was, Tov admits, actually no moment of textual unity, for there existed already by the time of stabilization other text forms and other "people" who used and deemed authoritative these other forms.

Alternatively, one might assume that transmission always relied on a combination of copying and authorial-editorial work, and that there were, from a time preceding any community's assent to authority—if such assent has been anything other than a gradual process—multiple textual traditions that continued along interwoven trajectories. Certainly corrections in the OG/LXX toward the MT, as well as recensions such as Aquila, Symmachus, and *kaige*-Theodotion and nonaligned texts at Qumran, reveal that text traditions were not sealed off from one another.[40]

Biblical texts remain open to change even now. Textual critics, for example, are busy creating new forms of the texts to represent older ones. The discovery of 4QSam[a] has convinced many text critics to count as authentic a section of text in between 1 Samuel 10 and 1 Samuel 11 that had been excised, presumably by scribal error.[41] While others have argued that the "lost" text is a late midrashic expansion and should not be included as part of the original text, Tov makes a convincing case that the variant appears early and that it was lost from the MT.[42] Thus, text critics, ostensibly looking for the original text, alter the construction of the stabilized text. As a result, some modern translations have added this once lost text to the end of 1 Samuel 10:27 (the NRSV, for example).

Though these scholars seek to find the final/original text, their scholarly work itself disturbs the history of the transmission of the text: grafting the extra text from 4QSam[a] onto the MT, as the NRSV does, likely creates a wholly new text that has heretofore not existed. Since MT 1 Samuel 16–17 contains additions not found in proto-OG texts such as 4QSam[a], yet the NRSV retains the MT for 1 Samuel 16–17, then NRSV forms a composite text type that likely presents an entirely new text. The point is this: the text is not yet done changing, because it continues to be read, copied, edited and studied. The concept of telos seems unhelpful here.

But Tov does not just argue for a moment of transformation in the history of the text; he also argues that a particular community had the authority to make one of the myriad variants the final and original text form, even though transmission-composition history continued to alter the text.

The Paradox of Authority

Tov also depends on the problematic concept of authority in order to determine which textual moment achieved finality/originality. Given the complicated trajectory of a text's development, a trajectory in which the text, at every attested stage, is realized in several divergent versions, which community has the authority to determine the point of origin for all other communities? And where does this authority come from? Many groups have considered biblical books to be authoritative in some way, and they have conferred authority on different editions. Not only is there a difference among the broad categories of Christians and Jews, but within these groups there are various subgroups that treat different texts—and even different canons—as authoritative.

For Tov, authority emanated from the Second Temple itself: "Although . . . textual plurality was characteristic for all of ancient Israel, it appears that in temple circles there existed a preference for one textual tradition, i.e., the texts of the Masoretic family."[43] Here, Tov relies on the work of Paul de Lagarde.[44] Like Rosenmüller before him, de Lagarde argued that every single manuscript representing the Hebrew Bible descends from a single model codex, the form of which was normative for rabbinic Judaism.[45] The evidence for this is primarily in the Talmud: Tov lays out several Talmudic references to *maggihim*, or professional correctors, employed to safeguard the text.[46]

Tov also argues for the authority of the proto-MT by pointing to the quantity of manuscripts found post-70 CE. The preponderance of texts found in the Judean Desert that date from the first century CE exhibit the proto-MT, and several Greek corrections toward the proto-MT date from near the same time.[47] Tov assumes that, since the proto-MT was copied quite often and showed a general consistency as a base text within the Second Temple period it must be identical to the texts claimed to emanate from the temple precincts.[48] In another publication, Tov elaborates on this claim: "Identity between two or more texts could have been achieved only if all of them were copied from a single source, in this case (a) master copy (copies) located in a central place, until 70 CE probably in the temple, and subsequently in another central place (Jamnia?). The textual unity described above has to start somewhere and the assumption of master copies is therefore necessary. The depositing and preserving of holy books in the temple is parallel to the modern concept of publication . . . ."[49]

There is, however, no direct evidence that one exact scroll representing the proto-MT held absolute pride of place in the temple.[50] Rabbinical texts, much like the Bible, cannot be cited at face value for their historical information: these are traditional texts that incorporate several layers of ideological and theological interpretation, and any historical conclusions drawn from them must be tentative.[51] Furthermore, rabbinic literature does not always seem to prove Lagarde's argument: *y. Ta'an* 4.68a seems to claim that there were conflicting versions of the biblical text used at the temple, and the priest Josephus—who claimed to use sacred books taken from the temple precinct itself—quoted extensively from a form of Joshua-2 Samuel derived from the proto-OG (attested by 4QSam[a]), not the MT.[52]

Thus if "publication" or "making public" was enacted by depositing a text in the temple, then several different texts seem to have been published.[53] Further, although certain types of proto-MT manuscripts seem to have been transmitted with impressive care, as John Van Seters helpfully notes, texts that "were most carefully copied and collated so as to avoid the usual copyist errors" are not necessarily of a universally superior text type.[54]

Tov himself suggests that a "conscious procedure [of choosing one master copy] never took place" since "different Bible texts continued to coexist with the master codex."[55] Perhaps the proto-MT scrolls do exhibit a striking similarity and thus might derive from one or more similar master copies, yet, if so, how does this justify the marginalization of the text forms used by others in the Jewish community and beyond at that exact time?[56] While the MT later became the privileged text within rabbinic Judaism, Ulrich points out that this selection happened quite late and was likely an arbitrary decision based not on textual purity—as proven by the difficult text of MT 1–2 Samuel—but rather on possession. That is, different sects simply used and later canonized the forms of the biblical texts that they had on hand.[57] Ascribing authoritative status and thus retroactive necessity to a particular text form developed and selected by means of a highly contingent set of historical circumstances is simply a theological gesture. It is not surprising that communities of faith accept this logic, but on what grounds can a post-Enlightenment scholar justify reproducing the theological gesture as a judgment that is *wissenschaftlich*? Or is it simply the case that choosing a text to be *the* text is an inherently theological gesture?

According to Tov, the identification of a particular text as authoritative changes the manner in which scribes treat a text. It cannot be redacted further, since it is authoritative.[58] This argument has, in recent decades, undergone significant critique, particularly in light of the textual pluriformity found at Qumran.[59] Again, Tov admits holes in this argument: "Many scribes took the liberty of changing the text from which they copied, and in this respect continued the approach of the last authors of the books. . . . This free approach taken by scribes finds expression in the insertion of changes in minor details and of interpolations."[60] Tov notes the vast number of minor alterations and interpolations in proto-MT Ezekiel; the proto-OG, an extant earlier edition that the proto-MT enlarged, is for Tov a "nonfinal" text.[61] Yet why should these late scribal exegetical interpolations be classified as authorial and part of pristine texts, while the scribes who altered the words "seventh day" to "sixth day" in proto-SamPent Genesis 2:2 be said to have created a nonpreferred reading?[62] Tov separates these two examples by claiming that the Ezekiel alterations function together as a "large-scale literary layer" and thus present a literary, as opposed to textual, alteration.[63] Yet the pre-Samaritan Pentateuchal redactions are clearly literary in the sense that they are a coherent exegetical redaction of a source text. Why, then, does Tov give the authors of the final layer of Ezekiel the freedom to alter the text while denying the possibility that the copyists of the pre-SamPent might have been creating a pristine or original or final text?

Perhaps Tov relies on the famed exactitude of proto-Masoretic scribes. Yet the pre-Samaritan edition was likewise "copied with great precision," after it underwent the redactional literary (or as Tov would claim, postliterary) development that created its textual tradition.[64] This precision still did not stop scribes from changing the text. Even after the formation of the pre-Samaritan text, the Samaritans redacted it again, and so did Masoretic scribes. How can one textual form be objectively final because of its authoritative status if the text was still in multiple modes of flux?

Modern considerations shape the concept of the final text as much as the content of it. Ultimately, Tov confesses that the norms of the religious tradition of Judaism are operative in his decision to define the final form as he does: "[Readings] created after the crystallization of the editions contained in M should not be brought to bear on the original text of Hebrew Scriptures. That corpus contains the Holy Writings of the Jewish people, and the decisions that were made within this religious community also determine to a great extent the approach of the scholarly world towards the text."[65] But even if the MT functions as the sacred scriptures of rabbinic Judaism, how is this one community's valuation determinative as an objective statement about origin? Already within the Second Temple period, some Jews within Palestine seemed to regard several textual traditions as sacred. Why are their views not considered normative? Moreover, Samaritans consider their own version of the Pentateuch to be authoritative; what status do these claims have for modern scholars?

If Tov claimed that his own religious identity was normative for his practice and the practices of those also in his religious community, this judgment would be compelling. Instead, Tov claims that "the approach of the scholarly world"—and thus the normative scholarly definition of the original text—is necessarily constrained by these religious norms. As in the canonical debate, should scholars prescribe rather than describe norms and, in the process, declare some textual traditions more right—or more original, more final, more pristine—than others?

Even if one grants the universal superiority of the particular biblical text used by rabbinic Judaism, one must deal with the temporal problem of granting authority to a particular form of a biblical text. The originality and authority of the proto-MT, for example, is a retroactive effect created by the practices of a number of diverse later religious communities that understood and used texts in a manner different from that of Second Temple Judaism. Judaism did not confer authority on the text form of the MT at one moment in time; rather, authority developed in a diffuse process that coincided with the construction of a legendary past explaining the origin and development of the text. Tov even admits to the diffuse nature of the MT and the diachronic diversity of the community that curates it:

> There has never existed any one single text that could be named the Masoretic Text. . . . In other words, although there indeed existed the express wish not to insert any changes in the Masoretic texts, the reality was in fact paradoxically different, since the texts of the M group themselves already differed one from the other. Thus there existed a strong desire for textual standardization, but this desire could not erase the differences already existing between the texts. The wish to preserve a unified textual tradition thus remained an abstract ideal which could not be accomplished in reality. Moreover, despite the scribes' meticulous care, changes, corrections, and mistakes were added to the internal differences already existing between members of the M group.[66]

As Tov notes, the manuscript record proves that no biblical text has ever been final in any sense other than a retroactively ideal form. It is quite clear that scribes continued, even through the Masoretic period, to add, subtract, and reconfigure elements of the text. Tov himself notes the various systems used to add vowels to the consonantal text, the addition of accentuation and division into sections, paratextual interpretive elements, and most important, the actual emendations to the consonantal text known as *tiqqunê soferim* as well as the inner-textual inclusion of variants known as *ketib-qere*.[67]

At work in Tov's conception of authority are powerfully linked concepts of legitimacy and filiation, the seemingly natural authorization of a historically contingent compilation of an uneven assortment of texts as bearers of the true lineage. Constructions of "legitimate" textual filiation, however, are necessarily retroprojections developed to protect the legitimacy of particular groups. According to many biblical scholars, the proper inheritors of the biblical text in its true form were the Masoretes, who were authorized by groups who derived from those who had already been legitimated before 70 CE, and therefore, they maintain, the Samaritans objectively do not use the real Bible. Yet this is unsatisfactory argument because it leads to an infinite regression of authority. Where did this chain of authority begin?[68] Moreover, this lineage is contested by the mere existence of other genealogies that authorize different texts, and even the existence of illegitimacies within any given tradition. How can one decide between them? In terms of the legitimacies of true variants and illegitimate ones, who can say which group got it right in anything other than a theological sense?

When the term "authority" enters into critical discourse, scholars should interrogate the source and extent of the authority cited. Authority creates norms and hierarchies that are self-justifying and turn the historically contingent into the necessary. Critical scholarship does not accept authority as an answer to a question; rather, it works to uncover the contingent conditions that allowed for the cultural arrangement within which particular voices bear authority while others babble on at the margins.

Tov's concept of the original text is based on a paradoxical moment of final originality, conferred by a mythical attribution of authority that somehow carries a universal force. Perhaps most surprising is Tov's frank admission of the roles played by paradox, myth, and contingency in his work. Given these limitations, Tov's concept of the original text seems an unlikely candidate to serve as a theoretical foundation for the division between biblical scholarship proper and reception history.

From Urtext to Archetype: Manageable Diversity

Not all textual critics eschew textual multiplicity: Ronald Hendel, the editor in chief of the Oxford Hebrew Bible project, currently in progress, has outlined an editorial theory of textual criticism that seems to offer a much different role for reception history.[69] The OHB project is unique, because it aims to be a genuinely eclectic edition of the biblical text. It will not adopt a single manuscript as the base and adding a critical apparatus underneath, as in a diplomatic edition. Eclecticism will allow it to pursue a reconstruction of the hypothetical "earliest inferable textual state," since it will not have to replicate any variants extant in a particular manuscript. Thus the OHB will be able to emend—or, in Hendel's words, "restore"—the text to its "earlier" state.[70]

Furthermore, "in cases in which . . . multiple editions are recoverable," each edition (e.g., the proto-MT, the proto-OG) will be represented in the OHB in the form of its own parallel column.[71] As far as possible, "a common ancestor to the extant editions will be reconstructed." Practically, each reconstruction will approximate the "archetype" of an edition, which is equivalent to its "earliest inferable textual state."[72]

At first glance, the OHB project appears to appreciate textual pluriformity and diachronic difference within the various textual traditions of the Bible. However, Hendel admits that the "original text" functions in his methodology as an "ideal goal or limit," and he even cites Tov's definition of the "original text" approvingly.[73] What distinguishes Hendel's approach is the object of recovery. He claims that the original is an "ideal goal or limit" that is "beyond our evidence," but the "archetype"—defined as the "manuscript at the top of the stemma"—is more achievable.[74] That is, Hendel claims that the original text existed but is unrecoverable based on the current level of scholarly knowledge. What scholars can do, however, is recover a particular form of the text that derives from the original text and yet remains the "ancestor" of known editions.

Hendel's goal, then, is to "determine or reconstruct the best set of readings," which are "the earliest or more original readings, approximating the archetype."[75] For Hendel, "Approximating the archetype is a step towards the 'original text.'"[76] Hendel illuminates the historical dimension of the quest for the "original text" when he forwards a theoretical justification for eclectic editing. Developing an idea from Pier Giorgio Borbone, Hendel notes that "a critical text is actually the opposite of eclectic, since it attempts to reverse the eclectic agglomeration—from diverse times, places, and scribal hands—of secondary readings in the existing manuscripts."[77] The goal of Hendel's eclectic method thus emerges in this description as a single, unified, historically located text that minimizes diversity within itself. One might say that it seeks the moment just before reception of the text, which inaugurated the "agglomeration" caused by the text's movement through "diverse times, places, and scribal hands" and thus produced "secondary readings."

I argue that substituting the concept of the archetype for that of the urtext does not much change the practice or the goals of textual criticism. Like Tov, Hendel still privileges "earlier" and "more original" readings and accepts them as the "best" readings.[78] To this end, Hendel claims that the text critic must "distinguish . . . primary from secondary readings" as such. Hendel defines "primary readings" as "earlier and text-critically preferable," whereas "secondary readings" are either "revisions" or "errors."[79] According to this schema, the primary readings are valuable for text criticism, while the secondary readings are of interest only "for the study of the reception of the biblical text."[80] Thus, Hendel draws a line between the original text and its reception, using the period of the "stabilization" of the MT in the late Second Temple period as a definitive dividing line. Hendel approvingly cites Tov's statement that a text is "finished" when it is "considered authoritative."[81] Like Tov, Hendel does not elaborate on what immanent criteria separates a "primary reading" from a "reception" other than its temporal location on the other side of the supposed stabilization of the biblical text. Thus, Hendel uses the traditions of particular, later religious groups as justification for locating the divide between original and reception where he does.[82]

The OHB will, however, represent within its own critical text multiple editions of biblical texts that clearly derive from before the period of stabilization. Hendel therefore agrees that the text underwent a long and varied process of composition and that this process had, at least sometimes, divergent end points. Yet he represents pluriformity in a highly limited way. Any readings that occurred after the creation of an archetype are declared "secondary" and ought, in his view, to be excised from a critical text. Instead of Tov's singular determinate original, Hendel argues for a limited number of determinate originals. Thus, each one of Hendel's archetypes faces the same problems as Tov's singular original.

In the case of Daniel 4–5, for example, the proto-OG edition and the proto-MT edition are both expansions of some now unrecoverable predecessor text (or texts). It is clear that the assumed predecessor text itself had had a long, complicated, unoriginal, and clearly unfinalized textual history by the time it was read and reworked by proto-OG and proto-MT scribes.[83] As John Collins concludes, "Both texts show signs of redactional expansion, and neither can be identified as the original form of the story."[84] Thus, before the original text of either the MT or the OG existed, two separate sets of authors-editors decided to add to, remove from, and rearrange the text(s), creating the OG and MT editions. These editions then were altered repeatedly, as witnessed by the history of their transmission and translation.[85] How are scholars to tell the difference between the primary and secondary interventions in a case such as this? Does one search for the text supposedly underlying the MT and OG? Hendel answers these questions by explaining that after the transition from composition to transmission, "some scribes became major partners once again, when the changes were so thoroughgoing as to create a new edition. In these cases, new textual production occurs after the period of textual transmission has begun."[86] Thus, some scribes managed to reopen the process of textual production, stepping behind the ontological divide that separates esteemed authors-editors from mere copyists. How did they do this without having their alterations deemed secondary? Moreover, does not "new textual production" describe the process that led from the presumed Hebrew text of Daniel 4–5 into the proto-MT and proto-OG editions, as well as to what the Samaritans did to the proto-SamPent, and also what happened with the well-known additions to Daniel? That which lies on the secondary side of Hendel's ontological divide seems suspiciously similar to the primary.

While Hendel includes limited pluriformity in his theory of textual criticism and acknowledges that the original text is unrecoverable, he implies that the original text nevertheless exists when he notes that "we cannot have unmediated access to the master text; it is beyond our evidence."[87] The "master" or original text is currently beyond our grasp, but it is not completely absent: it is mediated by its archetype—which is itself mediated by manuscripts. The absence of the original text is not an ontological problem for Hendel; it is an epistemic one.

Hendel critiques fellow textual critics Moshe Goshen-Gottstein and Shemaryahu Talmon on this very issue. Goshen-Gottstein claims that, in the absence of "strict philological evidence" to the contrary, "we have to look upon conflicting readings in our primary sources as alternative readings, none of which must be considered as superior to the other." Likewise, Talmon argues that the text critic must accept various readings as "pristine" because there is "no objective criteria for deciding which reading is original."[88] In response, Hendel notes that Talmon and Goshen-Gottstein are essentially arguing that there could be "objective criteria" and "strict philological evidence" to make these sorts of decisions, but scholars currently lack the data to do so. Hendel defers to the words of Tov: "One's inability to decide between different readings should not be confused with the question of the original form of the biblical text."[89] He goes on to explain that "in other words, Talmon has taken a methodological or epistemological problem (our inability to know which is the archetypal reading) and made it into a statement of essence or ontology (there is no archetypal reading)."[90] Thus, Hendel refutes Goshen-Gottstein and Talmon by noting a category error: they agree that there is an epistemological problem but end up instead making claims about the text's nature.

Perhaps, however, Talmon's and Goshen-Gottstein's epistemological assumptions are incorrect? The problem may stem from the supposed scientificity and objectivity of textual critical claims. Hendel asserts that we do not now have the ability to find or deduce the original text, but this state of affairs is our shortcoming, because (it is assumed) the original text really is out there, somewhere just beyond the limits of our knowledge. The paradigm of the asymptotic ideal archetype appeals to Hendel's assumed epistemology and ontology of the biblical text. But how does Hendel know this to be the case? If there really is a single pristine text of any biblical book, then it must have become pristine at some telic point during the long composition process. But who decides which point along the line is the pristine point? Here, Hendel must rely on Tov's concept of authority, with all its problematic assumptions.

Perhaps the notion of an epistemological shortcoming is not the real problem. Text critics note the structural impossibility of recovering the exact true words of the text and so consign themselves to asymptotic structures, aiming for a recovery the original text as far as is possible based on our limited knowledge. Yet if we had the knowledge, that is, if there were no epistemological shortcoming, we would then know how the original text or archetype read. But perhaps text critics cannot be sure of their full recovery of the naturally privileged form of a text because there is none. The problem is not with our perception of the history of the text. The problem is rather that the history of the text in itself presents forms of the text that both exceed the expected textual ontology and fall short of it. The surplus of variants and editions for the books of the Pentateuch exceed the concept of the single original text, and yet no particular manuscripts have been able to claim the title of the text of the Pentateuch. The question of how these excessive-yet-insufficient manuscripts relate to each other as well as the issue of how to regard the universals to which they supposedly correspond suggest that the field needs a developed ontology of biblical texts more urgently than it needs to discover even more manuscripts—as if more conflicting information would solve Hendel's so-called epistemological problem.

Hendel appears to argue, along with Tov, that whatever was "considered authoritative" by a community denotes the "primary" and "pristine," but he also agrees with Arie van der Kooij that the critic "should go as far back as the textual evidence allows and requires."[91] These are quite different and mutually conflicting ontological claims. Not only are scholars unable to pinpoint any specific moment at which the text became authoritative; it seems impossible for a scholar to make an ontological judgment that a traditionary text *actually became original* simply because a group of people felt that they were finished with changing it. By the time any group declared the text sacred in Second Temple–era Palestine, there were already multiple editions of biblical texts in many uniquely varying manuscripts available, and at least one community held multiple editions without classification—namely, Qumran.[92]

What would the archetype of the original text of the book of Daniel present? It seems clear that Daniel underwent several radical revisions over time. Loren Stuckenbruck has argued that at Qumran, texts found alongside copies of Daniel may simultaneously show something of the "tradition-historical background of the biblical book" (4Q242; 4Q530), "contemporary Danielic traditions" (4Q243–45; 4Q552–53), and "the creative use of Daniel" (1QM).[93] Moreover, with the help of higher criticism, scholars can comfortably assert that Daniel 7–12 reflects quite a different historical situation from that of Daniel 1–6 and thus the addition of

Daniel 7–12 to Daniel 1–6 constituted a later edition of the book of Daniel. It is, however, highly unlikely that any critical edition would not include Daniel 7–12 within its reconstruction of the book of Daniel.[94] Since the authors and redactors of Daniel 7–12 altered a text in order to compose and produce a primary, pristine edition, how is it that the authors and redactors of the story of Susanna and those redactors that connected this story to the book of Daniel were producing something secondary and less than pristine?[95]

And if the "additions" to Daniel (and how is it that Daniel 7–12 does not count as an addition?) such as the story of Susanna are considered in some way pristine, then which version is the pristine one? The likely older OG text, or the longer and more well-known edition preserved in *kaige*-Theodotion?[96] Both are certainly literary editions of the same story, but exhibit very important differences. For example, the famous bathing scene only occurs in Theodotion.[97] If the critical edition is to include these stories with the text of Daniel, even more ontological problems arise: the order of the stories could follow manuscript P. 967, in which Bel and the Dragon comes before the story of Susanna, or the Theodotion-Daniel manuscripts, which place Susanna's story before chapter 1. Narrative order is not inconsequential to the ontology of a book![98] If some of these editions are excluded, on what grounds are they inferior to Daniel 7–12? Yet if they are all included, does it not seem that the historical development of the biblical text demands a much more complex ontology than drawing a line between primary and secondary, or original and reception?

The text-critical epistemological problem is not that we do not have enough information to find the true, original text. The real epistemological problem is the assumption among critical scholars that these fault lines, these boundaries between original text and reception, between primary and secondary, simply occur as natural givens. How can one justify the ontological judgment that Daniel 7–12 is primary or pristine or original and that Bel and the Dragon is secondary?[99]

Hendel's methodology would support the inclusion of Susanna, since he holds that "the critical text includes all the textual compositions that are ancestral to the existing texts and editions."[100] Theodotion-Susanna most likely redacted OG-Susanna, and thus scholars possess the ancestor. Does Theodotion-Susanna merit inclusion as a separate pristine text, or no? At which point along the line does this more-than-secondary text have its pristine moment? This judgment requires an ontological distinction that has no clear epistemological justification.

Hendel seems content to recognize diversity by approving of a critical edition of multiple ancient editions of a given text, but this strategy in fact aims to limit and contain diversity. Text critics should, Hendel claims, find an original or archetype of each one of a small number of authorized, authoritative traditions.[101] Yet the book of Daniel, for instance, shows a vigorous complexity in its production-transmission history, over the course of which many hands and many traditions have handled and altered its contents. Where along these divergent historical lineages can one pick a point that is ontologically pristine? And how could one know, with objective epistemological certainty, that this point was "it," that any changes that occurred afterward were secondary and that they thus belonged to the history of reception instead of the history of composition?

Hendel's ontology of the biblical text, like Tov's, assumes determinate historical moments that held the embodiment of the full presence of the text itself. Moments beforehand authors had not yet formulated every essential element to the text, and thus there was still work to be done to bring the text into being. From what we can deduce about the history of the text, however, this moment is a chimera. There is no naturally occurring, hermetically sealed moment of pure textual presence, and it is probably not useful to posit an ideal moment in lieu of an actual one.

Imagining Intention

In an alternate presentation of editorial rationale for the OHB project, Michael Fox advances a critique of this very conclusion. He begins by distancing himself from the project of locating the urtext of Proverbs, pointing to its complicated and diverse history of textual production, which makes it impossible to locate one layer as the original text: "Anyway, in a sense the book of Proverbs is all additions, since it is an anthology of anthologies, themselves agglomerations of proverbs, epigrams and poems, some deriving from oral literature, others having antecedents in written wisdom. At what stage do "additions" become "later additions?" In the case of Proverbs, we are dealing with a snowballing text, and the Ur-snowball is not only beyond recovery, it is beyond conceptualization."[102] Here, Fox admits that one cannot assign various ontological statuses to different levels of revision within a textual history that is replete with revisions and that is, in some sense, all quotation. Proverbs are often traditional sayings in general use and thus are secondary even when first written down. Proverbs are not amenable to any discussion of originality. Furthermore, the collections of quotations obviously derive from various temporal, sociocultural and geographic locations.[103] In light of this evidence, no edition of Proverbs in its entire textual history could possibly be the goal of Hendel's "reverse eclecticism," because if it were, the whole book would have to be dismissed as secondary.[104]

But after this admission, Fox surprisingly asserts that what he is looking to reconstruct is a hyparchetype, or, quoting Paul Maas, a "reconstructed variant carrier."[105] That is, Fox simply displaces Hendel's displaced original text one step further, from archetype to hyparchetype. Like Hendel and Tov, Fox admits that his new object of study is also ideal: "Hence the text I am aiming at never had physical existence. It is a construct. It can be defined as the proto-MT as it should have been, what the authors, conceived as a collectivity . . . wanted us to read. This goal is, of course, heuristic, not fully attainable."[106] Just as Hendel claims that the search for Tov's urtext is not a practical goal, Fox calls Hendel's archetype a "phantom" for which any quest is "doomed."[107] Yet Fox declares the hyparchetype of proto-MT Proverbs his new goal while admitting that it, too, has the ontological status of a phantom. The aporia of the final/original text, which is the moment wherein production simply becomes transmission, forces anyone who attempts to conceptualize it into ideal, abstract territory. Fox here challenges Tov and Hendel's terminology but nevertheless repeats the structure of their concepts.

Fox also shifts from discussing the multistage snowball-like development of the book of Proverbs to selecting one "moment," albeit ideal, in this textual history as the privileged moment. Fox does not seem to weigh arguments for the relative merit of each version; the moment of the proto-MT "as it should have been" (but admittedly never was) carries seemingly natural superiority to the proto-OG. How did the hyparchetype MT simply become the object of study, especially since Fox seemed to be unsure about the possibility of locating a definitive layer of Proverbs to be the urtext?

It is not the lack of a Hebrew *Vorlage*. Fox agrees that there likely was a Hebrew text for the proto-OG and that it is in part recoverable: "There are a large number of LXX pluses, consisting of lines, verses, and even full poems. These are of considerable interest to the reception history of the book, but they are not part of the history of the hyparchetype under consideration and do not belong in the eclectic edition. Even when I think that they had a Hebrew basis and that I can retrovert them, I will confine them to the textual commentary."[108] Fox here excludes the Hebrew basis of the OG from the critical text, assigning instead it to the "reception history of the book." Pages before, Fox had built an impressive argument for considering the entire textual tradition of Proverbs under the category reception history.[109] How then did only the OG Proverbs end up on the reception side of the boundary between original and reception when the OG Proverbs amounts to a layer of additions to a text that is, at its core, an agglomeration of quotations?

One might assume that, as with Tov, the reason derives ultimately from religious identities. Here, I should be clear about my own role in this critique: I am no enemy of religious convictions. As a Christian, I hold many particular religious convictions myself, and so I am extremely sympathetic to the textual commitments of particular religious groups. But is the OHB critical edition of the Bible a theological project? If it is not concerned with presenting the text of a particular religious community, that is, if it aims to present not one religious community's reception of the text but rather the text itself or an objective, universally valid archetype or hyparchetype of the text itself, then what nontheological grounds can Fox cite in order to justify privileging one form of the text over the other?

Even if one grants the goal of labeling the ideal proto-MT as "the book of Proverbs," how does anyone know what the text "should have been?" That is, by what standards can one adjudicate the "correct hyparchetype of the Masoretic Proverbs"? One may suggest many possible answers to this question. Perhaps least controversially, one approach would be to emend obvious spelling errors and the like. But many variants present more complicated choices. Between two variant readings that equally seem to fit the literary context, does one decide on aesthetic merits or perhaps depth of profundity? Perhaps one could suggest that "the more original reading" should prevail, but this is a problem of infinite regression for the book of Proverbs.

To answer this difficult question, Fox points to the work of Thomas Tanselle, who argues that the editor must "use authorial active intention as a basis for editorial choice."[110] Fox first grants that there are "innumerable and indeterminate" individuals responsible for the formation of the text of Proverbs but then defines the "author" as a "construct comprised of that collectivity."[111] Thus, the text critic must divine or somehow reconstruct the collectivity of authorial intentions in order to select the appropriate variants. Fox explains that "Proverbs is the work of individuals who intended us to understand certain things. I don't know what we can read for—or write for—other than the communication of intention. . . . Nothing other than the intended text is worth the reader's time."[112] Several difficulties arise. Setting aside issues of simple error, every alteration to the text has some sort of scribal intention as a motivating factor. By obeying the agglutinative intentions of all authors, the text critic would create a textual monster. For example, the addition of several lines—probably, as Fox agrees, in Hebrew—to Proverbs 9:12 reflected in the OG certainly had as much authorial intention lying behind it as any other bit of Proverbs.[113] Yet this addition, in Fox's opinion, is reception and not composition.

Some sort of thought likely accompanied the gloss to Proverbs 5:22a that exists in the MT but not the OG or Peshitta, but Fox declares that he will "excise" this addition because "it was absent from the text when LXX's and MT's lines diverged."[114] Why is that moment of divergence given precedence but the divergences that occurred before it and after it deemed as belonging to composition or reception? And isn't this gloss part and parcel of the collective authorship of the book? Surreptitiously, borderlines have appeared in the midst of Fox's massive collective author that divide the actual historical authors into two camps:

legitimate authors and their legitimate intentions, and illegitimate authors and their illegitimate intentions. Does the moment of textual divergence between the MT and the OG really justify this sort of categorization?

And in any event, how can "recovering authorial intention" possibly be the goal of editing a book such as Proverbs, given that Fox has already outlined the secondary nature of every inscription of a proverb? Whatever Hezekiah's scribes had in their heads when they wrote down Proverbs 25–29 cannot possibly be the ultimate arbiter of the form or meaning of that section of text, let alone the definition of its correct edition. Even they did not assign themselves this responsibility. The scribes explain their own activity in Proverbs 25:1 with the word "העתיקו": that is, the scribes "moved" ("עתק") or "transcribed" the text of Proverbs 25–29.[115] The intentions of the scribes responsible for producing Proverbs 25–29 by no means define the nature of these words. Neither do the scribes claim even to be authors! Though they did doubtless think about how to arrange the various sayings that comprise Proverbs 25–29, this intention has been altered by scribes who inserted their work into a larger work, one that included diverse texts such as Proverbs 1–9 and Proverbs 31:10–31.[116] Why is it that the intentions of the scribes who inserted Proverbs 31:10–31 are considered part of the collectivity whose intentions are determined to influence modern scholarship's construction of the ontology of the book of Proverbs, but the scribe who added the gloss to Proverbs 5:22a is part of another collectivity altogether, that of the reception history of the text? These questions confront even the OHB, an edition that seeks to recognize a (limited) multiplicity of biblical text forms.

In defense of his methodology, Fox sketches a critique of the major alternative: what he calls the "relativistic acceptance of any and every text-form as a 'textual moment' of irreducible validity."[117] Fox wonders whether "if everything is equally valid for every kind of edition, is there any point in anything other than a Kennicott-Rossi type assemblage, indeed, whether there is sense in any editorial activity at all."[118] This defense is questionable on a number of grounds. First, the term "validity" allows for at least several different valences of meaning that are here conflated. Every textual moment may in fact be valid in the sense that it presents a text that is a priori equivalent in ontological status to all other textual moments, but this does not mean that every edition should contain everything or that there are no standards for editing at all. The accusation of relativism seems to imply a slackening of scholarly standards, but relativism does not necessarily engender such a state of affairs. Fox's response seems much like that of the proverbial parent who is upset that every child is called special, because that means no child is special at all. What this parent does not imagine is this: children can each be special, yet in very different ways.

One may claim that each text form is valid as a particular text form but that not all text forms are equivalent answers to any question asked about the text.

To return to the analogy of children: in order to find out what makes each child special, one needs to ask particular and limited questions, such as who is kind to their classmates or who enjoys reading or who runs quickly. Likewise, textual critics can examine a particular manuscript of Proverbs and ask in what way did, or could, this text function as the text of Proverbs. One can edit an edition of Proverbs that is meant to reproduce a text that was used by medieval Masoretes, or one can edit an edition of Proverbs that is meant to reflect an edition used by second-century BCE Alexandrian Jews. One can order texts by aesthetic criteria, brevity, theological profundity, or relative age. These are not exclusive choices, and one edition is not naturally better or worse.

What a "relativistic acceptance of any and every text-form" may instead imply for a scholarly community is the following: one must define each and every manuscript as well as every critical text as an ontologically limited presentation of the "text itself." Calling the proto-MT "the Bible" and the proto-OG "reception of the Bible" obscures the text at hand as well as the act of scholarly (re)production. If one is seeking to replicate an ideal form of the proto-MT, perhaps it should merely be labeled as such, and a quest for the proto-OG would only be reception history insofar as the quest for the proto-MT is itself reception history of texts and traditions from an earlier time. Or perhaps editions of known texts could be published alongside hypothetical, eclectic reconstructions of a text that predates any of them, and neither could be deemed less original. This is not "anything goes" relativism: on the contrary, it is far more historically specific and less arbitrary than privileging one contingent historical moment (or an ideal representation of one) as the original, the primary, the intended form, of the work. One may, for example, discuss actual historical texts and contexts instead of otherworldly apparitions such as collective authors and ideal texts.

In an epigraph to his article on the OHB, Hendel quotes Jorge Luis Borges on the topic of translations of Homeric epics: "The concept of the 'definitive text' corresponds only to religion or exhaustion."[119] Hendel returns to this quotation in the body of his essay in order to underscore his claim that the OHB does not seek to be the definitive critical edition of the Bible.[120] This stance is admirable in its humility, but it does not seem to take what Borges is suggesting far enough. When applied out of context to the critical edition, the statement implies that all modern editions are but flawed texts that seek to approximate the ideal work and as such can only asymptotically approach their goal. But it means something else altogether if it is applied to the source text, which is what the sentence immediately before it in Borges's essay seems to imply Borges had in mind: "'To assume that every recombination of elements is necessarily inferior to its original form is to assume that draft nine is necessarily inferior to draft H—for there can be only drafts."[121] Concerning the text of the book of Proverbs itself, and not merely the modern critical editions, there are only drafts, because no one person or group has had the authority to compel an end to the process of redrafting this text. One can claim that there was a universal end to this process of the development of the book of Proverbs, but anyone who does so is forced to speak only of the ideal realm. The material evidence to the contrary is inscribed into every variant manuscript, represented by the phantoms that haunt the critical apparatus clinging to the page's edge. The idea that scholars must accept a singular provisional edited text merely because we do not have enough information to find the true archetype sounds more like the result of exhaustion than religion, but in either case Hendel and Fox seem to think there is something other than a draft waiting at the hidden headwaters of the nilotic biblical text.

The Great Divide: An Ideal Stability

Moshe Goshen-Gottstein and Shemaryahu Talmon, the two consecutive chief editors of the Hebrew University Bible project, have started their text-critical venture from a different set of assumptions than either Hendel or Tov. Perhaps most important is their shared assertion that there is no recoverable urtext and that variant readings may therefore be regarded as equally acceptable. To make good on this claim, Goshen-Gottstein and Talmon give four separate apparatuses that include variants from the early translations of the biblical text, Hebrew texts from the Second Temple period, and medieval rabbinic manuscript readings.[122] A plethora of variants are offered to the reader, but the editors offer no judgments concerning their priority. No conjectural emendation, such as is found in the OHB, is allowed. As Goshen-Gottstein argues, the HUB will "present nothing but the facts."[123]

In this respect, both Talmon and Goshen-Gottstein can be said to be critiquing the urtext theories that derive from Lagardian textual criticism, but they both continue to use several concepts that nevertheless divide an original period from later reception of the biblical text. Important to both Goshen-Gottstein and Talmon are the concepts of a great divide that precipitated the stabilization and fixity of the biblical text and the establishment of the Masoretic tradition as the eventual telos of biblical development.[124]

Goshen-Gottstein and Talmon are both skeptical that any quest for the original text could be successful. As Goshen-Gottstein suggests, the "axiomatic assumption that there was such a thing [as *ipsissima verba*] and . . . the positivistic utopian effort to recover them remains a legitimate goal, though unattainable. . . . We do not look out any more for the *veritas* of an *Urtext*, but are satisfied with recapturing its reflex pragmatically, as far as our evidence allows."[125] Thus Goshen-Gottstein does not deny that in the distant past there may have been an urtext, but he sees the goal of textual criticism as a more pragmatic study of extant texts. It would appear that Goshen-Gottstein retains the concept of the urtext, but in a weak form. Though he allows for its merits, he has questioned the ideal quality of the goal of seeking an urtext: "We are allowed to ponder how large is the functional difference between the theologian's attempt to establish the 'true unchanged word of God' and the philologist's endeavor to recapture archetype or Urtext."[126] Goshen-Gottstein compares the attempt to recover the text to a purely theological task. In other words, the urtext seems to be a noumenal object. What besides theological convictions could divine the secret textual identity of the massive and pluriform biblical tradition?

It appears that Goshen-Gottstein shares the spirit of this theological venture. When discussing the relative text-critical merits of variant traditions, he remarks that "the Massoretic type appears to us to be a main current in the centuries before the period of the Destruction, but there are rivulets flowing side by side with it—and investigations have already shown that it is sometimes in them that the pure water flows."[127] Some of the metaphorical water is pure, and some is contaminated. Some of this contamination is within the Masoretic tradition itself and thus calls to be corrected. In other words, some variants are more equal than others. How is one to know what is contaminated and what is not?

Goshen-Gottstein claims that there are cases in which alternative readings should be allowed to stand as true alternatives and not be subordinated one to another. But Ronald Hendel keenly observes that Goshen-Gottstein's seemingly egalitarian textual ontology appears only where there is an epistemological lack. That is, various readings are only considered equal alternatives when there is no strict philological evidence to prove their inferiority. The American legal dictum "innocent until proven guilty" comes to mind: the alternatives are under temporary reprieve. As Tov sagely argues, for there to be secondary readings at all, there must be primary readings, and this judgment implies that Goshen-Gottstein thinks that there is, somewhere unbeknownst to us, proper philological evidence that could and would help scholars discern the secondary and corrupt readings and, by extension, the original or uncorrupted readings.[128] Yet in general scholars lack such evidence, and thus Goshen-Gottstein falls back on a default position of ontological openness to alternative readings.

Thus, the HUB admits to a practical textual pluriformity but subordinates that apprehension to the superior, yet unreachable, theoretical goal of recovering the true text. In his criticism of the HUB, Hendel notes this dissonance but uses it to argue for the necessity of positing an ideal text, whether achievable or not. It seems more prudent, however, to hold that there is not, and there never was, an objectively ontologically privileged form of these traditional texts. There are, to be sure, particular religious communities who have their own faith-based reasons for adjudicating between versions and editions. But these are not givens; these are not positions that are justifiable outside of a certain set of theological assumptions. Rather, they are theologically speculative. It is not that we do not know enough to judge. It is that the act of judging itself here requires a disavowal of the mantle of objective, critical scholar. One can only make these sorts of claims from an interested, committed, but limited viewpoint; the possibility of recovering an urtext persuades, as Goshen-Gottstein himself suggests, the theologian, not a putatively objective philologist.

In their editorial choices, however, Goshen-Gottstein and Talmon signal their communal commitments quite clearly. For the base text of the HUB that is then supplemented by the apparatuses, the editorial team chose the Aleppo codex, which is, according to Goshen-Gottstein, "the manuscript on which Maimonides relied, and that it is correctly ascribed to Aaron ben Asher."[129] This is in contrast to the first edition of Kittel's *Biblia hebraica,* which followed the rabbinic tradition of using the second Rabbinic Bible of 1525 as the *textus receptus,* as well as the more recent editions, *BHS* and *BHQ,* which are diplomatic editions of the Leningrad codex, the oldest complete Masoretic text of the Hebrew Bible.[130]

According to Goshen-Gottstein, the Aleppo codex should be used as the base text for scholarly editions because it is older and closer to Aaron ben Asher than Leningrad, though it lacks the Pentateuch up to Deuteronomy 28 and is missing several other sections. Nevertheless Goshen-Gottstein maintains that as it is the "oldest" text available, there is "no other codex more suitable to serve as the basic text. On this central question no other decision seems possible."[131] Goshen-Gottstein's categorical claims are puzzling for several reasons. First, why is the oldest codex the clear choice for a base text? Of course, this preserves a particular canonical context for these works, but codex qua bound volume seems like a strange place to look for the "best" base text of, for example, Isaiah, especially in light of the discovery of 1QIsa[a]. If age is a factor, why not use the Dead Sea Scrolls as much as one can for base texts, as they are available? Goshen-Gottstein explains that the Aleppo codex is "the most important witness in our possession of that type of Massoretic tradition which has become dominant throughout Jewry. In this case it must be regarded as the best 'substitute' for Aaron's manuscript which we ever shall be able to obtain."[132]

Here, Goshen-Gottstein lays his theological cards on the table. The true base text, which is (seemingly always, under any name) just beyond scholarly reach, is in Goshen-Gottstein's estimation the codex prepared by Aaron ben Asher that was then approved by Maimonides.[133] Goshen-Gottstein's approval of Aleppo as the essence of the Masoretic tradition leads him to downplay the importance of Leningrad codex, a "mixed" text corrected toward the ben Asher text form. Revealing a hierarchical determination that he justifies with objective text-critical metrics, he explains that "comparison showed the two codices for what they are: the Aleppo Codex—the perfect original masterpiece which authenticates itself by internal criteria; the Leningrad Codex—a none-too-successful effort to adapt a manuscript of a different Tiberian subgroup to a Ben Asher Codex. . . . No scribe in his right mind would go to the trouble to adapt an existing manuscript to another model [as in the case of L] unless he recognized its authority."[134] Goshen-Gottstein's "internal" criteria include the "almost complete harmony between text and massora," which validates the Aleppo's original status as the first production of a codex of the entire Masoretic Hebrew Bible.[135] But this is, confusingly, an emic evaluation that is used to justify an etic proposition. That is, Aleppo is pure and perfect only insofar as one accepts that the Tiberian subset of the Masoretic form of the Hebrew text of, say, the book of Jeremiah is somehow more pure than proto-OG Jeremiah. Leningrad's mixture of subtypes is only a lesser creature if we take the already mixed-up layer cake of a text that we call the Hebrew Bible as an unmixed whole. It is striking to think that a traditional compilation of heavily edited texts could, thousands of years into its textual development, finally find its most pure state in the hands of a particular group of medieval scribes. Perhaps it is true, but it would take more than "internal criteria" to prove that this is so. Goshen-Gottstein thus reveals one of the dividing lines by which he measures the true text over against the other, less pure, forms. To start one's search by looking for the most internally consistent Masorah in an early Masoretic codex of the complete Hebrew Bible is not to start on particularly objectively stable ground, since this origin is itself a complex amalgam of materials. Is this really "nothing but the facts?" The impassioned selection and defense of Aleppo reveals that the choice of a base text is not an insignificant detail. And the inclusion of all possible variants in critical apparatuses will not diminish the force of this decision.

Of course, Leningrad is not necessarily or logically superior, either; these two manuscripts are simply two manuscripts that represent the text in two different places at two different times. Perhaps one was written by a more proficient class of scribes, or one is in fact a mixture of two previous textual types, but how does one draw axiological implications from these conclusions? Clearly, even the best of the Masoretic scribes were preserving a so-called corrupt text of 1–2 Samuel; what is the ontological status of a pure and perfect copy of a garbled text?[136] Barring theological commitments, there is no more reason to base a scholarly edition of the text of 1–2 Samuel on the Aleppo codex than there is to base it purely on what remains of the texts of the Judaean Desert.

It is beyond question that the ben Asher school produced remarkable texts on many levels and that they are truly important to the development of the biblical text and the sustenance of the Jewish faith. The same can be said for Maimonides. But they hold no particular authority when it comes to selecting the most suitable base text for scholarly use. The emic religious convictions of these subjects/objects of study should not necessarily be allowed to set the terms for the modern scholarly field at large. By the time Aaron ben Asher and Maimonides produced the fruits of their thought about the relative purity of textual traditions, the text already existed in other "base" forms that they excluded a priori on religious, not textual, grounds.[137] Why should we, whoever we are, be bound by those decisions? But perhaps the act of presenting any singular edition of the Bible requires selecting some religious assumptions over others if one is to construct it in any way at all; in the end, one may be forced to rely on emic points of view, since there exists no objective, etic perspective on a socioreligious construction such as the Bible.

Goshen-Gottstein suggests an external metric, as well, for periodizing the textual history of the Bible, namely, the great divide that developed at the close of the Second Temple period: "The Destruction of the Temple . . . is the main dividing line in textual history as far as it can be recovered."[138] In this, Goshen-Gottstein agrees with Talmon, who calls this boundary the "crucial period of the Great Divide," which "decisively determined the totally different transmission of the biblical books by 'normative Judaism' and by the Community of the Renewed Covenant [i.e., Qumran]."[139] While Talmon emphatically asserts that "the textual multiformity" at Qumran "refutes modern views which profess allegiance to Lagarde's Urtext theory" and supports a theory of "various pristine texts," he then shifts to a discussion of "postdivide" textual transmission that (according to him) recognizes textual stability and is equivalent to the canonical and theological views of the rabbinic tradition.[140] In the "predivide" world, the text was pluriform and variable, existing in at least some Jewish communities in several adaptable forms; but in the postdivide world, these textual traditions became a "handed down corpus of biblical books, the culminations of a long process of growth of an earlier diversified biblical literature in oral and written transmission."[141]

True, the rabbinic tradition with its rhetoric of the fixed text developed a robust existence after the great divide, and the Qumran community and very likely other now-lost textually pluriform traditions did not survive, but the biblical text manifestly did not simply become "fixed" or "stabilized" as a whole in the "postdivide" period for at least two reasons.

First, the text had already developed into several different and still living traditions, including that of the Greek-speaking Jewry of the Mediterranean world, various early Christian communities, and the Samaritan community, and these different textual traditions continued to exist straight through the period of the great divide, providing multiple exceptions to the univocally stable text in the postdivide period (to say nothing of translation, which produces its own transformative effects that continued in these exceptional textual traditions).[142] Second, the text continued to develop even in the supposedly fixed textual tradition of "central Judaism" after the period of the great divide and into the period of the Masoretes.[143] The scribes retroactively adopted a "primary" text for each book and subsequently categorized and corrected manuscripts toward that particular text, as well as contributed to textual stabilization and correction through the use of technologies including new vowel systems, scribal textual interventions, direct scribal alterations such as *tiqqunê soferim,* the inscription of textual corrections into the margins of texts by means of *ketib-qere* and *sebirin,* as well as through the use of the technical apparatus of the Masorah itself as guard and pedagogue.[144]

As the observer effect would predict, the remarkable Masoretic work meant to stabilize the already fixed text in fact altered the history of textual development in its own way.[145] Moreover, variations even within this stabilization system ensured the variations that continued to appear throughout the medieval and modern period.[146] While there was a polemical and theological drive toward recognizing one pure form of scripture in the rabbinic tradition, there was simultaneously an "acute awareness of the existence of variants in manuscripts of biblical books."[147] This acute awareness and rejection of variant readings reveals their continuing existence post-70 CE; the variants found in Josephus, Philo, and Rabbi Meir's Torah are witnesses to this diversity.[148] As Gary Martin has demonstrated, even at the time of Aristeas the text was in considerable flux.[149] When it comes to traditional texts, stability and fixity are rhetorical devices, not ontological realities.

One might note here the similarities between the activities of modern textual critics and the Masoretes; for both groups, the creation of critical editions is a productive, not archaeological, activity. Correction requires a correction toward something else and thus assumes one privileged text form and ultimately one manuscript—either a diplomatic base text or eclectic edition—as a "center" of the manuscript group or groups. This moment of selection is itself a massive intervention into the history of textual development and imposes, rather than closes, an era of intense textual change. Is not the modern shift from local biblical manuscripts toward the text of the second Rabbinic Bible, then to the Leningrad codex, and now toward the Aleppo codex, proof that the text of the Bible continues to change?

Moreover, the variants found within the Talmud and rabbinic midrash itself signal that the text was not quite as fixed as some would have it: as the Tosafists explained, "Our Talmud disagrees with our Scriptures."[150] One may point to discrepancies between the order of books as given in the MT and the divergent canonical lists given in halakhah or to textual differences that are not merely the result of poor memory.[151] Even within "central" Judaism alone, the biblical text remained in flux and is still in flux today. Goshen-Gottstein's review of the history of text criticism recounts the many twists and turns of the modern quest for the best text of the MT, and this is itself a history of textual variation, not one of stability. If the text were so fixed, why would the work of modern textual criticism be continuing some half millennia later?

Of course, the quantity of textual developments decreased in the years after 132 CE. Yet Goshen-Gottstein, Talmon, Tov, Dominique Barthélemy, James Sanders, and many other scholars use this historical development to subtly assume the natural priority of the MT, and moreover of the Tiberian MT, after the divide. At the same time, these scholars seem conveniently to forget that other communities were still using the same text forms found at Qumran. Drawing the line of the great divide seems to justify an exclusion of non-Tiberian MT text forms and the shift from an acceptance of textual pluriformity to an aversion to it. Yet a decrease in the quantity of textual difference does not naturally grant one particular text form a hegemonic status. The meaning of the great divide must be imposed either by a theologically committed group at the time of its supposed rupture or by scholars from a more recent vantage point. The tolerance of textual pluriformity pre-70 CE allowed by Talmon and Goshen-Gottstein suddenly disappears, and thus the divide between original and reception reinscribes itself at the boundary.

One might push this point even further. Talmon remarks that, in contrast to the inhabitants of Qumran, who used various adaptations of biblical traditions, "the Sages adopted and promulgated one exclusively legitimate version of Scripture. The production and transmission of quasi-biblical compositions revolving on biblical themes and traditions was evidently discouraged."[152] This statement is consistent with the theological rhetoric of the rabbis, but it overlooks the lively and important "production and transmission of quasi-biblical compositions revolving on biblical themes" within rabbinic Judaism, namely, haggadic and halakhic midrash, including the Mišhnah and Talmud.[153] One may add to this, as well, the various Targumim. Perhaps midrash and Targum were not viewed by the rabbis themselves as scriptural, but they nevertheless attest to the continued life and development of these texts and traditions after the so-called great divide.

Thus, the very logic Talmon uses to critique the Lagardian tradition of urtext-oriented textual criticism can be directed against the "postdivide" period. Just as "we have no objective criteria for deciding which reading is original and which derivative" in the predivide era, we may say of the variants within and without the Masoretic tradition in the postdivide era that "both have the same claim to be judged genuine pristine traditions."[154] Just as "the earliest attainable biblical manuscripts give witness to a wide variety of textual traditions which were current in Judaism in the pre-divide stage of transmission," biblical manuscripts give witness to the continued existence of a wide variety of textual traditions in the postdivide stage.[155] Perhaps Talmon would agree with this line of reasoning. If he would, however, then why is there a base text of the HUB, and why would it be the Aleppo codex?

In terms of method, Talmon agrees with Goshen-Gottstein's practical reformulation of the project of textual criticism: "Ideally the critical analysis aims at recovering the original wording of the sacred writings. However, in actuality the target cannot be attained because of the unavailability of reliable ancient sources from a time close to the creation of a biblical book. Scholarly analysis can only attempt to recapture primary formulations underlying the current major Hebrew and translational versions, but cannot achieve the reconstitution of one primary text from which they derive, much less the biblical authors' *ipsissima verba*."[156] In other words, the text-critical project must recognize the asymptotic impossibility of the recovery of the original text and thus must allow for the diversity of ancient readings, which the multiple apparatuses of the HUB aim to represent. Yet in Talmon's writing, much like that of Goshen-Gottstein, one may find a certain textual preference that covertly manifests itself within otherwise "objective historiography."

For example, in his overview of textual criticism, Talmon tells the story of the composition and development of the biblical text by way of reference to four main stages, during the first of which, according to Talmon, "variant wordings" of the early transmission characterize the biblical texts and "multiformity" predominated over "uniformity."[157] Talmon here appears to lay aside notions of the "pure origin" of any biblical texts, but it quickly becomes apparent that he has simply displaced the *ipsissima verba* from a point of origin to a historical telos. The modern four-stage history of the text, he explains, delimits the text's "history" between two endpoints, namely, "between the inception at varying times of the books contained in the corpus and the stabilization of the text," which "probably achieved its essential form at the height of the Second Temple period."[158] Thus, the biblical texts have a particular stabilization point that marks the moment of their "essential form[s]." Of course, many of these texts had already been stabilized at other times and in other communities, but the unified and stabilized text that was generated by the community of normative Judaism serves as the natural bookend to this process. No doubt, factors such as the rise of the liturgical use of the Bible in the synagogue, the textual focus of rabbinic study, and the rabbinic concern that the world of the Bible had become something "different" from the world of the rabbis are extremely important. Nevertheless, their importance does not justify the scholarly conclusion that these moments are normative for the "text itself" and all communities.

In other words, the rabbis and Masoretes thought that they should not (openly) meddle with the text any longer, but why does this lead anyone to argue that the Aleppo codex is thus the natural choice for a base text of the Bible? Can a line really be drawn at the great divide that somehow legitimates the future Aaron ben Asher text and delegitimates other text forms, leading to the former being declared "the Bible" and the latter being relegated to reception? Does the canonization of the text in one particular religious group have retroactive significance for all previous stabilized and all future stabilized forms of the text? I argue that one cannot make universal judgments in this way. But perhaps there is another model we can use that would truly respect pluriformity in biblical textual criticism.

Pluriformity in Contexts

Eugene Ulrich is one of the preeminent readers and editors of Judaean Desert texts and has served as chief editor of the biblical scrolls for the Scrolls International Publication Project; as such, he has faced squarely the consequences of the textual pluriformity found within the scrolls. Ulrich's research focuses on the long, diverse composition process of biblical texts and the resulting variants at Qumran; these variants, variant editions, and parallel presentations of biblical traditions lead him, like Talmon and Goshen-Gottstein, to question not only the goals of textual criticism but the very existence of the original text.[159] Ulrich asks difficult questions about the ontological status of various textual editions and seems content at times to accept ambiguity and uncertainty.[160] Like Talmon and Goshen-Gottstein, Ulrich begins the process of rethinking textual criticism from the grounds of a pluriform text; these grounds are not entirely stable, but they seem to give rise to more honest and careful assessments of the historical record. But also like Talmon and Goshen-Gottstein, Ulrich at times—though it should be stressed, not often—establishes a boundary between the original and reception by positing an end to the process of textual development. Conceptually, this line functions in many ways as a structural analogue to Lagarde's line of origin.

Ulrich points out that the method by which a biblical text was produced should guide text-critical methods for delineating that same text. Israelite literature in general seems to have been woven together over time from a series of discrete oral and written texts that themselves came into being through their continual retelling in different contexts in somewhat different forms; thus text criticism should find a line between "text criticism" and "literary criticism" hard to draw. Even more difficult to locate would be any "original" text: Ulrich posits at least eight possibilities for the meaning of the term "the original text," each of which can be understood as a possible legitimate object of the text-critical search. One can for example, search for the source behind the biblical text (e.g., Canaanite stories "behind" the biblical texts), an original "document" (P, for example), the earliest complete edition of a book (e.g., the earliest connection of P and non-P material that became "Genesis"), the earliest moment at which the book became sacred, authoritative, or canonical (e.g., Genesis in the late Second Temple period), or perhaps only the proto-Masoretic version of the consonants, or otherwise a particular Masoretic version with vowels, punctuation, and interpretation added by the Masoretes.[161] More pointedly, one can look for an edition between any of these "earliest" editions—say, a later edition that was accepted as authoritative (e.g., Theodotion-Daniel), and not the "first" version that was accepted as such (e.g., proto-MT Daniel).

Ulrich gives as another example the development of the text of Exodus:

> After . . . repeated reformulations during the monarchic period and the early postexilic period, a Hebrew form of Exodus emerged that was eventually translated into Greek. That form can be labeled edition n+1, where n stands for the number of revised literary editions the text had undergone prior to becoming the Hebrew *Vorlage* of OG Exodus. A subsequent edition, n+2, was produced when some editor systematically rearranged the section with chapters 35–39 into the form present now in the MT. Yet another revised edition of Exodus, n+3, was formed when the many large expansions visible now in 4QpaleoExod^{m} were added to the text of edition n+2. The SP of Exodus may or may not be considered a new edition, n+4, dependent upon whether quantity or significance is the chief criterion, since there are only two or three small changes beyond 4QpaleoExod^{m}, but those changes determine the community's identity.[162]

Ulrich shows that neither the original text nor the final text are entirely determinable, since, on the one hand, the origins of the text lie in a traditioning process not compatible with the concept of originality and because, on the other, the text develops well past the form later associated with the MT and in several irreducible directions. Thus, Ulrich urges text critics to recognize the diverse forms in which these biblical texts exist and not to attempt to collapse texts into an "original" text that never existed as such. Qumran in particular reveals pluriformity of textual witnesses and is, according to Ulrich, likely "representative of the shape of the Scriptures elsewhere in Judaism."[163]

Yet Qumran is not alone in its witness: others, too—Josephus, SamPent, LXX, Philo, the New Testament, rabbinic quotations, for example—testify to a pluriform text continuing well into the "postdivide" era. Thus, according to Ulrich, the MT is "simply one form of that book as it existed in antiquity." Even rabbinic scribes were constantly "actively handing on the tradition," for example, by copying but also at times "attempting to make [the text] adaptable and relevant." This principle of "resignification," a term borrowed from J. A. Sanders, is the very mechanism by which the sacred text comes to matter to any community at all. The text is "capable of having new significance" in each new context in which it is read.[164]

Yet Ulrich, like Talmon and Goshen-Gottstein, posits a terminus ad quem of the end of biblical composition to replace textual criticism's terminus a quo of the original text. Ulrich points out that "the same process that characterized the composition of the Scriptures from their beginnings was still continuing all the way through the Second Temple Period."[165] Yet this "all the way through" has its limit at the end (or just after the end) of the Second Temple period: "It appears that the organic or developmental process of the composition of the Scriptures was brought to a halt," and the second Jewish revolt of 132 CE "appears to be a more likely setting for the crystallization of the view that a single form of the text was a necessity."[166] Thus, for Ulrich the end of textual composition is only "the abrupt interruption of the composition process for external, hostile reasons (the Roman threat or the Rabbinic-Christian debates)."[167] Ulrich explains that "it was not so much a 'stabilization' of the biblical texts as a loss of the pluriformity of the texts and the transition from a dynamically growing tradition to a uniform collection of 'Scripture.'"[168]

Yet pluriformity was lost only from the perspective of particular communities and not from the viewpoint examining the process of textual change itself. Rabbinic and early Christian communities developed preferences for particular sacred texts and grew to discourage altering them, but they talked about Scripture as if it were a fixed, stable text. This does not mean that something actually fixed and stable was objectively present, rather than something rhetorical, ideal, and sectarian. If something stable had arisen, then Origen's Hexapla and the Masoretic endeavor would never have been necessary. It seems rather clear from debates within and between Jewish and Christian communities that all parties acutely felt the continuing pluriformity of biblical texts in the supposedly stabilized period—whereas one can imagine indifference to pluriformity during the Second Temple period, as it was not yet a problem. But it certainly became a problem afterward.[169] This problem is fundamentally a conceptual one, namely, how do readers understand a sacred text that has several forms? The existence of the problem validates not the unmet ideal but rather the material inconsistencies that bedevil any attempt to fully reconcile them.

For his part, Ulrich concludes that the "object" of the text critical "search" should be "the text as it truly was," which denotes "the organic, developing, pluriform Hebrew text—different for each book—such as the evidence indicates."[170] What if the evidence indicates that the biblical texts remained developing and pluriform?[171]

James Bowley and John Reeves push Ulrich's arguments even further: "Succinctly stated, 'the Bible' is not and furthermore never was."[172] Since "canon" was not "a category employed by ancient Judaism" it is "therefore anachronistic" to think of Second Temple Jews having had a "Bible" as such.[173] To speak of the "original text of the Bible" is to "impose upon the texts' authors and/or readers alien categories" that were used only by later communities.[174] These texts were not held together, bound as a codex, and separated from all other texts; rather, from all archaeological remains, it appears that biblical texts were seen in the Second Temple period as a diverse collection of texts with rather hazy (or even nonexistent) "edges." Alternate editions, paraphrases, parabiblical narratives, harmonistic and creative editing of biblical texts, and commentaries were held together at Qumran without apparent distinction.

Bowley and Reeves also argue that Jubilees and 1 Enoch, for example, were not seen as "rewritten Bible" but were understood by many in Second Temple Judah to be as authoritative and sacred as Genesis itself. Thus, although later religious groups selected Genesis to be part of "the Bible" but saw Jubilees as "a later attempt to rewrite the Bible" (while keeping Chronicles, which is clearly a later attempt to rewrite the Bible, as a part of "the Bible"), we are not bound to retroject such selections back into the period of the composition of the biblical text itself. For this reason, Bowley and Reeves claim that "we can no longer speak of the 'final form' of any particular text." As they note, "Any particular text one might use is one exemplar from one stage in a long and complicated genealogy."[175] The methodological result is that scholars cannot talk about "the text" or "reading the text itself." Instead, any reading of any biblical text must be preceded by the choice of which particular form of a particular text one is to read.[176]

The principle of selection is not inherently given; there is no necessarily wrong or right, no pure or corrupt, no original or secondary texts to read. There are just texts, which can be sorted based on historical, social, aesthetic, theological, authorial, and any number of other grounds. But there is no given or necessary method by which to sort them. Even more than Ulrich and Talmon, Bowley and Reeves test the boundaries of the "great divide" between the "original period of composition" and the "reception" of biblical texts.

Though Bowley and Reeves offer a provocative and compelling argument, they seem to harbor something of a historical imposition in their own work. They claim that the concepts of canon and Bible are anachronistic, alien, and imposed by modern scholars because they were not used by the authors of biblical texts, who apparently fit within the category of ancient Judaism.[177] But if their arguments concerning the lack of finality of any biblical text are correct, then how is it that these texts have discrete authors, given historical contexts of production, and given historical categories that must be used to read these texts correctly?

Bowley and Reeves claim that "modern theologians and historians are not in a position to make demands of ancient writers."[178] Within this radical dismissal of boundaries between Bible and non-Bible, original and derivative, there suddenly appears a surprisingly strong division—a great divide—between modern scholars and ancient writers. How is this possible if the text never had a definite, given original or end point? In other words, it seems strange that the Second Temple–era precanonical scribes are granted the authority to create categories for texts that they were anachronistically resignifying—and thus not originating—while the textual judgments assigned by medieval scribes and modern scholars are so easily dismissed.

Several assumptions are at work here. One implicit assumption is that the authors of a text understand a text's ontology correctly. A derivative assumption is that a scholar must uncover an author's intentions or context in order to read the text in a sense that is unanachronistic, or perhaps "chronistic." Reading the text without these assumptions would violate the text's essence, resulting in a poor, garbled, or nonsensical reading. But why should the intentions, concepts, and reading protocols of one segment of ancient Jewish scribes be seen as the ontological arbiters for biblical texts?

Bowley and Reeves do not define the nature of biblical texts in terms of one particular textual moment in the midst of a given text's genealogy, but they do claim that some scholars read the text out of context—which assumes that there is a correct context within which to read each biblical text. But since there is no naturally privileged final historical form of a biblical text, it follows that there is no naturally privileged final historical context within which to read any biblical text. In the end, it appears that Bowley and Reeves do implicitly imagine that one particular period in the genealogy of these texts holds the key to their essence, and it is one before the end of the Second Temple period. The dividing line, in Bowley and Reeves's point of view, is one of proper historical context.

Miltonesque Textual Criticism

Though the scholarly search for the original text of the Hebrew Bible has taken many forms, some of which even disavow the term "original" while nevertheless retaining its function, these forms seem to share one underlying conceptual narrative. In schematic form, the basic narrative of the original text is as follows: at one point in time, there was a text—either an original text, an autograph, a pristine copy, an archetype, a text that was considered authoritative, a final form of the text or merely a relatively more original version—that stood at the end of a process of composition and simultaneously at the beginning of a process of copying. Everything was as it should be. It was, in some sense, perfect.

But at that paradoxical point in time, alterations to the text ceased to be compositional and henceforth became corruptions. Authors became copyists. From that point on, the long history of the postoriginal text becomes a history of transmission and reception. Thus, the perfect thing was not immutable. The many changes to the text in the last several millennia include both intentional and unintentional changes, expansions and emendations, translations and misspellings. But whatever their cause, they pose a problem for textual criticism by detracting from the purity and authenticity of the text. Paradise is lost. Textual critics mourn for the lost original and marginalize nonoriginal texts by means of several literary tropes: namely, the binary tropes of *degradation* (corrupt text, incorrect text, or errors versus pristine text or correct text), *marginalization* (secondary readings, inauthentic texts, or even daughter versions versus primary readings, authentic texts, or central texts), *pathology,* and *perversion* (deviating texts versus corrected texts or texts with textual integrity), and *decline* (transmitted text versus original text), among others.

Yet the narrative does not end with sadness. Paradise is not merely lost; it can be regained. Into the mess of textual corruption, the modern textual critic brings rational analysis and historical artifacts that allow him or her to discard the accumulations and confusions produced by the fallible transmission history of the text. With the swords of *recensio* and *selectio,* the textual critic cuts away the accretions of impurity surrounding the text. By analyzing the existing manuscripts and identifying corruptions, the textual critic retraces the history of corruption, hopefully finding vestiges of the moment of pristine textual origin that emanated from the hand of the author and offering an argument that justifies a particular reconstruction of the moment of origin.[179] "Recovery" is thus a key motif in the conceptual narrative undergirding textual criticism. Overall, this basic narrative of loss and recovery begins with purity, follows with a fall into corruption, and then advocates a method that will redeem the lost purity. This three-stage narrative should sound eerily familiar to those working in biblical studies, since textual criticism adumbrates the basic Christian theological narrative.[180]

Yet if this Miltonesque narrative does not adequately describe the biblical text or the task of textual criticism, is there an alternative construction that could clarify the boundary between an original and its reception?

TWO

Living in Pottersville: An Alternate Approach to Textual Criticism

> In actual textual criticism "original" . . . is used relatively: given the fact of different readings, a normal and probably a necessary way of ordering, classifying, and understanding them is to ask which of them may probably be considered secondary and derivative in relation to others; and what is thus perceived to be not secondary and derivative in relation to other readings is in that respect more "original." . . . [It is] doubtful whether any serious thinking about the text at all can be carried out without this piece of the conceptual apparatus.
> —James Barr

> Léfebure, ce n'est pas mal.
> —Jacques Derrida

Introduction: The Illusion of Borders

Some visual illusions play on the skill of the human brain, honed by many millennia of evolutionary pressures, to locate clear borders delineating objects.[1] In the case of the famous Kanizsa triangle, a white triangle complete with clear borders seems to emerge from the image. If one looks closely, however, it quickly becomes apparent that no borders are present. Our brains supplied them for us. What actually exists is the impression of a triangle, which then creates the impression of three circles—yet they are not, in fact, circles—and an underlying, black-bordered triangle, which is instead three open angles. When looking at the Kanizsa triangle, the viewer constructs a nonexistent border that not only brings into being a ghostly triangle; it also retrospectively alters all other objects in the frame.

In the practice of textual criticism, the emergence of the phantasm known as the original text—or one of its aliases, such as authoritative copy, archetype, or final form—not only constructs borders where there were none before. It also distorts what is actually there. Take, for example, the illusion performed by charts of the transmission of the biblical text. At the top of chart, placed before the variant Hebrew versions that became the SamPent, the MT, and the OG, one finds a Hebrew *Vorlage*. This implies the existence of a unified group of texts and a stable form of each biblical book. Yet this figure of uncomplicated, pure origin obscures the lines that actually exist. What is missing in this chart, and what has been tidily collected into a single category and given firm borders, is the variegated literary development of the Bible that contains no such set form. Origins are generally thought to be simple and pure, but when they are found, they are inevitably messy, complex things.[2] The Bible is no different.

To revisit the example of the book of Daniel: the proto-OG and proto-MT editions of the book of Daniel agree significantly—though, as always, with some variants—for chapters 1–3 and 7–12. Yet there are discrepancies between the agreed-on older and "more original" material, particularly among the proto-OG and proto-MT versions of Daniel 4–6. In chapters 4 and 6, the MT is much shorter than the OG, but chapter 5 exhibits a longer MT and a shorter OG. As a result, Ulrich and others have concluded that "in Daniel 4–6 *both* the MT and the OG are apparently secondary, that is, they each expand in different directions beyond an earlier common edition that no longer survives."[3] Moreover, the OG apparently translated a Semitic *Vorlage* that preceded it; in other words, we have two ancient versions of a now-lost base text that it would be impossible to reconstruct at this point.

Some might harbor the dream of recovering the lost base text of chapters 4–6 and using it as part of the "original" book of Daniel, but there is a problem. The older version would not necessarily be in any way superior to the later revisions, since it was clearly not the end of any process and was not adopted as stable or fixed by any known community—and certainly not the communities that altered it. Nor was it the "original" book of Daniel, since it is also clear that Daniel was written in historical stages, the Aramaic court stories (chapters 2–6) having been written earlier than the Maccabean-era chapters (especially chapters 7–12). At its origins the book of Daniel is irreducibly complex, but this complexity can be ignored if it is given the singular name of "the original."

When textual critics speak of redaction criticism, or source criticism, however, they readily disavow the concept of an original text. The great advances made in critical biblical study over the past few centuries derive from scholars slowly recognizing the complexity of even the earliest versions of the biblical text. Indeed, it was the discovery of the Bible's originary complexity that first led scholars to question the ideology of fully formed authorial as well as divinely issued texts. In 1753 Jean Astruc argued that the narrative repetitions and the existence of multiple names for the deity suggested that the composition of the book of Genesis must derive from multiple sources and that these sources likely came from diverse historical and cultural backgrounds.[4] The resulting field of source criticism sought to understand the diverse complexity of even these "original accounts."

Likewise, redaction critics pushed biblical scholars to carefully assess the way in which biblical authors and editors stitched together their source materials by focusing on how the biblical text functions together as a historical and literary patchwork. Even the strongest advocates for the unified authorship of the Yahwist, such as John van Seters, and the Deuteronomist, such as Martin Noth, admit that their original author incorporated earlier sources and traditions.[5]

Text critics, however, bracket these complications of origin in the tidy category of literary criticism that looks behind the veil of the *Vorlage*.[6] This bracketing maneuver allows the text critic to seek out an original text that paradoxically stood at the end of this long, fragmented literary process. Due to the surprising discoveries of texts at Qumran, it is now clear that textual pluriformity existed well before any canonization or completion. Yet the illusion of a unified "original text" that then fragmented into various lesser versions and translations continues to persist.

Like many illusions, the original text is difficult to grasp because it often seems so commonsensical. Karl Marx opens his critique of commodity fetishism with this observation: "A commodity appears at first sight an extremely obvious, trivial thing. But its analysis brings out that it is a very strange thing, abounding in metaphysical subtleties and theological niceties."[7] Marx does not attack commodities as being clearly metaphysical objects in order to strip away their presumed divinity. In other words, Marx does not imagine that you need to be disabused of a conscious notion that your watch is a magical object. No, he is aware that you consciously think that it is a lump of metal parts. On the contrary, Marx needs to convince you that underneath your conscious belief that the commodity is an inert product lies another belief altogether. We consciously think that commodities are simply things, but unconsciously commodities function for us like magical objects—which is why advertising can be effective even when we consciously think that the advertisements are ridiculous. Marx's revelation is that we unconsciously treat commodities as supernatural objects. We disavow this belief on the surface, but we act on it in practice.[8]

Why does this disavowed illusion continue to drive the field of textual criticism? Because it flows not from an objective analysis of the data gathered by textual critics but from the deeply held, rarely questioned general conception of what a biblical text *is*. In other words, the assumed ontology of the biblical text creates this illusion within textual criticism. In order to see the biblical text properly, one must enunciate an alternate ontology of biblical texts, one that affirms the processual and differential qualities of the biblical text, which might prove more productive for text-critical research.

Imagining a World without an Original Text

Can illusions prove useful? In the epigraph to this chapter, James Barr claims that text critics must organize texts into a hierarchy of "more or less" originality, concluding that it is "doubtful whether any serious thinking about the text at all can be carried out without this piece of the conceptual apparatus."[9] While Barr simply asserts his opinion and then moves on to other matters, permit me to pause for a moment and ask whether it is, in fact, possible to think without the concept of the original text. Like George Bailey in *It's a Wonderful Life,* can one imagine what the world would look like if the concept of the original text had never been born? Would it really be as foreboding as Pottersville, chock-full of chaotic nightclubs and lonely librarians? And on the other hand, is Bedford Falls as pristine as we once thought?

Emanuel Tov defines textual criticism as the field that "deals with the origin and nature of all forms of a text," which "involves a discussion of its putative original form(s) and an analysis of the various representations of the changing biblical text."[10] In Pottersville, this definition would be emended as follows: textual criticism deals with all forms of a text and analyzes the various representations of the changing biblical text. The text critic would look closely at the extant forms of a given text and still describe relationships of dependence, still date texts, and still attempt to discern where and when particular manuscripts were written. What would disappear is the evaluation of texts in terms of universal worth.

If there were no original text, then there would be a general acceptance that a biblical text could appear in various nonidentical guises. What a given scholar or critical edition in Bedford Falls offers as the original, final, stabilized, authorized, or published text would in Pottersville merely present one particular form of a text that a particular historical reader had selected to read at a particular time. This statement would hold for any determination of the proper canon of the Bible, the proper editions or text traditions of each book of the Bible, or the proper readings from among the many manuscripts in that tradition.

Each variant would represent a justifiably real yet different form of the text, and scholars would not make ontological claims about the relative purity, priority, or acceptability of it in universal terms. But this would not, as Barr claims, mean that one must abdicate thought altogether. On the contrary, when evaluating manuscripts scholars would simply have to specify what relative grounds they are using to justify limited claims. Without the concept of a hierarchy of manuscripts, answers to the question "What is the text?" would either be ad hoc (i.e., "Here's a version of this text, let's read this one"), local (i.e., "Our community reads this version"), or made by means of a specific limited criteria (i.e., "Here is the most literarily coherent, or theologically profound, or aesthetically pleasing version to me").

A given scholar may be looking for the most beautiful, or earliest known, or earliest known proto-Masoretic, or shortest text, and of course any scholar can justify prioritizing manuscripts among these lines. None of these attributes are necessary or universal. They are limited. To think in these terms, one simply has to take the extra step of proposing a limited set of criteria that can be used to draw distinctions. One would not stop organizing manuscripts into historical lineages or proposing dates and locations of production for particular manuscripts. But one would admit that stemmatics and historical information brings us no closer to knowing which text we should use at any particular time; it gives us no insight into the relative worth of texts.

Furthermore, while it is helpful that the OHB shows textual pluriformity by presenting side-by-side editions of the proto-OG and the proto-MT where they reflect different archetypes, the focus on archetypes and other ideal constructions continues to privilege a point of origin over derivative forms. This privileging undermines the representation of the pluriformity of biblical texts. Each edition—even the MT—existed in various forms that changed throughout time, and so in Pottersville one would not privilege an archetype of any manuscript group or tradition as natural or original.

Yet what about copying mistakes—surely poorly copied manuscripts are considered lesser beings in Pottersville? A Pottersvillian would respond that perhaps spelling errors or metalepsis exhibit poor copying skills, but a text that is copied poorly may still be—and may sometimes be *even more*—authoritative for a particular community precisely because of its alterations. What is from one perspective a scribal error can be, from the perspective of a community reading that text, divine writ. What is metalepsis from the perspective of the copyist might be beauty from the perspective of the poet. What is from one perspective the translation character of the LXX is, from another perspective, simply the text itself. Copying errors, translation errors, and the like only degrade the worth of a text if one seeks an original text. If there is no original text, then one might affirm the full existence and value neutrality of every aspect of the complex situation that we find in the world. Perhaps some would prefer to distinguish texts by means of the criterion of scribal mistakes. But to distinguish among texts in this way would not amount to making a universal statement of the absolute value of a text.

Not only is Pottersville a fine place to live—there is no Bedford Falls, and there never has been. It is an illusion. We have always been living in Pottersville.

There is no original biblical text, and any thought that has ever been thought about the biblical text has emerged in its absence. We have always been thinking without the original text: now we just have to think without thinking about the original text.

Barr claims that the concept of the original text is necessary because it allows for classification into primary and secondary categories. Here Barr hits the nail on the head: the "original text" serves only to create a hierarchical framework. Yet the resulting ethico-ontological axiology (that is, a hierarchy that assigns moral values such as "pristine" and "corrupt") is so pervasive and accepted that freeing ourselves of its illusive power is difficult indeed. For example, when Emanuel Tov introduces the sixth-century BCE silver rolls from Ketef Hinnom, which contain the priestly blessing from Numbers 6:24–26, he declares that "since these documents contain no running biblical texts, their contribution to textual criticism is limited."[11] At first glance, this argument makes quite a bit of sense. The amulets were not meant to be whole copies of the book of Numbers, and they differ from the MT as well. Yet it has biblical text on it. How is it not then a valued witness to the biblical text? Why would its limited textual scope necessarily limit its contribution?

It seems far more defensible to assume that every stage of the text's development and transmission is contingent, which is to say that its particular constitution is not logically justified. That is, there is no necessary version of the text, because any local necessity (e.g., the authority conferred by a particular group) it itself historically contingent. It could have happened that the Masoretes ended up with proto-OG Jeremiah, or that the Samaritans became the dominant religious group and their canon became the normative one. In the end, the only necessity is the necessity of the contingency of every particular instantiation of a biblical text.

To push Barr's point even further: text critics do not use the concept of the original text to sort texts into a hierarchy—no, they use the concept to create hierarchies. Text critics manufacture classificatory schemes as modern external supplements to the texts, and by their own logic these schemes are clearly unoriginal to the *Vorlage*. Even gestures toward ancient communities' conferment of authority as the moment of origin recognize a historical supplement as that which grants full originality to the text. Late Second Temple communities were as much historically removed inheritors of a textual tradition as are modern text critics, and thus their classificatory judgments (if they can be known at all) are also supplements. Strangely, these supplements seem to create the originality of that which they supposedly represent.[12] Authority cannot yield an original biblical text, but in its place modern scholarly as well as ancient communities produce an originalizing textual supplement that carries out its assigned task with varying modes of success.

To say there is no original, final, or privileged text is to embrace the identity of the biblical text and canon as pluriform, recognizing the lack of inherent universal value for each variant of the text. But is there nothing but variants, then? A truly pluriform text presents a difficulty: if countless uniquely different instances of the book of Proverbs are equally the book of Proverbs, then how does one read, analyze, and comment on the book of Proverbs at all? How does one get anything done in Pottersville?

The Ontology of the Text: Identity and Difference

How does a critic read a text when no two physical representations of this assumedly extant text agree? Scholars' responses to this problem flow from their general conception of what a biblical text is. In other words, one's ontology of the biblical text determines potential approaches to biblical criticism.

When trying to explain shared elements of identity between manifestly different things, biblical studies confronts one of the world's oldest conceptual problems: namely, the problem of universals.[13] Biblical scholars tend to think of biblical texts in essentialist terms. This is not surprising, since Plato and Aristotle, of course, were dealing with a problem very much like that of textual critics. For example, one might suppose that all circular objects share the property of being circular. Yet every circular object is different and differently circular in its own way. No circle is perfectly round, and circles come in different sizes; thus what *is* circle-ness? To rephrase the example in terms of text criticism: all manuscripts of the book of Proverbs share the property of being Proverbs. Yet every manuscript of Proverbs is different; thus what *is* Proverbs itself? How can one discern a core of identity that might stand behind observable variety?

Realism: Recovering the Ideal Work

Plato famously posited as his solution to this problem the so-called realist approach. He held that an ideal circle is a real thing, later called a "universal." Textual critics have tended to follow suit by thinking in terms of the ideal book of Proverbs, for example. Thus particular concrete objects, such as actual manuscripts of the book of Proverbs, instantiate to varying degrees their universal—in this case, the ideal form of the book of Proverbs.[14] That is, each manuscript of Proverbs stands in more or less of a relation to a universal form of Proverbs that exists on another plane, accessible only through the particulars that instantiate it.

Felicitously, Plato chose terms familiar to textual critics to describe his ontology. He called the ideal universal form the model, of which all local manifestations were merely copies. Plato argued that a copy should closely resemble the model; thus copies should be judged and ranked by their degree of similarity to the model. Authentic copies faithfully replicate the pristine model and thus minimize divergence from the ideal, whereas poor copies introduce differences, innovations, and corruptions. Thus Plato called these poor copies "phantasms," ghostly things, since they misleadingly simulated the essence or reality of, an ideal form. Today, this word is usually translated by the term "simulacrum."

Plato's ontology builds a qualitative hierarchy based on the degrees of resemblance to an ideal form, drawing an important moral distinction between good copies and bad simulacra. In general, for Plato copies that minimize difference are better than copies that innovate or introduce change. The strengths of Plato's theory are clear: this theory establishes how it can be that two concrete particulars can share in an attribute. Yet Plato's theory carries with it some unhelpful baggage. In particular, three aspects of this essentialist ontology are troublesome for biblical critics. First, this ontology imagines that identity is static, fixed in the ideal form, and thus invariant. Second, it judges the worth of objects by means of their degree of deviation from the ideal form. Third, it thinks about difference from the standpoint of identity and thus defines difference in a purely negative manner—as simply a lack of resemblance. For example, one might distinguish between a real postage stamp and an imposter (or counterfeit) postage stamp by means of their degree of resemblance to the ideal form of an authorized postage stamp. In Plato's world, differences are primarily evidence of a failure to resemble an ideal form.

Many influential textual critics tend to think in these essentialist terms, claiming that each biblical book has a single fixed form that defines the true identity of that book. This fixed form is variously referred to as the original text, the urtext, the final authoritative copy, the archetype, or hyparchetype. All of these ideal constructions play the role of a normative ideal form. Text critics sort and judge particular manuscripts as well as text groups and versions according to their degree of deviation from these normative ideal forms. For example, Tov asserts that the OG is of particular worth for textual criticism since it contains some original readings, whereas the so-called daughter translations of the Greek text have no "bearing" on textual criticism.[15] So the Armenian and Coptic texts are worthless for textual criticism because any differences they may present are surely novelties that occurred during the transmission of the text and are thus not part of the true identity of the biblical text. The daughter versions thus play the Platonic role of simulacrum, since they diverge from their ideal form and lose their identity along the way.

Michael Fox, following Thomas Tanselle, posits a Platonic distinction between the immaterial work (the ideal text) and the material text (the manuscripts). In this argument, all manuscripts of Proverbs participate to varying degrees in the ideal work of Proverbs.[16] According to Tanselle's logic, the texts inscribed on artifactual manuscripts are physical incarnations of the author's intentions; any instantiation of physical text is suspect and requires correction toward the work. Though the work has likely never existed fully in any manuscript—given that, for example, spelling errors may have infected it from the beginning—recovering the *work* is the goal of the text critic. As Fox explains, "Insofar as the result [of text-critical analysis] is accurate, it will represent a work, as Tanselle defines it: an 'ideal verbal construction.'"[17]

The work is ideal, Fox holds, because physical instantiations of it are liable to be corrupted: "It is very unlikely that there ever was a manuscript that held this text. That is because changes, deliberate and unintended, were surely introduced at different times, some even before the later parts of the book were added. Hence the text I am aiming at never had physical existence. . . . Texts go through transmutations; the work has sort of platonic existence, abstracted from any particular textual manifestation. The editor aims to reconstruct the text that best represents the work."[18] Where, then, does one look for this ideal text that has never existed? As Fox argues, one looks in the mind of the author. Boldly, Fox proclaims that his goal "can be defined as the proto-MT as it should have been, what the authors, conceived as a collectivity . . . , wanted us to read."[19]

Thus Fox deals with the classic philosophical problem of identity and difference by positing a perfect, nonmaterial, and atemporal ideal of an author's thought that may only be approached via the imperfect data transmitted by the sensuous manuscripts. Fox makes clear his a metaphysical assumption: there is one correct version of Proverbs, and a scholar may go about trying to find it. Here we see the hallmarks of essentialist ontology: a static ideal work exists apart from the manuscripts that attempt to represent, or resemble, it, with varying degrees of success.

If we follow Fox's claim, the result is that the clear textual diversity of the book of Proverbs evidenced in the historical record is but a phantasm, a corrupted witness to something far more real—the idea of the work—that is inaccessible from the historical record itself. That is, the text critic's reasoning power may find the work, but the senses cannot. One troubling aspect to this schema is its marginalization of all physical manuscripts: for Fox, the ideal work is the real thing, whereas the material representations are "not real" and thus have no identity proper to themselves. Manuscripts are only witnesses to the real, of which they are not properly a part. In that sense, they all bear more or less false witness, as they point imperfectly to the real thing. Manuscripts are like phantasms: ghosts, mere apparitions, and as such they do not have a proper identity of their own.[20] In Tanselle and Fox's point of view, the physical artifact and the text it presents are nonpresences, things that exist only as witnesses to something real, in the Platonic sense: namely, the intention of the author.

But manuscripts are clearly real things, and they have measurable effects on the history of a text. Kyle McCarter, following the Platonic work/text distinction, notes the dual promise of physical presence—both endurance and change: "Copying . . . is a source of both survival and corruption for a text; the very process that preserves the text also exposes it to danger. . . . [A] text, because it has been exposed so often to the danger of copying, is especially liable to corruption."[21] McCarter assumes that change in general is dangerous and that exposure to time and space leads to changes. Change introduces difference, and introducing differences threatens the purity of the identity of whatever it is that has entered time. In the words of text critics, changes are corruptions. This value-laden term demonstrates that the stable identity of the work is an important, precious thing that one must guard. Since any materiality necessitates change and thus difference—and thus a complex ontology—any pure identity can only be found in the ideal realm.

However, this bifurcation between real and phantasm poses some problems. For example, can we really believe that there exists, in the mind of some author or collective author, a perfect yet immaterial form of the book of Genesis? How could we think this, in light of the complex and multifaceted composition history of that text?

Nominalism: Every Manuscript Is an Island

While there is some upside to realism in light of text-critical editorial practice, one wonders if these metaphysical assumptions harm text critical scholarship more than they help. One alternative to realism is nominalism, which rejects the existence of universals altogether. Instead, the nominalist argues that only concrete particulars exist and that the apparent relations between these particulars are merely linguistic fictions. Thus the manuscripts are real, while the notion of a connection between manuscripts—such as the idea of a book of Genesis that transcends any two copies—is a phantasm waiting to be exorcized.

Fox offers a nominalist counterargument to his Platonic conception of text criticism. Fox mentions the so-called diachronic perspective, which holds that the work exists "in fluctuating and multiple forms, while each text-form is an autonomous 'textual moment.'"[22] He calls this an "extreme" position that he avoids. The diachronic perspective is, he suggests, a "relativistic acceptance of any and every text-form as a 'textual moment' of irreducible validity . . . one must query whether, if everything is equally valid for every kind of edition . . . there is sense in any editorial activity at all."[23] In short, Fox sees the main alternative to Platonic idealism as nihilistic and "relativist acceptance" of radical diversity with no room for identity.

While completely nihilistic relativism is hard to locate within the field of biblical studies, less extreme nominalism has been suggested by several scholars. As David Clines proposes:

> The old textual criticism was devoted to marginalizing and ultimately to ignoring all its actual evidence, which is to say, all the existing manuscripts, in favour of and in the quest for the presumed but never glimpsed original. A postmodern textual criticism invites us to a new adventure with manuscripts, to consider the extant manuscripts and their texts in and of themselves—for what they witness to, whether the conditions of their own production or the purposes for which they were produced. In a word, an interest in originals is a modern interest; an interest in copies is a postmodern interest. Or rather, it is a postmodern perception that the distinction between original and copy is problematic and one that needs wrestling with and not taking for granted.[24]

Clines critiques the Platonic structure of text criticism, envisioning instead an intense study of individual manuscripts and their historical and social locations. Such a mode of study is not to be discouraged, but one may ask what the precise relationship is between different manuscripts of the book of Proverbs. True nominalism would see each manuscript as an island unto itself, separated by its moment of (re)production. Yet does each act of copying Proverbs produce something entirely new? One might rather suppose that plenty of scribes throughout the history of transmission of the book of Proverbs did not reclaim every word for their own historical context. Abundant evidence exists of copyist-authors, befuddled by some obscure phrase or symbol, copying it down without any understanding at all.[25] If this is true, then the manuscript of a biblical text cannot be understood entirely in relation to its context of production, because the biblical text that it contains was not produced, at least in large part, in the particular context that produced the manuscript.

And yet the inverse cannot be true, either: biblical manuscripts are all in some way products of their contexts, and reference to a context can, at times, explain various marking, formatting, additions and other alterations. One must hold together both the biblical text's locality and its universality. The biblical text, as a traditional text, does not come from any one place, but is the amalgamation of various productive and reproductive efforts deriving from many different times and places. It is thus balanced carefully between the poles of alterity (the otherness of the tradition) and identity (the local reality of the manuscript and its peculiar features). But whereas the Platonic view of text criticism argues that manuscripts are nothing other than a witness to something that they are not, the nominalist view seems to tack too hard in the other direction, claiming that manuscripts are nothing more than what they are in and of themselves. Platonic realism posits that manuscripts are pure alterity and should be studied only for what they are not, while nominalism seems to argue that manuscripts are pure identity, and should be understood "in themselves" without reference to other manuscripts of the same biblical text. In short, Clines argues that "the conditions of [each manuscript's] production" will best explain that (copy of a) particular text.

In other fields, this same attitude has led to a revived interest in the material text, the study of bibliographic codes and manuscripts that seek to do away with the ideality of the Platonic ideal of the work. The nominalist emphasizes the material text and analyzes each seemingly unique textual product within its own context of production. Yet this does not solve the problems inherent in textual criticism; it only reinvents them under a different name. Nominalism overlooks the genealogical relationships between versions of each biblical book. For example, the author-editor-scribe who added Susanna to the book of Daniel did not create the book as a whole; rather, the scribe took something from the past and redeployed it. Are we to imagine that the redactor controls the meaning of everything inherited, without remainder?

Nominalist opponents of text-critical ideality have championed the study of the materiality of particular manuscripts as an alternative. In Jerome McGann's terms, textual critics can separate the "bibliographic code" from the "linguistic code" and study them separately.[26] The bibliographic code comprises the features of page layout, binding, font, cover, and so on, which certainly do impart information about the book, at least as it was presented at the time of a particular printing. On the other hand, the linguistic code presents the words of the text. This division helpfully highlights the signifying elements of the material aspects of the particular manuscript that have often been ignored in favor of the ideal work in textual criticism. These material aspects form the material context of each particular manifestation of a text, and they certainly influence the modes in which the linguistic codes are interpreted. For example, as Eugene Ulrich has shown, the material aspects of Qumran texts must inform our notions of the development of the biblical canon.[27]

Yet it would be unhelpful to assert any primacy of the particular context over the traditional character of a text. To separate every physical manuscript that contains a biblical text, find the date and location of its writing, and analyze each manuscript as a sui generis historical event, to be understood completely in light of its moment of production and its material construction and perhaps privileging the concept of "social production," which would prioritize the social nature of textual production and thus look to analyze any text within the social matrix of its production and reception, would be to ignore the fact that all bibliographic codes and all material aspects of manuscript production are themselves dependent on prior codes and patterns of producing manuscripts. The local context does not produce the format of a text anew each time a manuscript is copied. Should we look entirely to the context of a modern Jewish scribe copying the Torah in order to understand the Masoretic notations, or is this bibliographic code diffuse and dependent on the past(s)?

Rabbinicists are having these same debates: Chaim Milikowski and Peter Schäfer have exchanged articles in the *Journal of Jewish Studies* that adumbrate the larger conversation. While Milikowski defines textual criticism as the "essential task of reconstructing the text of the work as best as one can," Schäfer points to the rather open and mobile nature of rabbinic texts that undermines traditional text-critical ideology. "In rabbinic literature," Schäfer asks, "are there texts that can be defined and clearly delineated, or are there only basically open texts which elude temporal and redactional fixation?"[28] Schäfer then posits two options for text-critical work on rabbinic literature, of which he supports the second: either to look at rabbinic literature as a "whole" and assume the "synchronicity of all works" or to "reach back to the manuscripts," trying to fix each one in time and space in order to make "more concrete historical statements."[29] As Schäfer warns, the latter approach "would not lead to the Urtext" but it "would tell us something about the history of texts and their reception. This means that it is not 'the' text as such that is to be fixed in time and space, but rather the history of the text as reflected in the transmission of its manuscript traditions."[30] Schäfer thus tempers a full-on embrace of the materiality of the text and the historical contexts in which each text was written with his caution that the text cannot be reduced to "concrete historical statements" by being "fixed" in space and time.

While taking an interest in bibliographic codes yields important insights into the signifying structure of any physical text, the text's identity is not fully present in any one of its physical manifestations. The text written in a biblical or rabbinic manuscript comes from somewhere else and is going to somewhere else. If one cordons off a single physical manuscript in its context, then one ignores its primary function, which is to transmit traditional material from the past into the future. Any present is limited by the text's own journey through space and time. Also, bibliographic codes are themselves not fixed in one point in time—and neither is the social construct that McGann suggests gives "true" authority—because they, like the linguistic code, are semiotic codes "from" an earlier time.

Moreover, semiotic codes in general are composed of signifiers, which complicates any concept of the fullness of the "identity" of any particular manuscript. To think of a sign, or even a text, as something all by itself is, in the words of Ferdinand de Saussure, to "isolate it from the system to which it belongs," when in fact "the system as a united whole is the starting point, from which it becomes possible, by a process of analysis, to identify its constituent elements."[31]

In biblical terms, a tenth-century Masoretic manuscript of the book of Jeremiah does not "stand on its own," since it is not a function of merely that time and place. The book of Jeremiah functions as a part of a much larger cultural system that may include—but is not limited to—a linguistic context, the corpus of Israelite and cognate literature, and social practices such as prophecy. The tenth-century manuscript of Jeremiah carries resonances of this cultural milieu within it. The "positive," material elements of a tenth-century CE manuscript of a book whose production extends back to the middle of the first millennium BCE do not tell the full story.[32]

While nominalism dispenses with the elaborate hierarchies and ideal forms found in Platonic realism, it continues to think of difference as something purely negative. That is, nominalism understands differences between manuscripts as a lack of resemblance between disparate objects. Nominalism seems to retain the logic of essences but simply grants to each individual its own, self-identical essence that ensures its radical difference from its neighbors. In the end, the textual ontologies of realism and nominalism both depend on modes of essentialist thought, and as a result, neither has helped textual critics to better understand either the identity or the differences that one finds working with biblical texts.

Text as Process: Neither Realism nor Nominalism

It is necessary for textual criticism itself, as well as any theory of reception history, to construct a nonessentialist ontology of biblical texts. Among text critics working in fields other than biblical studies, there have been concerted efforts to enunciate more complex formulations. In medieval studies, text critics also work with traditional materials that exhibit many variants among different manuscripts. Two scholars, Paul Zumthor and Bernard Cerquiglini, focus on the particular innovations and alterations that appear in individual manuscripts and dispense with the ethico-ontological hierarchy that labels alterations as errors or corruptions.[33]

For Cerquiglini, both best-text editing and stemmatic, eclectic approaches that search for an ideal original text misrepresent the variance that is integral to the identity of such traditional texts. As he explains,

> In the Middle Ages the literary work was a variable . . . The fact that one hand was the first was probably less important than this continual rewriting of a work that belonged to whoever prepared it and gave it form once again. This constant and multifaceted ac-

> tivity turned medieval literature into a writing workshop. . . . *Variance* is the main characteristic of a work in the medieval vernacular; a concrete difference at the very basis of this object. This variance is so widespread and constitutive that, mixing together all the texts among which philology so painstakingly distinguishes, one could say that every manuscript is a revision, a version.[34]

Cerquiglini points to the *Song of Roland*, a medieval poem that developed over time through repetitive oral performance and exists only in irreducibly variant textual forms, as an example, asserting that one must hold together these disparate textual forms as realizations of the same epic, even through their differences. In other words, Cerquiglini argues that difference is part of the identity of these works: they exist in pluriformity, and to represent them otherwise is to misrepresent them. As he concludes, "To reduce this plurality into one unique and supposedly established text loses something that is there."[35]

Though his remarks are brief and often enigmatic, Cerquiglini offers resources with which to critique both essentialism and nominalism as they intersect with textual criticism. First of all, he argues that the identity of ancient and medieval traditional texts, including biblical texts, is *dynamic*, not static, and thus includes change over time. Their *identity includes variance*. Thus, he conceives of difference in a positive manner. The difference between manuscripts, like the temperature and pressure differential between a two air masses, can produce something new. Cerquiglini's differences are not simply phantasms or simulacra. A scribal addition is real; it can be a productive force, a dynamic and constructive element, precisely because it does not resemble its model. Scribal alterations produced the biblical text, so the productive power of difference has already proven itself. An important question is this: at what point do we imagine that the world lost this productive power of difference?

In a radical transformation, Cerquiglini thinks of texts as processes, not essences.[36] Unlike homogenous, unified essences, processes are typically divergent; the unfolding points of a process do not necessarily bear close resemblance to the origin of the process.[37] Moreover, the identity of a process is not fixed like an essence, and neither is it located at one point in its development; rather, the identity of a process is defined progressively, through time. Processes create no natural ontological hierarchy; the worth of contemporary moths, for example, is not judged by the moths' degrees of resemblance to the moths of ninety thousand years ago. Likewise, to pick one version of a text and claim that it is the natural endpoint of production and the natural beginning of reception is to disguise a process as a product.

Adopting this ontology in the practice of textual criticism would mean that the worth of manuscripts of biblical texts would not be judged by their resemblance to a textual form at another moment. Biblical texts were produced by means of lengthy processes, and those processes did not culminate in a clear telos of a naturally pristine version. Likewise, there is no more authentic version of the text, no more pristine version, no primary version, no necessary preference for earlier or later or finished forms, nor is there a version with more integrity, and there is no such thing as a corruption. There are scribal misspellings, to be sure, but even these are not bad per se. There are just differences.

One may be reminded of Saussure's disgust at the evolution through mispronunciation of a particular written name, Lefébvre, into a different written name, Lefébure. Derrida responds, asking, "Where is the evil? . . . Lefébure is not a bad name [Lefébure, ce n'est pas mal]."[38] The point is this: supposed deformations often are simply changes, and carry no natural ethical or ontological defect as such. There is no reason to be disgusted at Lefébure, just as there is no reason to be call any version of a text "corrupt." A scribal error such as haplography, dittography or misspelling could (and surely at times has) created texts that can be read, can be used liturgically, and so on. Where is the evil?

Thus, the identity of a biblical text is contested, defined by multiple versions that seem to be differing manifestations of the same object. We have enough information to know that, empirically speaking, the text never was and never will be singular. Thanks to Eugene Ulrich, biblical scholars are beginning to understand the irreducible pluriformity of the biblical text. Too often, however, this pluriformity is treated as a past phenomenon, spoken of in the past tense—for example, at Qumran, there was great pluriformity, but after the period of stabilization, there is now stability. Yet the text remains pluriform; these texts from Qumran continue to exist. The text remains pluriform as long as Samaritans read their Samaritan Pentateuch and Eastern Orthodox Christians read their Septuagint, as long as Syriac-reading lectors call out the words of the Peshitta. It remains pluriform as long as scholars create new critical editions, and as long as there continues to be variance even within the famously precise MT. As long as *ketiv* and *qere* stare at one another, we find pluriformity and variance even within a single manuscript. The period of stabilization gave us not a stable text, but at best multistable texts within multistable textual groups. The identity of, say, the book of Proverbs is a function of differences that are logically and ontologically prior to any such identity.

Both realist and nominalist formulations of textual criticism, therefore, deny plain facts: realists deny the very manuscripts they read, while nominalists deny the relationship between two copies of the same book. I am arguing that biblical scholars should instead conceive of biblical texts as processes—processes that we may imagine function in an odd way as an open, contingent universal.

Textual critics can then reconceive their task as a mapping of the process of textual development, a charting of the trajectories and changes that the form of the text has always undergone. Textual critics can dispense with the construction of ontological hierarchies and the unhelpful heuristics of originality and authenticity, since the biblical text is at its most authentic when it reveals its internal variance. Textual critics can offer a sketch of the differential identity of a text instead of imposing a procrustean ideal form in order to create substantial identity. Perhaps most importantly, textual critics can affirm the continued and continuing pluriformity of the biblical text, insisting that the SamPent, the Septuagint, the Vulgate, the Peshitta, the Targums, the so-called daughter versions, the nonaligned texts from Qumran, as well as the variants within and among all these groups, are not failed witnesses, phantasms, or simulacra but are rather fully legitimate expressions of an ongoing process of textual development.

This leaves many important details to be determined, including the question of identity. In order to clarify the identity of a process, or shifting network, we can approach the problem from another angle: what is a text, exactly? We could respond with the near tautology: a text is a network of signs. While this answer may not seem to help us much, textual critic Hans Zeller stresses that signs—that is, the things that make up texts—function in particular ways, and these functions impact the type of identity texts may have. "My conception," Zeller notes, "rests on the linguistic idea of the text as a complex of elements which form a system of signs. . . . Seen in this way, a version is a specific system of linguistic signs, functioning within and without, and authorial revisions transform it into another system."[39] Zeller points out that texts are comprised of networks of signs. Rearranging the network of signs in any way creates a new network that can be distinguished from the older one: "In principle a new version comes into existence through a single variant. Since a text, as text, does not in fact consist of elements but of the relationships between them, variation at one point has an effect on invariant sections of the text. In considering different versions one must therefore not confine one's attention to the variants. This is most clearly exemplified when the title of a work is altered. Fundamentally, therefore, whether the variants are numerous and of far-reaching effect is not a necessary condition for the constitution of a version."[40] Zeller points out something quite interesting about texts, namely, that they are not simply composed of self-contained linear blocks. Replacing one word with another changes more than that one word, because texts are a network of relationships. Signs are not hermetic; they are inherently relational, and work together as groups. If one were to remove one key block from a wall, it could cause the whole edifice to collapse.

The network of signs that comprises a text is entirely interrelated, and moving one small jot or tittle can remake the whole.

This insight, coupled with Cerquiglini's comments, recasts the ethics inherent in the practice of textual criticism. To collapse a literary tradition into one of its many forms, which is the goal of many textual critics, is to erase countless other ancient versions that likewise deserve a hearing. Although it is admirable that Tanselle, Fox, and McCarter are as concerned as they are to preserve and care for the authentic voices of ancients that are threatened by the corruptions of time, it is unfortunate that so many other voices must perish to save just one. Perhaps a large critical apparatus such as one finds in the HUB project gestures toward representing those lost literary voices, but as Zeller points out, the atomization of variants obscures the overall effect of one particular manuscript. Rather than treating variants as marginal fragments at the edges of an intact central form of the text, critics ought, Zeller insists, to look at texts holistically.

Yet the nature of signs also helps us to confront Fox's concern that respecting variants leads inevitably to textual nihilism. Fox wants to claim that a particular proto-MT manuscript of Proverbs and an LXX manuscript of Proverbs share some identity, albeit in a relationship of subordinated ontology—that is, as George Orwell might say, some texts are more equal than others.[41] Signs, however, present an alternative conception of identity that relies on the central role of difference. And this alternative conception of identity provides the building blocks for a new ontology of the biblical text.

In short, signs are useful precisely because they can be used over and again by various people in various circumstances and yet be recognized as the "same thing" in each instance.[42] Each use of a sign, then, will introduce some sort of variation: at minimum a variation of time, since one cannot utter something twice at exactly the same moment. But signs are recognized even at surprisingly high rates of variations, as in the case of speakers shakily conversing in a shared tongue alien to both. Because of the essential repeatability of signs, there is a potentially limitless variety of users of any system of signs—you cannot wear signs out!—and a limitless variety of situations in which the sign will function, as there is no space in which these words cease to be recognizable.

In theory, a sign will still function in any potential context emitted by any potential user. For example, if a robot on a space mission mindlessly scrawls the word "dog" on the surface of Pluto, this will not inhibit its function as a sign in the English language, and any potential space traveler might be able to read it, regardless of its author's intentions or its context of production.

Let us continue with the example of the particular linguistic sign "dog." This sign, like any sign, is useful precisely because we can identify it as the same sign even in its nonidentical repetitions, such as alterations in spoken tone, accent, and pitch or alterations in written handwriting or font. "Dog" is the same word as "dog," even though the first letter shape varies between the two signs, and "dog" is the same word as "*dog*," even though the letter shapes of the second sign are slanted in relation to the first.

I can likely rule out the Platonic thought of a "perfect form" of every sign that may be found in a nonspatiotemporal realm, of which all earthly manifestations are but shoddy representations. There is no one exact way to enunciate "dog," because neither the southwestern American or the northeastern American, the rural English or the urban Australian, the native French speaker or the native Urdu speaker, have the right to claim that there is only one acceptable sound pattern for the pronunciation of English words. Any claim of "standard dialect" is not descriptive but normative. Likewise, there is no "correct font" in which to write "dog," nor do serifs make a sign as unrecognizable when compared to the same sign sans serifs.

But I can also rule out radical nominalist claims that there is no shared identity between signs. There is certainly some sort of identity to the word "dog"—otherwise nobody could read it. But signs have an identity quite different from the concept of identity text critics often rely on when they posit a perfect, pristine, original, or central text. There is no perfect, pristine, original, or central way to pronounce "dog," because signs function by retaining their identity in spite of—but also only because of—differential repetition.

Saussure's definition of the linguistic sign posits an irreducible relationship of a signifier (i.e., the ideal sound pattern of a spoken word) and a signified (i.e., the particular concept associated with the sound pattern).[43] Saussure constantly reminds his readers that the signifier is *not* the precise material sound or shape of any particular enunciation, because these vary significantly. Instead, he uses the phrase "sound pattern" to evoke the generalized shape or sound of a letter. The "sound pattern," or signifier, is an ideality, Saussure concludes.[44] Yet this ideality is not the pure, privileged, fully unified transcendental ideality of the Platonic model. There is no one absolutely pure way to pronounce the word "dog," and thus we must find another way to think of this ideal identity of the signifier.

Problems occur when someone says something indistinct or says something that sounds indistinguishable from something similar—like "bog," or "doc," for example. We may say that the ideal of "dog" is not a singular positive thing: instead, the ideality of "dog" is merely the minimal differential space between any possible pronunciation of "dog" and anything else that it might be confused with—"bog," "doc," etc. In other words, the ideality of "dog" is not a determinate, measurable entity. Signifiers, as Saussure notes, "are constituted solely by differences which distinguish one such sound pattern from another. . . . [A]lthough in general a difference presupposes positive terms between which the difference holds, in a language there are only differences, and no positive terms."[45] Thus, the ideal sound pattern of any word is nothing but the space one may make for it that is not currently occupied by other sounds. Saussure explains that "what characterizes these units is not, as might be thought, the specific positive properties of each; but simply the fact that they cannot be mistaken for one another. [Signifiers] are first and foremost entities which are contrastive, relative and negative. . . . The values of letters are purely negative and differential."[46]

Thinking of identity by means of difference creates an alternate way of thinking about what a text "is." This is a difficult way to think of identity, to be sure, but it rewards the careful reader. If we begin to think of the identity of a given text—texts are, of course, composed of chains of signifiers—as in some sense purely differential, it will allow us to analyze biblical texts while avoiding the traps into which textual criticism seems to keep falling. In particular, text criticism has a difficult time thinking of identity and difference because its logic, method and vocabulary derives from a metaphysical system that determines things in terms of presence. For instance, the term "variant" presupposes that there is some positive, present, and knowable constant from which one may measure deviance. By thinking in terms of differences, we can say that there is no positive, unified transcendental work by which one can measure variances in particular empirical manuscripts—because there are only variants.

But this does not relegate us to nihilism, as Fox worries: the word "dog" can be thought and recognized despite variations, so long as it is distinct from other words. The text of the book of Proverbs can also be thought and recognized despite variations so long as it is distinct from other texts. The ideal "book of Proverbs" inheres within the borders between historically extant versions of the book. Thinking about the text as a differential ideal can challenge text criticism in many ways. Most importantly, any proposed ethico-ontological hierarchy can no longer organize the mass of manuscripts, since the privileged lynchpin of the system—the transcendental, ideal version of the text—cannot be said to exist in any meaningful sense. There is no substantive center; there are only differential relationships. The identity of each biblical book is a function of its own internal differences, and the limits or edges of its identity are functions of the differences between its self-differential identity and other self-differential identities (i.e., other biblical books) that are recognizable as something else.

Instead of picking one side in the debate between de Lagarde's "from the one to the many" stemmatic reconstruction and Kahle's "from the many to the one" *vulgaretexte* theory, I would push textual critics to think in terms of "from the many as one to a different many as one," emphasizing that the "one" is a purely formal category suggested by the closely related but nevertheless different witnesses.[47] For this reason, the replacement of the concept of autographs or an actually recoverable original text with the asymptotic ideals of the archetype, hyparchetype, and so on is not sufficient, since an ideal limit can function as a lynchpin as much an empirical object can within an ethico-ontological system. Replacing a real despot with an idealized despot is not the same thing as instituting democratic reforms.

Perhaps some text critics will still want to think of literary identity in a positive manner—namely, they will want something to point to in order to say "*this* is the book of Daniel." But the relationship between the OG and MT of Daniel does not allow for this solution: clearly chapters 4–6 are a part of the book of Daniel, but the only versions we have are already secondary. Should we then cut out chapters 4–6 from our critical editions of Daniel or only publish parts that agree with both versions, since the resulting part will be beyond doubt entirely from "the [real] book of Daniel"? This, too, would be strange, since from the start chapters 4–6 have been part of the book of Daniel; the problem is that they only exist in variants, and there is nothing but variants. If we take seriously Zeller's argument that differences in one part of a literary text affect more than just the immediate vicinity of the differences, then these variants are not confined to chapters 4–6; they impact the rest of the book, however it is constructed.[48] There is, then, no "center" to the pluriform versions of the book of Daniel, but this centerless field is still made up of the varying versions of the book of Daniel. OG and MT editions are quite different, but the two of them can be distinguished from other biblical stories and thus are still one (self-differential) book.

Concerning the problem of the identity of the Bible, James Bowley and John Reeves claim that "instead of 'the Bible,' there are 'Bible*s*,' containing particular forms of certain texts in one or more specific arrangements used in individual communities. Nothing of a concrete nature warrants the common use of the singular number and the definite article as if there was an inalterable form and content to 'the Bible.' Succinctly stated, 'the Bible' is not and furthermore never was."[49] They are correct that there is diversity among different communities' canons of the Bible (hence, the nominalist "Bible*s*"). But this diversity is then contrasted with identity understood as specifying something with "a concrete nature" that would have "inalterable form and content." Using Saussure's discussion of differential identity, one can say "the Bible" to signify the differential field of various constructions of "the Bible," much as one can say "the book of Daniel" to signify not one concrete and inalterable text, but rather a pluriform field of texts that are minimally distinguishable from other texts. There are other alternatives to positing a concrete identity besides positing various concrete subidentities. By saying "Bibles" instead of "the Bible," one has merely substituted the problem of identity writ large for the problem of identity writ small. We may say "the Protestant canon," for example, but this would only replicate the problem of identity in a more circumscribed way. The alternative to one unvarying and concrete biblical canon is not just many smaller unvarying and concrete biblical canons. The concept of differential identity allows us to speak of the Bible without compromising or invalidating each other's differing constructions of the object.

Since realists believe that there is some determinate true content that "is" the text of each biblical book that may be discovered, they hold that extant conflicting manuscripts may be categorized and measured by how close they approach (or how far they deviate from) that content. Nominalists, on the other hand, defuse the conflict between conflicting manuscripts by pluralizing their terms (Bibles) and denying any relationship between the conflicting particulars. Perhaps there are no ideal, Platonic universals, but the differential network may be said to function *as* a universal, a concrete universal.[50] Any particular exemplar will of course not quite fulfill the whole breadth of the universal (for example, OG-Daniel and MT-Daniel contain both pluses and minuses). Irreducibly different particulars create the productive field of differential identity in their very dissonance.

Every particular manuscript of every biblical book falls short of functioning as the exemplar of its entire genealogy. Daniel is not summed up within the borders of the MT, nor is Daniel summed up by the OG or Theodotion. These variations struggle to be the center that the book of Daniel lacks, and any attempt to either deny their relation or raise one up as the universal will overlook the quasi-ontological structure of the "book itself." As Derrida explains, the "text" is "henceforth no longer a finished corpus of writing, some content enclosed in a book or its margins, but a differential network. . . . Thus the text overruns all its limits assigned to it so far (not submerging or drowning them in an undifferentiated homogeneity, but rather making them more complex, dividing and multiplying strokes and lines)."[51] McCarter was right about the dangers of writing, but perhaps this situation is not merely dangerous to any particular enunciation. It is also the way that any enunciation comes to be. We must be careful to see that the very corruptibility that text critics bemoan is the ground of possibility for what they are trying to recover and protect; the only problem is that this openness is structurally impossible to close, and this means that texts remain open to rereading and rewriting without possibility of complete stabilization or absolute finality. The gap between original and later, between composition and reception, seems to be largely mythical and a function of a particular metaphysics. Instead, the gaps *within* each differential textual identity and the spaces between one such textual identity and others seem to be more fruitful. Relocating the gap or divide from the moment of pure presence to the internal and external differences of texts could push biblical scholarship past now stale, unhelpful debates.

Yet even if one grants my thesis—namely, that there is no original or final or necessarily privileged form of a biblical text but only differential networks—one may think that the divide between original and reception lies somewhere other than in the material text. Many biblical scholars claim that their goal is not to find the original text per se but rather to reconstruct the historical context that produced a particular version of the text. In this model, there is a historical moment that defines the utterance of a text, which allows the scholar to pin down what it meant. The divide between reception history and the original, then, would not be a divide in the form of the text but rather a divide in the *meaning* of the text: that is, reception denotes an understanding of the text that is qualitatively different from the original because it was read in a different context. What, then, is the nature of this divide in the context of production and the context of reception, and how does it allow a methodological line to be drawn?

THREE

Anchor or Spandrel: The Concept of the Original Context

> The prophetic books of the Hebrew Bible have also been interpreted in creative ways and made to refer to whatever crisis people in any given time have found themselves in. But it seems clear that both prophecy and apocalyptic originally had a specific reference in mind, anchored in the period of writing.
>
> —John Barton

> Only something which has no history can be defined.
>
> —Friedrich Nietzsche

Introduction: The Anchor and the Spandrel

In light of the biblical text's pluriformity, textual criticism cannot identify the boundary between the original text and its reception. Alternatively, many scholars locate the boundary between original and reception by means of the concept of the original context. The concept of original context allows scholars to select a particular meaning of a particular text and declare it to be original. A historical context allows scholars to separate meanings proper to an original setting from later, unoriginal meanings that a text could not have had within that context. Original meanings are defined variously as the author's intention, the understanding of the original audience, or more broadly the interpretive possibilities opened by the semantic, cultural, and historical context of the text's production. All of these definitions posit a boundary dividing the proper meaning of the text from later meanings, the former constituting the domain of biblical criticism and the latter constituting the domain of reception history. If there is such a boundary, then what forms the barrier between the original context and later contexts? The answer, if deduced, would allow for a rigorous formulation of reception history.

But what if this idea of context is incorrect? Modern criticism has shown decisively that biblical texts are composed of many sources, traditions, and redactions, so the boundary between any original and later meaning is bound to be muddled. Just as textual pluriformity complicates any boundary drawn by textual criticism, the layered and multicontextual biblical text may confound contextual criticism. In order to condense the confrontation between these two points of view, I here juxtapose two tropes: the anchor and the spandrel.

When defining the relationship between a text and a historical context, biblical scholars tend to rely on metaphors of anchorage. According to John Barton, "In reading a text, one needs a sense of its anchorage in a particular period."[1] Likewise, F. W. Dobbs-Allsopp uses a related image in describing biblical texts as "past texts that remain tethered in important ways to that past."[2] Other scholars link text to context with images of pinning, rooting, or containment.[3] The semantic field of anchorage connotes a fixed location, a lack of change, and thus stability and integration with the surrounding environment. According to this logic, the failure to respect such fetters leads inexorably to misreading: as John Barton warns, "Some readers detach the Bible from its historical moorings and allow it to float freely in a timeless realm, thereby making it unable to exist 'back there,' at the beginning of the tradition, and so witness to the tradition's roots."[4] Three assumptions undergird this trope of the anchor: that every biblical text is a form of utterance in that it has a specific historical context to which it belongs; that every biblical text must be read in this context if it is to be understood properly and thus yield the meaning that is truly original to it; and that every biblical text has already escaped this context and now is to be found outside of it. The inherent tension between the first two assumptions and the third assumption creates the central problem of so-called historical-critical biblical research and, one may venture, all criticism and interpretation of texts and other artifacts.[5]

Following this logic, biblical criticism is the task of reading a text within its now-disappeared historical point of origin in order to determine what it did mean or could have meant and, subsequently, to separate this hermeneutical wheat from the chaff of later misunderstanding.[6] If one "weighs" the textual anchor by reading the text in another context, this leads to anachronism and interpretive chaos, leaving the text with no stability whatsoever, drifting aimlessly on the surface like a castaway on a plank. Texts were not made to drift: instead, as Barton claims, "witnessing" to its anchor-like "roots" is the true task of any text. Yet it is evident that biblical texts are instead always found drifting though history, seemingly unanchored, usually witnessing to something else. As a result, biblical scholars must return the drifting texts to their proper harbors and restore the missing anchors. John J. Collins describes this procedure as "placing the Bible in its historical context."[7]

Yet perhaps a biblical text cannot be fully contained or explained by any single context. As any visitor to Rome's *centro storico* has doubtless noticed, the city displays an impressive collection of ancient structures that over time have been converted from temples to churches, theaters to palaces, and markets to convents to museums.[8] At times, the ancient architecture seems to integrate gracefully with its more recent brick and stucco surroundings, while at other times one notices fragmentary arches that jut out unneeded into space, walls that slice through otherwise orderly floor plans, and columns that extend past the roofs they seem otherwise to support.

As a result of their piecemeal conversion over thousands of years, the adapted ancient ruins have at least several historical contexts in which they function as meaningful parts of a larger whole. To focus solely on their ancient origin is to ignore that they have more than one origin. Every architectural recontextualization reproduces the ruins, granting them another context of production.

Stephen Jay Gould and Richard Lewontin have referred to these sorts of architectural recontextualizations in their critique of adaptationist theories of evolutionary development. Noting that adaptationist theories tend to break up an organism into various traits and propose disconnected narratives that explain the necessary development of each trait, Gould and Lewontin favor an alternate paradigm, later dubbed "exaptation," which emphasizes the contingent and retroactive aspects of Darwin's theory.[9] Whereas adaptationism assumes that every existing trait appeared and was selected in order to ensure the success of the species within its environment, exaptationism argues that traits tend to find uses for which they were never selected, since organisms repurpose traits to cope with always-changing environments.[10]

Gould and Lewontin use the architectural feature of three-dimensional spandrels in Byzantine architecture as an example. Even though one may look on the central dome of San Marco in Venice and marvel at how the mosaic program seems to integrate perfectly with its Byzantine architectural canvas, the "traits" of the mosaic program did not evolve in lockstep with the architecture. Instead, the architectural programs developed first out of preexisting forms, and then the artistic program developed in light of the architectural constraints.[11] Thus the choice to create mosaics of the four Evangelists in the spandrels under the dome did not then lead to the selection of a dome as the architectural form of the ceiling; rather, images of the four Evangelists presented a convenient solution to the problem of four awkwardly shaped spandrels that resulted from the building of the dome.[12]

Likewise, Gould and Lewontin point to biological traits that organisms developed that were later repurposed and became quite useful: for example, flightless birds first developed feathers for warmth and only much later repurposed them as a mechanism allowing for flight.[13] Furthermore, some traits are genetically linked in such a way that selecting one trait necessarily selects another useless trait that only later may prove of some use—or hindrance. Vestigial organs, for instance, are examples of still extant but no longer adaptive traits. It would be a mistake to assume that the vestigial organ is an evolutionary dead end, since a change in our environment may allow for their repurposing, perhaps rendering these traits highly important to the survival of our species. In other words, the meaning and proper function of a trait is never a settled matter.

When we look at organisms and their traits in relation to a larger ecosystem, we find that traits are not anchored to a particular function within an unchanging environment but are constantly fluctuating just like their environment. Both the organism and its environment are always in the process of finding new purposes for their existing traits even as they develop new, underdetermined traits.[14] On closer inspection, what may seem like a perfectly ordered adaptationist teleology looks like a protean chain of chaotic contingencies forming and reforming meaningful patterns throughout; all organisms are always open to reforming their traits as well as the meaning or purpose of those traits. In the same way, the function of any architectural feature can be changed via adaptive reuse, and some features may be unused for a time before they are repurposed. What we find with both of these examples is an essentially open relationship between elements of a structure and their individual purposes (or what one might call their meanings). Spandrels are not fixed; they travel through always new contexts and are always open to being repurposed in new structures. This does not mean one can do just anything with a spandrel. Careful repurposing requires attention to what a trait can do and what it cannot. But what the spandrel teaches us is that it can do many things, even some things that are as-yet unthought.

Questions concerning the concept of textual recontextualization or adaptive reuse confront the biblical scholar in the same way that they confront the architectural historian studying the Markets of Trajan, which were repurposed in the early medieval era as various palaces, then as a garrison, and still later as the Convent of St. Catherine of Siena. The foundations of modern biblical criticism consist of the discoveries of various literary strata within the structure of each biblical book, and it is the continuing task of biblical criticism to explore the issues that result from this discovery. Biblical criticism acknowledges that biblical texts have been subject to adaptive reuse, but many scholars argue that the adaptive reuse of a given biblical text has limits and that there is a boundary point at which rereading and repurposing meaning turns from redaction into reception.

I argue that the internal content or meaning of each instantiation of a biblical book cannot be divided into original meaning and reception. Just as concepts such as authority, stabilization, and finality give textual critics an excuse to present a given form of a biblical text as objectively original, the concept of context and its correlates, authorial intention and original audience, generally confuse discussions concerning the meaning of biblical texts. My argument is that spandrels, not anchors, are more helpful generative metaphors for biblical scholarship.

The Role of Context in Biblical Criticism

So-called historical criticism is alive and well in the field of biblical studies.[15] Despite various apocalyptic warnings to the contrary, even many so-called postmodernists accept the normative claim that within scholarly discourse a text should be read with reference to its context of production. There are, of course, scholars who claim otherwise; critics engaging in reader-response or philosophical hermeneutics have generally stressed that readers have no choice but to admit that their own contexts influence their reading practices. But overall, the vast majority of biblical scholarship seems to operate under the assumption that the context of a biblical text's production should determine its analysis.

This line of thought rests on two simple wagers: first, that contexts function roughly like linguist Ferdinand de Saussure's concept of *langue*. For Saussure, individual speech acts (*parole*) are comprehensible because they derive from the overall linguistic system (*langue*). Since the synchronic linguistic system is already known to the speaker and audience, the utterance emanates from and is constrained by the linguistic system.[16] In the same way, biblical scholars tend to assume that the context makes the utterance comprehensible while also constraining its potential meaning. Context holds the proper code by which to read a given text.[17] Thus, a valid interpretation can only be secured by first locating the proper context. One must know where to drop anchor; returning the textual boat to the wrong harbor is the same as setting it adrift. In other words, if the wrong code is consulted, the text produces garbage.

As for the second wager, biblical scholars often assume that biblical texts are utterances akin to Saussurean *parole*, or individual events of language use emanating from a particular subject located at a singular point in time and space. Locating the source of an utterance in a subject allows for internal coherence or meaning, while locating the utterance at a precise moment ensures its place within a specific synchronic linguistic structure as well as its possible reference to a certain representable state of affairs.

John Collins, for example, explains his basic practice as follows: "I view the text in its historical context, relating it where possible to the history of the time and respecting the ancient literary traditions."[18] Here, Collins gestures toward the three main ways through which biblical critics "contextualize," or anchor, a text, namely, by attempting to read a given text within the linguistic parameters that existed at the time of its inscription, by reading the text as a species of a cultural genus such as a genre in order to clarify the intentions of the author and expectations of the audience, and by reconstructing the "history of the time" to clarify the text's historical referents and the nature of the cultural practices, economic processes, and political structures that are represented in the text. In short, a biblical scholar contextualizes by means of reference to semantic structures, generic expectations, and historical circumstances. All of these modes of contextualizing a text have the same goal: namely, to reduce the ambiguity of a text's sense and reference, rendering the correct meaning of the text. I analyze each of these three modes in turn.

Semantics as Context

In *The Semantics of Biblical Language,* James Barr insists that biblical studies recognize Saussure's absolute distinction between the synchronic and diachronic aspects of the study of linguistics.[19] In the diachronic mode, a linguist may study morphological, syntactical, or lexical changes within a language over time. In contrast, synchronic linguistics takes as its subject a language state, or a language as it existed "during a certain span of time during which the sum of the modifications that have supervened is minimal."[20] In other words, synchronic linguistics studies a static model of a given language at a given point in time. Saussure argues that true semantic analysis can only take place within synchronic linguistics, since the meaning of a word in the distant past—its etymology—does not likely influence the meaning of a word at the moment it is spoken. For instance, contemporary English speakers do not consider the word "silly" to really mean "lucky" merely because of its etymological roots in a West Germanic term for happiness (it is after all a distant cognate of German "selig," or "blessed"). What matters in synchronic analysis is function of that word within its language structure at the moment of its utterance.

What is perhaps less obvious is that this model presupposes a moment of enunciation by a single speaker, based on Saussure's presupposition that the speaking subject is the true subject of linguistic analysis. Saussure presumed that texts are dubious bearers of linguistic information: writing, as a durable image of the spoken word, exposes the utterance to all sorts of diachronic changes.[21] Yet here we find the central tension within the practice of the contextual analysis of texts, a paradox of diachrony and synchrony: writing remains, but its context quickly disappears. Thus the assumption of a unitary and singular historical moment of a speaker's enunciation becomes crucial for Saussure's analysis, since his very separation of diachronic from synchronic rests on it. At the moment of enunciation, a certain linguistic structure existed that was not subject to the nonsemantic whims of diachronic change, and if one can reconstruct this synchronic system, then one can pin down the semantic value of the utterance.

As a result, according to Barr, a given text "means something only as a functioning unit within the synchronic language system of a certain time."[22] Since one truism of biblical literature is that every biblical text is to some extent a composite text, this statement necessitates the division of biblical texts into various strata, each of which emanates from a single delineable historical moment. Thus

Genesis must be divided into redactional layers therein. Moreover, each strata must be assigned a relatively identifiable time and place of enunciation within a relatively consistent synchronic linguistic structure. Barr clarifies this interpretative approach by noting that "the words of (say) the prophet Amos must mean what they meant in the language system of the time of Amos, [but] the words of a commentator or glossator three centuries later must be understood as they functioned in the language of his time."[23] The primary critical task confronting biblical scholarship, therefore, is the identification of various unified textual strata, while the derivative tasks involve identifying each strata's historical context of production, re-creating the synchronic language systems of those contexts, and then reading these texts within the semantic constraints of those language systems. If the scholar fails to do so properly, disaster awaits: "Serious mistakes can be made by reading biblical Hebrew words with the sense that the same word had some centuries later."[24]

Barton agrees with Barr's approach: "Criticism certainly entails situating texts in the context of their origin," which then allows the critic to access "the sense that the text has when considered in its own historical setting, rather than as taken by later generations."[25] Barton dispels any simplistic critiques of this practice: "Where we do not know who wrote the text or what he or she meant by it, we may still be able to say that the text 'could mean A' or 'could not mean B' on the basis of our knowledge of the language in which the text is written. . . . So-called 'historical criticism' has the task of telling the reader what biblical texts can or cannot mean, not merely what they did or did not mean; to say of this or that interpretation, 'No, the text cannot possibly mean that, because the words it uses will not bear that meaning.'"[26] Barton claims that even if an author or determinate meaning cannot be ascertained, the biblical scholar may adjudicate the limits of possible meanings of a biblical text by means of the linguistic structure as it existed during the production of the text. One still, however, needs to know the general time and place of enunciation in order to avoid making what Barr calls "serious mistakes" of anachronistic interpretation.

John Collins also takes the notion of synchronic contextualization to be fundamental to historical-critical methodology: "Historical criticism so understood strives for objectivity by assessing the plausibility of any interpretation in light of historical and literary context, including historical philology, or the range of meanings that may be assigned to a given word in a particular context." It restricts what can be plausibly claimed "by limiting the range of what a text may mean in a particular context."[27] In Barr's, Barton's, and Collins's estimations, historical-critical scholars work by locating the limits of the possible range of meanings of a text. These limits simultaneously function as boundaries dividing what their field from other disciplines, such as reception history or theology.[28]

As an example of this practice, Barton uses the particular instance of nineteenth-century English novelist Anthony Trollope: "In the novels of Trollope we often find a female character saying that a male friend 'made love to her the whole evening.' It is crucial in understanding Trollope to realize that in his day this expression meant showing a romantic or sexual interest in someone, not having sexual intercourse with them. Otherwise, we would get a very distorted idea of what happened in Victorian drawing rooms."[29] It does seem rather clear that Trollope did not intend to portray drawing rooms as bordellos, since the context did not allow for that meaning of the phrase "make love." The text is an utterance by a temporally and culturally located subject, and the context has well defined and known rules that make plain what can be meant and what cannot.

But the example of Trollope is hardly analogous to a biblical text. Trollope wrote his works within the span of a few decades. In contrast, Genesis is the product of hundreds of years of varied types of oral and written processes that span cultures, space, time, theological structures, and more. From which of these contexts does the text emanate as an utterance? Where can one drop an anchor in this discontinuous seabed of tradition? Conceptualizing biblical texts as historical utterances banishes the diachronic from view in hopes of finding a pure synchronic meaning. This is easier to accomplish with texts clearly written by one person at one time. But with complex compositions such as biblical texts, it is impossible to ignore that any biblical synchrony is already shot through with splinters of diachrony.

The problem of the text is ultimately a problem of internal recontextualization, which is a serious issue for biblical scholars, since even the largest anchor cannot stop movement within an object. James Sanders has dubbed this phenomenon "resignification," while other scholars use the term "relecture."[30] Biblical texts are, for all intents and purposes, palimpsests, textual forms of spandrels, bearing the marks of multiple reinscriptions well before any supposed state of finalization. Recall Barr's example of the book of Amos: Amos's words *must* mean what they meant at the time of Amos, and the glossator's words *must* be understood in the language of that later time. But what does one do when the same words are the words of Amos and the words of a redactor? How does one adjudicate the ownership of the same set of words that have been used twice, in different ways?

John Sawyer provides a compelling example of this very problem by noting a scribal rewriting within the biblical text that divides Amos's meaning from a later reading:[31]

> What does *wehelilu širot hekal* in Amos 8:3 mean? It seems likely that *wehelilu šarot hekal* "the palace singing-girls will wail" is what Amos actually said, and that he was addressing this judgment oracle

> to the high-living royal establishment at Samaria. The reasons for the change to *širot hekal* in the Masoretic tradition would then be straightforward: *hekal* in Jerusalem denoted "temple" rather than "palace," . . . and while there may have been *širot* "songs" in the temple, there were certainly no *šarot* "singing girls." For the Masoretic tradition, followed by AV and RSV, the original meaning of these words, as they were understood in Samaria in the eighth century BC, would have been of purely academic interest, whereas the words as they stand are addressed to Jerusalem and foretell the destruction of the temple in 587 BC. . . . The decision on what it means today [i.e., in translation] depends on arbitrary considerations.[32]

Sawyer here demonstrates the recontextualization and thus multiplicity of semantic possibilities for a single text within the production history of the biblical text itself. Amos was describing Samarian female palace singers, but the redactors certainly understood this phrase—and the Masoretes pointed it—as a description of laments ringing through the temple, understood to be a reference to the temple in Jerusalem. Barr's distinction between Amos's words and the glossator's words is misleading, since the same words were sedimented with multiple meanings before the book of Amos was "finished." And what if Amos was quoting words from an entirely different source with a different meaning, or what if they were added or changed by an early scribe to enhance Amos's words? How many other meanings are historically sedimented within those words that remain invisible to the modern scholar's eye? This question brings to the fore all quotations and interpretations within and between biblical texts: for instance, are the words of Isaiah 11:6–9 that are quoted, centuries later, in Isaiah 65:25 the words of Isaiah or the later Isaianic author?[33] One could here cite a plethora of examples of resignification, all of which demand a reconsideration of semantic synchrony.[34]

Perhaps a more striking example is provided by Barton himself when he refers to Borges's "Pierre Menard: Author of the Quixote." Borges's text is a fictional literary review of modern French writer Pierre Menard's fragmentary line-for-line "recreation" of *Don Quixote*.[35] Borges compares quotations from Menard and Cervantes's works, noting semantic differences between passages composed of identical words. According to Barton, Borges's story shows that "the meaning [of a text] is historically bound," and the fact that it is means that "the provenance of a text should be taken into account."[36] Barton's conclusion, however, may take for granted something that Borges's story calls into question: namely, the identity (or difference) of Menard's and Cervantes's words. It is perhaps important that Menard does not simply either recopy the *Quixote* or happen to write the same words in a completely different text. The narrator of the story explains that "those who have insinuated that Menard dedicated his life to writing a contemporary *Quixote* calumniate his illustrious memory. He did not want to compose another *Quixote*—which is easy—but *the Quixote itself.* Needless to say, he never contemplated a mechanical transcription of the original; he did not propose to copy it. His admirable intention was to produce a few pages which would coincide—word for word and line for line—with those of Miguel de Cervantes."[37]

In short, Barton too quickly assumes that this story shows that the same words mean different things in different eras. On the contrary, what this story shows is that the *Quixote* itself can be read within different semantic contexts, as the narrator claims to do: "Shall I confess that I often imagine [Menard] did finish it and that I read the *Quixote*—all of it—as if Menard had conceived it? Some nights past, while leafing through chapter XXVI—never essayed by him—I recognized our friend's style and something of his voice in this exceptional phrase: 'the river nymphs and the dolorous and humid Echo.'"[38] A close reading of this short story does not allow for Barton's conclusions: rather, "Pierre Menard" provides an examples of the same text read within different synchronic moments, much like the text of Amos does in Sawyer's account. What Menard suggests is that the redactors of the Pentateuch were reading and rewriting the same text that was written by P, for example, but that they were probably reading it quite differently than P. Thus, these differences are not foreign to the text at hand but rather are internal to it. The point is that Amos, for example, did not become a different work when copied and pointed by the Masoretes. Instead, the Masoretes revealed semantic possibilities inherent within the text itself as it existed in their era.

A biblical text is not equivalent to an utterance. It cannot be read wholly unanachronistically, since even one supposedly "synchronic" edition of a biblical text or one manuscript copied at a precise point in time carries the sedimented languages, meanings, and contexts that comprise its extended contexts of production.[39] As Collins argues, some historical critics appreciate ambiguity, but even those critics "often argue that one meaning is primary—either the author's intention or what the text would have meant in its original setting."[40] I, however, have argued that there is ample reason to question the concept of "original setting" for complex traditional texts and thus to question the concept of their hierarchization into "primary" (and presumably secondary) meanings. Moreover, even if one accepts that there are several possible semantic contexts that are acceptable for biblical criticism to study, then how does one differentiate between those multiple possible meanings that a given biblical text "originally" had at various points during the context of its production and receptions, which are meanings that come after the putatively original ones? Barton and Barr have tried to draw this line with purely semantic boundaries—"the words of Amos," for example. Yet biblical texts traverse semantic boundaries and multiply semantic possibilities, and therefore some other principle must govern the placement of the boundary between original and reception.

Genre as Context

Historical-critical scholars have also argued that a text must be read within the generic expectations of the broader culture that exists at the moment of that text's enunciation. For Barton, this is in fact the essence of biblical criticism: his first thesis concerning the "nature" of biblical criticism states that "biblical criticism is an essentially literary operation, concerned with the recognition of genre in texts and with what follows about their possible meaning."[41]

Form criticism contributes much to the study of ancient texts. Socioliterary conventions function much like linguistic structures in that genres allow readers to exclude some meanings as invalid within the specific context of the text's utterance.[42] Yet for this very reason biblical texts, which as complex traditional texts are unlike utterances, cannot be easily collapsed into one particular temporal manifestation.

In her article "Spying out the Land: A Report from Genology," Carol Newsom surveys various theories of genre, arguing that "genres are dynamic" and that as a result "some of the most interesting issues in genology are precisely those of genealogy."[43] Yet not only genres have a genealogy: texts, too, have genealogies that include several genres in which they have participated during the course of their production. As such, these genealogies cast doubt on genre's ability to demarcate an original meaning from a reception.

Since its inception, form criticism has argued that genre provides the anchor with which to moor a text in its appropriate context. Hermann Gunkel, for instance, argues that each genre of psalm derives from a particular cultic setting, shares a set of thoughts and moods, and shares formal elements.[44] Though the genres of psalms "arose from the cult," Gunkel studies their diachronic development. As Gunkel argues, psalms later "turned their back on [the cult]," and poets began writing "mixed genre" psalms so confused that "here and there a complete formlessness occurred."[45] Showing his preference for the "original" genres, Gunkel admonishes students to begin thinking in terms of "pure genres" and only after these are "clear" to allow oneself to read mixed-genre psalms such as Psalm 119, which derives its odd construction from the shift away from production in the cult toward "individual poets."[46]

Gunkel's distaste for diachronic shifts in genre are well known, but more pressing for my concerns are generic shifts undergone by particular texts.[47] For example, according to modern scholarship, Psalm 30 is an individual thanksgiving psalm commemorating a recovery from illness, yet its superscription declares it to be "a song of the dedication of the house" ("שיר־ חנכת הבית"), presumably a communal function unconnected to illness.[48] Thus, in every extant manuscript containing this psalm, we find a superposition of at least two generic matrices. Since the superscriptions are generally understood to have been added after the composition of the poem, many scholars assume that this psalm was retroactively reread as a communal thanksgiving.[49] Concerning Psalm 30's apparent genre, Gunkel remarks that "later usages prove nothing about the origin of the poem. In Ps 30, an individual 'song of thanksgiving' has been used at the temple consecration, apparently at a time much later than the time of its origin. So if one wishes to research the type of a literary branch, one may not begin with its last tributary. Rather, one must begin at its origins. If we are to make any progress, we must immerse ourselves in the oldest worship service."[50]

Gunkel, like Barr, argues that the genre of a text at its moment of enunciation holds the key to the text's original meaning and that later developments are more akin to a fall from grace than a progression or unfolding. Barton too supports this view: "It is not too much to say that it is impossible to understand any text without at least an implicit recognition of the genre to which it belongs . . . the meaning depends on the genre."[51] A text belongs to a genre; when confronted with a text that traversed multiple genres during the literary production of the text itself, Gunkel, like Barr, regards the earlier version as superior. Likewise, Barton describes how recognizing genre requires detecting the "discrete earlier existence" of "texts that have in each case a particular genre."[52] Other than the assumption that "an origin is more authentic than a development," what reason is there to prefer the earliest genre among the choices? Clearly the structures and genres of Hebrew psalms derived from still earlier Mesopotamian hymnody; should we then leave behind the Israelite worship service in favor of locating the original branch from which the Israelite worship service, including its songs, is merely a tributary?[53]

Israelite cultic song genres, to be sure, were influenced by and derived from earlier songs and worship rites. But in the same way that the etymological fallacy insists that the origin of a word is not necessarily present in nor definitive for any particular use of that word, the supposedly original *Sitz im Leben*, literary structure, or constraints on meaning imposed by a particular historical moment in the development of a genre cannot be definitive for later derivative genres or texts. This is even more important in light of the diachronic development of biblical texts, since genres developed, were created, and were forgotten during the development of the text itself.

In another example, the intrapsalm prose text called David's Compositions (11Q5 27.2–11) found in the Psalms scroll 11QPs[a] suggests that at least some

Second Temple reader-redactors recontextualized psalms as participants within prophetic and wisdom rather than cultic genres:

> ויהי דויד בן ישי חכם ואור כאור השמש ו סופר
>
> (And David, son of Jesse, was wise, and a light like the light of the sun, /and/ learned. [11Q5 27.2])
> כול אלה דבר נבואהב אשר נתן לו מלפני העליון
>
> (All these [psalms] he [David] spoke through prophecy, which had been given to him from the Most High. [11Q5 27.11)])[54]

David, cast as a prophet and sage, is named author of the known psalms (and thousands of others), thus authorizing a particular set of reading practices that are not included within the various contexts generally attributed to psalms. Moreover, based on the position of "literary" and "didactic" psalms such as Psalms 1, 73, and 119, it does appear that other Second Temple–period reader-redactors understood the book of Psalms primarily as a text meant for intensive private study, effectively divorcing the texts from their cultic settings.[55] Yet it is also likely that these selfsame psalms continued to be used within certain cultic settings throughout the Second Temple period.[56] All of these genres reflect particular settings, proving not the fixedness of a text within a genre but rather the fundamental openness of texts to new settings.[57] Even during their process of composition, the Psalms were already circulating among various genres. Any line delineating genres, like that of semantic structures, runs precisely through the biblical text. If texts are only understandable within their genre of enunciation, then whose enunciation, among the various enunciations of these texts, counts most?

Thus, Barton's claim that "literary competence" is defined "principally as the ability to recognize genre" runs aground on the multiplicity of genres to which these texts have already opened themselves even within their context of production. It seems unjustifiable to create a hierarchy of genres by which to separate the "original" from nonoriginal ones. Perhaps genre functions not as a contextual anchor fixed to one determinate point in time but rather as a spandrel. As the selfsame text moves between different contexts even within the "biblical" period, it may resonate with various genres and settings. Psalm 30, for example, may be actualized in at least several genres, but perhaps it contains the resources to actualize itself in genres not yet developed. Such an understanding of genre at least accounts for the development of the biblical text itself, and should that not be of primary interest to historically minded biblical critics? If there is a line separating the original meaning of a text from later meanings, genre determination cannot adjudicate the placement of this divide.

History as Context

Collins claims that another important aspect of "viewing the text in its historical context" is the practice of "relating [the text] where possible to the history of the time."[58] In its most broad outlines, biblical criticism "relates" the text to history by reconstructing the text's referents and situating the text in its general cultural milieu.

For example, when readers know the geographical locations of particular places referred to in biblical texts, this creates a richer experience, and it may reduce ambiguity in certain texts. Moreover, knowledge of ancient Near Eastern political and military history can help one read the prophetic counsels of Isaiah with more historical precision. In the same way, knowledge of general cultural customs, ritual practices, economic realities, literary motifs, and other aspects of the broader cultural "reservoir" may also reduce textual ambiguity or reveal semantic subtleties. This practice of clarifying the particular referents and general milieu of biblical texts carries great importance in the field of biblical criticism. At times, "viewing the text in its historical context" requires knowledge of cultural, political, or economic realities in place at the time of the production of the text but were not referents of the text per se. For example, knowledge of the scribal class in Jerusalem as it existed in the Second Temple period may help "contextualize" biblical texts that do not mention scribes or even writing at all.

There are, to be sure, several problems that confront any biblical critic looking to contextualize a text. Most striking are the epistemological problems: how does one (1) identify the temporal and social location of the text's production, (2) determine what the text is actually referring to, and (3) discern which "background" details are important or necessary to read the text?[59]

Identifying the sociocultural location of a biblical text is extremely difficult, primarily because ancient Near Eastern authors did not sign their literary products. Moreover, later ascriptions of authorship to important ancients seemed to be part of literary convention rather than due to the presence of a historical signature.[60] Mostly anonymous scribes produced, compiled, and redacted literary, legal, and religious texts alike. Even general identifications of authorship are quite difficult, since traditional texts such as the Bible see the hands of many scribes in many different temporal and geographical locations. Some scholars use the criteria of literary cohesion to identify "J" as an author of the J document in the Pentateuch, but even if this unitary author existed, naming when or where is by necessity speculative.[61] Many such guesses rely on identifying either datable real referents or datable displaced referents in the text.[62] Yet these identifications must remain epistemologically tenuous, since literary works do not necessarily refer to realities outside the text. As Sándor Hervey observes, "The analysts' formulation and reformulation of contexts of situation in such a way that they meet explanatory needs constitutes a form of begging the question."[63]

For example, it is as possible to write about a divine promise of land in a context of landlessness (i.e., exile) as it is in the context of newly acquired land (i.e., Persian period) or disputed land (i.e., the period of Seleucid and Ptolemaic competition for Palestine). Or the book of Job could be seen as an exilic text because it "relates" to the pain of the exile, but it could equally be seen as a post-exilic text because it "relates" to the pain of Persian-period disappointments or it could "relate" to the period of suffering under Neo-Assyrian domination, say post-701 BCE. Moreover, the suffering may not be societal; perhaps the book of Job "relates" to a personal episode of suffering or to a purely theological crisis.

The problem is simple: many biblical texts relate so easily to different societal, historical, and personal circumstances that it becomes nearly impossible to prove which circumstances are the "right" ones. Very likely, these texts' method of production itself caused this problem. The book of Psalms, for example, has clearly been edited to make the poems easy for almost anyone to appropriate.[64] And perhaps the lengthy and uneven editorial process that a text such as the Pentateuch underwent makes it all the more relatable to many, not just to one or even a delimitable few, contexts.

Even if one discerns the proper identity of a single speaking subject responsible for the text, another problem immediately arises: how does one discern which circumstances determine the text?[65] Which circumstances are simply white noise? Even before the observer enters the picture, we seem to face a difficult choice between an infinite regression of inclusion or an "arbitrary reductionism" of exclusion.[66] This dilemma renders problematic the representational or referring function of texts. Texts do not merely refer to an already fully given context; they relate particular linguistic and nonlinguistic elements to each other, sometimes in novel ways. As Frederic Jameson writes, a text is a "simultaneous production and articulation of 'reality.'"[67]

Barr struggles with this very issue in his vast work on biblical theology. In his introduction, Barr notes that much of the "biblical theology" movement seeks to read biblical texts "outside" of their "original contexts," a mode of interpretation that ignores theology "as it existed" at the time the text was produced. But as he explains, "The term 'biblical theology' has clarity only when it is understood to mean theology as it existed or was thought or believed within the time, languages and cultures of the Bible itself."[68] Barr stresses the importance of maintaining the divide between the original context and later contexts that undergirds modern biblical scholarship: only by so doing can biblical theology's "difference from doctrinal theology, from later interpretation, and from later views about the Bible be maintained. What was thought about the Bible by Irenaeus or by Calvin is thus something quite other than biblical theology as here understood. What we are looking for is a 'theology' that existed back there and then."[69] Barr then defines reception history as a focus on the "history of the effects of writings rather than on origins," a methodology that examines texts "after they were composed, after they were finalized."[70] At the moment of composition, finalization, "back there and then," lies the domain proper to biblical criticism. Just after that moment and also everything long after that moment constitutes the domain of reception history.

One problematic fact troubles this clean distinction: biblical texts are not utterances of individuals emanating at singular points in time for specific purposes but are rather fluid texts formed from amalgams of discrete traditions, genres, and materials that themselves are obscure or otherwise complex at the moments of their own origins. Knowing this, Barr hedges his concept of "back there and then": "If it is asked how closely we define 'then,' e.g. whether we refer to the time of the events referred to, or to the time of the original writing of the texts, or to the time of their finalization, the answer is that any or all of these are included or may be so. All of these count, for my purpose, as 'biblical times and cultures.'"[71] Implicitly, Barr agrees that biblical scholars are aiming at a moving target: "back there and then" encompasses a wide variety of settings, a long scope of time, and a rather broad array of literary, linguistic, and social contexts. With this hedge, Barr is at odds with his own comments on semantics: "back then and there" could encompass both of Sawyer's reconstructions of Amos 8:3, one describing the palace girls and one foretelling laments in the temple. Multiplicity remains within the text. The doctrinal is already within the biblical.

Another problem confronts Barr's division: there is no "back there and then" that can function as a discernible unit. Differences between pre-exilic, exilic, Persian, and Hellenistic periods cannot be synthesized into one block of "biblical cultures" that allows for a clear differentiation from later "doctrinal" readers. For example, were the Qumran interpreters "back then and there" practicing "doctrinal" or "biblical" theology with their *pesharim*?[72] If Qumran is not part of the "original context," then Qumranic rewritings of biblical texts would be considered "doctrinal," but how does that square with the fact that the similar act of compiling and rewriting various Pentateuchal sources in the Persian period is considered "biblical"?

Ultimately, the question is this: how does one justify a separation between the variegated "back then" from everything else that has come after? Barr calls the time of textual "finalization" a "biblical time." Following Ulrich, Tov, and Talmon, this period of "finalization" lasted between 70 CE and 132 CE. How is it that Irenaeus is so clearly something other, more "here and now" than "back there and then," though he himself was born in 130 CE?

It is clear that Irenaeus was a Christian, and so he was certainly reading the book of Daniel in a Christological sense that was not possible when the court stories of Daniel 2–6 were written, likely some four hundred or so years before Irenaeus's time.[73] Perhaps Barr could argue that Irenaeus's reading is "doctrinal" because it takes into account concepts that were not available in earlier contexts in which the text was written and read (and rewritten). But the same could be said for Philo, or Josephus, or any of the various sectarian elements that composed late Second Temple Judaism, though that period qualifies as "a biblical culture" in Barr's sense. Most late Second Temple–era Jews were closer in reading practices and theological presuppositions to Irenaeus than to the much more ancient author(s) of Daniel 2, let alone P or J.[74]

Moreover, what would Barr say about the Tannaim, since they coexisted with the "finalization" of the biblical text? Are they then "biblical," and are their beliefs in resurrection, strict monotheism, the oral Torah, and so on "biblical?"[75] Or, is Josephus's understanding of Daniel 8:11 as referring to the events of 70 CE a part of "biblical times?"[76] Perhaps in Barr's estimation these views are too late to be "biblical," but then, problematically, the stage of "finalization" would not itself be biblical.

Of course, one need not even leave proto-MT Daniel to feel the tension between "back there and then" and "here and now." Individuals unquestionably within the realm of "biblical cultures" read and rewrote Daniel in ways unavailable to previous readers-writers of the book; Daniel 12:1–3 itself presents a theological thought, namely, resurrection, that was not thought by the readers-writers of earlier elements within the book of Daniel.[77] It is likely that readers from the time of the composition of Daniel 12 would have found precedent for their ideas in earlier biblical literature that originally did not connote resurrection; for example, Daniel 12:1–3 draws on earlier texts such as Ezekiel 37 and Isaiah 52:13–53:12. Though when produced, Ezekiel 37 and Isaiah 52–53 described the political revival of Israel, by the time of Daniel 12:1–3 they were read as a description of revivification of the dead. How can such an "out of context" application nevertheless be "biblical?" If it is "biblical," then how does one exclude Philo for just this sort of "doctrinal" activity? In short, the contextual differences internal to "biblical times" are as extensive as differences between "late biblical times" and "early nonbiblical times," casting into doubt the periodization itself.

Barr's framing is not objective: rather, by constructing a contradiction it seeks to protect an ideology of reading that valorizes the concept of origin over anything derivative. Where nothing quite original can be found, and where no clear hierarchy between different derivative forms or meanings presents itself, the historical-critical method posits its presuppositions as regulative ideals, bringing to life specters of "the original text" and "the original meaning" that thereafter haunt scholarship. Just as with semantic and literary structures, the "historical context" does not provide a clear or internally consistent justification for distinguishing between original meaning and receptions. Biblical texts such as Psalms reveal the openness of the "biblical period" to the spandrel-like retroactive recontextualization that constitutes just the sort of activity that Barr, Barton, and Collins are trying to dismiss from the practice of biblical criticism.

Strangely, the practice of "contextualization" in historical-critical biblical studies generally avoids an analysis of the concept of context itself. Though modern biblical scholarship has advanced our knowledge primarily because of its concern for historical contextualization of texts, "context" often functions as a catchall term that at times references linguistic synchrony, at other times references literary conventions, and at yet other times references the world of historical events, including authors and their intentions. Perhaps the concept of "context" has eluded analysis because it is, to the observing scholar, a horizontal phenomenon: "Like the horizon or peripheral vision, it by definition eludes direct examination; when examined directly, it is no longer peripheral."[78] In the next chapter, I develop a concept of context that takes into account the production history of the text. By necessity, it draws more on the metaphor of the spandrel than on that of the anchor.

FOUR

On Tigers and Cages: Rethinking Context

There is always another town within the town.
—Gilles Deleuze

If I can caricature a little and say that the historian will always want to *put it back into its context* (the tiger is out of the cage, the historian always wants it put back inside), then Derrida will always also be urging the question: "How did it escape in the first place?"
—Geoffrey Bennington

Introduction: Biblical Zookeeping

Biblical scholars often claim that the original context holds the proper meaning of a text. Michael Fox, for example, claims that his "main concern in approaching a text is essentially . . . to ascertain the meaning of the text, which is to say, the authorial intention."[1] For many, the meaning of a text is singular, and it is equivalent to the intentions of an author as they existed in the original context. Thus the original context holds the key to a text's meaning.

Imagine biblical scholarship of this sort as a zoo in which all the textual animals keep escaping their contextual cages, and we scholarly zookeepers are kept very busy capturing and returning them. So busy, in fact, that we have not often asked why it is that the cages do not ever seem to fulfill their assumed function of containment. The truth is that texts always leave their contexts, especially their putative original contexts, and contexts never seem to do anything to stop them. Actually, the situation is even worse: original contexts simply disappear into the mists of time while the texts romp around in the present. Biblical scholars are not only busy catching escaped texts but are even more busy (re)building their proper habitations from the fragments that remain. How do texts escape in the first place? Is there something about contexts, or texts, that prompts this escape?

Yes, there is something about texts or contexts that prompts this escape, since one of the defining characteristics of text is its *durability*. That is, texts are things that remain readable long after any act of inscription. The skill of escaping contexts is not an anomaly or problem but in fact a central feature of texts.[2] Escaping contexts is simply what texts do, and if they did not do this very thing, then they would not be very useful at all. Letters, rituals, poems and laws are written precisely to be taken and read out of their original contexts and in other contexts, to be understood in light of the contexts of the readers as well as the writers.

At times biblical scholarship focuses so much on the moment of the inscription of a text that it overlooks the moment of reading, which generally occurs well outside the context of inscription. The very function of a text is to be readable outside of its context of production.[3] As Geoffrey Bennington writes, "Reading [is] what opens texts up always beyond their historical specificity to the always possibly menacing prospect of unpredictable future reading."[4] Any historical specificity in texts is already disturbed by their opening toward a reader—any reader.

Some biblical texts thematize this uncageable contextual openness of reading. Deuteronomy 5:3, for example, claims that "לא את־אבתינו כרת יהוה את־הברית הזאת כי אתנו אנחנו אלה פה היום כלנו חיים" ("YHWH did not make this covenant with our ancestors, but with us, ourselves, these ones here today, all of us who are living"). Taken literally within its narrative world, Moses's statement is untrue: he speaks these words to the "new generation," the people who most certainly were not present at the mountain. Here, Moses presents the covenant as something radically unanchored from its context of production, so unanchored that in fact it did not address those who first heard it. Rather, the true addressees of the covenant are "us," the ones "here today." And who are "we," and when is "today"? Perhaps one could claim that the true addressees are those characters in the text, the new generation poised to take possession of the land. Yet Deuteronomy 5:1–5 may well have been written during the period of the exile, and if so the true addressees were the rhetorical targets of the Deuteronomists, namely the exilic community, poised to return to the land.[5] And yet the hortatory style of Deuteronomy seems designed not merely to address the one generation living during the writing of the book but, as Deuteronomy 4;9 says, "your children, and your children's children" (cf. Deuteronomy 4:10, 25; 6:2, 7, 20–21; 11:19–21).

Deuteronomy's reliance on deictics, also called indicators or indexicals (e.g., "here," "now," "this," "you," "us"), is telling in this regard. Indicators have no constant referent; what is the meaning of "I" except, as Émile Benveniste writes, "the person who is uttering the present instance of discourse containing I?"[6] Instead of providing concepts, indicators "provide the instrument of a conversion that one could call the conversion of language into discourse."[7] Indicators allow for the reappropriation of language itself, and Deuteronomy exploits this feature of language in order to open itself up to reappropriation beyond the borders of any named addressee, beyond the borders of any context, cage, or harbor. In the case of Deuteronomy 5:3, indicators simply pile up in an ungrammatical mess, comprising the entire second half of the verse. To what do these indicators refer? To nobody in particular—and thus precisely to anybody who reads them, since this hortatory function seeks to preach to unknown generations yet to come. Emphatically, Deuteronomy shows us, whoever we might be, that some textual tigers were never meant to be held in contextual cages.

In order to theorize reception history, biblical studies requires a more robust understanding of context. To this end, I analyze three linked concepts: (1) *text* and *context,* (2) *author* and *audience,* and (3) *meaning* and *significance.* A close look at these concepts shows that the historical-critical scholar rightfully asks questions about contexts, authors, meaning, and history. But when these concepts are asked to play the part of the zookeeper—that is, when scholars claim that only authorial intentions are meanings or that texts can only be read within one particular context—then these concepts obscure more than they reveal. Choosing to read a text as one imagines its author understood it or choosing to read a text as a particular recipient might have understood it is a contingent, not a necessary, choice.

Text and Context: Determined or Determinable?

While scholars use the term "context" in various ways, the general concept presupposes a distinction between a focal point and the surrounding environment.[8] Context re-presents the familiar problem of parts and wholes, or how individual elements relate to larger systems. It implies that the meaning of an individual element of a system is ambiguous unless it is considered in light of its environment.[9]

Literary contextualization asks how a given passage hangs together with the rest of the text. It is assumed that the meaning of particular parts of a text must be comprehensible in light of the other parts of the text and in light of the text as a whole.[10] Context, understood as the network of circumstances surrounding and producing an utterance, may take into account the macrocontext of broad categories such as the language of the utterance, cultural significations, or extant political and social networks. Circumstances can also include microcontextual data such as paralanguage (gestures, intonation, expressions, or font and formatting in written texts). Inquiry into the particular thoughts or intentions of a writer as they relate to a written text developed as another facet of the circumstantial context.[11] Some scholars search for "actual" intentions, or the thought process of the historical author, while others search for the intention as represented in the text regardless of the psychological process of the author.[12] Overall, the concept of context relies on the assumption that a proper reconstruction of this state of affairs will reduce the number of valid meanings that an utterance may have.

Contexts Are Open, Not Closed

Consider the commonly held view that ancient contexts cannot be reconstructed in their totality. One cannot know everything there is to know about the ancient context, since the historical record remains fragmentary, and extant ancient texts present only biased snapshots.[13] These critiques assume that a real past context empirically exists, albeit beyond the limits of reconstructive efforts.

Yet reconstructing a context is an act of creation, not just reproduction. As systems theoreticians G. Spencer-Brown and Niklas Luhmann have shown, the act of drawing distinctions must precede any act of indication, description, or analysis.[14] For example, it is only by externally articulating a "Second Temple period"—a variegated period to say the least—that one can organize a study of it. Once delimited, scholars must determine what data inside the frame counts as signal and what is noise. As Howard Eilberg-Schwartz argues, "Cultural wholes are complex and thus there are numerous ways in which the interactions among cultural elements can be construed. Since it is impossible to see everything as related to everything else, the interpreter is forced to make a decision as to which elements in the system are related."[15]

Contexts do not come prepackaged with directions for assembly. Even at the time of an event's occurrence, the identity and significance of all of its elements and the relations between them are *underdetermined*.[16] What elements are related in a given context, and what is the nature of these relations? There is no singular correct answer to that question. An underdetermined context may be experienced or explained—that is, determined—in irreducibly conflicting ways.

This is not to say that elements and their relations are open to any determination imaginable. On the contrary, as Eilberg-Schwartz argues, each element of a context can play multiple roles—but not just any role. Contexts are not like a puzzle in which every piece has only one place to fit within the larger picture. Rather, contexts more closely resemble a set of particular building materials the contours of whose elements allow for certain connections, but not others. You can build many different things with a set of wood planks, a hammer, and some nails, but you cannot build a skyscraper. The structural contours of the set of objects and their potential relations allow for a multiplicity of constructions.[17]

Consider a hypothetical element, such as a particular American flag, within a hypothetical context, such as the courtyard in front of a federal government building in Washington, D.C., during the spring of 2003. Even at the moment when the flag was "in its context," its identity and meaning were underdetermined. Was that flag a symbol of liberty and peace or of hegemonic dominance and empire? Or was it a meaningless fixture, a rallying place, a pretty pattern, or the site of ironic gesture? What did it refer to—did it connote the institution of the military, or the American people as a whole, or the notion of freedom, or radicals protesting war? What were its true relations—that is, who owned it, who wanted it, who took care of it, who noticed or made a fuss about its presence, who ignored it?[18] Any historical figure who attempts to determine the meaning and relations of that flag at a particular moment in time—say, a student protesting a contemporary war in front of it—did not and could determine the essence of the flag for all observers. Instead, the flag always remains open to counterdeterminations at that precise moment. The flag was determined in a particular manner for a particular war protestor, but the flag remained open for others, such as an apolitical passerby, to determine differently.

In any context, the American flag may be determined in disjunctive ways. The significance of the flag is thus metastable, allowing for alternate determinations, none of which are necessarily superior to the others. What those parties as well as any scholarly (re)constructors lack is a clearly objective, singular determination of that flag.[19] Moreover, the flag is only one element of this framed context. *Every* element within that same context lacks a universally definitive determination. Not only is the scholar unable to ascend to a transcendental position from which to objectively adjudicate such a dispute; more importantly, there *is no such position,* since the truth of the context *is* that the elements and their relations are open to dispute. In other words, there is no single real meaning or real set of relations lurking behind—or defining from above—any context or any element or relation in a context.[20]

As an example of a context that presents several incompatible but nonetheless irreducible determinations, consider the conflicts in Jerusalem between 168–164 BCE. When scholars reconstruct this context, they must refer primarily to the texts that describe it. A number of Jewish writings from this time period, including the Enochic Animal Apocalypse and the Apocalypse of Weeks as well as Daniel 7–12, take a distinctive perspective on the conflict.[21] Moreover, several later Jewish historiographical works, such as 1–2 Maccabees and the works of Josephus, also determine the events differently, as do some later Greek and Roman historians such as Diodorus and Tacitus.[22] While these various sources agree at points, several irreducible historical problems remain, most notably the causes and meaning of Antiochus IV's religious persecution.[23]

The historiographical problems do not rise merely from garbled source material or historiographical errors. Several factions understood the same elements and relations in contradictory ways. Elias Bickermann argues that at least four versions of the persecution exist. Pro-Seleucid sources claim that Antiochus IV merely stopped in Jerusalem to put down a local rebellion. Anti-Jewish sources, on the other hand, argue that Antiochus IV was provoked only by the particularism of the Jews.[24] Meanwhile, Jewish eyewitnesses such as the author-redactors of Daniel 8–12 place the full blame on Antiochus IV and hardly mention intra-Jewish or Jewish-Hellenistic conflict. 1 Maccabees, however, stresses the Jewish-

Greek divide as the source of the conflict, and 2 Maccabees focuses more on intra-Jewish conflict as the source of the persecution.[25] So as Bickermann argues, one underdetermined event—the rededication of the Jerusalem temple to Zeus Olympios in 167 BCE—was determined differently by Hellenistic Jews, Jews resisting Hellenization, Seleucid authorities, and Seleucid-Syrian soldiers stationed in Jerusalem.[26]

Historians often compare these accounts in order to re-create what "really happened." While this is often a very productive endeavor (even if it cannot be conclusive), it is very likely that no particular participant in these events would recognize the bare facts of the matter as "what really happened." Each group determined their situation by means of different symbolic worlds.[27] Would a completely objective recreation of the true events of 168 BCE fit cleanly into any single or communal perspective on the events? The bare, underdetermined facts of what happened were not real for anybody living at the time.

Of course, something really did happen in Jerusalem in 167 BCE, but the fundamental identity of those acts was open to different determinations. Were the actions taken in the Jerusalem temple a sacrifice or a desecration? If one offers an answer, by what authority does one derive that answer? Any answer concedes something to one committed viewpoint over another. An ontology of Antiochus's act only emerges once a side has been taken.[28] If one attempts to describe events in their underdetermined state, perhaps by saying "a man slaughtered an animal in a building," one does not reconstruct a context or contextualize a text. Reconstructing a context requires selecting elements to include in the frame and excluding others, and it also requires characterizing these elements and their mutual relations. If one could even conduct such a thing as a neutral survey, it would do none of these things.

But one could attempt to write a *dialogic* account of the event, representing "the point of intersection of several unmerged voices" that appears within "a concrete event made up of organized human orientations and voices."[29] A dialogic text does not provide an overarching point of view that sublates various perspectives or reveals the universal truth of the situation that was hidden from all embedded perspectives. On the contrary, a dialogic representation juxtaposes perspectives. It refuses the position of objective transcendence, limiting itself to an immanent perspective. As Derrida argues, "There are only contexts without any center or absolute anchorage," since no observer can claim the authority to impose his or her center as necessary for all other observers.[30]

This unfinalizable dialogism does not necessarily include a bridge of mutual understanding between various conflicting spaces. Rather, it presents these perspectival differences as constitutive of true reality rather than as mere distortions of it. Of course, there can be historical distortions: 1 Maccabees, for example, clearly reflects a pro-Hasmonean bias. This bias certainly alters the way it tells its story, even perhaps to the point of deliberately misrepresenting the situation by ignoring the rebellion of 168 BCE.[31] But "behind" all the ideological distortions, I am arguing, there is no purely objective, natural account that may allow for a dismissal of all perspectives as merely distortions themselves.

It is not historically accurate to say that Antiochus IV either sponsored an "abomination" ("שקוצים" [Daniel 9:27]) or called for a proper sacrifice. On the contrary, Antiochus IV sponsored an abomination, *and* he called for a proper sacrifice. And more. A rift runs down the middle of this single historical event that multiplies its contextual potential. This boundary does not separate "the real event" from its later misinterpretations. It separates various possible construals of the event from one another, even at the moment of its historical occurrence.

Contexts host differences and tensions between perspectival positions instead of resolving them. As Michel Foucault writes, "History appears then not as a great continuity underneath an apparent discontinuity, but as a tangle of superimposed discontinuities."[32] Gilles Deleuze calls this tension a space of "disjunctive synthesis."[33] If any context is an underdetermined multiplicity, and if all texts are in some way dependent on their contexts for meaning, then this requires historians to admit that texts are themselves underdetermined in their meaning. At the moment of a text's initial circulation no less than at the present moment, it is underdetermined. Thus the text is always able to be read in different ways by the various disjunctive points of view already comprising its context.

As a result, the act of "contextualizing a text" can include the practice of mapping a text's own disjunctive synthesis of various perspectives. How might Daniel 7–12 be determined differently by Seleucid officials, the *maśkîlîm*, and Hellenized Jews? It matters little if we have historical evidence of Seleucids ever reading it. Daniel 7–12 was a text that existed in the late Second Temple period and as such it could have been read by Seleucids, Hellenizers, and many others. Its own openness to reading constitutes part of its context. Daniel 7–12 is dialogic not just because it represents different perspectives within itself; it is dialogic because it performs dialogism, as it has proven time and again.

Methodologically, the upshot of this conclusion is twofold. First, scholars create contexts by choosing their boundaries, selecting "important" elements, and interpreting them and must take responsibility for doing so. Furthermore, scholars must respect the fact that there are plausible justifications for drawing the lines differently. There is no scholarship without drawing lines, but there are no natural, self-justifying lines to simply respect. Second, even after drawing lines, reading a text "in its historical context" does not naturally lead to the discovery of "an original meaning," since the originating context is always already a multiplicity, not a unity. Contextualization must be at least open to the multiple points of view present in any context of utterance. As a result, one can read a biblical text from multiple perspectives and still be "within" the context of production, however narrowly that context is drawn. This conclusion complicates a neat semantic division between "the original meaning" and "receptions." Reception history, or the study of things other than the original text in its original context, may be all that has ever existed.

The Inside of a Context Must Already Be on Its Outside

So we have established that contexts are not pregiven wholes. Rather, contexts must be determined by the individuals and groups living within them just as they must later be (re)determined by the scholars who study them. Thus, when historians place a text back into its context of production, there are always already multiple irreconcilable points of view from which to read it and determine its meaning.

My argument thus far is essentially synchronic and leaves untouched the temporal, diachronic dimension of contexts. As Valentin Voloshinov points out, "Contexts do not stand side by side in a row, as if unaware of one another, but are in a state of constant tension, or incessant interaction and conflict."[34] In other words, even if every context were to exist as a pregiven, already interpreted and determined whole, history cannot be understood as a succession of contexts objectively separated from one another, each containing a decodable meaning and self-determinate content. Every moment requires traces of other past and now absent moments that constitute its very identity.[35]

Even speaking of the "elements" within a context assumes that these elements already have some intrinsic identity apart from their relations. For example, in the context of Jerusalem in 167 BCE, one could recognize the acts of the Seleucids at the Jerusalem Temple as either sacrifices or abominations (or even perhaps other things). Perhaps these interpretive possibilities existed because the acts in question looked and functioned much like sacrifices familiar to Seleucids or Syrians, while they were vastly different from the sacrifices familiar to Jews. They were familiar—and thus identifiable as something—because they "cited" previous sacrifices, copied them up to a point, repeated them with minimal differences. Thus, the interpretability of those acts depended on their degree of difference from previous acts, and confusion sets in when Jews and Seleucids or Syrians interpret the same act by means of different sets of previous comparable acts.

One recalls the famous lines from Epictetus: "This is the conflict between Jews and Syrians and Egyptians and Romans, not over the question whether holiness should be put before everything else . . . but whether the particular act of eating swine's flesh is holy or unholy."[36] The debate about the identity of a particular act—what does it mean to eat swine flesh—can only be presented with reference to the historical traditions of those communities.[37] In other words, the identity of the act in part depends on its relations to past events, customs, and significations that lie outside of the immediate context of 167 BCE. The traces of these extracontextual elements, their ghostly presence, allowed individuals to recognize and interpret their present. By this same logic, the great problem surrounding Antiochus's acts is the lack of continuity between the persecution of Jews and the official Seleucid position of general religious tolerance.[38] This example demonstrates that the elements of a context are each composed of a network of referrals to other elements of other contexts. As such, the dimension of time enters into our discussion of context.

If every moment requires traces of other past and now absent moments for its very identity, then the act of framing must allow for porous frames. The moment of a speech act relies on the supertemporal *langue* as well as the unframeable entity of culture and elements from other historical moments—past conversations, for example—that are required for anything like meaning to occur within the speech act. In the words of historian David Harlan, the relevant context for an utterance "may include all of . . . civilization. And more."[39] Every element of a context's meaning cannot be determinate strictly within the temporal bounds of its context.

The future complicates every present, as well. Events are notoriously difficult to understand as they unfold. Consider the fall of the Iron Curtain in Eastern Europe. The situation was largely undeterminable, and historians kept cautioning that we would have to "wait and see" what had actually happened or whether anything actually had.[40] Rather than introduce a determinable identity into the world, the event of the fall of the Berlin Wall instead added tremendous uncertainty to the political situation. At its moment of coming into being, the situation was fluid, impossible to comprehend. Even after much time had passed, what had actually occurred might be drastically reevaluated depending on later events. Was it a failed revolt, or a moment of madness, or a peaceful demonstration, or a shift in the world order itself? It is hard to say if even now, more than twenty years later, we yet know what the fall of the Berlin Wall actually was.

Statements of identity and meaning can be provisionally formulated, even in fairly stable ways, but such accounts always carry the qualification that the future may destabilize them. The "full," unquestionable meaning must be continually deferred, theoretically to the point at which nothing more may happen to destabilize it.[41] As Zhou Enlai may have replied to Henry Kissinger when asked to describe the significance of the French Revolution, "It's too soon to tell."

In other words, the identity and meaning of events and contexts depend on future events and contexts. Freud called after-the-fact restructuration

"Nachträglichkeit," "deferred action."[42] Meaning of any sort is thus a retrospective effect; even an author's meaning is often something that emerges during or even following, not only preceding, the act of writing. In this way, history is never a closed book. The meaning of a context is often only found outside of that context, out of context itself, past and future.[43] As 1–2 Maccabees show, the meaning and identity of Antiochus IV's actions were open for later generations to rethink, and they themselves could not close the case. Since "the end" has not yet come, there is no possibility of summing up the identity or meaning of any event, and as such the supposed whole *does not exist as a whole.*[44] Constructions of the meaning of a given context are simply more elements. They are provisional, local, contingent, revisable. No context is closed; all are structurally open and constitutively heterogenous.

Thus, if a scholar claims that the original context fixes the original meaning of a text, one may respond that the original context is not original, since after all it derives its identity from the past. And the context is always not yet determined, since its meaning is open to the future in general. Contextualization cannot simplify the text or determine it. It combines the text with a complex set of temporally underdetermined elements and thus multiplies its own possibilities. Independent of an observer's particular perspective, contexts are neither original nor determined.

Texts as Exemplars of Contextual Mobility

Up to this point, I have highlighted the complexity of "the historical context." As for texts, or that which biblical scholars try to "put in" a historical context, they are peculiarly difficult things to contextualize. This difficulty, I claim, is constitutive of textuality itself, because a text is always, from the start, a recontextualization of other text. That is, the elements of any specific text—the words, phrases, motifs, genre, gestures, formatting, and so on—are cited from other contexts previous to the "original" context of enunciation. As Bakhtin argues, every text is composed of citation from various sources outside the moment of enunciation: "Prior to [the] moment of appropriation, the word does not exist in a neutral and impersonal language . . . but rather it exists in other people's mouths, in other people's contexts, serving other people's intentions: it is from there that one must take the word."[45] Texts are primarily acts of adaptive reuse, not pure invention. It is precisely for this reason that language is useful to a broad variety of speakers over a long span of time. In order for language to function, signs must be both repeatable in various contexts and identifiable in different local manifestations. The signs and structures that comprise a language must be flexible enough to allow the speaker to adapt that language to her own environment, but the language must also remain identifiable to others at the moment of its enunciation.[46] For a listener to identify the signs used by the speaker, the listener must already have access to the signs, deriving this access from previous enunciations. What allows for language simultaneously deprives it of full originality.[47] As a result, signs sit somewhat uneasily within contexts of production: they always come from somewhere else, and they are always flexible enough to be regrafted onto other contexts.[48]

Written signs are not only repeatable; they are also durable. That is, a written text remains long after its context of production has passed away. Durability has long been noted as a productive feature of writing: writers write things down precisely so that readers can read them outside the situational context of writing. Even if I write myself something personal and temporary like a grocery list, I write it so that I can read it in another context—namely, at the store, when I have already forgotten what I need.[49] Any text is useful insofar as it can be read outside of its context of production, leaving behind the singular events of its composition. In other words, writing is useful precisely because it does not lose its readability when it is transported elsewhere and read at another time, even when it is radically separated from its context of production.

The book of Psalms, for example, trades on this feature of texts. The poems that constitute the book of Psalms were not originally composed as a part of the book of Psalms. They were written for other contexts, both literary and circumstantial. The "publication" of the book of Psalms offered a set—or, more appropriately, various sets—of previously existing psalms and even of previous collections of psalms that were further arranged and edited.

Thus, the origin of the book of Psalms is unoriginal, already a secondary origin, which is to say it is not an origin at all.[50] Perhaps one might claim that the oldest discernible setting of each individual psalm constitutes its "original context." So, Psalm 15 *is* an ancient cultic entrance liturgy. But surely this is not the original context of the book of Psalms, since the entrance liturgy has little to do with the book qua literary work. Moreover, each individual psalm is composed of words, phrases, motifs, and formal elements that predate even that "original" setting of the psalm. Which context, then, is the "right one" in which to read the Psalms?

Perhaps this is the wrong question, since the book of Psalms is composed of prayers that have already been decontextualized so that they may function as prayers suitable for people in many different contexts.[51] Patrick Miller explains, the Psalms "were composed, sung, prayed, collected, passed on because they have the capacity to articulate and express the words, thoughts, prayers of anyone. "[52] Decontextualization seems to be the origin and purpose of the book of Psalms. How does one then read it in context? And even if a specific context for a psalm were miraculously found, as Miller comments, "the sealed poem breaks out of its context even when given one."[53]

While my particular example of the book of Psalms highlights this feature of decontextualization and recontextualization, all texts continue to find new contexts regardless of writerly, readerly, and scholarly attempts to pin them down. This is how texts function. De/recontextualization explains precisely how any biblical text came to be. During this lengthy process there is no single necessary, natural, objective "original context" for a biblical text, since there is no necessary, natural, objective hierarchy of author-redactors. One cannot "contextualize" a composite text that underwent significant redactional work without choosing one particular, highly contingent moment to become the moment when the text was "finished."

How does one justify the placement of the boundary between the original meaning and the first reception? Some scholars here invoke the ethical discourse of "respect": a reader should respect ancient authors' words, just as he or she would desire that his or her own words be respected.[54] But here one may ask who we choose to respect out of all the voices reflected in, and hands that have contributed to, the formation of the text.

Author and Audience: Who Is Talking Now?

For many biblical scholars, the author defines the original meaning of a text.[55] To cite Barr, "Who, for example, would read with respect an account of Paul's theology which made it clear from the start that for this depiction of the theology it was of no importance whatever what Paul actually thought or intended?"[56] This argument assumes that Paul's composition signals his authorship, which in turn ensures his hermeneutical control over the contents of his text. In other words, an author is the source of the text and the guarantor of its meaning. "The reader," E. D. Hirsch claims, "should try to reconstruct authorial meaning," which is equivalent to the author's "intention."[57] Biblical critics have offered sores of proposals for defining, measuring, and discerning authorial intentions, but in general these proposals share the beliefs that intentions present a standard by which one can judge a reading as either faithful or treacherous and that the goal of reading is to approximate these intentions. Intentions can be imagined as particular mental states of a writer, as goals and schematic plans, as strictly that which is realized in the text, and as fictions attributed by a reader.[58]

Yet an approach like this to texts such as Genesis or Proverbs takes the concept of authorship *out of context,* because the ancient notion of "the author" was quite unlike our modern concept. Anonymous, honorary, attributed, and pseudonymous authorships were the norm.[59]

Authorship in/and Biblical Contexts

Michel Foucault helpfully argues that the concept of "author" varies widely depending on one's cultural location.[60] Foucault points out that the modern conception of "author" acts as a safeguard of textual coherence and an anchor to a historical moment.[61] Authors in this sense function as tools used by literary critics to solve textual contradictions, explain stylistic differences, and allow for historical mooring; thus one may appeal to an author's drafts, or his or her other works, or biographical details to explain an ambiguity in the text. By this method some meanings are validated and others are deemed impossible. Thus, the author "is a functional principle by which, in our culture, one limits, excludes, and chooses; in short, by which one impedes the free circulation, the free manipulation, the free composition, decomposition, and recomposition of fiction. In fact, if we are accustomed to presenting the author as a genius, as a perpetual surging of invention, it is because, in reality, we make him function in precisely the opposite fashion. . . . The author is therefore the ideological figure by which one marks the manner in which we fear the proliferation of meaning."[62] Foucault notes two significant differences between ancient Near Eastern and modern conceptions of authorship. First, the biblical text developed precisely by means of "composition, decomposition, and recomposition." Their practice of producing texts suggests that ancient Israelite and Judahite scribes did not observe nor expect the sort of reading prescribed by Hirsch.Second, throughout the ancient Near East, texts functioned as sites of immense productivity, yielding a superabundance of meaning that surpassed any particular signifying intent of a single scribe.[63] In the ancient Near East, scribes were not generally seen as the hermeneutical or productive force behind their writings.[64] Signs were understood to be generative throughout the ancient Near East, including in Israel and Judah.[65] As a result, ancient readers and writers did not rely on the intentions of the inscribing agent as a tool to exclude meanings or as a guarantee of contextual and hermeneutical singularity.[66]

Biblical scholars have long argued that, in various ancient Near Eastern cultures, "certain words were thought of as having power inherent to them," especially in royal, divinatory, and cultic contexts.[67] Though many explanations of such power have overstepped the bounds of evidence, biblical texts do depict certain situations wherein words function as "an objective reality endowed with a mysterious power."[68] That is, signs could do things; they had the ability to produce an illocutionary force that finds its source in divine, not merely social, power. One may note descriptions of such supposed power in texts such as Psalms 73:9, 147:15, and 109:17–18, Proverbs 18:7 and 18:20–21, Jeremiah 1:9–10, and Isaiah 55:10–11. This linguistic effect occurs in texts such as Numbers 5:16–

31, in which written words are described as having the potential to cause pain and damage specific organs, and Numbers 11:26, in which people not present at Moses's blessing were nevertheless given a portion of Moses's spirit merely by having their names inscribed in a list.[69] This view holds that signs not only carried power: they also could produce effects independent of their author or utterer. Even though Isaac did not intend to bless Jacob, the utterance produced the irreversible effect of blessing Jacob (Genesis 27:34–37). Likewise, Nehemiah can ask that his enemies' taunts "be turned on their own heads" (Nehemiah 4:4).[70]

Scribes throughout the ancient Near East mined the shape of the written sign as well as its web of lexical values for referential significance. Babylonian and Assyrian scholars "regarded the overabundance of possible meanings associated with the polysemy of the cuneiform writing system as an inexhaustible source of knowledge and wisdom."[71] Ancient Mesopotamian and Egyptian scholars were nervous about this "potentially dangerous" overabundant productivity, especially with respect to omens or other "divine signs," but their method for dealing with such overabundance was interpretation: the "act of interpreting a sign" limited "that power by restricting the parameters of a sign's interpretation."[72] In the Hebrew Bible, evidence of this practice may be found in Amos 8:1–2 and Jeremiah 1:11–12, in which the phonic similarities between signs reveals the interpretation of the divine message. As Noegel shows, biblical narratives depict Israelites divining messages in ways consonant with other ancient Near Eastern practices, such as by creating the effect of the message through the interpretive act.[73]

Thus ancient Israelites and Judahites assumed that written texts, particularly texts thought to be imbued with divine power, could easily be separated from their original context of production and applied to different contexts, producing different meanings in each case. This assumption undergirds Daniel's expectation that Jeremiah's prophecies continued to speak about events beyond the exile in Daniel 9, the conviction that biblical texts described present events in the Qumran *pesharim*, and interpretation of ancient law in Second Temple halakhic texts as statements about contemporary situations.[74] One may also look to 1 Maccabees 3:48 and 2 Maccabees 8:23, which both "present the Torah scroll as a book that could be consulted as an oracle by opening it at random," demonstrating the assumption that biblical texts functioned in ways unimaginable by the scribal agents who wrote them.[75] Within the "original context" of biblical texts, "the author" did not function as a hermeneutical source or goal; if anything, the status of the pseudonymous or attributed author ensured that the selfsame text would continue to function as an agent of new and helpful meanings.

More broadly, as Armin Lange and others have shown, the very composition and development of biblical prophetic texts witnesses to a shift from "written prophecy," in which oracles were understood to refer to the time of the prophet, to "literary prophecy," in which "the redactional reworking of prophetic texts is a prophetic process in which new meaning is gained from the already written prophetic tradition."[76] As "oracle collections were recontextualized and reapplied to timeframes later than their place of origin," the "surplus of meaning" within the prophecies themselves came to "transcend their original contexts and meanings."[77] Thus, to read these texts is to hear at least two voices, that of the historical prophet and of the literary prophet, speaking to Second Temple audiences and beyond.[78]

But, as Martti Nissinen asks, "The dilemma is this: Who is talking now?"[79] Perhaps we hear two voices, and perhaps even more. The redactors of these texts assumed that prophecy contained a structural openness, an expectation that the text itself was always able to reach beyond its context. Reading these texts in context would require assuming, like a good Second Temple Judahite, that the words of the prophet have never yet exhausted themselves.[80] For biblical texts, at least, authors and their intentions do not differentiate original meanings from receptions.

Intentions and Significances

One cannot, however, follow in the footsteps of the New Critics and simply banish the author in favor of the "text itself."[81] Many different local manifestations of biblical texts coexist, and as such any "text itself" must be selected or constructed amid the variants that comprise the text. And it is just as arbitrary to dismiss authorial intentions as it is to valorize them. Writer-redactors who produced biblical texts constitute a valid area of scholarly inquiry. Yet scholars who are interested in intentions must look the evidence squarely in the eye. While it is very likely true that the writers of the Bible had intentions when doing so, doubtless many of these intentions were conflicted, unfinished, or unconscious. Biblical texts, like all authorial products, contain half intentions, unintended effects, nonsense, absentmindedness, and intentionless rote recall. Moreover, the things used to transmit these intentions—words, phrases, motifs, characters, settings, other versions of stories, and so on—necessarily come sedimented with layers of previous intentions that any author is unable fully to recognize, understand, or master.

Herschel Parker notes that "familiar literary texts at some points have no meaning, only partially authorial meaning, or quite adventitious meaning unintended by the author or anyone else."[82] For example, during the piecemeal composition of *Pudd'nhead Wilson,* Twain transformed the character Tom from a white thief into a mixed-race slave but did not edit to reflect this change. Parker notes the result: "As it turned out, Twain got an accidental bonus on the level of local meaning, for any reader of chapter 11 will think that Tom snatches away his hand so the palm reading Wilson will not find out that he is part black and a slave, not merely that Wilson will find out that he is a thief. Judging from the abundant evidence that Twain did not read entirely through what he salvaged as *Pudd'nhead Wilson,* he probably did not ever specifically "intend" the new meaning of the gesture, even retroactively, although he would have been delighted to get something for nothing."[83] Authors are not in full control of what they write. What Eco calls the "intentio operis," or the "text's intention," may assume a different form from the "intentio auctoris," or the "author's intention."[84] Biblical literature is most likely full of these "accidental bonuses," and it would impoverish our reading to deny them as plausible effects. For example, several scholars have proposed compelling readings of the redactional shape of the psalter. Though no redactor may have intended these particular effects, such "accidental bonuses" should not be ignored simply because the redactor did not notice them.[85] Even scribal errors may lead to "accidental bonuses."

MT and OG-Jeremiah 23:33, for example, present two different versions of a joke: both are effective for different reasons, though one probably formed through scribal error.[86] Should the text read, as the response to the question "What is the burden of YHWH," "*What* burden?" ("אה־מת־משא,"), as MT-Jeremiah has it, or "*You* are the burden!" ("ὑμεῖς ἐστε τὸ λῆμμα" = "אתם המשא"), as in OG-Jeremiah? Both versions are quite humorous, though in different ways. In my opinion, MT-Jeremiah is more humorous: YHWH identifies those seeking "burdens" (or oracles) as burdens themselves, as in OG-Jeremiah, but only in retrospect after having already brushed off the barely noticeable burden. Yet MT-Jeremiah 23:33 is most likely secondary. Must we do away with this accidental bonus merely because it is attributable to unintentional scribal error?

To this example of serendipitous authorial confusion, compare the distinction Barton, following Hirsch, makes between "original meaning" and "later significance": "The significance may vary from one generation to another, but the meaning remains constant throughout."[87] For Hirsch, the "meaning" can only ever be the "author's intention," albeit an intention that is expressed in the text itself and that is not recoverable from the author's biographical details. The ontologically lesser category of "significance" contains other interpretations. One may here note that if Hirsch is correct, then the Hebrew Bible is itself constituted by invalid means, since much of it developed from diverse oral traditions and all of it was subjected to repeated redactions. From the moment of their inscription, these texts never had meaning but only significance.

If we must read for the author's intention but the author's intentions cannot completely control the text, then we will never actually be able to read anything. In this paradoxical state of affairs perhaps the problem lies with the dominant ideology of reading. Readings that do not ask about authorial intention are valid. One may of course seek intentions because various sorts of intentions do exist, to be sure. Even Derrida acknowledges that "the category of intention will not disappear, it will have its place, but from that place it will no longer be able to govern the entire scene and system of utterance. . . . What the text questions is not intention or intentionality but their *telos,* which orients and organizes the movement and the possibility of fulfillment, realization, and actualization in a plenitude that would be present to and identical with itself."[88]

Intentions are not bad, nor nonexistent. They simply do not, and cannot, play the role of telos for all reading, even all scholarly reading. Authors do not necessarily control everything their works say, mean, or do. As such, biblical authors' intentions do not constitute or justify the divide between original and reception. As Derrida argues, it is the very structure of signs that precipitates the lack of total authorial control. The *iterability* of signs—that is, the ability of the same signs to appear in many contexts, albeit in slightly different forms—requires signs to cite occurrences exterior the context of enunciation. Derrida argues that texts are useful precisely because they can be read in the complete absence of their author, as in the case of a letter. Even in the event of the biological death of the writer and the complete obliteration of the context of the text's production, the text will nevertheless necessarily continue to function as a network of signs.[89] For example, both Voyager spacecraft, by now abandoned to the drift of interstellar space, hold inscriptions that are readable and recordings that are decipherable even in the radical absence of all authorial presence. Perhaps some scholars lament the fact along with Socrates that all written texts are at some point abandoned by the author, set adrift, left anchorless and orphaned with no father to answer for them.[90] But whether this is a bad or good quality of texts, it is not merely contingent or restricted to marginal, poorly written texts. Rather, *drift is an essential characteristic of text itself.*[91] Think of texts as tigers on the loose or as spandrels, not anchors. They are not encoded intentions. And even if they were, these intentions would themselves have to be signs to be readable, and thus they would be subject to the very same drift.

Audience and Author

Some scholars have proposed taking the audience into account in order to admit the openness of the text beyond authorial control while retaining historical contextualization.[92] In general, scholars discuss the audience either in an abstract sense, as the matrix of possible readings at the time of production, or in a concrete sense, as the reaction of specific readers or listeners to a text. Both possibilities introduce another variable into the archaeological search for authorial intentions, namely, a receiver of the text. This receiver does not play a merely passive role; rather, the recipient of a text must read the text, which requires an active engagement. Reading inserts an unstable, unprogrammable, dialogical element into the stable algebra of interpretation.

Perhaps one takes "audience" to mean "addressee," a determinate person or people expected to read the text and thus included within the sphere of the author's intentions, safeguarding the hermeneutical sanctity of the text's meaning.[93] These "first audiences," it is argued, hold a privileged position in the history of interpretation due to their contextual proximity to the production of the text.[94] By this logic, other, later, unintended audiences create significances through their encounters with the text.[95] For his part, Barr clearly states that this division between original audience and later audiences is a "boundary point" for biblical scholarship.[96] In this line of thought, however, one immediately encounters practical problems of authority and theoretical problems of spatial and temporal delineation: where is this line to be drawn, and who draws it?

Even if a certain audience can unquestionably be called "the original audience," audiences are not often unified in their reception of texts. Even within the first audience of a text one can expect to find a multiplicity of understandings. The line distributing different meanings runs through the midst of an audience, not behind it. And as for temporal delineation, when is this line to be drawn? In the weeks following this first reading, are original audiences still to be found? What about years later, even generations later?[97] Opening up the text to include "audiences" (something every text by definition does simply by being a text) simultaneously makes it impossible to close it off to certain audiences and contexts.[98] As Bennington writes, "Reading would be impossible otherwise: from the moment one manages to read a text, even at a level of elementary decipherment, one is, however minimally, part of its context."[99]

Psalm 137:3 stages a readerly confrontation internal to the "ancient audience" itself: "For there our captors asked us for songs, our tormentors for amusement: 'Sing for us one of the songs of Zion!'" Here, the victorious Babylonians demand that the vanquished Israelites sing triumphant Zion songs in order to amuse the Babylonians. Perhaps some Babylonians were amused by the dissonance between the downtrodden Israelites and the jubilant words and tune of their Zion songs, but perhaps others merely found the songs aesthetically appealing. As a result, the out-of-context Babylonians became the audience for a Judahite text. Here we see a multiplicity of historical and cultural contexts, meanings, and audiences for the Zion songs jostling each other within the original context itself.This multiplicity also finds expression in Lamentations 2:15, where passersby mock Judahites by recontextualizing part of a Judahite Zion psalm found in the book of Psalms (MT Psalm 48:3). The audience for the phrase "the joy of all the earth" in this case is not just those participating in a cultic rite; the "original contexts" of this text must also include both the mockers and the lamenting Judahites.

Perhaps biting irony and dejected lamentation were not intended by any putatively original author of Psalm 48, but these meanings were always a possibility of the text, from the moment of its first inscription: the shift in audience does not create this function of the text.[100] Rather, the shift merely actualizes a property of signification inhering in the text. And where does this activity stop? Just as any text functions in the radical absence—even the death—of its author, texts continue to function beyond any determinant addressee. The "context of production" never quite closes, since the text itself is a productive force.[101] One may choose certain contexts in which to read a given text, and one may analyze it from the perspective of certain writers or readers, but these are choices, not necessities, and they reflect contingent perspectives, not necessary ones.

Meaning and Significance: Original or Reception?

Do texts mean anything one wants them to mean? No, a text does not just mean anything. But it most certainly does not only mean just one thing. Many biblical scholars agree that texts are *polysemous*, that they can mean several things.[102] It is more appropriate to say that the number of meanings a text has is always yet to be determined.

For all of the weight it carries within biblical criticism, the term "meaning," much like "context," remains ironically undefined. What does "meaning" mean?[103] Of course many different answers have been offered to this question, but broad agreement can be found on several fronts. Most importantly, contrary to the beliefs of many ancient and early modern philosophers, meaning is not a definite property of particular phonemes, words, or even phrases, and neither is meaning something inside a word or a phrase. Rather, like context, meaning is "a set of relations" between parts and wholes, "not a possession."[104] It is for this reason that contextualism has become so important: if meaning is a product of the word's relation to other words and to nonlinguistic situations, then the context, or that to which a word relates, plays a part in the creation of meaning itself. As Moisés Silva concludes, "The context does not merely help us understand meaning; it virtually *makes* meaning."[105] This insight guides diverse modern approaches to meaning such as the Wittgensteinian concept that "meaning is use," J. L. Austin's speech act theory, and even verification theories.[106] All of these approaches assume that meaning emerges from a relationship between language and other elements that comprise a context.

Meaning as a Function of Relations

Saussure's model of the linguistic sign presents this relationship as internal to each sign, the signifier aspect of a sign referring to the sign's concept, or its "signified."[107] As an example, Saussure offers a diagram of the linguistic sign in which the signifier is represented by the letters that spell "tree" and the signified concept of tree is represented by a small image of a tree.[108] While Saussure claimed that the identity of the signifier was composed of pure "differences without positive terms," his conception of meaning is entirely positive: Saussure argues that signifieds simply exist.[109]

Derrida applies pressure to this concept of the signified, asking what exactly a signified is and where we can find one. To answer these questions, perhaps we should follow Wittgenstein's injunction: "If you want to understand the use of the word 'meaning,' look for what are called 'explanations of meaning.'"[110] Consider the following: when asked to give the meaning of a biblical text, a scholar will inevitably produce a linguistic explanation, such as a commentary. But surely this explanation is not the signified, as the commentary is simply another string of signifiers similar to the text in question. Similarly, when an individual wants to find the meaning of a word, that individual might turn to a dictionary, wherein no signifieds are contained: definitions are merely strings of other signifiers.

To recall Saussure's discussion of signifiers, each signifier's identity emerges from its purely differential relation to other signifiers—that is, the sound "dog" does not naturally mean anything, but it is merely distinguishable from other sounds. Derrida argues that this differential identity is precisely the way that signifiers mean as well. In other words, there are no such things as signifieds; the little picture of a tree in Saussure's diagram does not help us escape this conclusion, since it, too, merely substitutes a verbal sign of a tree for a pictorial sign of a tree. Essentially, meaning is only an act of *substitution*, a sort of translation of signifiers. As Bennington writes, "If, for example, I wish to give the meaning (signified) of a given signifier, all I can ever do is produce more signifiers, organised in such a way that one or more of them count as a signified."[111]

For Derrida, the dictionary is a massive organizational device: it produces a network of signifiers, arranging them in certain patterns that create a self-referential system. Perhaps the reader has had the experience of looking for the meaning of a word in a dictionary, only to realize that the meaning of several other unfamiliar words in the definition must be sought in the same book. Diving into a new field of scholarly literature usually presents much the same problem: one must discern within a body of related literature what "they mean" when they say X and Y, since it is somewhat different from what "we mean" when "we" say X and Y. Moreover, many scholars take words in wide circulation and "reposition" them within a discourse; Heidegger, for example, worked hard to redefine the word "Being" in philosophy and was in large part able to do so by organizing large groups of other signifiers through his books and lectures. Thus, meaning is an effect of organizations of signifiers, "a set of relations."

Derrida notes that any commentary, rephrasing, or attempts to define or fix the meaning of statements "in other words" creates a "textual supplement" that itself calls for further comment or definition with further supplements, and so on.[112] Even authors who wish to explain their work are limited to creating supplementary signifier organizations ("What I mean to say is . . .") How is an author's explanation different in kind from a critic's explanation rather than simply different in degree? Both are supplementary linguistic structures that seek to reposition the elements of the text so as to account for its structure; neither has an objective, necessary privilege over the other. "Putting a text in its context" would require recognizing that the author does not have complete control of the text even from the start, that the author's intentions, however whole, cannot organize the entire context and text in such a way that he or she absolutely overdetermines the meaning effect that the text will produce, that there is no necessary boundary between meaning and significance, and thus that the very boundary between "biblical criticism" and "reception history" is founded on a fundamental misconception. Perhaps Derrida, Wittgenstein and Stout are correct: "Meaning" as Hirsch understands it does not exist.[113] There are only significances, significations.

Presenting a meaning, then, requires actively reorganizing the text in a manner that attempts to account for the "position" of the signifiers in the text. Put in simpler terms, readers must be able to justify their reading by showing how their reading takes account of the various elements of the text as it reorganizes it and substitutes some words for others. In this way, the reader must rewrite the text in another mode. The reader must become an author, just as the author surely became his or her own reader during the writing process. We can thus conceive of the position of the author as "the one who holds the meaning" as a structurally open space, able to be occupied by any reader who may try to make sense of the text.

Thus no participant in the textual process (author, reader, the context of writing, the context of reading) has a right always to dominate all other readings. But none of these participants can ever be fully excluded from readings. Moreover, no scholar can know the number of acceptable meanings that a given text has, since future readers and future contexts may hold as-yet unknown resources with which to read any text. Of course, some readings are questionable, and others are poor. Nevertheless, there is not only one correct way to read any text, nor has any text, if it is still readable, yet seen the last acceptable reading.

Context and Meaning

Many biblical scholars nevertheless argue that the meanings of biblical texts are contextually determined, that is, that one can discover an utterance's particular meaning by analyzing the context in which the utterance is given. In other words, although the signifying relationships within an utterance are underdetermined, the external situation surrounding the utterance determines it.

For this to be true, the external situation must itself already be determined so that it may determine the text. However, as we have seen, the relations between elements within a circumstantial context are not objectively predetermined; any context must be constructed by relations between elements being assigned, either by participants or later scholars. A text is a part of a context, and as such both text and context must be constructed with reference to each other and with reference to the other elements of the context. Context does not naturally overdetermine text, and text does not overdetermine context: both context and text are underdetermined in relation to each other, until they are respectively (re)constructed and read. However, texts function precisely by moving between contexts, and so any text is itself open to reading in various contexts. Even if a scholar offers a particularly convincing "contextualization" within one context, traditional texts are particularly potent exemplars of a constitutive multicontextualism. Biblical texts, therefore, always mean more than can be determined within any one context.

Conclusion

In summary, the concept of the original meaning of the text, supposedly found only in its original context, runs into several problems. First, the "original context," even for those living within it, is a site of underdetermined multiplicity; it must be framed and the relationships between its elements determined before it can function as anything resembling a "whole" into which the text can be "put." There can always be other frames and other determinations; for this reason, the task of framing and determining contexts is in principle infinite. The boundary between "original" and "reception" is thus not a pregiven reality.

Second, however one frames them, the production of the biblical text doubtless flows through various contexts; this processual movement bars any single context from the status of "original." As such, each physical manuscript of a biblical text bears not just the context of its moment of production but carries with it sedimentations from its past. A biblical text always sits somewhat uneasily within its context, always pointing to previous contexts and always moving on toward new ones. It can never be constrained, or objectively reduced to, any one set of contextual relations.

Third, the author of a text cannot claim a position of absolute dominance over the productive powers of his or her text, nor can the audience be delimited in a necessarily objective manner so as to give theoretical clarity to the concept of "original audience." Texts are open to reading, which is to say texts are productive, not reductive, even at the moment of inscription.

Fourth, meaning is an effect of signification produced by reading and is not an inherent property of any text. There is no necessary priority ascribed to any particular individual's construal of a text, and thus the boundary between "original meaning" and "receptions," just like the boundary between "original text" and "corruptions/additions," is a construction of biblical scholars. Removing this boundary does no damage to the text or violence to any of its readers; it only acknowledges the purely contingent nature of the boundary.

With respect to methodology, I conclude that reception history is nothing if reception history is understood as studying that which comes after the original. There is no such thing, since there was nothing original in the first place. In the first place, there was the secondary. But everything is reception history if reception history is understood as studying how unoriginal audiences take unoriginal texts and give them unoriginal meanings, which is simply to say if it is understood as "people taking a text and doing something with it." Text criticism, source criticism, redaction criticism, rhetorical criticism, canonical criticism, tradition history, comparative studies: these approaches all look at how people take texts, contexts, and traditions and do different, and sometimes relatively new, things with them.

Yet if it is true that all biblical scholarship is reception history, then how does one actually go about reception history?

FIVE

Mapping the Garden of Forking Paths: A Nomadic Reception History

> In all fiction, when a man is faced with alternatives, he chooses one at the expense of the others. In the almost unfathomable Ts'ui Pên, he chooses—simultaneously—all of them. . . . All the possible solutions occur, each one being the point of departure for other bifurcations. Sometimes the pathways for this labyrinth converge. For example, you come to this house: but in some possible pasts you are my enemy: in others my friend.
>
> —Jorge Luis Borges

Introduction: What Can a Text Do?

In "On the Genealogy of Morality," Nietzsche outlines the basic rationale for a process-oriented study of cultural objects. The meaning of any cultural object, Nietzsche argues, is not defined or contained at its point of origin; rather, the cultural object transforms as it traverses contexts: "The origin of the emergence of a thing and its ultimate usefulness, its practical application and incorporation into a system of ends, are *toto coelo* separate; that anything in existence, having somehow came about, is continually interpreted anew, transformed and redirected to a new purpose."[1] In these few lines, Nietzsche issues several thoughts crucial for reception history: (1) an origin does not explain any current meaning or function; (2) all things are eventually repurposed and thus reinterpreted; and (3) this reinterpretation often ignores and obscures the previous uses and meanings of the adapted thing.

With regard to biblical studies, the last few centuries have proved Nietzsche right in every respect. Though many biblical scholars continue to argue that the origin of a biblical text holds the secret to its true meaning, the data amassed by biblical scholarship points in the opposite direction. Biblical texts never stay put, and their contexts of initial production, as well as their author-redactors, prove hopelessly unable to contain them or restrict their function. Would it not make more sense to explain the form and meaning of a biblical text as a changing process, thereby incorporating variation within the definition of its form and meaning? Following Gilles Deleuze's lead, I propose that biblical texts are not objects but are instead objectiles, object-projectiles, that must be studied as something for which movement and variation is a necessary quality and thus for whom any static identity is an always contingent predicate.[2]

Biblical studies must move beyond essentialism, which holds that a thing is defined by the static set of its distinctive characteristics. For example, essentialists have historically claimed that humans are defined as "rational animals," since rationality is the characteristic that distinguishes humans from other sorts of beings. Thus, rationality functions as the essence of humanity. In contrast to essentialism, Deleuze proposes a "mannerism" that focuses on the capabilities of a thing as opposed to its predicates or essences. Things should be distinguished by their capacities—*what they do*. Instead of asking what the essential feature of a human being is, Deleuze turns to Spinoza's question of what a human being can do.[3] Of course, the essentialist has a point: the power for rational thought, to be sure, is a true human potential. But one must also admit that the power for irrational thought is a true part of human beings, as well. So, irrationality constitutes a part of the answer to the question "What is a human?" Deleuze thus focuses on *capacities* when attempting to understand the identity of an object. And capacities can change over time. Several millennia ago, the potential actions of a human were quite different. Who can say what humans might be able to do even a hundred years from now? "For indeed," Spinoza remarks, "no one has yet determined what the body can do."[4]

Biblical texts are much the same. Too often, biblical scholars ask, "What is the essential textual form of this biblical text? How *should* this text look? How *should* it be read? What *does* it mean?" Instead, we should think in terms of a text's potential. What *can* it look like? What *can* it do? The point of biblical scholarship is not containment. It is knowledge—to know what a biblical text *is*. And the only way to know what it *is* is to see it in many different contexts doing many different things. Reception history asks precisely these questions.

And instead of treating capacities as a predicate of an object, we should treat them as an event or action. For example, instead of answering the question "What color is the sky?" by responding that it is blue, Deleuze would argue that one should assert that what occurs at a given moment is the action of the *sky bluing*, which is but one of the coloring powers of the sky.[5] That is, one particular power of the sky is the manifestation of the color blue, and this is best seen not as a property of the sky but rather as something it does. As Deleuze would say, "The sky blues."[6]

One could argue, of course, that "blue" is a cultural construct, and that various cultures distinguish the color "blue" in quite different ways.[7] Furthermore, the color blue results from a specific interaction between the human eye and particular frequencies of electromagnetic radiation; the wavelengths comprising the color blue do not necessarily interact with other animals or even inanimate objects in such a way that the "bluing" of the sky could be universal.[8] Yet setting aside the question of the identities of various sorts of colors and the varieties of perceptions of color that different people or species can have, we may still agree that colors emerge from a spectrum of electromagnetic radiation.[9] Human perceptions of color emerge from the relationships between the light effect in the atmosphere, the structure of the human eye, and the human brain. One could ask many questions about the differences between various human observers, the differences between human and nonhuman observers, and so on, but these questions are ancillary to the question about the powers of the sky to emit particular patterns of radiation.

In short, humans generally see the daytime sky as blue because of "Rayleigh scattering," in which electromagnetic radiation disperses when it encounters small particles.[10] Sunlight scatters when it encounters particles in the earth's atmosphere, becoming diffuse sky radiation. Since shorter wavelengths are affected more than longer wavelengths, the electromagnetic radiation occurring within the visible spectrum that English speakers refer to as "blue" appears to cover the sky. Whatever one calls it, and however one perceives it, the sky is doing something. Thus, one can conclude that the sky is not blue, as if its color is a property or predicate—rather, the sky produces a bluing effect.

Yet the event of the "sky bluing" occurs only in certain sets of circumstances. At noon on a clear day, for example, the sky blues. In other circumstances, such as at morning or evening or night or during a storm, the sky shows that it can manifest other colors, since it has other powers. Due to the varying composition of the atmosphere, the relative position of the sun so on, the sky can also orange, red, yellow, black, grey, white, and brown. Moreover, the sky "is" not cloudy: the sky clouds, since the production and dissipation of masses of suspended water droplets is another power of the atmosphere. If one says, "The sky *is* blue," one perhaps unwittingly claims that a particular set of circumstances are the natural circumstances in which the sky reveals its true essence. Storms and sunsets, from this vantage point, are lesser aberrations.

When one asks about the powers of a thing, rather than its essence, then unusual events that occur at the limits of experience take on a much different significance. For example, the coloring power of the sky known as the aurora borealis, or northern lights, can only perceived in particular latitudes and at certain times. Yet in these contexts, the sky greens or reds with bursts of intensity. Thus, it is clear that both bluing and flashing green are among the coloring powers of the sky. The sky is *not* blue. The sky is something that can blue, black, grey, orange, red, green, sparkle, flash, cloud, precipitate, and much more.

Likewise, particular interpretive meanings are contingent productions of texts, contexts, and readers. Texts may reveal surprising capacities when read in particular circumstances. For example, a liberatory capacity of the text of Exodus emerges within the history of African American discourse, but others of its powers emerge in a modern Egyptian context. Similarly, the book of Joshua may reveal certain capacities when read in a Zionist context and others when read by Native Americans attending Puritan schools in seventeenth-century Massachusetts. A focus on the powers of the text, rather than on the conditions within which the text manifests those powers, allows one to analyze a text's reception history.

Stanley Fish's interpretive communities and their "systems of intelligibility," much like Foucault's discursive formations and epistemes, certainly do influence the potential capabilities of a text.[11] Yet for Foucault and Fish, the episteme and the interpretive community serve as the protagonists of their scholarly work. The variations between epistemes and communities provide the focus. In contrast, a focus on the objectile-text would lead to questions about the textual capacities revealed under the conditions of various epistemes and interpretive communities. Moreover, we must always hold a place for readings yet to come and contexts yet to emerge. In the example of the sky, if the chemical composition of the air changes drastically, this event will influence the capabilities of the coloring power of the atmosphere. Likewise, the continuing reading of biblical texts will doubtless produce new forms of meaning, since their ongoing development of signifying power depends on their relationships to changing contexts and changing readers.

Framework for a Processual Reception History

As an open-ended process, a biblical text has no moment of purity, origin, finality, or true meaning that could constitute a necessary, universally valid boundary between the text and its later receptions. In order to reconceive reception history along these lines, I have followed the work of philosopher Gilles Deleuze. Three of Deleuze's concepts have proven fruitful: (1) the distinction between the virtual and the actual, (2) the inversion of the relationship between problems and solutions, and (3) a topological approach to structure. I introduce each of these concepts in turn.

The Virtual and the Actual

Perhaps Deleuze's most helpful contribution to reception history is his distinction between the virtual and the actual. This distinction allows biblical scholars to regard the Bible as an underdetermined objectile-text that moves and changes but that has local determinations, or particular texts and readings.

Textual and historical scholars tend to think of texts and meanings in terms of the binary pair of the possible and real. The possible consists of whatever is permissible according to known facts and the rules of logic. For example, it is possible that Nehemiah is the author of at least part of the book of Nehemiah, but it not possible that Pharaoh Ramses II is author of the book of Nehemiah, since he was not alive at the time of its initial production. Thus, one can exclude impossibilities, enumerate possibilities, and then arrange possibilities according to probability. Yet one of these possible states also happens to be *real* as well as possible. That is, one possible state also holds the additional attribute of being real. There are many possible manifestations of the color of the sky (e.g. red, blue, yellow), but only one color also has the quality of being real that is added to it in each moment of space and time.

According to this line of thought, one may be able to enumerate all of the logically plausible meanings of a particular text and chart them. For example, Michael Fox, the leading authority on Proverbs, offers three possible meanings for the Hebrew word "אמון" in Proverbs 8:30: "artisan," "constantly/faithfully," or "nurturing/growing up." Of the three, Fox selects "growing up," reading the word as an infinitive absolute functioning as an adverbial complement.[12] While Fox agrees that it is possible to construe the text in a limited number of ways, he assumes that one reading in particular is not only possible according to the historical context, including its semantics and syntax, but also that that reading also existed in reality. Thus, one of the limited number of possible states is also real by virtue of its extra component of existence.

While this approach does offer the reader a decisive answer to the question of a text's meaning, it is difficult to determine what "reality" means in this case. In his discussion of Proverbs 8:30, Fox enumerates the possible meanings and proves that they all function perfectly well within the semantic and syntactic structure of both the language system and the text. If all of these readings exist—they were enumerated, so clearly they exist—and are defensible, what makes one of them *real*?

Alan Lenzi offers a more nuanced approach. He argues that several senses of "אמון" in Proverbs 8:30 are real but that readers should see "the meaning 'artisan/advisor' or, as I prefer to translate, 'master,' as the primary sense of the word."[13] According to Lenzi's argument, more than one possible meaning of אמון may have been implied in its original context, but only one meaning—namely, the obscure use of the word to mean "master"—is objectively privileged. It is *primary*, while other possible meanings are secondary. But who has the authority to arrange these meanings into a hierarchy of denotation and connotation? Does the author or the scholar have this authority? Or does a nonhuman entity such as "the rules of grammar" have the agency to discern primary meanings? How would we know if it did?

For reception history, another problem looms larger. If the ancient context or the initial author sets the boundaries for the possible meanings of the text, and one or more of these possible meanings are real, then how do new readings emerge? Fox and Lenzi argue that one must discern the correct readings from within the subset of possible readings. What, then, can one say of readings that are not even within the set of possible historical readings? For example, the ability to read Amos 8:3 as a reference to the Jerusalem temple as opposed to the palace at Samaria only appeared after the word "היכל" took on the semantic value of "temple," long after Amos had died but still before the Masoretes pointed the text.[14] Thus, a new potential meaning emerged in the flow of history. The meaning ascribed to the text by the Masoretes was not a transcendental form waiting to be discovered by careful readers. Instead, it was constructed using materials that had not existed at the time of that text's inscription. What can scholars who think in terms of the real and the possible say of new readings? The response must be that these new readings are not even possible.

Instead of thinking in terms of the possible and real, Deleuze urges us to think of existence in terms of the virtual and actual. This is no mere shift in jargon. Unlike the distinction between the possible and the real, that between the virtual and the actual allows for the production of novelty within history. In brief, Deleuze asks us to think of potentialities, capacities, and powers as real things: an incredibly strong individual's potential to inflict bodily harm, for example, is palpably real, and surely affects the reality of those who come into contact with such an individual. Such a fully real potential is, in Deleuze's terms, virtual until it is made actual by it being acted it out. Texts, I suggest, should be thought of in similar terms. One might reinterpret Michael Fox, for example, to name several virtual powers of the text when he discusses Proverbs 8:30, but in the end he selects one as his actual reading. All of those readings, however, are real.

Whatever exists in the world of our experience, including all determinate objects, comprises the realm of the actual. The virtual, on the other hand, refers to the formal, structural conditions and capacities that generate the actual and allow it to transform. When one looks at the sky one experiences the current "actual" color of the sky. But we would be wrong to think that the current color of the sky exhausts the reality of the coloring power of the sky. On the contrary, the potential power of the sky to turn a wide variety of colors, even surprising or unusual ones, is just as real as the actual color that is manifest at any present moment. Deleuze names this very real, but never quite present, matrix of potentiality a "virtual multiplicity."[15] This multiplicity consists of the potentiality available to a particular body.

Whenever a thing changes, we may think of this change as the virtual dimension of the object generating a new actual state of affairs from its potential powers. When the sky turns from blue to yellow, the potential yellowing power of the sky emerges. Since this process makes actual a particular potential power of a virtual multiplicity, Deleuze calls this process "the actualisation of the virtual," and he calls the new manifestation "the actual."[16] Thus, the process of the sky transforming from blue to yellow—that is, the sky shifting from bluing to yellowing—is an actualization of a virtual power of the sky.

Yet the virtual multiplicity that conditions the actual coloring of the sky is not identifiable with any particular color, nor is it merely a tracing of all colors the sky has turned in the recent past. Neither is it a monstrous agglomeration of all the colors the sky might turn. Rather, the virtual is the structure by which the sky has color at all.

The virtual is always a field of *differential relations* rather than fixed identities. Likewise, the virtual multiplicity of the coloring power of the sky is not a set of colors. Rather, it is system composed of, among other things, the differential power of atmospheric pressure that drives the process of atmospheric changes. These pressure changes govern the emergence of particular weather conditions that we perceive as the "sky greying." Hence, particular weather conditions constitute an actualization of differential forces. Yet this differential power of atmospheric pressure interacts with other differential elements, such as the position of the sun as it changes in relation to a particular rotating point on the earth's surface, to create effects of light. Thus, *differential elements* (the atmospheric composition, the quality of light entering the atmosphere, the position of the light source relative to an observer) form a system of *reciprocal relationships* that produce the coloring powers of the sky. Accordingly, a virtual multiplicity is an ever-changing structure of potential powers defined by differential elements in reciprocal relationships. From this structure, actual—and sometimes novel—things emerge.

A text can also be thought of as a virtual multiplicity. The differential relations between lexemes, sentences, and paragraphs, for example, creates a potential field of reading that can be actualized in divergent ways.[17] These differential relations within the text must be set in play with the system of culture within which one reads the text, including the semantic, generic, and historical sets of relations that determine the context of reading. Together, these differential relations comprise the powers of a text. These powers include its hermeneutic potentials but also embrace all affectivity a text might create. For example, the mere sight of a Bible might cause fear, bring comfort, or elicit boredom, regardless of its semantic potential. These are some of the Bible's many capacities.

As helpful as it is to catalogue possible meanings of a text in the ancient world, this approach cannot help us to understand readings that emerge without precedence. Thinking of the biblical text as a dynamic virtual field, however, explains its generative power. The virtual is a dynamic, rather than static, structure. Virtual multiplicities change, and, as they change, so do the capabilities of their actualization. In the case of language, over time particular structures of graphemes transform. Lexemes and grammatical rules also change, and the virtual structure of linguistics shifts with them. Since Deleuze posits the virtual as a dynamic process by which every actual thing emerges, the concept of the virtual can in this way help us to explain the emergence of novelty.[18]

For the reception history of the Bible, Deleuze's distinction between the virtual and the actual has several important implications. First, no single form of a text, and no single reading of any form of a text, exhausts that text's potential force. Every biblical text is surrounded by a "cloud of the virtual" that is every bit as real as any historical instantiation of that text or its meaning. Second, this virtual text, like a context, is determin*able* but is not given as already determined, and any determination is a limited, provisional manifestation. Texts are also determinable in a nonsemantic sense, as well: a text may serve as a doorstop or a fetish object without ever being read. These uses are just as real as a hermeneutical use of a text. Third, the virtual most often actualizes in divergent ways. That is, we should not expect most readers in the history of a particular text to arrive at the exact same determination of the elements of that text, because processes tend to give rise to different actual manifestations. Fourth, the virtual conditions a process, not a final product. Scholars should expect to find a broad diversity of readings of a biblical text whose forms change throughout time, just as evolutionary biologists should expect to find a broad diversity of mammals whose forms change throughout time. As a result, no particular actualization is intrinsically better than any other, since there is no ideal form or essence that conditions the process. In the same way, no human is more human than any other human, as there is no origin or telos to the genetic process of humanity. Within this process, we may see divergence as a mode of experimentation with form. Last, the virtual is itself a process, but one separated from the process of any particular actualization. That is, two processes are at work: the process of the developing text and the process of any particular reading or use. When a reader approaches a biblical text, for example, that reader seeks to actualize the virtual semantic capabilities of the actual manuscript at hand. This reading process is an actualization of the virtual. Yet every biblical text is also itself a process, as its own text undergoes forces of composition, redaction, alteration, emendation, canonization, standardization, translation, citation, commentary, and enculturation. These forces alter the virtual capabilities of the text, but the continued coexistence of actualizations of earlier forms of the text make revisiting previous modes of its structure possible. In this way, each reading actualizes a text, giving it local significance by making manifest a particular construction, or determination, of the various elements that compose a particular edition of a text.

Problems and Solutions

Deleuze also rethinks the relationship between problems and solutions.[19] In general, problems represent a gap or lack in the sense of the object of study. For example, the question "What is the meaning of the book of Job?" expresses the lack of a clear singular meaning. The problem requires a singular solution, so the reader must determine and then narrow a set of logically possible solutions. According to this point of view, a problem is merely a question that has not yet found its correct answer. Solutions are the primary focus of inquiry, and as such problems exist only to be extinguished.

The prevailing logic of problems and solutions drives textual criticism. The original model for each biblical text is taken to define the identity of local texts attempting to represent it.[20] Good copies exemplify the original manuscript, while bad copies lead the readers astray because of errors, additions, and so on. The problem can be formulated as a question of which text is closest to the model. This particular problem determines the nature of its solutions in advance—that is, the solution must be a singular text that most closely resembles the model. Likewise, many biblical scholars have understood the problem of reading to be determining the meaning of a given text. In turn, the solution to this problem is the reading that most closely approximates the meaning.

Deleuze argues that the virtual/actual distinction asks us to see the concept of problems and their solutions in a different way. Instead of imagining that problems are merely simple questions that have yet to find the single correct solution, we ought, Deleuze suggests, to consider problems as fields of inquiry and experimentation. If we consider problems in these broader terms without assuming that a single predetermined solution, or even a preextant hierarchy of solutions, will extinguish the problem, then we can think more clearly about processes and the means by which they evolve.

For example, Deleuze proposes that all local populations of biological species present different solutions to the general problem posed by their environments. There is no "correct" species and no natural hierarchy of species. The conditions of the environment problem engender a "domain of solvability" that is "relative to the process of the self-determination of the problem."[21] As the problem changes, in other words, the types of potential solutions change as well. If a species fails to solve the environment problem, or if environmental changes alter the local terms of the problem and the species cannot adapt to solve the new terms of the environment problem, then the species will no longer exist.

Yet each species that survives continues to testify to the many different ways in which one might solve the environment problem. As Deleuze writes, "An organism is nothing if not the solution to a problem, as are each of its differenciated organs, such as the eye which solves a light 'problem.'"[22] The overall "light problem," which compels species to find ways to capture and process the information that light provides, can be solved in many different ways, as attested to by various types of animal eyes, as well as light-sensitive photoreceptive proteins employed by bacteria.[23] The light problem not a particular question with a particular answer. By shifting the focus on solutions to a focus on problems, one may investigate the ways in which the construction of a particular problem creates a particular field of acceptable solutions. And when one analyzes a virtual problem through its field of actual solutions, one may then discern the general structure of the problem.

Deleuze offers an interesting example of the problem-solution relationship: "Learning to swim or learning a foreign language means composing the singular points of one's own body or one's own language with those of another shape or element which tears us apart but also propels us into a hitherto unknown and unheard-of world of problems."[24] In this passage, Deleuze asks us to think, among other things, of the event of swimming. Imagine "swimming across a lake" as a problem. Doubtless, it can be solved in many ways. There are certainly infinite ways to fail at this task—one might not move one's arms and so begin to sink—but are there not as many ways of successfully crossing?

What conditions, then, must be satisfied to solve the problem? In swimming, one must compose the "singular points," or particular elements, of one's body in such a way that they coordinate with the opposing element of the water. In this way, the problematic field is composed of both the general conditions, such as gravity and the composition of the human body, as well as the particular conditions of the particular human body in question (its particular strength and capabilities, its buoyancy) and the particular body of water (its turbulence, density, or size). These conditions of the problem specify the field of solvability for this task, providing the conditions for success as well as failure.

Yet one always has to hold open the possibility of surprising solutions emerging from changing conditions. The conditions of the problem may change at any moment: if a storm whips up, the solutions given at one time may no longer work—a swimmer must adapt to the conditions in the water. Or a solution adopted for a problem may even be so influential as to change the sorts of solutions for that problem that are deemed acceptable: the introduction of the front crawl stroke, for example, changed the very field of potential solutions for the event of crossing a lake.[25] If a system changes over time, then it makes sense to think of that system as an open-ended problem. Thus, individual solutions only offer local, contingent, and provisional resolutions to the problem. The search for solutions requires repeated experimentation that seeks to stretch the borders of a problem's solvability.

Consider the problematic character of a historical context. The events leading up to the Maccabean revolt, for example, constitute a problem with many potential solutions. This problematic situation faces the participants in the events in Jerusalem of 167 BCE as well as any contemporary observers or later historians. Some construals of that context fail, just like some biological species fail to meet the conditions of their problematic field. But surely in the chaotic world of Jerusalem in 167 BCE, the perspectives of the several groups formed mutually exclusive (or "incompossible") worlds, in which "several worlds appear as instances of solution for one and the same problem. . . . These diverse events form so many instances corresponding to the problem and determining the genesis of the solutions. We must therefore understand that incompossible worlds, despite their incompossibility, have something objectively in common. . . . The incompossible worlds become the variants of the same story."[26] One does not simply construct the problem and its solutions from thin air. On the contrary, one must locate the contours of a particular problem in order to discover any feasible particular solution.

The process of the composition and formation of a text and the history of the reading of a text are problematic fields not unlike the lake crossing—that is, they are not simple questions. Individual manuscripts and individual readings constitute particular solutions to the problematic field of a biblical book. The problematic text calls for a limitless series of potential solutions, and since the problematic text itself changes over time, and the contexts in which it is read also change over time, there is no telos for this process. If the conditions of reading a text change as a text travels through various contexts, the field of solutions itself changes, much like the rules of swimming change when one moves from a freshwater river to a saltwater ocean. In different contexts, the text is capable of manifesting different sorts of capabilities.

There are always many different ways of actualizing the text's virtual dimension. Each event of editing or reading a text offers the writer or reader the chance to engage in an open-ended process whose end result is neither necessary nor predetermined. A reception historian, then, surveys the many different solutions to the problematic field of the text and attempts to discern patterns, tendencies, and limit cases within this field, without drawing firm boundaries or creating putatively necessary hierarchies between solutions.

Moreover, if we think of a biblical text as a virtual problem, then we may avoid the serious charge that a text might as well mean just anything at all. Since the text is a problematic field, the reader must account for its various parts for it to be an actual solution. The structure of a particular virtual problem, such as a biblical text, conditions its own actualization. That is, the process of producing a particular solution, such as an actual reading of a biblical text, is determined by the structure of the text. Also, the local conditions of the problem, such as the readers, their interpretive communities and reading protocols, and the general historical context, work together to further define the structure of a particular problem. In regards to biology, the general environment problem may appear in radically different ways to different species—surely the problem of the rainforest manifests itself differently to spiders than it does to birds. Likewise, texts may pose their virtual problems to different communities in very different guises, but the virtual structure of the problem may be (virtually) identical.

Topology and Readings

Some readings are successful, and some are failures. How may one discern between solutions and nonsolutions? Deleuze would likely urge one to think in terms of *topology*.

Take, for example, the game of chess. In order to play the game of chess one must have a chess board and various pieces. No chess piece necessarily "means" anything in particular outside of the structure of the game of chess. These pieces and the board are what Deleuze calls "differential elements" that find a particular identity, or significance, within their set. The rules of chess stipulate a particular manner of relation between the chess pieces: knights may move a certain way, and so on. Thus, the chess pieces exhibit a particular set of differential relations. These are considered "differential" relations because these movements make sense as a set of relations: the way a knight may move makes sense only in relation to the pawn's movement, the rook's movement, and so on.

To this field of differential elements and the field of differential relations, Deleuze adds "singularities."[27] In Deleuze's writings, singularities are sensitive points in a system: the boiling and freezing points of water act as singularities, for example, since water radically changes at these points. Singularities often function as rules or as the "tendencies of a system."[28] For example, one could call the boiling point of water "the rule of boiling."

In chess, the set of differential relations proper to chess tells us how a knight moves. When a knight lands on another piece, something sensitive, or special, occurs. At this point, a piece is captured, and the pieces move in a manner not accounted for by the relationships of piece movements during play (for example, when a bishop is captured, it does not move diagonally but instead moves off the board). One could call this singularity "the rule of capture." Another singularity emerges at the point of the king. When the king is captured, the game ends. Likewise, one could call this "the rule of the king." According to Deleuze, any such set of differential elements, differential relations and singularities constitutes the structure of a virtual multiplicity.

Chess, then, presents a problematic field that may be solved in countless ways. How might a chess game be played? There is no limit to the permutations a game might take, and no model or match that each individual match attempts faithfully to replicate. Indeed, some players might even invent new techniques and new strategies that would upset commonly held assumptions about how a chess game must look, which would then alter the problematic structure of the game for future players.

Yet we know that structures are not static. Even the rules of games undergo changes, mutations, and mistaken applications. How might the structure of chess submit to forces of change? Imagine, for example, playing chess with someone who accidentally moved a pawn like a rook. You might say, "That's not right." A use of a differential element, such as a chess piece, in a manner that ignores its differential relationship to the other elements produces a disruption of the process of a game of chess. This disruption might, if allowed, expand or alter the virtual field of chess. Now, imagine your opponent refused to allow you to move your pawns two squares forward on their opening move. When you objected, your opponent might say, "Well, the way I play chess, pawns are not allowed to move two spaces, ever." Here we would see a slight difference in the rules between the players, but we might not necessarily claim that they are playing an altogether different game. These sorts of small adjustments can slowly change the structure of games, languages, cultures, and even biblical texts. And as they change, the potential powers, and thus actual products, of these structures change as well. At some point the chess pieces may move in different patterns.

But suppose your opponent said, "Every time you take a piece, you must then hold a spelling bee to decide if the piece survives or not." Perhaps you might agree to play the game with these newly negotiated rules, but at that instant you would have stopped playing chess. Of course, this new game would be related to chess, possessing a related virtual, problematic field. But it would nonetheless constitute a different game. From this example, we might deduce that a change in the structure of singularities can produce a new virtual field. In turn, this new virtual field would engender different capacities and powers and would incarnate itself in different ways than the virtual field produced by the previous configuration of singularities.

Deleuze calls slight differences (i.e., a different way to play chess or a different chess game) different actualizations of the same virtual multiplicity. At the point at which we begin to play a different sort of game altogether, Deleuze claims that we find a distinction between two different virtual multiplicities.[29]

In terms of reading a text, one can think of different readings as different actualizations of the same virtual field. Deleuze calls the process of rereading in such a way as to produce a quite different but technically compelling account of the text a "counteractualization."[30] Likewise, one can think of simple misreadings as disruptions of the text, and one can think of a reading that seems to reconstruct the text in a manner unlike itself as the production of a different virtual field. None of these activities is naturally good or bad, and none is necessarily better than any other. They simply perform different tasks. Disruption can be as productive as it is mistaken; this process undergirds humor, paradox, and nonsense. Creative distortion can prove fruitful; this process guides the best sorts of "remakes" in film, for example. But how does one distinguish between readers' disruptions, distortions, and countereffectuations of a text?

In order to conceptualize the boundary point between reading and reconstructing, we may find it helpful to think in terms of topology, or the study of the variable actualizations of virtual shapes.[31] Topology is a branch of mathematics that studies the properties that are preserved when an object is deformed, as if by stretching, but without any aspects of its surface being torn or sutured.[32] If we imagine the space of a rubber ball, its topological features would be those that do not change even if I deform its shape by stepping on it or throwing it forcefully against a wall. This approach to space is quite different from that of Euclidean geometry. From a Euclidean perspective, when I step on a rubber ball, it takes on a different shape than it had before that event. It goes from being a sphere to an oblate spheroid. Or as Levi Bryant explains using a triangle as an example, taking it

> as a being composed of three singularities or points along with three relations, a Euclidean view emphasizes the static form possessed by the triangle, its formal identity, while a topological point of view emphasizes the dynamisms or adventures the relations between these singularities are able to undergo. Thus, for instance, a Euclidean view is prone to emphasize the different types of triangles such as right, isosceles, and equilateral triangles, while topology thinks the manner in which these triangles can be transformed into one another and other shapes through operations of stretching, pulling, and twisting.[33]

Thinking in Euclidean terms, we may imagine that there are a pregiven number of possible chess games that exist in invariant forms; in topological terms, we may imagine that part of the excitement of chess derives from its dynamism, or the "adventures" that a contingent game of chess might undergo.[34] Topology helps us to rethink identity and the boundaries between structures in a new way. Instead of looking for a close resemblance of form, topology pays attention to the general coherence of the structure. Two objects that look quite different may in fact be "homeomorphic," or topologically equivalent. An old joke claims that topologists cannot tell the difference between a doughnut and a coffee cup, because the two shapes can be morphed into each other without any tearing or suturing: thus, the coffee cup and doughnut are topologically equivalent.[35] While topologists can, of course, differentiate between the two objects, they nevertheless posit no topological distinction between the two. But if one bends the structure to the point that it rips or breaks, that is when the identity of the structure changes. If one wanted to turn a sphere into a coffee cup, one would have to tear a hole to create the handle.[36]

Topology is also a very interesting and useful metaphor because it pays close attention to the context of a set of points. Euclidean geometry assumes that all shapes exist within the featureless space of a flat plane. Topology, on the other hand, asks about the ways a form changes as it is embedded within a variety of curved and folded spaces. Thus, topology gives us a way to imagine one form as it traverses a series of different contexts. A spherical space, for example, alters the local neighborhood of points surrounding a triangle's singularities: that is, the lines between the corners of the triangle are bent by the space in which the triangle is embedded. If that same triangle were embedded in a space shaped like a crumpled-up piece of paper, the lines connecting its corners would have jagged edges and protrude at points along with the space itself.

We can use topological thinking to break away from Platonic theories of reading and translating. Instead of asking whether a commentator has provided the correct meaning of the text or whether a translator has given the right translation, one could ask a more topological question, namely, how one might bend, stretch, and fold this text in order to read it differently without destroying its form.

If one encounters a particular reading of a text that does not account for an important feature of that text, one could certainly argue that the reading has undergone a "structural mutation." Say, for example, that one encounters a reading of the book of Job claiming that Job never complained. This reading seems to actualize a different text than the well-known book of Job; it manifests a different set of singularities and thus emerges from a distinct virtual structure.

Or, with respect to context, instead of asking what the correct context is in which to read a text, one might ask in what ways a particular context reshapes the reading of the text. Clearly noticeable topological stretching of texts occurs at points in space and time during which great change altered the terrain in which texts could be read. For example, the Shoah has most certainly shaken the fabric of the biblical text by changing the problematic field in which religious texts may propose their meanings. As a result, this event and its aftermath have forced readers to ask different questions and seek different answers when reading biblical texts.[37] Other world-changing events have altered landscapes, as well: the event of the Renaissance altered the structure of cultural space in which biblical texts could be read, giving critical scholars a different problematic in which to ask new questions and seek different answers.[38]

Yet the space in which a reading occurs does not determine the reading by itself. One can challenge and sometimes even change contexts. Readings can be novel and thus destabilizing. In part, this is because the space of a context itself must be determined. The jagged shape of a post-Shoah context for a contemporary European Jew may appear quite different to a historically illiterate neighbor oblivious of those recent events. If that neighbor learns of the events of the twentieth century, however, it is possible for he or she to reconstrue his or her context. Of course, readings cannot occur outside of contexts, and contexts do impact reading, but context cannot alone determine the reading, because context itself must be determined and can always be redetermined. One could characterize this reciprocal relationship as "dynamic coemergence," in which context, text and reading progressively specify each other without any necessary hierarchy between the three being posited.[39]

As one might imagine, determining the relationship between text and context is less clear-cut than determining the topology of a triangle. Nevertheless, the metaphorical shift from Euclidean to topological thought would help us to think less in terms of accuracy with respect to a predefined meaning and more in terms of the various powers or capabilities of a text. Reading a text requires, to some extent, transforming it.

When we look at how a text produces meaning in various settings it tells us more, not less, about the nature of that text. Thus when one reader carefully shows that Exodus is a liberatory text, and another reader carefully shows that Exodus is a text concerned with proper modes of servitude, we may affirm this divergence without contradiction.[40] Both John Collins and John Levenson, for example, make defensible—and yet irreducibly different—arguments that take into account the structure of the text of Exodus. These readers, in my opinion, show that Exodus may properly "stretch" in particular ways and instantiate different meanings without tearing.

A Nomadic Reception History

These Deleuzian concepts—the virtual and the actual, the problematic field, and topological identity—together form the basis for a processual theory of biblical reception history. They allow one to assert both the identity of a text and its many different textual manifestations, uses, and divergent readings over time.

It should be noted that one could structure the practice of reception history in many different yet defensible ways, and so what I offer here is not a normative description of the essence or nature of reception history. Instead, what follows is my attempt to provide an account of biblical reception history that focuses on the development and capacities of the text in question. Since I am a textualist working within the field of biblical studies, my textual focus should not be surprising.

Other reception historians may be more interested in the readers or reading practices themselves, and still others may be more interested in shorter durations of time and geographically or culturally delineated spaces of reception. A cultural historian, sociologist, or theologian might find it more helpful to begin at another starting point or to ask different sets of questions.

The Four Processes: Text, Reading, Transmutation, and Impact

On the one hand, reception history should trace the production and continued development of a biblical text by means of textual criticism without creating a hierarchy of forms. On the other hand, reception history should trace the production and continued development of readings and other uses of the biblical text. As a biblical text develops, at every moment its process of textual formation and alteration serves as the ground of another process, namely, the process of its production of significance.

Straddling these two categories are the liminal cases of translations. From the perspective of the source text, translations are readings. But from the perspective of other readings and the readers themselves, the translation often *is* the source text. One might study the Greek Septuagint version of the book of Exodus, for example, from both perspectives and even take note of the difference between these perspectives: that is, the analysis of the translation will certainly differ from the analysis of the translation qua communal text.[41]

Every source text holds within itself internal differences. For example, the composition and redaction histories of Daniel reveal an active reading process that exists internal to any manuscript that may be named the "source text," and thus reading and textual development propel each other.[42] Daniel 7 clearly reads and rewrites Daniel 2, yet the book retains both the "source text" and the "translation."

Likewise, the book of Proverbs is always already both text and translation. To prove the point quickly, I note that that the Instructions of Amenemope, an Egyptian text that served as a source for Proverbs 22:17–23:11, is not written in Hebrew, that Proverbs itself is clear that Hezekiah's scribes "translated" ("העתיקו"), or moved, chunks of the book from other sources (25:1), and that many sayings found in the book of Proverbs were likely in circulation well before their inscription within Proverbs and thus were translated from the oral sphere to a written one.[43] In light of these facts, it becomes clear that the problems assumed to be proper to translations are, in fact, merely the problems posed by texts in general. At least for biblical texts, the processes of textual development and reading are always intertwined; separating them will forever be a heuristic, yet necessary, procedure for reception history.

From the dual processes of textual development and reading, it seems helpful to distinguish at least two additional processes. I call these the processes of transmutations and nonsemantic impact. At every point, these processes all affect each other, and in the case of biblical texts, these processes doubtless split and recombine in fascinating patterns that have yet to be clarified. Each process has its own virtual and actual dimensions, and each process has its own sort of singularities. I first sketch the processes of transmutation and nonsemantic impact and then turn to the processes of textual formation and reading in more detail.

The Process of Transmutation

While I do not find it helpful to attach values of "good" or "bad" to particular reading procedures, I do recognize a helpful distinction between readings that play by rules and readings that play fast and loose. The former category I call "readings, "and the latter I call "transmutations."

I use the term "transmutation" in the sense provided by Roman Jakobson, who organized translation into three categories: intralingual, interlingual, and intersemioic transmutation.[44] Since all reading requires a substitutionary reorganization of the text that results in a statement purporting to say "what the text says," the motif of translation can prove quite helpful to reception history.

According to Jakobson, intralingual translation, or "rephrasing," occurs when a reader creates a text within the same language as the original text that "translates" it, or produces a meaning for it. This process transpires in the practice of reading, as well as the production of commentaries, explications, paraphrases, descriptions, and so on. Just as there is no perfect or primary translation of a text, and yet translations can be more or less accountable to the source text, readings can prove more or less accountable without being organized into a value-laden hierarchy.

Whereas intralingual translation names the process of reading within a single language, interlingual translation names the process of interpreting signs of a source text by means of another sign system of the same class, as occurs during the translation of Hebrew into English. This form of language transformation is equivalent to the typical notion of translation. To this taxonomy of translation, Jakobson introduces a valuable third term, "intersemiotic transmutation," which describes the interpretation of signs of a source text by means of another sign system of a different class. Intersemiotic transmutation gives rise to visual depictions of textual narratives, musical adaptations of images, and so on.

Jakobson's taxonomy distinguishes types of translation by means of the semiotic systems used in various translation processes. Jakobson asks what type of sign systems the source and target languages are. As almost all biblical reception will require interlingual translation, a theory of biblical reception history would be better served by distinguishing among types of translations by other means. Since reception history inquires into the ways in which texts and readings change throughout time, the modes of change could guide its taxonomic structure. For this reason, I distinguish between readings and transmutations. Readings produce sign systems that carefully account for the elements of the source text as they reorganize them, forming a topologically homeomorphic text, while transmutations engage the text but do not read it per se. I do not think it wise to treat readings as necessarily *better* than transmutations merely because they engage the text more closely; transmutations can at times be more beautiful, more theologically profound, or more historically influential than any particular reading.

Jakobson's category of intersemiotic transmutation may include transformations of the biblical text that focus less on translation and more on creative expansion and adaptation or even outright topological "tearing." Since I want to track the ways biblical texts manifest their significative capacities, it would be odd to sort receptions into categories based on their medium of presentation. By dividing the presentation of a text's reception into sections that treat commentaries, visual art, music, and so on as discrete groups, a reception historian emphasizes the medium in which a text reveals its capacities rather than on the capacities themselves. Such categorizations can prove quite interesting, but a work of visual art that interprets a biblical text may have more in common with a particular musical adaptation as a reading or as a transmutation than it does with any other work of visual art. As a result, I find it more helpful to distinguish between the types of textual capacities that receptions express. Within each process, I group receptions that seem to manifest similar expressive powers of the text in question.

Particular transmutations may find their roots in the text or in particular readings, while others emerge from a mere passing familiarity with the source text and its readings. Some transmutations even emerge from clear misreadings or misapprehension of the readings of others. Particularly creative translations may cross the line from the status of "reading" or "text" into transmutation. As far as how organizing transmutations and presenting them, sorting them into categories of "almost readings" and "clear misreadings" and the like would be far less interesting than sorting them into categories of "powerful" or "troubling" or "life affirming" or "effective." That transmutations do not adhere closely to the text is not necessarily a problem, and a lack of conformity to the model of reading does not constitute failure.

As a biblical scholar, my focus is on the capacities of the text, so I sort transmutations into categories that attempt to reflect the sorts of capacities a text exhibits. Let us consider a brief example of a transmutation. The eponymous character of the book of Job often appears in the histories of art, literature, philosophy, theology, medicine, and other discourses in ways that develop rather than exegete the book of Job.[45] In one such example, Job became one of several patron saints of medieval musicians.[46] Even though this development may find its origin in a reading of the text of the book of Job, or of related texts such as the Testament of Job, the trope of Job and the musicians began a life of its own that did not necessarily continue to rely on readings of the text to sustain its elaborating.[47] Thus "Job and the musicians" emerges from the history of the character Job, but it functions in a manner tangential to the semantic concerns of the text of the book of Job.

This operation should be of interest to biblical reception historians, since it is clearly a product of the text in combination with readers and contexts, although it is a diffuse and distended product from the point of view of a textualist. But to judge the cultural manifestations of the trope of "Job and the musicians" by its faithfulness to the book of Job seems to miss the point. Transmutations allow for a text to connect to various communities, organizations, traditions, and discourses. Many of the examples of this motif either show musicians increasing Job's pain, or they show musicians soothing Job's pain; thus the motif of the musicians shows connections to certain semantic nodes of the text—namely, *Job's pain*—as they also demonstrate the flexibility within these semantic nodes—for example, *increasing* or *decreasing* Job's pain.[48] One could analyze the ways in which these transmutations interact with the text, how they draw power from the text, and how they creatively expand this power.

One could then pivot to consider how these capacities interact with other elements in the world: what sorts of things do these transmutations do? Through the trope of Job and the musicians, for example, the text of Job is extended (and distended or perhaps torn) so that it might function as a legitimating authority for the foundation of musicians' and instrument makers' guilds.[49] By means of the transmutation "St. Job," musicians associated their trade with a religious icon and thus the power of the church and the protective blessing of the deity. The text alone cannot do this, but the transmutation of the text can extend the text's capacities. Thus, the process of transmutation produces linguistic and other semiotic structures, such as music and visual art, that extend a text's capacities beyond what its semantic structure allows. Readings, on the other hand, express the capacities proper to the text through the production of linguistic and other semiotic structures.

Thus, the transmutation of a text produces actualizations of the emergent virtual capabilities of that text: the text really can function in ways that extend, rather than contain, its semantic potentials. A reception historian, in turn, can trace the problematic structure of the text by charting how that text transforms and extends itself and how it might do so further.

The Process of Nonsemantic Impact

Reception historians can also trace the history of the nonsemantic impact of a text, which is comprised of the impact of a text beyond its hermeneutical function. Many scholars working in reception history locate their theoretical resources in philosophical hermeneutics, so it should not be surprising that nonsemantic, or nonhermeneutic, uses of a text are not often studied with the same intensity as semantic-hermeneutic uses. And yet the nonsemantic impact of a text can often overshadow its production of semantic significance.

One example of this process would be the nonsemantic impact of the Rosetta Stone, whose semantic context is not necessarily of great interest to the modern world but whose nonsemantic functions opened Egyptian hieroglyphs to the possibility of modern reading, played a role in British and French colonial rivalries, and currently attract droves of tourists. Biblical texts function in similar nonsemantic manners. Psalm 91, for example, has functioned as an apotropaic text since at least the Second Temple period, as attested by 11Q11 at Qumran.[50] Of course, the particular images found in Psalm 91 contributed to its use as an apotropaic text, likely as a result of the reading process, but its apotropaic function is itself something distinct from reading.

Texts are often powerful even when they are not read; the Jewish practice of binding tefillin, found even in the Second Temple period, exemplifies this, as does the writing covering the monumental art of the ancient Near East.[51] Even today, politicians, judges, and witnesses often swear while touching a Bible. Of course, the Bible only has nonsemantic power because it (ostensibly, at least) carries semantic power. But this is not always the case, and it might be that the semantic powers of texts are less responsible for their nonsemantic powers than scholars imagine.

Though textualists are right to care deeply about the semantic production of texts, they often ignore the powerful force of nonsemantic impact of those same texts. A text's nonsemantic impact comprises part of the text's virtual capacities, and these capacities are actualized at every moment. At the very minimum, any manuscript, as an extension in space-time with particular qualities, manifests this power. The problematic field of a text's nonsemantic power opens it up to experimentation. How might this text impact its surroundings without or beyond functioning in a semantic fashion?

The Process of Textual Formation

In the field of biblical studies, reception historians often focus on the process of reading the biblical text and downplay the process of the development of the text itself.[52] Yet it seems rather clear that the history of the development of a biblical text constitutes an important part of that same text's reception history. For this reason, reception historians should look to the fields of source criticism, redaction criticism, form criticism, textual criticism, and tradition history in order to consider the process of the formation of the text.

The actual text of a biblical text consists of the actual physical manuscripts, while the virtual text consists of the cloud of potentialities that manifests between different manuscripts and that surrounds each of them. That is, each manuscript of the book of Job, for example, is marked by the differences between itself and the other actual members of the general series "the book of Job." Even if the reader is completely unaware that the particular version of the book of Job in their hands is unlike many others, the capabilities and potentialities of that particular text are limited or expanded depending on the version. A manuscript of the book of Job that ends abruptly at 42:11, which may be the case for the Qumran Targum (11QtgJob), alters the capabilities of that text and is thus marked by its difference with respect to other manuscripts.[53]

This process of textual formation is of course open to changes and the introduction of novelties. The OG translation of the book of Job greatly altered the text and yet remained a text of the book of Job; centuries later, this alteration was itself altered again in Origen's Hexapla to bring it more in line with other known versions.[54] At each of these points, the virtual potentials of the text changed in response to the actual changes undergone by the actual text. The virtual powers of a text are not static: the virtual is not a Platonic Idea but an ever-changing process. One might imagine the virtual multiplicity of the text of the book of Job as a vast enmeshed field that includes the potentials of the many manuscripts of the book of Job. In other words, each actual manuscript has certain actual features that do not exhaust the potential that may be manifest by the book of Job.

One might ask what the text of a biblical book looks like. Particular manuscripts are contingent, local actualizations of a text's virtual structure. We may analyze the various extant manuscripts and translations and in turn offer a topological model of the ways the text of the book of Job has been stretched and twisted. Finally, we may be able to indicate points at which the text seems to "tear" or "suture" in a way that alters its identity. At these points, we may posit that the text becomes "something else." Biblical scholars can then map the forms in which texts have appeared, providing a clearer picture of the texts that produced particular readings.

The Process of Reading

Readings begin with an encounter with an actual manuscript, or various actual manuscripts, and thus the reading process emerges from a particular point or set of points within the process of textual production. From an actual manuscript, the event of reading begins with the virtual significatory capabilities of the text and then proceeds to produce an actual reading, or "meaning."

Since an objectile always harbors more capacities than it can manifest at any point in time, we may think of reading as a series of limiting selections or choices that continue to narrow the potentials of a virtual multiplicity until what emerges is an individual reading. Deleuze encourages us to think in these terms through his references to Borges's short story "The Garden of the Forking Paths," which describes a labyrinth-book, written by an author named Ts'ui Pên, in which "all possible outcomes" of every event occur.[55] As the narrator remarks, "In all fiction, when a man is faced with alternatives, he chooses one at the expense of the others. In the almost unfathomable Ts'ui Pên, he chooses—simultaneously—all of them. He thus creates various futures, various times which start others that will in their turn branch out and bifurcate in other times."[56] Thus every reader of the labyrinth-book must confront these forks, choosing some at the expense of others, until one coherent version of the story emerges. When reading a given text, one confronts a semiotic garden with a succession of forked semantic paths. If one reads the word "אמון" in Proverbs 8:30 as "artisan," one then opens potential semantic paths while closing others, whereas if one reads the word as "faithfully," one actualizes a different relationship between that word and other words around it. In this way, a reading progressively limits and thus clarifies a particular capability of a text even while forcing many others to remain obscure.[57] A reading reorganizes a text, and any act of organization means that each element of a unit will be embracing only a very limited rage of its potentials. For example, a corporate office is composed of many people who each have many different talents, but the organization of the office requires that people employed there explore only a very limited range of their capacities. One may be a championship frisbee golfer and also a decent cook, but the title of "accountant" requires that one forgo these potential activities and focus on the accounting until one leaves the sphere of power of the corporate office. Likewise, reading requires selecting paths, exploring some and shutting down others for the sake of the unity and productivity of the organized meaning of the text. Reception history, on the other hand, involves mapping the garden in which the paths fork.

It is important to note, however, that in Borges's story, Ts'ui Pên had not already mapped out in advance all possible meanings of his own story. On the contrary, Borges characterizes the activity of this book as a "creation" that is ongoing, a "branching out" and "bifurcation" that continually develops. The garden of forking paths portrays *genesis*, not origin. The labyrinth-book does not possess its semantic secrets at the moment of its authorial origin. It actively produces novel futures that emerge from the text. The genius of the author is to produce a text whose virtual capacities allow for the creative experimentation of readers to construct ever-new actual meanings. The garden, in other words, is continuously forking.

Gilles Deleuze helpfully calls the process of producing an actual thing from a virtual multiplicity a "dramatization."[58] As James Williams explains, "By dramatisation Deleuze means a new way of playing a given relation of expression and expressed, that is, like the director putting a new version of a play, the expressor must take something that already determines this version, but that must also be given a new and re-invigorating slant."[59] An actor receives a script much like a reader receives a text, yet the actor must create the dramatization of the script and in the process produce the character who speaks the already written lines.[60] Crucial to this process is the process of selection and thus exclusion: the actor must give the character determinations by choosing to speak each line in one particular way to the exclusion of other possible ways. Likewise, an actor who takes part in a remake of an earlier film must "counteractualize" the role by thinking of the role in a different way from the previous actor.[61] Actual things can only express "certain relations or certain degrees of variation," while the counteractualization of those things allows for a greater expression of these degrees of variation.[62] Each dramatization will be to a greater or lesser extent influenced by local patterns of reading, local intertexts, and local discursive formations. By taking a broad look at many such local dramatizations, a reception historian may be able to discern more global patterns of dramatization that suggest contours of a text's virtual semantic structure.

Every fork chosen can be justified by means of many criteria, none of which are naturally superior to any other. These criteria often derive from the prevailing discourses available, but one can always attempt to recover criteria from other discourses particular to other spatiotemporal and cultural locations. Sets of scholarly, aesthetic, or theological criteria are historically contingent and themselves constitute changing processes and are thus not universal or transcendent. Any use of any criteria will itself be a divergent actualization of a virtual multiplicity.

In this way, "a medieval Rabbinic reading," or "a patristic Christian reading," or "a modern scholarly reading" will select particular Jewish or Christian or scholarly modes of reading and emphasize some of their intrinsic criteria over others. Intertextual relations, as well, must be selected according to particular criteria, as must standards of coherency. Yet none of these selections provides a necessary mode or a determinate solution to the problem of the text: there can be countless "modern scholarly readings" of the book of Job, and as a result the production itself—namely, the reading—provides a more compelling objectile of study, at least for the textualist reception historian, than the set of reading practices or particular subjectivity involved. Some choices will open certain areas of the text's capacities, and simultaneously close others. Only a panoply of readings can begin to offer a glimpse of the text's fluctuating wealth of powers.

Reception History as the Story of the Text's Capacities

My particular construction of reception history focuses on the development of the text and its productive capacities. The task of the reception historian is thus to produce a history of this development. Since history is something of a story, reception history must at minimum locate a protagonist, a plot, and a point of view for its particular form of storytelling. I name the textual process as my protagonist and the unfolding of its significatory, transmutational and nonsemantic powers as my plot. As a result, in my concept of reception history I emphasize the global tendencies of a text's production of significance and deemphasize concerns with mapping a particular context's general reading tendencies, analyzing particular readers, and meticulously constructing local contexts.

Since a global view of the reception history of a text spans many contexts, cultures, horizons of expectation, and reading models and strategies, these broader tendencies reveal more about the process of the text than do the local patterns of reading. By tracing readings from many diverse contexts, a reception historian can locate various semantic nodes through which clusters of readings converge. One way to locate singularities is to observe various examples of a particular process and map them, noting the crucial points of attraction.[63] For example, one cannot discover at what temperatures water will undergo its various phase transitions simply by looking at it, but repeated experimentation with water will eventually locate its freezing and boiling points. In different conditions, including under different pressures, in different altitudes, and in different chemical contexts, the boiling and freezing point of water will change. But nevertheless, the system has tendencies that one could map through repeated experimentation.[64]

Biblical scholars can map readings of biblical texts over time and discern long-term tendencies. For example, are there particular phrases that are construed in wildly different ways? I have found it helpful to try to determine "singularities" that seem to determine general patterns of reading and use throughout a text's processual life. Each singularity functions as a node that constitutes a center around which the given text can be organized. For example, as we have seen, one semantic node of the Exodus story is "liberation from oppression," while another is "proper modes of servitude." Scholars can see this not only by reading the text. The *history* of readings of Exodus reveals these tendencies—as well as other tendencies that may be less obvious to those simply observing the text. The task of reception history is to map the various trajectories as they reveal the capacities of that text.

The Nomadic Distribution of Reception

Deleuze is quite interested in problems of categorization. We must categorize or else we experience pure chaos. But categorizations often rely on preconcieved notions of identity, and this tendency effectively freezes our conceptions of the world. We cannot perceive newness and change if we keep cramming things into the same boxes. In order to address this problem, Deleuze opposes "nomadic distribution" to "sedentary distribution."[65] Sedentary distributions arrange the world according to preconceived categories. Most reception histories categorize by means of sedentary distributions, such as "Christian" and "Jewish," or "Western" and "non-Western," or "ancient" and "modern." These are categories imposed from without.

Nomadic distributions categorize based on immanent criteria alone.[66] Whereas a scholar using sedentary distribution might look at a particular reading and say, "It's written by a medieval Christian, so put it with the medieval Christian stuff," a nomadic distribution would require one to *analyze the reading first*. Once one saw what the reading *did* with the biblical text, and what capacities of the biblical text it exposed, then one could put it with other readings that acted in a similar manner. Thus nomadic categories might contain readings from Jews *and* Christians, ancients *and* moderns, westerners *and* easterners *and* southerners. Each category would contain readings that actualized similar virtual capacities of a given biblical text.

Along with a subject and a plot, one needs to determine a point of view. Deleuze asks us to think about the "point of view" like a camera shot: we can, through film, see a field of variation through a particular vantage point that is open to anyone.[67] It is not my place, even if I temporarily occupy it. The camera offers a structurally open point of view, a primacy of viewpoint over viewer, that allows us to see variation from different vantage points. Each vantage point, Deleuze argues, offers a particular mode of organizing the chaotic world, or "determination of the indeterminate," which is "a condition of the manifestation of reality."[68] In this way, a point of view opens a reading by organizing the text in a particular manner. Viewpoints organize and imply particular "modes of existence" but do not emanate from individual subjectivites.

In short, the biblical reception historian asks what a text can do. Here is the mandate: demonstrate the diversity of capacities, organize them according to the immanent potentialities actualized by various individuals and communities over time, and rewrite our understanding of the biblical text.

SIX

Justice, Survival, Presence: Job 19:25–27

The suggestions [for Job 19:26] are endless.
—Norman Habel

Of the excessive production of texts, there is no end.
—Qohelet 12:12

Introduction

As I construe it, reception history is not primarily an interpretative practice (i.e., "What does this text mean?"). Rather, reception history creates a model of repeated textual experimentation (i.e., "How might this text function?").[1] To be sure, creating a model of textual experimentation does require much reading, but this reading is of a different sort from interpretation. Instead of reading one version of a text and producing a meaning, reception history as I understand it would read—that is, organize and thus make sense of—the history of a text's unfolding capacities. This kind of historical survey would thus produce a map of the text's ever-expanding potentials.

To illustrate this theory of reception, I offer here one such mapping. I have chosen Job 19:25–27 as my test case, for several reasons: (1) it is widely accepted in critical scholarship as an important yet difficult set of verses within its larger literary context, (2) I am aware of its exceptionally broad and diverse history of reception in Jewish and Christian communities as well as outside of them, and (3) it is a short text, and thus its readings may be traced more clearly throughout history. This exercise functions as a suggestive example, not an exhaustive account of the text's history.

In this mapping exercise, I analyze the text and its contexts and suggest several semantic nodes, or general patterns of meaning or use, that emerge from this analysis. As one does with any simple narrative, I will begin at the beginning, with an analysis of the presumably earliest Hebrew text of Job 19:25–27 in what I believe to be its initial context of production. I begin with the initial context for the sake of the narrative presentation of the textual process and not because it holds any special secret or privileged meaning. Potentials that emerge only after the initial context are for my purposes just as important as those available within it.

The Question of the Initial Context

It is difficult, however, to discover the origin of the book of Job—or, more precisely, it is difficult to know if there is anything that can be called the origin of the book of Job.[2] For centuries, biblical interpreters have struggled to understand the compositional fault lines that seem to run through this text.[3] The earliest textual witnesses, which are among the texts found at Qumran, generally align with the MT. But evidence internal to the text suggests several stages of development. Most importantly, the book of Job contains a prose prologue and epilogue (1:1–2:13; 42:7–17) that differ from the poetic section (3:1–42:6) in form as well as content, which suggests stages of textual growth. Scholars have argued for the priority of both the prose and the poetry, but no clear victor has emerged.[4]

Yet the text is far more complex than the poetry/prose dichotomy suggests. For example, the prose section itself developed over time: the epilogue (42:7–17) does not discuss the events of the divine council in chapters 1–2, and it does not mention the satan at all. Moreover, some scholars have argued that a redactor added the friends to the prose narrative, which seems to separate them from the story of Job's disintegration and reintegration with his family (cf. 2:11–12 and 42:7–9).[5] Regardless of the accuracy of any of these claims, it seems clear that the text developed over a long period of time. Thus, the book of Job's "original context" might extend from the exile until the Hellenistic period.[6]

Yet the story of Job precedes the entire biblical text that bears his name. The character Job, though likely not the biblical book, was known before the exile. Ezekiel mentions Job as a famous hero (14:14, 14:20), but his comments are at odds with the biblical narrative (Job 1:18–19), implying that the biblical book of Job rewrote an earlier tradition.[7] It may well be that the prose sections of the book of Job modify an already existing folktale; thus, the origin of the book of Job is already secondary.

It is thus impossible to locate a single literary, generic, or historical context for the book of Job. What is more, the book exhibits interesting effects of linguistic dislocation. Edward Greenstein argues that the book of Job, while markedly unusual in its diction and spelling, is not written in a particular dialect.[8] It is written in that style, Greenstein maintains, in order to produce the effect of foreignness. In modern American cinema, this same foreignizing effect is achieved by means of British accents: characters in American films set in the ancient world usually make it sound as if the Acropolis were adjacent to Trafalgar Square. In the book of Job, many of the Aramaic-like qualities fail to approximate actual Aramaic, and thus it appears that the book of Job exists in a linguistic netherworld. It is original to no existing semantic context except for its own, which is itself multiple.

And yet it remains possible for readers in many different contexts to read this noncontextual—perhaps multicontextual?—semantic system. The book of Job signifies in spite of, or perhaps because of, its clear internal dislocations. Many recent biblical scholars, such as Norman Habel, Carol Newsom, and Davis Hankins, have read the book as a literary whole in ways that nevertheless take account of its internal differences in style and substance.[9] Thus, the dislocations within the initial context(s) of the book of Job do not disable its signifying function any more than the differing initial contexts of the words in this sentence disable its signifying function in whatever contexts it may be read.

The Initial Context(s) of Job 19:25–27

We have little to no information concerning the reading of Job within its presumed context of production. There are neither commentaries nor even translations that survive from the Persian period, nor do we find anything other than brief recountings of the prose tale, assorted translations, narrative retellings, and individual quotations that remain from the Hellenistic world. What modern scholars mean, then, when they claim to be reading a text in its ancient context is that they are attempting to read it as if they were ancient peoples. The product of such readings cannot be anything other than a modern product, albeit a modern product designed to mimic presumably ancient products.

Even this goal is itself a thoroughly modern one, since ancient and medieval readers were in large part quite uninterested in reading texts as if they were other people. Perhaps one might think that I am disparaging modern interpreters and critical study, but the opposite is true. This entire book is a paean to the thoroughly modern goal of using one's imagination to read the text from different perspectives. Yet I am also arguing that no particular perspective is naturally superior to any other. One must ask particular questions to discover which particular vantage points provide significant answers to those questions. Different questions would produce quite different results.

Moreover, the imaginary displacement of critical reading produces thoroughly modern things, albeit modern things that seek to represent past things. Scholars find themselves in the paradoxical position of consulting new critical editions, fresh linguistic analysis, recent commentaries, and new historiographic syntheses in their attempts to reach the furthest back in time. Perhaps *BHQ* is closer to the text of the Second Temple period than anything before it, but nevertheless it remains a codex with a critical apparatus. It is, like the book of Job, an *archaistic*—not an archaic—document.

Thus, our beginning looks surprisingly like the ending to our story. In this chapter on the ancient context of the book of Job, I focus mainly on recent scholarly readings from Norman Habel, David Clines, and Choon-Leong Seow, among others. These modern readings emerge from within the process of the reception of the texts that they try to read as if that history did not exist. But this odd juncture of ancient and modern is not merely a "fusion" of two horizons that ends in a moment of understanding. Rather, these archaistic readings display the semantic divergence and novelty that the biblical text produces. We must imagine that, even in its initial context, as in every successive context, the text of Job 19:25–27 overflowed with different semantic potentialities.

Since I do not suppose that the text of Job 19:25–27 is a direct citation from an older text—though it has been suggested that it is—the literary location of this text in the book of Job works as a defensible initial literary context.[10] I take the presumed Hebrew text from the Second Temple period to be my point of literary departure and the general cultural milieu of Persian-period Israelites and the necessarily vague borders of "classical Hebrew" to be my historical and linguistic contexts, and I offer a reading of Job 19:25–27 that seeks to locate its various semantic potentialities in light of these contexts.

Determining Literary Contexts

Biblical scholars often imagine that literary contexts are "given."[11] If they were, biblical scholars would spend less time constructing them and there would be fewer arguments about them. Contexts do not simply appear: we must discern them, which is another way of saying that we must construct them.

As for Job 19:25–27, what is its literary context? Here is one answer: Job 19 constitutes a speech given by the character Job. It occurs in the second of three rounds of dialogues between Job and his friends (chaps. 15–21). By this point in the book, the dialogue has turned from a conversation into something more resembling a shouting match. Eliphaz, Bildad, and Zophar take turns accusing Job of sinful activities that have brought about his justly deserved punishments, and they repeatedly associate Job's plight with the "fate of the wicked," who invariably descend to Sheol (cf. 15:20–35, 18:5–21, and 20:5–29).

In contrast, Job appropriates the language of lament in his speeches of the second cycle (16–17; 19; 21). As Gunkel argues, one of the forms appropriated in particular by Job is the lament; he notes a strong connection in 19:7–22 to the genre of individual lament poetry.[12] In these speeches, Job relies heavily on what Adele Berlin has named "the trope of death"—a common trope in lament poetry of the ancient Near East—to describe his suffering.[13] The images forming the constellation of the trope of death are rather consistent throughout lament and thanksgiving genres and occur in less consistent forms elsewhere throughout the Hebrew Bible.

The shared imagery between Job 19, Psalm 88, and Lamentations 3, for example, is uncanny. In all three poems, the sufferers imagine themselves in darkness (Lamentations 3:2; Psalms 88:7,18; Job 19:8) and complain that their bodies have been decimated by God (Lamentations 3:4; Psalms 88:10; Job 19:20), that they are surrounded and walled in by God (Lamentations 3:7,9; Psalms 88:9; Job 19:8), that their glory or respect has vanished (Lamentations 3:18; Psalms 88:9; Job 19:9), that they have been separated from their communities (Lamentations 3:6; Psalms 88:9,19; Job 19:13–19), and that their cries for help have been rejected (Lamentations 3:8; 43–44; Psalms 88:10,15; Job 19:7). All three contain the vivid image of God besieging the individual (Lamentations 3:5a; Psalms 88:17–19; Job 19:10–12). These images—of immobility, dismemberment, and darkness—suggest identification with buried corpses and thus the inhabitants of Sheol. In short, these three poems employ the elements of the trope of death.

There has been much debate over whether or not the ancient poets understood these poems as metaphorical. Regardless of the answer, the sense of death in them extends far beyond its biological determination. As Jon Levenson argues, "Whereas we [moderns] think of a person who is gravely ill, under lethal assault, or sentenced to capital punishment as still alive, the Israelites were quite capable of seeing such an individual as dead."[14] The trope of death expresses physical, emotional, and religious devastation, which reflects the poet's distance from life, order, and God.

Further, there are clear references to the underworld itself in Lamentations 3:55 (שאול) and Psalm 88:3 (בור). It is fitting, then, that Job 19 also contains references to death and the grave. For example, in verse 10, Job cries, "He breaks me down on every side, and I am gone," using the verb "הלך," which here seems to refer to impending death (cf. Genesis 15:2, Psalms 39:14, 1 Kings 2:2, and 2 Chronicles 17:11).

Chapter 19 is not alone in its use of the trope of death. In fact, all of Job's speeches in the second cycle abound in death imagery, for example, in "He slashes open [יפלח] my kidneys, and shows no mercy" (16:13), "My spirit is broken, my days are extinct, the grave [קברים] is ready for me" (17:1), and "My eye has grown dim [תכה] from grief, and all my members are like a shadow [צל]" (17:7). While Job and his friends all seem to focus on Sheol throughout the second cycle, in terms of genre, they all speak past one another. The fate of the wicked emphasizes the awful but deserved unalterable conclusion to an evil life. In contrast, the lament psalm stresses the pain of the speaker, which is necessary to move the deity into action and moving the deity into action in turn requires that the speaker's location in Sheol be known. It seems that, in the second cycle, Job and his friends carry on an indirect argument about where sufferers end up, why they end up there, and the possibility of salvation. Job expresses an impossible desire to be recovered from Sheol in 14:1–22. In response, the friends claim that the wicked go down early to Sheol and cannot return (see esp. 15:30, 18:19, and 20:26). The friends argue that Job's experience of Sheol in life is evidence of his wickedness and that he will soon be forever lost. One might construe the lament-genre trope of death as Job's response. As he mimics the one in Sheol who does not belong there and can potentially envision a restoration, Job offers an alternate conception of his predicament. Perhaps this is an indirect struggle for control of the language of death—and thus of the language of ontological finality.[15]

It might seem that what I have been doing is simply telling you what is clearly there. And yet what I have actually done is carefully select particular images and intertexts to focus on in order to justify a particular perspective on this text. I have clearly set up this text as concerning death and Sheol as well as a struggle for the language of death. This construction of the literary context allows me to move to a discussion of the recovery of life from the jaws of death, which is a common motif in lament and thanksgiving psalms. Of course, this context informs just one reading of Job 19:25–27. As for the many other elements of the text and the other potential intertexts, I have hidden them from view. There is no other way to determine a context; reductionism is required to establish it. As a result, one could always determine a context differently by highlighting other elements.

For example, to begin again, differently: Job 19 constitutes a speech given by the character Job. It occurs in the second of three rounds of dialogues between Job and his friends (chaps. 15–21). By this time, the dialogue has turned from a conversation into something more resembling a shouting match. Eliphaz, Bildad, and Zophar take turns accusing Job of sinful activities that have brought about his justly deserved punishments and repeatedly associate Job's plight with the "fate of the wicked," who invariably descend to Sheol (cf. 15:20–35, 18:5–21, and 20:5–29).

Throughout his speeches of the second cycle (16–17; 19; 21), by contrast, Job returns to his appropriation of the language of the courtroom.[16] In chapter 9, Job uses forensic language to argue with his friends' pious encouragements to pray for renewal. Job's forensic language conveys his inability to pray: God is his adversary, not his advocate. In 9:2b, Job subverts Eliphaz's rhetorical question in 4:17 ("Can a human be in the right before God?") by asking "How can a mortal be justified before God?" Job here twists the word "צדיק" from its ethical or religious sense to its forensic sense. For Job, the question is not one of his righteousness, because he is righteous. In the following verse, Job asks about contending with God in court (לריב עמו), suggesting that traditional supplication would not work in his peculiar case.

Job's recourse to legal metaphors is quite powerful, in fact: since the legal system serves to mediate disputes and restore justice, Job has at his disposal a discourse that disarms the pious niceties of his friends. The courts have an important function in the community and are a viable source of tradition, a tradition that sets aside a priori knowledge and looks to the facts of each particular case in order to render a proper judgment. The legal tradition requires that charges be made public, and it then offers both parties a chance to speak and for the accused to defend herself or himself. Thus, the legal system would offer Job the perfect communal space in which to confront God, since he believes that God has attacked him for no cause (2:3; cf. 9:22).

As a result, Job develops an elaborate courtroom fantasy. In chapter 9, Job realizes that it would be too difficult to take God to court, because God would then be prosecutor, defendant, and judge alike (9:15–16, 9:32). In light of this paradox, Job wishes that there were an arbiter (מוכיח) that could keep God from abusing and intimidating Job (9:33–34). If this could happen, then Job would be free to testify and tell the truth about his awful condition, including the fact that he has done nothing to deserve it (9:35). In chapter 16, Job offers legal testimony describing the attacks of his assailant (16:9–16) and protesting his own innocence (16:17). Job even imagines that God has managed to force Job's shriveled body to testify against Job himself (16:8). In turn, Job asks for his innocent blood to cry out for justice (cf. Genesis 4:10). Job then proclaims that his "witness is in heaven" and that "the one who vouches for me is on high" (16:19) before wishing again for arbitration (ויוכח) (16:21). In chapter 19, Job begins his testimony again: he accuses his friends of attacking him (19:2) and then recounts God's assaults (19:6–12) and God's destruction of Job's community (19:13–19). Job then wishes to write down his legal testimony for all to read (19:24, reading "witness" with the LXX for "עד") before declaring that his kinsman-redeemer will soon rise up to vindicate Job (19:25).

Both of these constructions of context are acceptable, justified by the semantic, generic, and intertextual structures that existed in ancient Israel. Thus, we can see that context is constructed and that any particular construction of a context is contingent. But one must read in a context (that is, one cannot read entirely "out of context"), and so context is necessary.[17] When analyzing the potentials of a text, one must remember that the context is not given, and therefore one must ask, even when thinking about the context of a text's production, how the text functions in the midst of various contexts.

Semantic Nodes: Justice, Survival, Presence

The early versions do not seem to presuppose significant consonantal variation.[18] It is likely that the earliest recoverable consonantal text is minimally different from the text found in the Aleppo codex and Leningrad codex, which are in agreement. That text, written in Aramaic script, is as follows:

(25) ואני ידעתי גאלי חי ואחרון על־עפר יקום
(26) ואחר עורי נקפו־זאת ומבשרי אחזה אלוה
(27) אשר אני אחזה־לי ועיני ראו ולא־זר כלו כליתי בחקי

A comparison of two English translations highlights some of this text's flexibility. Here is the NRSV:

(25) For I know that my Redeemer lives,
and that at the last he will stand upon the earth;
(26) and after my skin has been thus destroyed,
then in my flesh I shall see God,
(27) whom I shall see on my side,
and my eyes shall behold, and not another. My heart faints within me!

And here is the NJB:

(25) I know that I have a living Defender
and that he will rise up last, on the dust of the earth.
(26) After my awakening, he will set me close to him,
and from my flesh I shall look on God.
(27) He whom I shall see will take my part:
my eyes will be gazing on no stranger. My heart sinks within me.

After surveying the patterns of semantic dispersion in the reception history of this text, I propose to divide readings into three separate *semantic nodes,* each of which gathers together an interpretive trajectory, which exemplifies the procedure I am calling "nomadic distribution."[19]

My mental image for this procedure is as follows: it is as if each reception of Job 19:25–27 were a marble, and taken all together, they were a giant bag of marbles. If one were to drop a bag of marbles on to an old wooden floor, perhaps no two marbles would end up in exactly the same place, but the contours of the floor would herd the marbles into a general pattern of distribution. Once one took a look at the pattern, one would perhaps draw contingent boundaries between different groups of objects.[20] Say, for example, that some marbles congregated by the low point near the door and others clumped in a depression near the kitchen table. One might think of the former group as "the door group" and the others as "the table group." From this exercise, one might be able to locate the basic contours of the floor, picking out the almost imperceptible ridges and ascertaining which way the different floorboards tilt.

Likewise, when sifting through the receptions of Job 19:25–27 that I had found, I noticed that some readings congregated around the semantic field of justice, others around the semantic field of survival, and still others around presence. Each of these categories relies on a different general construal of the text. By analyzing each of these "semantic nodes," I intend to explore the basic contours of this text.

These three nodes are as follows:

(1) Job envisions an extralegal avenger, or perhaps a courtroom scene, that will result in his justification before God; readings of this sort coalesce around a semantic node of justice, and are found sporadically in Jewish and Christian contexts from the ancient world to the modern.
(2) Job describes an experience of near death and subsequent healing; readings of this sort participate in the theme of survival, and while they are most commonly found in Western Christian contexts, they cross religious, cultural, and geographic boundaries.
(3) Job predicts a theophanic meeting with God; readings of this sort are concerned with presence, and tend to emerge in rabbinic Jewish and Middle Eastern Christian contexts, but can also be found far removed from these religious groups and geographic locations.

I treat each of these general readings in turn and then briefly trace each interpretive trajectory from the ancient world to the modern.

Justice

The semantic node of justice gathers together several strands of reading. One such strand is the forensic reading, which understands Job 19:25–27 to describe courtroom proceedings, with either Job as the plaintiff, a powerful arbiter as the prosecutor or judge, and God as the defendant or with God as the prosecutor and/or judge, Job as the plaintiff, and Job's friends or more vague foes as the defendants.[21] A different strand reads the גאל as an extralegal avenger, a גֹאֵלהַדָּם, who attacks either Job's friends or God on Job's behalf, perhaps after Job has died. Both of these general approaches understand the text to describe a vision of justice being meted out to those who deserve it, as well as Job's deserved vindication.

Recently, the prevailing scholarly reading of Job 19:25–27 has argued that this text presents Job's wish for a victorious lawsuit against the divinity. Clines, for example, explains that Job 19 is spoken in the waiting room between the time he issues the summons and has his case called.[22] In order to justify their determination of a forensic context in chapter 19, readers point to a particular reading of the words "גאל" and "קום," both of which can be found in forensic contexts (cf. Psalms 119:154 for "גאל" and Psalms 27:12 for "קום").[23] Many interpreters suggest a forensic sense of "אחרון" as well. It very well could signify the "last" in any context, including a forensic one, though this use in this sense would be unique in biblical Hebrew.[24] These words can inhabit a forensic context, but they alone cannot justify an exclusively forensic context, since all three of these words are only forensic in a secondary sense. That is, if they are already understood to be in a forensic context, then they can function as forensic terms in that setting. But when one hears "קום" in the context of "גאל," must one think "rise up in court"?

Habel gives a slightly more detailed argument for the "forensic context": "Given the legal context of this verse (cf. vs. 3, 23, 29) and especially the explicit juridical role of the 'witness' (16:19–21), with whom the redeemer is presumably to be identified, it seems preferable to view the verb *qwm* as a legal expression."[25] Yet 19:3 and 19:29 are hardly enough to establish an exclusively legal context for the verse within the chapter, and it is difficult to understand what Habel is even referring to. Verse 19:3 includes the words "כלם" and "בוש," but neither necessarily indicates a courtroom setting. Verse 19:29 does include the juridical word "דין," but verse 29 as a whole seems to describe not a court case but an extralegal persecution.

Habel also asserts that "the explicit juridical role of the 'witness' (16:19–21)" should convince readers that it "seems preferable to view the verb *qwm* as a legal expression."[26] That is, Habel argues that the general context of Job's arguments, and especially the intertext of chapter 16, overdetermines the meaning of "קום" in 19:25. There is no doubt that Job elsewhere explicitly states his desire to take God to court, especially in chapters 9 (cf. 9:3, "לריב לעמי") and 23 (cf. 23:4, "אערכה לפניו משפט"), and that in chapter 16 he imagines a courtroom scene that includes the word "קום," also found in 19:25 (16:8, 16:19). But Job also at times imagines decidedly nonforensic encounters with God. The most famous example of this is found in 14:7–17, at which point Job wishes that God would hide him in Sheol until God's own wrath passed over him (14:13). In verses 15–17, Job imagines that God would then "remember" ("זכר") Job and "yearn" ("תכסף"; cf. Psalms 84:3) to establish a relationship characterized by "communication" ("ואנכי אענך תקרא") and "tolerance" ("על־חטאתי לא־תשמור").[27] In chapter 14, then, we find Job wishing that God would sabotage God's own destructive power in order to renew Job's life and restore his relationships. Furthermore, we may find lexical correspondences between 19:23–27 and 14:7–17: "עפר" (14:8 and 19:25), "קום" (14:12 and 19:25), "מי יתן" (14:13 and 19:23), "חיה" (14:14 and19:25). One may thus construct contexts other than a forensic one using the lexemes in the text as well as intertexts.

Habel, among other interpreters, introduces another set of intertexts that, he argues, overdetermines the context in favor of an exclusively forensic signification. As he puts it, the "obvious resolution of the [semantic] problem is to identify the *go'el* with a figure like the celestial witness (16:19) and 'arbiter. (9:33)'"[28] Certainly, several times in the dialogues Job seems to imagine an unnamed figure that could help him mediate his dispute with God (9:32–35, "מוכיח" ["arbiter"]; 16:18–22, "עד" ["witness"]; 19:25–27, "גאל" ["redeemer"]; 31:35–37, "שמע לי" ["one who hears me"]). As Clines puts it, "It ought to be unmistakable that the *gō'ēl* of ch. 19 is the same as the 'witness' (*'ēd*), the 'advocate' (*śōhēd*) and the 'spokesman' (*mālîṣ*) of ch. 16."[29]

But how do we know that the גאל ought to function like the עד, and who or what would even have the authority to determine this in an absolute sense? How did the fact of Clines's reading (an "is" statement) become normative (an "ought" statement)? These texts could potentially read in such a way that the גאל and the עד are the same figure, but it is also possible that these are completely different flights of fancy—just as it is also possible that the image of the גאל can lead us to rethink our evaluation of the "עד" in a less forensic sense. And, fascinatingly, Clines shortly introduces another reading:

> A second reading, in which the end of the book is allowed to resonate here also, superimposes a new level of meaning above the meaning intended in these lines by the character Job. It is an irony, though not at all a bitter irony, that Job's words have a meaning other than he envisages. The truth is that, though he expects God to be the last person who would vindicate him, God does indeed in the end become his vindicator, and that on earth (42:10, 12). Job's desire to 'see' God is fulfilled to the letter (42:5), and the belief and the desire of those verses, here so antithetical to one another, are shown in the end to be identical. In the end, Job does not see his hope fulfilled, for he has no real hope; but he sees his words, hopeless but desirous, fulfilled with unimaginable precision.[30]

Clines here admits that there are at least two meanings struggling within Job 19:25–27, but he wants the reader to privilege the sense that does not "allow" the end of the book to resonate. God is, at least in light of 42:10–12, Job's גאל. The problem is that, according to Clines, God ought not to be. Yet why would we not allow foreshadowing and retrospective irony to influence our reading of this passage? And, moreover, is it not permissible to push back against this retroactive identification of God as גאל—that is, may we doubt that Job's restoration is, in fact, a full vindication?[31] Perhaps more importantly, Clines here privileges the intent of the speaker over the other meanings that those same words might have. Clines does offer a strong argument that, if we have decided to model the character Job's intention in our reading, then there is a good case to be made that the גאל is the מוכיח and the עד. But even in that reading, the retroactive identification of God as the גאל breaches this hermeneutical boundary, revealing the gap that separates Job's intentions—and all of ours—from his words. This is, of course, the same boundary that runs not in between "original" (here, what Clines understands as Job's intention) and "secondary reception" (here, the ironic reversal at the end) but rather through the midst of the textual fabric, even within its initial context.

In any event, these readings are contingent, and there is no heavenly ought that holds the true interpretive answer. Who could hold the right answer to the question of the meaning of this text, if even the character Job himself is not in control of its signification? To quote Job, "There is no arbiter between us who might lay his hand on us both" (9:33). No transcendental signifier, such as a particular construction of "authorial intention" or "the intention of the text" or even "the intention of the character," holds absolute authority. These terms merely lend a veneer of authority to what is, ultimately, the interpreter's own semantic organization of the text.

Habel and Clines—like many biblical interpreters—here construe the readerly task as one of providing ultimate solutions, as if the text requires the correct contextual key to unlock its true forensic secret, which would render the task of reading complete. Yet as Deleuze explains, thinking in terms of problematic structures may help encourage biblical interpreters to propose readings that do not seek to dominate the field of interpretation or too hastily declare other readings anathema. Very often, this solution-based approach to interpretation manifests itself subtly: for example, Clines simply asserts that because the forensic context can be determined, all other potential constructions of the literary context must be ignored. The correct response to this sort of argument is, in general, to reject this construction of the reader's task and instead to assert the problematic structure of the biblical text. That is, readers can either simply justify a nonexclusive particular reading or analyze the ways in which the text both supports and restricts any one of these potential constructions. Like biologists exploring the problematic structure of a particular ecosystem, we can analyze the various solutions to the problem of the environment without deeming one solution the answer to its many questions.

Along with thinking in terms of solutions rather than problems, biblical scholars also often think in terms of the possible and the real instead of the virtual and the actual. One can see this tendency clearly in Habel's and Clines's comments. In this line of thought, an interpreter deems one particular reading of a text "more probable" than all others since its semantic construction or literary intertexts is the most obvious. Usually this argument is accompanied by statements that a particular construal of context, or a particular choice of intertext, or a particular meaning is explicit, given, or obvious. The implication is that less obvious or explicit contexts, intertexts, and meanings are less probable, and thus are not really what the text means to say. But why are only the most obvious (to us) meanings the real ones or perhaps the most real ones? And who is that gives a particular construal of a context that we call given? Whose hand extends this gift? Why are subtle meanings or obscure intertexts impossible readings, to be discarded in favor of obvious ones?

In order to sidestep these impossible questions, biblical interpreters can instead think in terms of Deleuze's concepts of the virtual and the actual, both of which are real and neither of which is entirely given. In this mode of thought, we would read texts with an eye for the many diverse potentials that it may manifest through the process of reading. In other words, Clines's reading actualizes a very real potential of the virtual dimension of this text, but his actualization does not exhaust or diminish the manifold resources that the text always continues to offer to readers.

Clines's reading of 19:25–27 is as creative as it is compelling. He posits a separation of time, viewpoint, character, and scene in between 19:26a and 19:26b, a point that many recent interpreters follow him on.[32] He assumes that the *waw* opening 19:26b is disjunctive and that what follows may be understood as a completely different train of thought.[33] Thus, in 19:23–24 Job wishes for his own testimony to be carved on a mountainside so that his fight can be carried on until he is acquitted, while in 19:25–26a he expresses a conviction that his case will indeed be won, albeit after his own death. Then, in 19:26b–27, Job expresses his desire for the legal confrontation to occur in his lifetime but subsequently confesses his inability to believe that this could ever happen (19:27c). In Clines's reading, since Job has been abandoned by God and all fellow mortals (19:13–22), Job's גאל must be his own "cry" (cf. 16:18–19). With no one to save him but himself, Job remains his only hope.[34] Clines's solution allows him to admit that 19:26b–27 envisions a reunification with God while also permitting him to assert at the same time both that Job sees God as an enemy *and* that Job is not inconsistent on this point.[35]

Those of the many readers who, like Clines, are attuned to the thematic of justice want to hear Job's full-throated cry in all its unorthodox anger.[36] Furthermore, they do not want to accept weak theological apologies that obscure the painfully obvious divine source of Job's sufferings that even YHWH admits were inflicted "for no reason" (cf. 2:3, "לבלעו חנם"). In the book of Job, YHWH acts in ways that clearly violate the shared norms of behavior that guide human ethics of all stripes, and these violations, many readers claim, must be prosecuted. It is, of course, true that a great many readers throughout the centuries have worked hard to make Job's lamentations look as pious as possible. Readers such as Clines provide a very valuable corrective to this dominant mode of reading. Indeed, those who construe this text as a struggle for Job's legal vindication themselves struggle in many ways to redeem the radical and liberative dimensions of the text from the snares of complacent piety.[37]

Survival

Many readers have understood Job to address not the theme of justice but rather issues of survival. These readings generally do not concern themselves with the vindication of Job's righteousness or other moral concerns. Instead, they read this text as a vision of a return of vitality, a restoration of damaged relationships, and a recovery of ability in disabled body parts. The semantic node of survival gathers together many disparate readings that nevertheless construe the text as a description of a recovery, or continuation, or carrying on, of life. I offer one such reading that seeks to respect the contours of the text.

Readers of this text may determine the immediate literary context of 19:25–27 to be a form of a lament psalm (19:7–20). Here it seems important to note that a commonly occurring corollary of the trope of death in thanksgiving psalms is a recovery-of-life trope.[38] Many different metaphors represented in the Psalms fulfill this function: some envision a spatial ascent from underground Sheol back to the topside-world of the living (30:3; 30:4; 40:2; 40:3; 41:10), some use sight language to describe a vision in the temple that would likely bring healing (11:4; 11:7; 17:13; 17:15; 63:2), some describe body parts recovering their functions (13:4; 30:3; 71:20; 80:18; 85:6; 119:25), and still others use forensic language to describe a retrieval of wholeness (9:4; 18:44; 31:20; 119:154). The return-to-life trope may signify a recovery of individual integrity, bodily ability, legal status and communal reintegration or a desire for one or more of these things. Moreover, any one aspect may metonymically represent the reintegration of one's entire life (e.g., "going up" may signify a recovery of life in many different senses) or metaphorically represent another single element displaced by the image (e.g., "winning a court case" may signify recovery from a disease). One need not, then, posit an anachronistic doctrine of resurrection in order to imagine that, even in its ancient context of production, this text may have spoken of death and the recovery of life.

In the context of an extended trope of death, the sudden discursive shift in 19:23–24 may alert readers to a potential shift in tropes as well. In this light, 19:25 seems to be packed with words that signify a recovery of life: "גאלי," "חי," "יקום"

almost jump off the page. Job "knows" that a "living" "redeemer" will "rise up" "against the dust," perhaps referring to Sheol ("על-עפר"; cf. 17:16 and 21:26).[39] If one imagines that in 19:7–20 Job speaks of the collapse of every aspect of his life and casts this collapse as a movement toward Sheol, then this language sounds rather like a defiant proclamation of Job's hope in the restoration of his life. Following on this verse, Job then may be understood to describe his flayed carcass (אחר עורי נקפ) at the moment that he encounters the healing power of Eloah (מבשרי אחזה אלוה), thus contrasting his death-like state with his restored vitality at the moment that he begins his recovery.

Moreover, in the context of lament psalms, the verb "חזה," which Job uses twice in this text, often "signifies not so much an actual looking at God as an experience of a close encounter of salvific divine power."[40] While it is possible for "חזה" to mean simply "see" (Exodus 18:21; Song 6:13), the word is overwhelmingly associated with nonphysical sight, such as the visions of a seer (Numbers 24:4; Isaiah 1:1), the "sight" of thought (Job 34:32), or the experience of God's saving help (Psalm 17:15). For the lamenting psalmists who are metaphorically in Sheol, "seeing" the saving presence of God is often associated with renewal of life, akin to resuscitation (Psalms 30:3 and 86:13).

In addition, in verses 26–27 we see a litany of bodily references: Job mentions his skin (עורי), flesh (בשרי), eyes (עיני), kidneys (כליתי), and chest (חקי). These repeated enumerations of body parts, as well as the reference to God's proximity, may also suggest a restorative encounter, since psalmists at times refer to their restored body parts when describing a recovery of life or its maintenance in the face of death (56:14; 92:11; 16:9–10).[41]

The progression from חזה in 19:26b–27a to ראה in 19:27b underscores the motif of sight, which highlights the appearance of the formerly estranged divinity. Reversing his lament that he finds himself estranged from all vestiges of a community (19:13–22), Job finds himself next to God, and "not a stranger" ("זר-לא"). Job seems to relish his personal restoration, as suggested by his piling up first-person references in 19:27a: "I-I-for me-my eyes!"

In combination, these literary effects allow one to justifiably read this text in terms of a recovery-of-life trope, especially in light of the context of lamentation and death in chapter 19. In this reading, Job imagines that YHWH will someday restore his body and his community and end his alienation from the divine. To be clear, the Christian doctrine of resurrection is not imported into the text in this particular reading. Rather, Job sounds like an unfairly condemned death-row inmate, on his way to his execution but rebelliously imagining his salvation. Like a "dead man walking," Job imagines his hope that the mysteriously absent and ambivalent governor will wake up and grant an eleventh-hour pardon—which, if received, might restore Job's life, his freedom, his legal standing, his social relations, and his honor.

This reading understands this text to be describing the survival of Job, but there are other potential readings concerned with survival: for example, this text might also be read as a description of the survival of the גאל. As the petitioner, Job is expected to envision his own resuscitation. Yet, if the pair of words "קום" and "חיה" do signal a context of healing, as Michael L. Barré argues, one might construe the subject of the verb "יקום" and the adjective "חי" to be the redeemer, not Job.[42] Many clever rereadings of this passage demonstrate its unsettling effect: the Vulgate outright changes "קום" into a first-person verb ("I will be raised" ="אקום"), and Barré himself proposes to read the causative form ("יָקִים," "he will make stand").[43] These interpreters rightly note the appearance of resuscitation language in 19:25 but shy away from applying it to the גאל. But if one reads the גאל as YHWH, this text could then be understood to be describing the recovery of YHWH's life.

Emil Kraeling, for one, suggests that Job in 19:25 envisions the resuscitation of the redeemer, which represents God's mercy.[44] Kraeling finds support for his reading in analogous literary descriptions of gods returning from the land of the dead. In the Ugaritic Ba'al cycle, for example, El dreams that Ba'al, who had descended into the land of the dead, had returned to life. El's cry that "I shall know that Mighty Ba'al lives" ("wid' kḥy aliyn b['l]," CTU 1.6.III.8) exhibits lexical and thematic similarities to Job's declaration in 19:25. Perhaps Job imagines that the reason for the prolonged absence of divine help is that YHWH has departed for the land of the dead. The recovery of YHWH's life, then, would here be described with language similar to Ba'al's return to the land of the living.

While of course it is highly unlikely that Persian-period and Hellenistic Jewish readers of Job would link these two specific texts (Job 19:25 and CTU 1.6.III.8–9), it would be hard to imagine that those same readers would not be familiar with the idea of a god who returned from the underworld, since this theme is rather common in ancient Near Eastern and even Greek thought. Thus, one could construe this text as a parody of the return-to-life trope used by psalmists: that is, Job uses all the words one would use in such a context to signify hope in one's own recovery, but they can only be understood to be expressing hope that God will be revivified: "My redeemer is living, because at last he rose up from Sheol."

Bruce Zuckermann reads the reference to the dying-and-rising god motif as an attack on a belief in resurrection or Yahwism; this may be more or less defensible, but it is simpler to argue that Job here makes a point: namely, God, not Job, is the one who must change.[45] Once God's proper character returns, God may then do what is right and restore Job (which would then be described in 19:27). In retrospect, this reading construes chapter 19 as a long setup to a quick reversal: Job explains in detail his metaphorical death, but in the end, it is God who must be pulled up from the pit first.

There are, of course, many other readings that one could gather up in the semantic node of survival.[46] For example, Matthew Suriano suggests an interesting reading of Job 19:25–27 that centers on the question of Job's proper burial. Suriano argues that Job describes a loyal kinsman's production of an epitaph that memorializes his name and thus ensures the survival of his name for future generations:

> What Job pleads for is the recognition of his innocence and the rehabilitation of his status in society. Concomitant with these provisions would be a proper death. . . . This theme of death and disinheritance is implied throughout chs. 13–21 and is made explicit in certain passages, notably 19:23–27. In particular, these verses express the sufferer's confidence that a kinsman will step forward and perform the necessary actions to afford Job justification in death. According to this ideology of death, the fate of the individual was directly related to concepts of collective identity tied to kinship and patrimony. Thus, the defunct individual's identity was preserved within a larger framework of ancestry. This belief was reified through cultural practices such as communal burials inside family tombs and was affirmed by writing the name of the dead in an epitaph.[47]

Suriano's proposal is intriguing, but perhaps he goes too far when he claims that it alone provides the "proper context" for reading this text.[48] As he explains, "Because scholars have not recognized the cultural context of Job 19:23–27, they discuss the figure of v. 25 in terminology that is incorrect. The context for Job's kinsman-redeemer is not a courtroom drama set in the divine realm, but rather Job's death and burial."[49] Suriano assumes that there is a singular proper cultural context for the word "גאל." This is not a tenable proposition. "גאל" can certainly carry a forensic valence, since the word has no "proper context"—it is a word and as such can be used in limitless contexts, such as this one right here. Moreover, even the context of production of Job 19:25–27, this word had a wide array of "proper contexts," such as forensic action, extralegal vengeance, levirate marriage, divine liberation from oppression, and many others, none of which were or are "incorrect."[50]

Yet in his analysis, Suriano opens up another understanding of survival: the survival of one's name, the continuity of familial descent, and the maintenance of proper ritual observance that seeks to extend the life of an individual beyond the borders of death. This is a part of the struggle to live on in some sense past one's death. And those interpreters who try to close off readings that highlight Job's struggle for survival surely do a disservice to the vast array of this texts' potentials.

Presence

It is also possible to read this passage as a description of a theophanic encounter with God that does not necessarily help Job to survive or resolve any of Job's legal claims. Job's stress on the motif of seeing God (אחזה/ראו), his emphatic repetition of the first person, and the physical proximity connoted by the phrase "not a stranger" ("לא־זר") lend textual support to this point of view. Some readers have suggested that Job's words could reference the actual ending of the book of Job (38:1–42:6), in which Job encounters YHWH "in the flesh," as it were, in the midst of a theophanic storm that rises on the dust of the world. Job's response to YHWH's theophany includes the words "But now my eye sees you" ("עתה עיני ראתך"), which parallel "my eyes see" in 19:27 ("עיניו ראו"). The speeches from the whirlwind, however, have confounded many interpreters: what, exactly, do they do for Job? They seem to bring little comfort, or restoration, or healing, or vindication in themselves.[51] Thus, a third option would be to read this text as a call for the divine presence and as expressing an ambivalent attitude toward the potential legal or life-giving consequences of that meeting. Seow offers intertextual support for a reading of 19:25–27 that stresses theophanic presence: "Job's language [ויחזו את־האלהים] is, in fact, used of theophany, as in the encounter between Israel's leaders and God on Mount Sinai (Ex 24,11)."[52]

One particular strand of this interpretive trajectory found immense popularity in nineteenth- and early twentieth-century biblical criticism. In this general reading, Job expresses an expectation that he will encounter YHWH only after his death, and though he has no hope of earthly healing or restoration at this meeting, Job nevertheless desires to be in the divine presence. According to Heinrich Ewald,

> *werde ich* dennoch *schauen—Gott,* die Wonne der Erscheinung und unmittelbaren Nähe Gottes auch als Richters und Vertheidigers meiner Unschuld, die ich vor dem Tode des Leibes nichtmehr geniessen kann, dann noch empfinden! und zwar dann, wie vonselbst hieraus erhellet, mit geistigen Augen, nicht mehr mit den jezigen, und doch so gewiss und so klar und fühlbar als möglich. Wer Gott schauet, wird das reine Licht die klare Wahrheit und das ewige Leben gewahr, garkeine Trennung und keinen Zwiespalt mehr zwischen sich und Gott fühlend, also auch keinen Schrecken, keine Furcht noch Strafe: im leiblichen Leben dies zu können hat Ijob hier längst vollkommen verzweifelt, aber er weiss nun dass er es auch nach dem äussern Tode geistig könne und sicher werde.[53]

Ewald argues that Job, like any mortal, cannot withstand the immediate presence of the divine (cf. Exodus 33:20). Yet emphatically in 19:26–27 and elsewhere in his discourses (23:3), Job expresses a desire for an encounter with God "in the flesh." Ewald argues that Job knows that this encounter is not possible while he is alive, but he hopes that, when he leaves his mortal coil, will be worthy of participating in YHWH's (albeit ghostly) presence. One very important component of this reading is the privative sense of the preposition "מן" in the phrase "מבשרי" in 19:26b and another is the meaning he ascribes to the verb "חזה." Bernard Duhm offers intertextual support for this reading: "'Ohne meinen Leib' d.h. obwohl ich tot bin. Der Körper bleibt ja unter der Erde, Hiob selber aber wird als Geist, etwa wie Samuel I Sam 28 . . . aus der Erde steigen, und eben als Geist Gott selber sehen. חזה wird bekanntlich mit Vorliebe vom ekstatischen Schauen gebraucht."[54] Yet while this reading is compelling in a number of ways, it also has its share of weak points. More recent interpreters have asserted that ancient Israelites did not believe that humans continued to exist in the form of spirits after death, and so this reading might seem strange to them, but Duhm shows that, at least on the margins, ancient Israelite texts did acknowledge that the spirits of the dead were available for meetings (1 Samuel 28). Should we be so quick to think that Job could not imagine that a spirit of the dead could confront YHWH? Though Job at times wishes for the rest provided by Sheol (3:21–22), at other times Job seems to imagine that no one can ever escape the invasive divine presence, even those in the depths of Sheol (26:5–7).

If understood as a call for a theophany, Job's request does not seem like an appeal for a simple restored relationship, since Job never seemed to see the divinity before his misfortunes (1:1–2:13). It seems even less like an appeal for a recovery of health, since biblical theophanies are famous for their destructive and dangerous effects (cf. Psalms 29:5–9).

And here, too, we find the same exclusive interpretive mentality at work. Ewald, perhaps the first major biblical critic to endorse this view, notes, concerning other commentators at the time and their construal of the literary context for Job 19:25–27 that "allein viel schlechter, ja gänzlich falsch ist die Ansicht vieler, vielleicht aller neuern Gelehrten, dass Ijob hier eine irdische Hoffnung habe und von der Zeit nach dem Tode gar nicht rede. Diess ist schon gegen die Worte, es ist gegen den Zusammenhang der Gedanken, es fehlt gegen den Sinn des ganzen Buches und gegen den deutlichen Fortschritt von 14, 13–15 bis 16, 18 ff. und endlich bis hieher."[55] Ewald's claim that the semantic nodes of justice and survival are "totally false," "opposed to the words themselves," and ultimately "sins against the meaning of the whole book" participates in the same fundamental assumption that we found at work in Clines and Suriano. Interpretation is a battlefield, these interpreters claim, and there can only be one victor. It must be said that, in light of the literary context that Ewald has constructed, the other interpretive nodes do not seem as convincing. But it is always possible to determine the context in a different manner. If one does so, the other interpretive nodes will not seem as offensive.

One might also notice that the various semantic nodes shade into one another. For example, the node of presence seems present, albeit in a ghostly manner, in the other readings. The nodes of justice and survival both imply that the divine will have to be present in some manner, and thus all three readings implicate each other. Due to the use of the word "גאל," Job's hope could be seen as a forensic hope; due to his use of "קום" and "חי" in parallel, he could be interpreted as appealing to a revivification trope; and, due to his seeming use of a sight-as-healing metaphor and a stress on "חזה" and "ראה," he could easily be understood as voicing a desire for an encounter with God. And since lament and thanksgiving psalms more often than not blend these metaphors, it would be hard to construe one and not admit the existence of the others.

In all, most scholarly readings tend to draw too strict a distinction between courtroom and revivification metaphors. In many instances in lament or thanksgiving psalms, forensic language is not meant as an exclusively literal image; it often refers to God's saving activity from immanent peril. For example, in Psalm 9 the forensic metaphor is quite fluid: the psalmist proclaims, "You have maintained my just cause!" (4), but the vindication is later presented as a return-from-Sheol motif: "You are the one who lifts me from the gates of death" (13).

Consider several other examples. The poet of Lamentations 3 complains of residing "in the depths of the pit" but conceives of salvation in forensic terms, exulting, "You have taken up [רבת] my cause [ריבי], O Lord; you have redeemed [גאל] my life [חיי]" (3:58). Psalm 143 contains the metaphor of the poet's suffering and impending doom as existence in Sheol (143:3,7), along with revivification language (143:11), and forensic language (143:2). Psalm 71:13 mentions "my accusers" ("שׂטני נפשי") as the cause of suffering while incongruously asking YHWH to "revive me" ("תחיינו") and "bring me up again from the depths of the earth" in 71:20.[56]

Thus, these interpretive distinctions are effects of our reading, which is nothing more than the actualization of a solution from a problematic structure. Let us not forget that, when we propose a reading, we are offering something smaller than the problem, offering something that could never cover over the problem like putty over a crack in the wall. The problem always survives our attempts to kill it; its presence continually evades our grasp.

Moving on from the Initial Context

Thus, within its initial context, one can trace a general virtual structure of the text that may help in classifying its diverse readerly actualizations. I have proposed a procedure whereby the reader determines the degrees of freedom provided by determinations of the text's historical and literary contexts as well as its semantic structure. In other words, I have analyzed some of the text's structural potentials that allow for the production of different, yet equally justifiable, readings.

In the process, I have discovered that the constitutive boundary—the one separating production from reception—runs straight through the text's initial context, as well as its potential meaning. That is, from the very beginning, the text of Job 19:25–27 was a complex dialogue of production and reception, of offering and taking: the writer produces but also receives from the context and past texts. The reader always receives the text from someone else, and that reader always lives within a context that in part determines her or him; but this same reader also must determine the text's contexts and produce a reading from the elements of it that are given and yet underdetermined. What results is a processual system with emergent properties, that is, a problematic virtual multiplicity.

SEVEN

Trajectories of Job 19:25–27: The Example of Survival

> To articulate the past historically does not mean to recognize it "the way it really was" (Ranke). It means to seize hold of a memory as it flashes up at a moment of danger. . . . The danger affects both the content of the tradition and its receivers. . . . In every era the attempt must be made anew to wrest tradition away from a conformism that is about to overpower it. The Messiah comes not only as the Redeemer, he comes as the subduer of the Antichrist. Only that historian will have the gift of fanning the spark of hope in the past who is firmly convinced that *even the dead* will not be safe from the enemy if he wins. And this enemy has not ceased to be victorious.
>
> —Walter Benjamin

Introduction

In this final chapter, I offer a glimpse of Job 19:25–27's problematic structure, manifest in its reception history. I have chosen to focus on the semantic node of survival simply by virtue of its breadth of receptions, but I also offer a brief sketch of presence and justice. While I briefly touch on transmutations and nonsemantic effects as they occur in the history of this text's processual development, the greater part of these fascinating stories receive short shrift. I have selected to discuss receptions that demonstrate various capacities expressed by the text within various contexts.

Survival

To survive is to remain alive or to endure in spite of resistance. Survival presupposes a simple narrative structure: a life is threatened with death, and yet it subsists.[1] Survival does not entirely evade the threat of death: the specter of death always lives on, if only in memory. It is not merely a triumphant narrative. Death as well as life have starring roles in the drama of survival. A survivor is always a survivor of something, and from that something the survivor can never fully escape.

The book of Job resonates strongly with Tod Linafelt's concept of "literature of survival."[2] Though death besieges Job, he manages somehow to escape its clutches. Yet even in the happy conclusion, readers have noted that Job's restored family surely could never erase the memory of the lost children on whom Job doted so much and about whom he worried (1:2, 4–5). In the epilogue to the book of Job, the narrator never mentions relief for the many physical ailments he endured (cf. 2:5–8, 12–13). At the level of the narrative, Job's wounds remain.

Like Job, all survivors must learn to live with their wounds, which testify to the enduring existence of death even in the midst of life. For the survivor, life and death have crossed each other's sovereign borders, complicating any attempt to identify one without reference to the other. Linafelt calls this the "paradoxical dynamic of survival: death in the midst of life, life beyond the borders of death."[3] For the survivor, there is neither death nor life but rather life-death.[4]

And yet not all who have survived an encounter with death survive in the same way. As Timothy Beal explains, "Surviving is, most literally, 'living over' or 'living through.' Living through is very different than living beyond. Living beyond is forgetting, living in oblivion. So survival is in some sense about not forgetting, resisting oblivion. The survivor takes something of what she or he survives into the present."[5] But surely some survivors do live in oblivion by forgetting what has happened. Are they really surviving? Is one living at all if one lives in oblivion? Is not living beyond—forgetting, oblivion—more akin to death than to life?

Some scholars object to the term "reception history," preferring the labels "afterlife" or "survival," implying that the text has somehow managed to escape its own historical oblivion and find itself before our eyes.[6] How is it that this set of marks on a page will most certainly outlive me, their author? And of all the texts from the ancient world, most of which have perished, how is it that the ragged, difficult text that is Job 19:25–27 has managed to escape and subsist for all these years? In the case of Job, its raggedness, its seeming incompleteness, has in fact only served to encourage its life. As Linafelt argues, "To imagine a text existing complete in and of itself is to imagine not 'survival' but a 'lifeless' state of preservation. Paradoxically, the 'unfinished edge' of the text . . . allows it to go on, endure, by calling other texts that respond to it. It is the unfinished edge's refusal to be finished that converts the death sentence to a suspension of death."[7] This same struggle for survival—that is, the struggle between death and life, oblivion and resisting oblivion, forgetting and remembering—repeats itself throughout the history of the reception of Job 19:25–27. Many have read 19:25–27 as a triumphalistic rejection of death that proclaims an otherworldly resurrection, allowing the faithful to "live beyond" the struggles and pain they have endured in this life. At the same time, however, others have struggled to read this text as part of Job's passionate fight to recover his life by "living through" his traumatic experiences. Both of these viewpoints on Job 19:25–27, along with many others, intersect in the semantic node of survival.

In this section, I trace the struggle between life and death in Job 19:25–27. I begin with the OG translation and go on to sketch the actualization of survival through early Christian readings, performance in liturgy, monumental inscription, and artistic illumination. The semantic node of survival gathers together a broad array of readings of 19:25–27 that refer to Job's holistic recovery of the various aspects of his shattered life. Throughout the centuries of the Common Era, examples of this construal of the text are quite easy to find, and yet they also exhibit significant internal diversity.

Old Greek Job: Recovery of Life

The OG version of Job, a translation made in Alexandria in the second century BCE, is perhaps the earliest known translation of the book of Job.[8] It exhibits a refined literary quality in Greek, which is unusual for OG.[9] Since the text of OG Job is 20 percent shorter than the MT version, some have suggested that the Greek translation reflects a Hebrew version that differs from that of the MT.[10] Yet an intriguing pattern emerges from the particular differences between the text of the MT and the OG: the often confusing later chapters of the book of Job, especially the lengthy and tedious speeches of Elihu, are much more likely to be absent in the OG. A full 35 percent of Elihu's speeches are not represented in the OG, whereas only 16 percent of God's speeches in chapters 38–42 are unaccounted for in the OG.[11] Since Job was not used in Alexandrian Jewish liturgy, the idea that the translator might have been catering to a popular audience is plausible.[12] OG Job omits 16 percent of MT chapters 15–21 and the percentage of omissions after chapter 21 climbs higher, but it is striking to note that only two half verses are omitted from all twenty-eight verses of chapter 19. The translator's attention to the preservation of this chapter might signal a concern for proper translation due to the text's early importance.

The text of OG Job 19:25–27, as reconstructed in the critical Göttingen edition, and a translation and critical notes follow.[13] One may wish to skip this technical section and proceed immediately to next section, where I draw broader conclusions.

> (25) οἶδα γὰρ ὅτι ἀέναος ἐστιν ὁ ἐκλύειν με μέλλων ἐπὶ γῆς.
> (26) ἀναστήσαι τὸ δέρμα μου τὸ ἀναντλοῦν ταῦτα· παρὰ γὰρ κυρίου ταῦτά μοι συντελέσθη,
> (27) ἃ ἐγὼ ἐμαυτῷ συνεπίσταμαι, ἃ ὁ ὀφθαλμός μου ἑόρακεν καὶ οὐκ ἄλλος· πάντα δέ μοι συντετέλεσται ἐν κόλπῳ.

> (25) To be sure, I know that he who is about to unloose me on earth is everlasting.
> (26) May my skin which patiently endures these things rise up; for these things have been accomplished on me by the Lord—

(27) things I am conscious of in myself, things my eye has seen and no other; and all of them have been accomplished for me in my bosom.[14]

The most striking choice by the translator of OG Job is to read "יקום" with "עורי" as its subject. This decision links "עורי with a masculine singular verb instead of the difficult plural "נקפו," but it introduces a new problem, namely, the intervening *waw* and preposition "ואחר." As it is difficult to find any trace of them in the Greek, Samuel Driver and George Gray, as well as Édouard Dhorme and others, have concluded that the OG translator entirely omitted the two words.[15] It is possible, however, that the translator read "ואחר" as an epexegetical *waw* and temporal adverb, and that in turn may explain the replication of an imperfect verb ("יקום") with an optative aorist verb ("ἀναστήσαι"), thus understood as a jussive.[16] The Hebrew imperfect with a parenthetical temporal phrase—"that is, afterward"—may have prompted the modal Greek verb.

OG Job's reading of "יקום" left "אחרון" without a clear function. OG Job seems to render both "חי" and "ואחרון" with "ἀέναος," construing the two words as predicative adjectives in hendiadys or perhaps as a syntagm connected with an epexegetical *waw,* thus resolving the syntactical difficulties of the masculine "אחרון."

Verse 26b presents an array of fascinating readings. OG Job appears to represent "נקפו" with the verb "ἀναντλοῦν," a present active nominative or accusative singular participle.[17] For the confusing plural subject, the translator has substituted a verb conjugated in the singular with a fitting subject: "τὸ δέρμα μου." The switch to participial form requires "קום" to continue to be the finite verb in the sentence, at the same time allowing "נקפו" to modify the subject ("my flesh").[18]

This move permits OG Job to use "זאת" as the object of the participial clause, thus making sense of difficult syntax. While the Hebrew singular is rendered with the plural "ταῦτα," OG Job regularly performs this substitution in accordance with Greek style (cf. 5:27). The verb "ἀναντλέω" occurs in the LXX only one time, in Proverbs 9:12, translating the word "נשא." In that context, the word elliptically refers to sufferings borne by a scoffer. As Driver and Gray note, "Whether G read נקפו . . . and, if not, what exactly it read instead of these words, is uncertain" due to the conceptual difference between "to hack off" ("נקף"-I) or "to surround" ("נקף"-II) and "to endure" ("ἀναντλέω").[19] If OG Job read "קנפו," however, it is very possible that the words are redivided into "נקפ וזאת," with the *waw* functioning either emphatically or epexegetically.[20] Thus OG Job would read and adequately represent a singular Hebrew verb. Furthermore, the phrase could be understood as such: "even these things (="these sufferings") [which my flesh] circles around." In order to smooth out the complicated syntax and highlight the connotation of Job's body revolving around (orbiting, and thus under the influence of, or bearing) suffering, the translator used the verb "ἀναντλέω."

In this instance, perhaps a translator perceived a poetic metaphor, and concretized and simplified it. At least, this is a defensible reading of the text.

It appears that the Greek translator read "ומשדי" ("παρὰ γὰρ κυρίου") for MT "ומשברי" and "אלה" ("ταῦτα) for "אלוה." It is unlikely that either is necessarily preferable to the MT, because both words find parallelistic complements—"בשר" in the former and "אלוה" in the latter line. It is, however, interesting to note that OG Job likely read a Hebrew manuscript with fewer *matres* and no pointing; thus the reading of "אלה" could have been supported by the same logic, as a semantically parallel intensification of "זאת."[21]

Previous studies of OG Job have not accounted for the verb "אחזה" in 26b. Several scholars have assumed that the word did not influence the translation and that "συντελέσθη" is purely interpretive.[22] In OG Job, "συντέλεω" represents "כלה" (cf. 19:27b and 21:13, reading with *qere*), "נקף-I (1:5), and "אבד" (30:2). Discussions of OG Job seem to have agreed that the appearance of "συντέλεω" in Job 14:14 is superfluous. As Hervé Tremblay writes, "Le traducteur y a inserté le verbe συντέλεω alors qu'il ne se trouve pas dans l'hébreu."[23] There is, in fact, an appearance of "כל" ("all") in 14:14 that is read by the OG translator as a form of "כלה" and translated as "συντελέσας." In Job 19:26b, however, the translation of "אחזה" is less wooden. OG Job likely considered the phrase "and by the Lord I have seen these things" to be too elliptical to be rendered woodenly in Greek. The more direct Greek rendering retains the first person on the verb with the independent dative personal pronoun "μοι" while exchanging the motif of sight—which connotes the reality of the suffering from Job's vantage point—for a descriptive perfect passive verb that connotes the reality of Job's suffering from an objective viewpoint. While the Hebrew text is more literarily artful, the Greek text is more easily understood. Sight here connotes the reality of the experience, and this connotation is foregrounded in the Greek.

The same strategy seems to have guided OG Job in verse 27a. According to the OG Job's reading, Job claims to have seen his many sufferings (elliptically referred to as "these"). Instead of rendering this metaphorical "sight" into Greek, OG Job does away with the metaphor: Job "knows" ("συνεπίσταμαι") for himself ("ἐμαυτῷ") these "things." Since Hebrew "חזה" often connotes the metaphorical sight of visions (Isaiah 1:1; Amos 1:1), dreams (Daniel 2:26), and theophanies in the temple (Psalms 11:7 and 17:2), OG Job renders the conceptual difference between the "literal" sight of ראה and that of חזה by converting metaphoric language into concrete terms.[24] Finally, OG Job reads 27c ("כלו כליתי") as "all of them ["כֹּל"] have come to an end for me [יִכָּלְיָתִי]."[25]

Overall, the translator's decisions to read "חי" ("living") as a predicative adjective of the substantive participle "גאל" ("the redeeming/avenging one") and the ensuing use of "יקום" ("he/it will rise up") as part of verse 26 constitute the most consequential differences between the Masoretic reading, preserved in the

MT tradition, and OG Job. If "יקום" ("rise up") applies to Job's skin, then Job likely envisions a miraculous healing as a deliverance from his suffering. Furthermore, while "ἀναστῆσαι" can mean simply "to rise," its use in this context is similar to its use in OG thanksgiving psalms, which connotes a recovery of life and health. This reading envisions Job's restoration as a return to full life from his sufferings, which have been cast as a death-like experience. Thus, OG Job seems to notice a similarity to tropes in thanksgiving psalms, as in OG Psalm 40:9–11 (=MT 41:9–11). In this psalm, the speaker uses the trope of death to express suffering and then uses the word "ἀνίστημι" to describe recovery.

I understand OG Job 19:25–27 to be saying the following: Job claims to know that the "everlasting" one (i.e., God) is about to "unloose" him, or, in other words, liberate him from his miseries (19:25).[26] Then, Job expresses his hope that God will heal, or "raise up," his body, which has patiently endured his sufferings (19:26a). This healing, Job reminds his listeners, is the work of God (19:26b). Finally, Job expresses the intimate and exclusive knowledge that he has of this future healing (19:27).[27]

And yet one may find ample degrees of semantic freedom within OG Job 19:25–27 that would help one fashion a counterreading. While the word "ἐκλύω" in Koine Greek most often signifies "to be set free" (cf. Tebtunis Papyri 49.6), in the Old Greek translation this word commonly signifies "to be weak" (LXX 2 Samuel 16:2; 17:29, 1 Maccabees 3:17, and Testament of Job 30:1), "to lose courage" (LXX Deuteronomy 20:3 and 1 Maccabees 9:8), or "to dread" (LXX Proverbs 3:11). This translation choice seems odd: in the entire Septuagint tradition, the word "ἐκλύω" translates "גאל" nowhere other than in Job 19:25. Yet, since the Greek text of OG Job is of a high literary quality, the frequent use of "ἐκλύω" to signify "to be set free" in Greek literature may justify a similar reading in this instance (cf. Theogonis 1339, *Phaedrus* 67d, and *Odyssey* 10.286).

Yet, again, the various translation options depend on different construals of their broader literary contexts. If one reads this passage in the context of Septuagintal literature, one may then read with Claude Cox, the translator of Iob in the NETS, who translates "ἐκλύω" as "undo me" (19:25).[28] In Cox's reading of OG Job, Job declares that God is about to finish him off, but Job hopes that his body can continue to endure God's relentless attacks (19:26). Moreover, Cox reads "συντετέλεσται" in 19:27 as "come to an end," rather than "accomplish." In Cox's reading, God's action is the "undoing" of Job, and thus things seem to have "come to an end." That is, Job will soon perish at the hands of God, unless his body can continue to endure God's torments. Cox's reading of "συντέλεω" finds ample support throughout the LXX and pseudepigraphal literature (cf. Jeremiah 14:12, Ezekiel 7:15, and Testament of Levi 5:4).

Yet one might argue that in none of these cases does "ἐκλύω" translate "גאל" and thus that reading "ὁ ἐκλύειν" as "he who is about to undo me" is an incorrect reading. In this line of thought, one must try to discern the meaning implied by the translator's act of translation. While this is a perfectly reasonable project to undertake, it ignores the status of OG Job and the later LXX Job as fully authentic and legitimate texts of the book of Job. Once OG Job has been translated, it then functions as the book of Job itself and may be read just as one reads the Hebrew text—that is, it may be read as a text and not simply as a translation. The Greek text, no less than the Hebrew text, harbors its own capacities for multiple readings. Moreover, it is just as groundless to privilege the complex, partially derivative Hebrew text of the book of Job in all instances. It is a version of the book of Job in its own right. In short, OG Job functions as both a translation of the book of Job and as a text of the book of Job, and both constructions of its identity may produce justifiable, but different, readings.

This is an unsettling state of affairs. For example, the introduction to the NETS expresses the committee's desire to represent "what the original translator thought his text to mean" as opposed to "what later interpreters thought the text to mean," thus producing "a new translation of the (original) Septuagint—that is, a translation of a translation."[29] According to this introduction, the modern English translators of the Septuagint have "decided to focus on the most original character of this collection, namely, that of interlinearity with and dependence on the Hebrew, or, from a slightly different angle the Septuagint as produced rather than as received," and thus "characteristically for interlinears, one should read the Septuagint as produced."[30] Perhaps the translators of the NETS aimed to translate for this purpose, but it seems like a difficult task to try to parse out the elements of the Septuagint that are "production" from those that are "reception." This borderline runs through the middle of the Septuagint. One may read a translation as it relates to its source text, and one may read a translation as a text in its own right, but these choices are interpretive strategies adopted for the sake of the reader and do not necessarily correspond to any intention in the mind of a translator. Who should have the final word on what it means to "read" the Septuagint, whether it is to read it without reference to the source text or not?

Nevertheless, the continuing development of the process of textual formation led to ever-changing capacities, as shown through the development of the process of the text's reading. Translation is, in many ways, the mode of literature's survival, but it would be impossible for the translator to not change the translated text. Survival requires change: as Walter Benjamin writes of the word "trans-lation," "No translation would be possible if in its ultimate essence it strove for likeness to the original. For in its afterlife—which could not be called that if it were not a transformation and a renewal of something living—the original undergoes a change."[31] Even within the history of the Septuagintal text, several variants show how the survival, and thus transformation, of the text both reflects and alters its history of reading. For instance, LXXa Job 19:26, a later recension of OG Job, reads: "ἀναστήσει δέ μου τὸ σῶμα" ("But my *body* will rise").[32] It is a statement about Job's *body* rather than his "δέρμα," or "skin," which is a more literal translation of "עורי" as well as "בשר." This alteration makes sense if it reads Job 19:25–27 as a description of resurrection of the actual body rather than of an afterlife of the soul.

Yet one might also see in this alteration a slight reticence to identify resurrection with lowly flesh; a textual emendation from "skin" to "body" would allow one to read this text as a description of a transformation of the body into something less identifiable than material flesh. This line of thought seems quite similar to Paul's description of resurrection in 1 Corinthians 15:39–40 and 50, where he differentiates a "spiritual body" from the physical, fleshly body. Is this an intimation of an ideological struggle already occurring over this verse? If so, it suggests that the immanent fleshiness of Job 19:25–27 was causing problems from the very start within the ideological construct of the doctrine of resurrection.

An addition to the last verse of OG Job, 42:17, reads "γέγραπται δὲ αὐτὸν πάλιν ἀναστήσεσθαι μεθ' ὧν ὁ κύριος ἀνίστησιν" ("And it is written that he will rise again with those whom the Lord raises up").[33] This addition seems to have influenced the development of the Testament of Job, which mentions the "resurrection" ("ἀνίστησιν") in 4:5, and the further development of the postscript in manuscript V, which adapts the addition to OG Job 42:17.[34] All of these additions use the verb "ἀνίστημι," which is only used in the context of rising from troubles or suffering elsewhere in OG Job, except in 14:12, where it is negated. These additions find reason to interpret the word "ἀναστῆσαι" in the Greek versions of Job 19:25 as a supernatural rising. We can see a general shift toward concretizing metaphors as one reason for this development; from this shift in semantic context, new textual potentials emerge.[35] As the concept of resurrection developed in Jewish and Christian communities, it found textual resources in the psalmic, metaphorical motifs of a descent and return from the land of the dead.[36] When read in a concrete manner, these proclamations of a return from the land of the dead, which is one way of reading Job 19:25–27, came to be associated with the resurrection.

Reading Survival: The Immanence of Resurrection

Emerging from LXX Job's reading of Job 19:25–27, the interpretive trajectory of survival generally construes this text as a prediction of Job's renewal in the form of resurrection.[37] This trajectory manifests itself in early Christian texts, since early Mediterranean and European Christianity almost exclusively read the LXX in light of nascent Christian theological claims.

The earliest known citation of Job 19:25–27 occurs in 1 Clement, written to the Corinthian church near the end of the first century CE. In 1 Clement, these verses function exclusively as a scriptural support for the final resurrection (26:1–3).[38] It is clear that the author of 1 Clement understands Job 19:26 as a recovery-of-life trope similar to those found in lament and thanksgiving psalms: the two other biblical texts cited in support of resurrection (LXX Psalm 27:7 and 3:6) are individual lament psalms. LXX Psalm 27 mentions a descent to Sheol (1) and hopes for healing and restoration (7–9), and 1 Clement reads the description of sleep and waking in LXX Psalm 3 as a subtle reference to death and revivification. While this is not likely the intent of any putative author or even translator of this psalm, the mention of sleep in lament psalms can signify the "sleep" of death (LXX Psalm 12:4 and 87:6). Thus, in light of the context of the book of Psalms, 1 Clement construes sleep in LXX Psalm 3 as a metaphor for death. As the theological concept of resurrection evolved in the Greco-Roman era, the already established construal of Job 19:25–27 as a recovery-of-life trope allowed it to manifest a new meaning, namely, as prophesizing the resurrection of the righteous.

Concerning the final resurrection, the author of 1 Clement writes: "Do we then think that it is so great and marvelous that the Creator of all things will raise everyone who has served him in a holy way with the confidence of good faith? . . . For it says somewhere, 'You will raise me up and I will praise you,' and, 'I lay down and slept, and I arose, because you are with me.' And again, Job says, 'You will raise this flesh of mine, which has endured all these things' [καὶ πάλιν Ἰὼβ λέγει· καὶ ἀναστήσεις τὴν σάρκα μου ταύτην ἀναντλήσασαν ταῦτα πάντα]."[39] This textual form of Job 19:26 is not attested elsewhere, but its status as a citation of Job is not in doubt. Some scholars have argued that, prior to 1 Clement, these texts already existed in an oral *testimonia*, or a stock group of scriptural citations that support a particular theological conviction, concerning the resurrection. It is more likely, however, that this citation comes from memory and has been altered either by the author of 1 Clement or by the sources from which the author drew.[40] Either way, this text was undergoing changes outside of the "textual tradition" of the book of Job, and as such it constantly retained the potential to transform.

Perhaps the most striking part of this citation is the transformation of "τὸ δέρμα μου" ("my skin") or "τὸ σῶμα" ("the body") into "τὴν σάρκα μου" ("my flesh"). Though the word "σάρξ" does not pervade the New Testament literature concerning resurrection, the phrase "resurrection of the flesh" came to dominate the discussion of the theology of resurrection in the Christian community by the second century primarily because of its emphasis on corporeality.[41] It is here, in 1 Clement's citation of Job 19:26, that we find the earliest known reference to the "resurrection of the flesh" as well as the first known use of "σάρκα" in Job 19:26.[42] One can only speculate about the author's purpose concerning this transformation in 1 Clement, but its effect is clear: Job 19:25–27 becomes an important advocate for the immanent aspect of resurrection.

1 Clement addresses a Corinthian church divided into schismatic groups (1–3), which the author seeks to unify by, in part, explaining the basic theological structure of the author's Christian faith.[43] Fundamental to this structure is the role of the resurrection (24–27), which the author claims "is at all times taking place" (24:2) and can bring new life to situations in dire need of renewal. The author looks to nature and finds resurrection, understood as the renewal of life, constantly at work precisely where death and darkness seem to have eclipsed life and light: "Day and night declare to us a resurrection. The night sinks to sleep, and the day arises; the day [again] departs, and the night comes on. Let us behold the fruits [of the earth], how the sowing of grain takes place. The sower goes forth, and casts it into the ground, and the seed being thus scattered, though dry and naked when it fell upon the earth, is gradually dissolved. Then out of its dissolution the mighty power of the providence of the Lord raises it up again, and from one seed many arise and bring forth fruit" (24:4–5).[44] 1 Clement's reading of OG Job 19:26 follows this same line of thought: Job declares that at the moment of bodily, emotional, and communal dissolution (19:2–22), he awaits the one who will renew all of these things. Within 1 Clement's overall message, Job 19:26 functions as both a scriptural proof text for the theological principle of resurrection and as a proclamation that resurrection "is at all times taking place," even perhaps within the fractured community of faith in Corinth.

Some readers might resent the focus on postmortem resurrection in interpretive trajectory of survival, since the angry Job of the dialogues would not accept his unjust state of suffering as only a momentary hardship before an everlasting life of otherworldly bliss.[45] Any displacement of Job's hope into a spiritual afterlife seems to "tear" the text, as it would be difficult to construe differently Job's commitment to the immediacy of his struggle and his clear hope for the restoration of his world throughout the second cycle (cf. Job 16:18 and 17:13–16).[46] Moreover, the restoration that does come is, at least in the Hebrew text, not primarily that of a beatific afterlife (42:7–17, but cf. LXX Job 42:17a).

Yet many Christian interpreters have downplayed Job's attachment to the material things of this world—including his family—despite his repeated claims that he resents losing his life "for nothing" and very much wants his old earthly life restored, including his possessions and his social role (29–31). For example, Jerome claims that after losing his children and possessions, Job "flinched as little as the sage of whom Horace writes—'Shatter the world to atoms if you will/ Fearless will be the man on whom it falls.'"[47] In this line of interpretation, Job's solid faith in the afterworld leads him to care little about the injustices and struggles of this life.

But Clement shows that the interpretive trajectory of survival may in some ways respect Job's concern for this life, for this world, this body, and this community.[48] While the resurrection is, of course, an eschatological event in Clement's mind, it is also something that "is all the time taking place" (24:3). Resurrection, Clement reminds us, is also an immanent-imminent event that heralds the renewal of life, where before there had been no hope of recovery. Resurrection is not only an eschatological hope—in the guise of radical transformation, it permeates the fabric of the world. It may be found in the dead seed producing new life as well as in the fractured community suddenly restoring its sense of collectivity and vocation.[49]

There is, of course, a way in which the discourse of resurrection can smother hopes for immanent change and material transformation. But there are manifold potentials offered by the discourse of resurrection, among them the image of "living through." As Christian theologian Catherine Keller has argued,

> Yet even if new wounds cease to happen and old ones to hurt, the hells on earth created by the dealers in death will not disappear along with them. Like the old scars in Jesus' hands, the new creation must surely retain the scars as marks and monuments. . . . This would entail accepting the tragic dimension of the universe, . . . not by miraculous restorations but by the restorative activity of history itself—that is, in precisely the sense that time can heal if we let it. The mothers of the dead in El Salvador with whom I have communicated . . . [wish] for the realization in history of the hopes for which they struggle, a realization not at all utopian and absolute but of a decency that would have allowed their children to live full lives and die nontragic deaths.[50]

Within Christian theological notions of the resurrection of the flesh, we find an idea of survival that holds in tension a desire for a replacement of this world and a desire for a transformation and renewal of the material conditions of this world. When early Christian authors ruminate on the restoration of the flesh, they picture the things of this material world, yet in their most utopian guise.[51] This tension is the struggle between, in Timothy Beal's words, "living beyond" and "living through," which Keller's allusion to the unsettling status of Jesus's still-wounded hands crystallizes (John 20:27).

Yet this is not only an issue for Christian theology. This same tension disturbs the book of Job. The description of Job's very material restoration fails to mention the lives of Job's former children and servants, who will not be restored (1:2–3; cf. 42:13). Does Job live beyond or live through? Does he forget his children, as does the narrator, or does he silently remember? Is Job's desire to "see" God "not as a stranger" (19:27) a desire to reclaim his life or to move beyond it? Is Job offering to revoke his lawsuit if God will appear as a גאל? How do we know?

Perhaps this text pulsates with the potentiality of this tension; perhaps Jesus's mangled but still-living hands express the same tension of survival displayed by Job's mangled but still-beating heart.

Though for some time after 1 Clement no readings of Job 19:25–27 remain, starting within the third century CE the flood of interpretive energy begins to swell. Almost all Greek-speaking early Christian interpreters read OG Job 19:25–27 as a prediction of the resurrection, including Origen (ca. 250 CE), Julian the Arian (ca. 375 CE), Cyril of Jerusalem (ca. 375 CE), Epiphanius of Salamis (ca. 375 CE), and Hesychius of Jerusalem (ca. 450 CE).[52]

Origen's use of this text may provide an index of its dominant function in the context of second- to fourth-century Christianity. Throughout his writings, Origen expresses the need to defend himself from interlocutors who attacked his conception of the resurrection by claiming that he denied the resurrection of the flesh. Origen uses the Sadducees' denial of the resurrection of the body in Matthew 22:23 as a pretext to explain his view of the resurrection. Judging from the textual location of this defense, it seems quite possible that Origen's complex and quite inventive conception of the resurrection had already been caricatured as "Sadducean."[53] Origen concludes his explanation with the following, quoting LXX Job 19:25: "Nor are we, in saying this, showing a lack of belief in this passage from Isaiah: 'And all flesh shall see the salvation of God,' or in what was said by Job: 'For he is eternal who is to save me on earth and resurrect my skin which is suffering these things' [ὅτι ἀένναος ἐστιν ὁ ἐκλύειν με μέλλων ἐπὶ γῆς ἀναστῆσαι τὸ δέρμα μου τὸ ἀναντλοῦν ταῦτα]."[54]

When elaborating his own doctrine of resurrection in a positive manner in his extant works, Origen never quotes Job 19:25. It only enters his text here, where he asserts that his doctrine does not violate its sense. Origen's rhetorical move suggests that his opponents had used this text against him, or perhaps that he felt vulnerable to such criticism. As Reimar Roukema notes, "Il est manifeste qu'Origène ne polémique pas ici contre les hérétiques, mais contre ceux qui n'acceptaient pas son approche de la résurrection des morts, qui était elle-même considérée comme hérétique. Pour s'approcher formellement de la compréhension majoritaire de l'Eglise, il termine cette digression en témoignant que, lui aussi, il croit aux paroles . . . de Job."[55] Thus, when Origen needs to affirm his commitment to the survival of the material world, he swears on Job 19:25–27.

Through the pre-Vulgate Latin Itala translation, others read a Latin translation of LXX Job and generally came to similar interpretive conclusions.[56] By the fourth century CE, Job 19:25–27 appeared quite often in Greek and Latin religious texts. Following 1 Clement, several of these early interpreters justified their readings by construing the literary context of 19:25–27 as a psalmic trope of death. For example, the fifth-century patriarch Severus of Antioch comments on Job 19:25–27 as follows:

> In consequence of so great a trial [Job] had in a sense gone down to Sheol and final destruction, so that even his name should thenceforth be extinguished, as he himself said when he was being tormented by the pains, and suddenly he arose as from the dead, and put off the unsightliness of the sores, and he was comely in body, as in the bloom of youth, and everything ended for him in a change to the best fortune. . . . That he endured such pains, not because he looked to the things that were given him in this world, but to the hope of the great and wonderful resurrection, concerning which also he said, "For I know that he will ever be revealed who shall release me upon the earth. He shall raise my skin which endures these things" (Job 19:25–26). The words which are before us for the purpose of interpretation were used by the author with reference to the general resurrection which is expected by everyone.[57]

Severus begins this passage by reading Job's cries as metaphorical descent to Sheol ("had in a sense gone down") and likewise reads Job's restoration as a metaphorical return to life ("he arose as from the dead").[58] In this text, Severus reads the restoration of Job's material condition as an experience of resurrection. Yet Severus also claims that Job's endurance derives not from "this world" but rather from his belief that there will be a "great and wonderful" resurrection, thus implicitly reading Job 19:25–26 also as a prophecy of Jesus's resurrection.

John Chrysostom (ca. 375 CE), however, famously wavered in his opinion of whether or not Job hoped for a bodily resurrection. In a letter to his friend Olympia, Chrystostom points to Job 14:12 and 19:25 and claims that "Job . . . had no idea of the resurrection."[59] But in his commentary on Job 19:26, Chrysostom demurs: "Did Job know of the doctrine of the resurrection? I think so, and even in the resurrection of the body, unless we should say that the resurrection he is referring to is a deliverance from the evils which held him."[60] Chrysostom, like Severus, construes Job's words as a plea for a renewal of his current life, but he cautions that one's use of this trope does not necessarily indicate that one is referring to a resurrection after the cessation of biological life. Yet Chrysostom allows that it may be a possibility: "I think so," he says, "unless . . ." Chrysostom's words have been taken as an outright by rejection by many biblical scholars, but he seems rather to affirm the multiple semantic potentialities of this text.[61]

Is Severus's reading unjustifiable? The initial author of Job 19:25–27 did not have resurrection in mind and certainly was not thinking of the specific Christian proclamation of Jesus's resurrection. But we have already seen that OG Job understood the trope system of Hebrew, and slightly later readers (such as the LXX^{A}) concretized the trope and applied it to a developing doctrine of the resurrection. Thus, one of the potentials on this text includes the ability to shift from signifying a return-to-life trope in Persian-period Yehud to signifying a concrete return to life in the Hellenistic period. While it is anachronistic to read this text as a statement of resurrection in the Persian period, it does not seem anachronistic in the Greco-Roman period, let alone late antiquity, to read this text in light of the concept of a concrete recovery of life, since in these historical contexts the word "ἀνίστημι" signified, among other things, the resurrection of the dead (cf. Testament of Job 4:1).

Within the semantic and cultural context of Severus of Antioch, this text most certainly had the potential to signify resurrection. If this seems to push the interpretive envelope too far, one might also ask whether during the early production history of the book of Jeremiah it was possible for the "seventy weeks" to signify the time of Antiochus IV (cf. Daniel 9:2). Surely not—and yet, in the Seleucid period it was most certainly possible to read it as such. From the Iron Age to the Hellenistic world, Jewish readers compiled and edited prophetic collections so that they could be applied to later contexts.[62] Likewise, early Christian readers assumed that scriptural texts *should* be read within their contexts—and in Severus's context, these words could signify resurrection. As Severus claims, the "words which are before us" are "for the purpose of interpretation," and interpret them Severus did.

Greek-speaking readers tended to follow the trajectory of survival. Yet for the growing numbers of readers who did not read Greek, other translations soon filled these linguistic voids. Perhaps the most important biblical translation in history is Jerome's translation (ca. 390), known in later centuries as the Vulgate. Almost immediately, Jerome's Vulgate became one of the most important texts of the book of Job, and thus the potentials of Job 19:25–27 expanded with this development of its textual forms.

Though the Vulgate was supposedly a return to the Hebrew text of the Old Testament, at times it bends the Hebrew text to conform to the dominant Christian interpretations of particular passages.[63] Jerome pushes LXX Job's revivification trope even further, altering 19:25b in the process: "in novissimo de terra surrectus sim" ("at last *I* shall rise upon the earth"). The Vulgate text of 19:25–27 and my translation read as follows:[64]

> (25) scio enim quod redemptor meus vivat et in novissimo de terra surrectus sim
> (26) et rursum circumdabor pelle mea et in carne mea videbo Deum
> (27) quem visurus sum ego ipse et oculi mei conspecturi sunt et non alius reposita est haec spes mea in sinu meo

> (25) For I know that my redeemer lives, and at last I shall rise upon the earth,

> (26) and again my skin shall be encircled, and in my flesh I shall see God,
> (27) whom I myself shall see, and my eyes shall behold, and not another; this my hope is laid up in my bosom.

Already OG Job read "עורי" as the subject of the verb "יקום," but Jerome bends (and perhaps rips) this text into a prophecy of the final resurrection of the righteous by reading "אקום" for "יקום."[65] This was not, as some have claimed, the decisive historical moment wherein Jerome, for the first time, associated this text with the resurrection.[66] Driver claims that the OG Job, Pesh Job, and Rabbinic Targum "do not justify the conclusion that the translators detected a reference to experience after death: on the other hand, the Vulgate, with all clearness, does so and even introduces the idea of the resurrection of the body."[67]

Yet the idea of the resurrection had already been introduced by 1 Clement, and many Greek exegetes had read this text as a statement concerning bodily resurrection. Jerome amplified this exegetical tradition with his translation—and alteration—of the text. Jerome did so, however, because he had already read this text as a statement of the resurrection, when, a decade earlier, he had produced a Latin translation of the LXX.[68]

Moreover, this passage was important for Jerome's theology.[69] It was important to him especially because it seemed to espouse the resurrection of the flesh, in contradistinction to alternate forms of Christianity that denied the resurrection of the body itself.[70] As Caroline Walker Bynum explains, for early and medieval Christians the resurrection redeems "a psychosomatic unity, a person, fully individual both in its physicality and its consciousness."[71] In 397 CE Jerome wrote a scathing attack against John, the bishop of Jerusalem, who apparently taught that the flesh was not raised in the resurrection:[72]

> Job said: "And I shall be surrounded again with my skin and in my flesh I shall see God" (Job 19:26). . . . Does it not seem to you, then, that Job writes against Origen and for the truth of the flesh in which he sustained torments? For it grieves him that the suffering is in vain if another rises spiritually when this flesh has been carnally tortured. . . . If he is not to rise in his own sex and with the same members that were thrown on the dung heap, if the same eyes are not opened for seeing God by which he saw worms, where therefore will Job be? You take away the things in which Job consists and give me empty words concerning resurrection.[73]

Thus, Job 19:25–27 provides the exegetical support for the survival of the immanent materiality of the human body in the resurrection. In Jerome's reading,

Job's persistent references to his body parts signify their restoration, which reveals the continuity of the material world and of the human body even after the eschaton. Jerome insists that Job's bodily sufferings, his "carnal tortures," will be vindicated when his body—and not another (19:27)—revives. In this debate, Job 19:25–27 plays the part of the materialist counterweight to the neo-Platonic disgust with the world of matter. Its textual capacities help Christianity in its attempt to insist on the importance of the human body and, by extension, the material world.[74]

For early and medieval Christians, Job 19:25–27 teaches that "the heavenly self is no ghostly vapor, no mere collection of memories; it is the resurrected body—glorified, hardened against physical change or decay, yet beautiful and burning with desire."[75] Job retains the tension between "living beyond" and "living through" in Christian conceptions of survival. Both Jerome's translation and his supporting comments led to Job 19:25–27 forming the backbone of Christian appeals to the Hebrew scriptures for prophetic support of the resurrection of the flesh.[76] Throughout the centuries, in the context of Western European Christianity this text functioned as proof of the importance of materiality. In the twelfth century a story arose concerning Maurice de Sully, the bishop of Paris, who worried about rising doubt in the resurrection of the body. When he died, Maurice asked that the text of Job 19:25–27 be written on a card and placed on his chest during the exhibition of his body in order to remind the viewers that he shared Job's hope for immanent survival.[77]

The Christian preoccupation with Job's fleshly survival continued in what is undoubtedly the most influential engagement with the book of Job: namely, Gregory the Great's thirty-five volume *Moralia in Job,* which was completed in 595 CE.[78] Gregory's lengthy and wandering homiletical trek through the book of Job exerted a tremendous influence not only on the history of Christian interpretations of the book of Job but also on Christian exegesis and theology broadly construed.[79] In his reading of Job 19:25–27, Gregory expounds on Job's use of "skin" and "flesh" ("pelle" and "carne" in the Vulgate).[80] For Gregory, Job offers a rebuttal to theologians such as Eutychius, bishop of Constantinople, who claim that in the resurrection, human bodies will be "impalpable."[81]

Like 1 Clement, Gregory in his discussion of Job 19:25–27 emphasizes the repetitive immanent and material adumbration of the resurrection: "For what does the universe every day, but imitate in its elements our resurrection? Thus by the lapse of the minutes of the day the temporal light itself as it were dies, when, the shade of night coming on, that light which was beheld is withdrawn from sight, and it daily rises again as it were, when the light that was withdrawn from our eyes, upon the night being suppressed is renewed afresh."[82] But for Gregory, this is merely an adumbration, since he understands Job to say that the human body alone is the locus of the effect of resurrection. Like Jerome, Gregory points to Job

19:25–27 as the exegetical lynchpin that forces Christians to confront the material aspect of their hoped-for renewal:

> But see, I hear of the resurrection, but it is the effect of the resurrection that I am searching out. For I believe that I shall rise again, but I wish that I might hear what kind of person; since it is a thing I ought to know, whether I shall rise again perhaps in some other subtle or ethereal body, or in that body wherein I shall die. But if I shall rise again in an ethereal body, it will no longer be myself, who rise again. For how can that be a true resurrection, if there may not be true flesh? . . . But in this too for us, O blessed Job, do you remove these clouds of misgiving, and . . . [you] show in plain words if our flesh shall really rise again. It follows, And I shall be again encompassed with my skin. (Job 19:26) Whereas the "skin" is expressly named, all doubt of a true resurrection is removed.[83]

In Gregory's interpretation, the word "pelle" (translating "δέρμα," translating "עורי") in Job 19:26 justifies his claim that the "effect" of resurrection is not a metaphor, like "a new day has dawned," nor is it a disjunctive hope in a spiritual ascent that leaves behind the world of matter. For Gregory, these are not "true" resurrections. The fleshly focus of Job 19:26–27 leads Gregory, like Jerome, to assert that the resurrection is a radical transformation and yet preservation of the immanent world, such that the "world to come" will be, according to Gregory's reading of Job 19:27, a utopian transmutation of this world: "Both the same and different—the same with respect to nature, different in respect to glory; the same in its reality; different in its power. So it will be subtle."[84] Perhaps it should not surprise us that Gregory's understanding of the resurrection looks much like Job's restoration in the book of Job: a subtle, uncanny difference separates Job's initial state (1:1–5) and his postrevivification state (42:7–17), in the middle of which appears a pained expression of hope (19:25–27). One might say with Gregory that the beginning and end are "both the same and different—the same in reality; different in power," which is another way of saying that the book of Job ends with a "second naïveté": the "scars of hurt and doubt that have been voiced in the complaints" remain, albeit transformed.[85]

Performing Survival: Liturgy

Job 19:25–27 was not, however, only of interest to professional theologians and exegetes. A great many early Christians encountered this text as it was performed in the liturgy, in particular in liturgy dealing with death.[86]

Death liturgies are a set of survivor's practices whereby those who have survived a member of their community attempt to live through the trauma of severed relationships. These practices seek to reassure the community that though death rips a person from his or her community, the missing member is not, and will not ever be, entirely absent. For early Christians, the proclamation is twofold: the community will not forget the deceased and the loved one will not enter an oblivion of utter extinction.[87]

At the very least, the deceased will survive in the community itself. Death liturgies provide the space wherein the community can promise not to "live beyond" the deaths of its individual members. In the wake of the death of Hans-Georg Gadamer, Derrida quoted a poem written by Paul Celan, whose final line reads "die Welt ist fort, ich muss dich tragen" ("the world is gone, I must carry you.") As Derrida remarks, "The survivor, then, remains alone. . . . In the least, he feels solely responsible, assigned to carry both the other and his world . . . there where he speaks, in us before us."[88] Through liturgy, the early Christian church sought to "carry" others even after their death, to carry them over into whatever might come next, and to begin to learn how to carry them, their memory and their legacy, and their "world" in their ongoing lives and as a community.[89]

Early Christians also claimed that in death not only were individual members of the community able to be restored but also the community as a whole. In a study of eighth-century Christian liturgical practices, Richard McCall notes that the early Christian liturgy is a "performance that is also an enactment, a remembrance that is also a construction . . . [that] enacts a world that is both the world of the everyday . . . and the new world of church constructed by its gathering, praying, hearing, offering, feeding, and worship."[90] The early Christian performance of death liturgies, then, attempts to carry the deceased while transforming the world that survives. In this striving to "live through" death, perhaps it should not surprise us that Job 19:25–27 finds a place of honor, particularly in the Latin West.

The earliest known Latin death ritual appears in various collections of Ordines romani; the oldest of these collections date from the eighth century, but they most likely reflect a much older ritual matrix.[91] Within the ordines one finds versions of the Old Roman Ordo defunctorum, the "order of the dead."[92] According to Frederick Paxton, "the general nature and structure of the Roman *ordo* as it probably emerged in the fourth and fifth centuries are clear. The ritual was built around a coherent set of actions—viaticum as the rite for the dying, the chanting of psalms, triumphal processions—and infused with a spirit of optimism concerning . . . the resurrection of the dead."[93] Damien Sicard has organized this ritual, which may be found in many different versions in various manuscripts and whose performance varied each time, into a basic schema.[94] First, the dying individual takes communion and hears the Gospel accounts of the Passion read aloud until death arrives. At communion, a prayer claims that "the communion will be his defender and advocate at the resurrection. . . . It will resuscitate him."[95] As Paxton explains, "The ritual connection between *viaticum* [communion] given on the deathbed and the resurrection was rooted in the Christian understanding of the redemptive power of Christ."[96] The community then offers a prayer, a psalm (usually 113 or 114), and an antiphon, after which the attendants wash the deceased body and place it on a bier in order to transport it to the local church. Before the body left the house, the priest was instructed to recite the following antiphon: "De terra formasti me et carnem induisti me redemptor meus domine, resuscita me in novissimo die" ("My redeemer, you formed me from the earth and dressed me in flesh; Lord raise me up on the last day").[97] Joseph Ntedika points out that this antiphon was inspired by Job 19:25–27: "redemptor meus" ("my redeemer") and "novissimo die" ("the last day") occur in the Vetus Latina and the Vulgate, and the phrases "resuscita me" ("raise me up again") and "carnem . . . me" ("in flesh . . . me") occur as variants in both traditions.[98] Here Job 19:25 marks the moment that the body of the deceased crosses the threshold of both house and life. Someone speaks in the voice of the deceased, reminding the deity that the body beginning its process of decomposition was tenderly formed once but will now return to dust (cf. Job 10:9). Yet the hope for survival continues to hold death and life in tension: "Raise me up," the community calls out, thus "carrying on" the liturgical action on behalf of the deceased.

According to the ordo, the body is then carried to the church, accompanied by psalms and antiphons. When it has been placed in the church, the people are instructed to chant psalms, responses, and "lessons from the book of Job" until the burial.[99] Though no specific readings are listed, Ntedika is confident that Job 19:25–27 was always among them, since that text commanded such an important place in later liturgy.[100] As Paxton explains, the presence of the Joban readings in the liturgy offers a "tradition of direct confrontation with God—of the creature's right to remind the Creator of the essential realities of their mutual relationship—which gives special force to the confidence in salvation expressed in the ritual as a whole."[101] Thus, Paxton argues that the Ordo defunctorum construes Job's passionate speeches as an attempt to remind God to act as God should toward the world. This resonates with Seow's reading of "גאל" in 19:25: that is, Job must "remind the deity of a role abandoned that must be taken up again."[102] Ntedika points out that in one early Spanish liturgical text in the ordo that does name specific passages to read aloud, the texts chosen include both the bleak Job 7:1–10, in which Job seems to slide into oblivion, and the energetic 19:25–27, in which he vigorously fights to live on. Thus, in the ordo Job continues his role as preserver of the tension between Christian conceptions of death and the recovery of life.[103]

Resurrection was even more a focus of the Iberian Visigothic, or Mozarabic, liturgy, and as a result Job 19:25–27 is nearly ubiquitous in Mozarabic liturgies for the dead.[104] The use of Job 19:25–27 in Mozarabic liturgy likely began before the sixth century, since by that time it had already inspired a funerary inscription of this text near Cordoba.[105] In one particular liturgical manuscript, we find "credo quia Redemptor meus resuscitabit me, et in carne mea videbo Dominum meum" ("I believe that my redeemer will raise me to life, and in my flesh I shall look upon my Lord").[106] This text quotes a version of the Vetus Latina text but substitutes "credo" ("I believe") for "scio" ("I know"). It is likely that this alteration of the text borrows "credo" from the ecumenical creeds of the church, especially "credo in resurrectionen mortuorum" ("I believe in the resurrection of the dead.")[107]

Though this shift may seem to turn Job's cry into an inflexible doctrine, it is perhaps interesting to notice that recent commentators on the book of Job have shifted their own interpretations of the epistemological status of Job's "knowledge" in a similar manner, coming to understand it as belief instead. Until the twentieth century, almost all interpreters saw in Job 19:25 a proclamation of sure knowledge: "I know that my redeemer lives."[108] But recently, interpreters more reticent to see the Job of the dialogues as an orthodox pronouncer of pieties have argued that there are significant semantic degrees of freedom for the word "ידע." David Clines, for example, argues that it introduces what Job "knows, or believes," which is "that God is his enemy."[109] In this interpretation, "belief" is different from "knowledge": Job believes that his champion is alive, but he does not know this.[110] In other words, the shift from "scio" to "credo" in the early centuries of the Common Era parallels the epistemological shift from knowledge to belief in modern commentaries. Thus, the association of Job 19:25–27 with the Nicene Creed through the word "credo" in liturgical practices and funerary inscriptions does not necessarily mean that the passage amounts to a simple profession of dogma: in many ways, belief is something *less* sure than knowledge.

In the following centuries, the liturgical presence of Job 19:25–27 grew. By the tenth century, throughout the Latin world one may find the Officium defunctorum, or the Office of the Dead, which included a reading of Job 19:25–27. By the later medieval period the Office of the Dead had established itself as the "main funeral service" for the Roman Catholic Church, and many clerics and monastics chanted the office daily.[111] Since the Office of the Dead was chanted, it was set to music. In the later middle ages and the early Renaissance, composers often scored new melodies for the readings from the Office of the Dead, and thus Job 19:25–27 found another rich context in which its capacities could be explored.[112]

During medieval funerals, after the body had been placed in the local church, the mourners would recite the prayers, lessons, and responsorials that composed the Office of the Dead. And lest one imagine that the community would soon "live beyond" that death, the mourners would repeat the Office of the Dead on various anniversaries of that death, thus ensuring the survival of mourning.[113]

The most striking section of the office is comprised of nine readings from the book of Job.[114] The nine lessons comprised a large portion of the office, and as a result "the office contributed to a wide and detailed familiarity with Job," especially among the monastic communities that prayed the office daily.[115] Surprisingly, these readings focus almost exclusively on Job's anger toward the deity and the seemingly pious theology of his friends.[116] The only potential note of hope comes from Job 19:25–27, which is included four times in the office, once as a reading and three times as a responsory.[117] Yet it does not have either the first or the last word—it is flanked on all sides by Job's angry accusations. Hope does not triumph in Job's discourse, at least as presented by this liturgy. Instead, the final office reading closes with gloom: "I go, and return no more, to a land that is dark and covered with the mist of death, a land of misery and darkness, where the shadow of death, and no order, but everlasting horror dwells" (10:22).[118] And Job's famously pious declaration, "the Lord gave, the Lord took away, blessed be the name of the Lord" (1:21) is not to be found. Roger Wieck argues that "the 'I' of the readings ceases to be Job, ceases to be the person reading the Office and, instead, becomes the voice of the dead man himself, crying out for help. Pity and mercy are continually asked for throughout the lessons, but through a veil of near despair."[119]

According to Knud Ottosen, the Office of the Dead not only continues the complaint tradition established in the Ordo defunctorum—it radicalizes it and insists on the subsistence of the deceased: "In particular the many readings taken from the book of Job give expression to the complaints of the dead toward God. The dead person, on behalf of whom the prayers are spoken, is not in fact regarded as dead; he is still living. He cries out, complains, he suffers, he proclaims his confidence and faith in the mercy of God and he demands forgiveness for his sins. . . . At the same time, the Office of the Dead was also—from the very beginning—a prayer *for* the dead."[120] Thus, the dead demand that God act as גאל and that the community carry on repeating the demand in the place of the deceased. In this liturgical dramatization of Job 19:25–27, the community itself—that is, the collective of kinsfolk-redeemers—takes up the mantle of the גאל, struggling to ensure that God restores the departed.

Inscribing Survival: Funerary Monuments

In Job 19:23–24, Job utters the following words immediately before issuing his cry for a redeemer: "If only my words were written down! If only they were inscribed on a monument—with an iron pen and with lead they were engraved on a mountainside forever!" Faced with the immanent threat of death (19:2–22), Job suggests that, if only his words were inscribed on a cliff for all to see, then his complaint could survive the event of his own extinction. As long as it is legible, writing never ceases signifying; it does not extinguish itself when it reaches a particular addressee, and it does not fail to function even when the one who wrote it is absent.[121] An inscription survives both its author and any particular readers, including us. Here we find the fundamental thematic of writing: Job wishes that his words could escape his own context and continue to signify in his absence—even in the radical absence of his own death. Job 19:23–24 teaches us that "writing remains in a monumentality . . . linked to death."[122]

In my translation, I read "forever" with MT ("לָעַד"), but Theodotion understood this same phrase to read "as a witness" ("לְעֵד").[123] Perhaps one can assert the truth of both readings: Job desires to inscribe his words because writing *survives,* and what writing preserves is its *witness,* or its signifying function. Yet for the same reason that writing survives—namely, its ability to escape contexts and continue to signify even in the event of the author's death—Job's witness survives, undertaking a life of its own and evading the hermeneutical clutches of any who seek to control it.

Job's wish has not gone unrealized. Millennia later, the book of Job continues to survive as literature of survival. One of the book's most fascinating potentials manifests itself in the world of funerary epigraphy, or inscriptions marking an individual's death. From quite early in the medieval period and continuing through the present, readers of the book of Job inscribed versions of 19:25–27 on their own monuments of stone in order to continue witnessing, even after their death, to their faith that they will yet survive. Some readers have linked 19:23–24 to verses 25–27, assuming that Job desires the inscription of his cry for a גאל. But whether or not these juxtaposed verses inspired the history of funerary inscriptions bearing 19:25–27, these inscriptions continue to function for precisely the same reasons that Job wishes for his words to be engraved for all to see.

It is also important to note that while many of these early inscriptions mark the tombs of clerics and theologians, as the centuries progress many more mark the tombs of the laity. The tenacious persistence of this verse testifies not only to Job's cry but also to the lively reading tradition these verses enjoyed beyond the confines of the monastery scriptorium. As Bynum remarks, "Medieval debates over bodily resurrection involved more than theology and philosophy. Mystics, poets, hagiographers, sculptors, and tellers of folktales ruminated about what a body could do, wherein lay its significance, and how it might be redeemed."[124] From the sixth century onward, we find many such funerary inscriptions that cite Job 19:25–27 in order to express hope in the resurrection of the flesh.[125] One of the earliest known inscriptions of Job 19:25–27 marks the tombstone of a woman named Justa from Cordoba whose title of "famula dei" ("handmaiden of God") signified her membership in the Christian community. Dating from the sixth century, her epitaph contains almost exclusively the words of Job 19:25–27: "Credo quod redemptor | meus vivet et in novissimo die | de terra sussitabit pelem meam | et in carne mea videbo domi|num. Iusta famula dei ("I believe that my redeemer lives, and in the last day my skin will rise up from the earth, and from my flesh I will see the Lord. Justa, handmaiden of God").[126] Justa's tombstone, like many others, cites the liturgical formula found in the early Visigothic death liturgies and also in the later *officio defunctorum:* namely, "Credo quod redemptor meus vivet" ("I believe that my redeemer shall live") As Job 19:25–27 crossed the boundary from liturgy to monumental inscriptions, it opened itself up to even further textual variation. Some of these variations may have derive from local manuscripts of scripture, others may have derived from the liturgical or oral traditions, while still other novel textual forms may have emerged from contingencies related to the inscription process, such as the tastes of the patron or the engraver.

In the context of funerary inscriptions, Job 19:25 also found itself mixed with other texts, such as in the sixth-century epitaph of Bishop Flavian of Vercelli. Flavian's tomb severs the text at the beginning of 19:27 and appends Psalm 30:6 (=MT 31:6): "In manus tuas commendo spiritum meum; redemisti me, Domine Deus veritatis" ("Into your hands I commend my spirit; you have redeemed me, O Lord of truth").[127] In Flavian's epitaph, it seems that Vulgate Psalm 30:6 provides the response to Job 19:25–27. Job calls for the renewal of the flesh, while the psalmist asks God to protect the now-fleshless spirit in the meantime. Of course, this juxtaposition also recalls Luke 23:46, in which Jesus, at the moment of his death, quotes the same psalm as Flavian ("into your hands I commend my spirit.") Flavian, like so many before him, proclaims the paradox of survival: "death after life" (Luke 23:46), and yet "life after death" (Job 19:25–26).

Even as the text of Job 19:25–27 metamorphosed throughout the early centuries of the Common Era, these inscriptions nevertheless continued many of the interpretive traditions that are gathered together by the semantic node of survival. In particular, these inscriptions proclaim the resurrection of the flesh, thus emphasizing the "physicality" of *carne* rather than the "spirit" or "soul." Justa's choice of a "fleshy" text to serve as her surviving witness, for example, links the solidity of the rock-hewn inscription with her belief in the enduring renewal of the physical world, including her very body.

Another Christian epitaph dating from the sixth century was, along with many other early Christian epitaphs, recycled as landfill in the medieval period to fill in a section of the Augustan Forum in Rome.[128] It was discovered in 1933 by Roman archaeologists, who were hastily recovering objects threatened by the construction of Mussolini's grand parade route that led from the Vatican to the Coliseum. The three extant fragments read:

> [—-pec]cator | [—-? scio enim quod] redemp | [tor meus vivat e]t in novis[simo die de ter]ra sur|[rectus s]im et|[in carne mea] vid[ebo] | [deum—-]
>
> [the sin]ner . . . | [I know (believe?) that] my rede | [emer will live a]nd in the la[st day I will be li]fted up fro[m the ear]th, and | [in my flesh] I will se[e | God . . .]

Perhaps the anonymous individual marked by this epitaph would marvel at the ability of this text to survive grave robbers, vandals, the elements, fragmentation, reuse as rubble, and the whimsies of a fascist dictator. And yet the inscription lives on, bearing the scars of its travels, its words broken to pieces (cf. Job 19:2) but nonetheless continuing to signify its testimony to the endurance and even renewal of the physical world.[129]

Yet "witness" does not exhaust the activities requested of these funerary inscriptions. In a ninth-century tomb from the monastery church of San Felice in Pavia, for example, the text of Job 19:25–27 exhibits some nonsemantic aspects of biblical reception.[130] Like other Carolingian-era tombs, the inside of Ariperga's casket is painted in bright colors and decorated with striking imagery. On the end of the casket behind Ariperga's head is a bright red cross, signifying the victory of Christ, with vegetal tendrils sprouting forth in new life.[131] At Ariperga's feet is a large image of the "hand of God" that symbolizes the divine presence that remains with the flesh even in death.[132] Underneath the image of the hand of God, one may read a smattering of words from Job 19:25 ("credo . . . r . . . emptor vivat"), and on the sides of the tomb the text of Job 19:26 appears. Alongside these biblical texts are apotropaic inscriptions that ask for angelic protection.[133] In this context, the crucifix, as well as the hand of God, likely functioned as an apotropaic symbol. For the Carolingian faithful in Lombardy, these powerful images ensured that the body of the deceased would, as Ariperga herself asks, "requiescat in pace" ("rest in peace") and thus remain suitable for resurrection.[134] Thus, in Ariperga's tomb, the words of Job 19:25–27 functioned as part of an apotropaic matrix that warned away evil spirits and claimed the power of the redeemer on behalf of the human body.

Nearly a century later, the famous Saxon bishop and patron of the arts, Bernward of Hildesheim (ca. 960–1022 CE), actualized Job 19:25–27 in a manner similar to that of Ariperga.[135] As Thangmar, Bernward's student and author of his vita tells us, before his death Bernward designed his own tomb and selected his epitaph in order to display his hope for bodily restoration.[136] Surrounding Bernward's sarcophagus, engraved along each of the edges of two of its sides, is the text of Job 19:25–27.[137]

This inscription frames two recessed planes that depict nine nimbed angels, four on one side and five on the other, each flanked by flames. These nine angels signify the "nine choirs of angels" led by Michael the Archangel that surround the throne of God, and the seven flames on each side represent the seven lampstands (Revelation 1:20). On one end of the sarcophagus, a medallion shows a cross-nimbed Lamb of God (cf. Revelation 7:7). Thus Bernward's design is consumed with the eschatological and otherworldly imagery of the apocalypse. And yet again, with its focus on the restoration of the dead human body from the dirt of the earth, the text of Job 19:25–27 plays the materialist counterbalance to the imagery of spiritual ascent. On Bernward's sarcophagus, we see again the desire to hold together both the hope for "living beyond" and the struggle of "living through."

Bernward's arrangement of the text is another striking element of his design. In Bernward's cultural context, Job signified the potential for liberation from disease and suffering of all kinds.[138] Throughout his life Bernward had struggled with poor health, but in his last years his body grew even more frail.[139] Perhaps it is significant that Bernward positioned the text of Job 19:25–27 so that it wrapped around his body, thus adumbrating the content of Vulgate Job 19:26 with the form of the text: "Rursum circumdabor pelle mea ("I will be encircled again with my body") After a lifetime of disabling sickness, Bernward's tomb holds out hope that one's own *pelle, carne, oculi,* and *sinus* will "rise up" with restored abilities.

While these monumental inscriptions are almost exclusively found on Christian epitaphs, the text of Job 19:25–27, like any biblical text, finds a way to overrun any boundary. In 1934, the Jewish biblical scholar Umberto Cassuto, noted for his work in both the Pentateuch and Italian-Jewish history, published an edition of Hebrew inscriptions from a long-vandalized eighth-century Byzantine Jewish graveyard in Venosa, Italy.[140] Like other Jewish scholars influenced by the *Wissenschaft des Judentums* movement, Cassuto sought to recover Jewish history from dominant Christian narratives that either demonized or ignored the rich history of Jews in Europe.[141] One important practice of *Wissenschaft des Judentums* is the resurrection of the memory of the deceased by means of the documentation, recovery, and preservation of tombstones.[142] Cassuto transliterates the eighth tombstone in his study as follows:

> [ha]-miqdash ha-qadosh she-[yi]bba[neh]
>
> . . . .

[ti]sh'im shanah wa-ani yada'[ti]
[go]'ali chay we-achar[on 'al 'afar]
[ya]qum

the holy sanctuary, which will be rebuilt . . .

. . . .

ninety years. But I know
that my redeemer lives, and last upon the dust
he will rise.[143]

How shall we read this tombstone? The reference to the rebuilding of the sanctuary signals an eschatological context, but its fragmentary state gives us little surety that this context extends to the citation from Job. Even if the full literary context were available, it might not extend to the citation, since the disjunctive shift from temporal information to biblical quotation ("ninety years/ But I know") seems to set the citation apart from the rest of the epitaph. Cassuto offers no suggestions other than noting the reference to Job 19:25–27.

In his encyclopedic study of medieval Jewish tombstones from Italy, David Noy argues that a belief in bodily resurrection is mentioned only a handful of times, perhaps even just once, among known inscriptions.[144] And while Jewish tombstones often borrow the Latin phrase "hic requiescit in pace" ("here rests in peace"), there is little other in the way of Jewish inscriptional appropriation of Christian language.[145]

The use of Job 19:25–27 was so prevalent in Christian funeral liturgies and inscriptions and so absent from Jewish funerary practices that it seems hard to believe that this was anything but an act of appropriation. But since Jewish funerary epigraphy almost by rule does not mention the bodily resurrection, and since this tombstone was written in Hebrew, perhaps this tombstone appropriates Job 19:25–27 from Christian practices and yet does not refer to the resurrection. Unlike the Vulgate and the LXX, this Hebrew inscription reads "he will rise up" ("יקום") with the MT; thus the redeemer "rises up last upon the dust," perhaps not in the sense of an attorney but rather as a "kinsman-redeemer" who will preserve this individual's name and ensure the continuance of the family estate.[146]

This appropriation might share some affinities with the interpretation of Saadiah Gaon (ca. 930 CE), which may also be gathered up in the semantic node of survival.[147] Saadiah's translation emphasizes the essential role of the community in the survival of legacies, memories, and stories:

(25) I know that the favored of God will survive,
and others after them will arise upon the soil;
(26) and after my skin is corrupted,
they will gather around this story of mine,
and from the ills of my body I shall show signs of God,

> (27) just as I witness myself, and mine eyes see nought that is foreign,
> when my piercing glances pierce my breast.[148]

Saadiah explains his reading in detail in his comments:

> I referred *And I know that go'ali liveth* to human beings rather than God, linking it to his prior statement (vv. 23–24), in which he wished his words to be transmitted, so that he might have a lasting remembrance that the favored among the faithful and further successors among their offspring in this world would pass on his story, as he says, and others after them will arise on the earth (v. 25). His object is to publish and make known to humanity the power of God. . . . That is why he says, *and from my flesh I witness to God,* meaning, I reveal him to humanity.[149]

In Saadiah's reading, the rock-hewn words of Job mentioned in 19:23–24 ensure the transmission of his story to the future generations that, as גאלים, survive him and pass on his story themselves, presumably to those who will carry it on after their own deaths. Perhaps the mutilated but still signifying tombstone in Venosa participates in this same project: the survival of the signifier. It seems as though someone from the Jewish community at Venosa took up the role of the גאל himself or herself in order to redeem the text, recovering it for Jewish use. Like Cassuto himself, as well as the broader field of *Wissenschaft des Judentums,* the anonymous Venosan Jew struggles with the past in order to redeem it and give it new life: a survival, perhaps even a type of purely immanent resurrection.

Though this brief study has only scratched the surface of the interpretive trajectory of survival, perhaps it may suffice to demonstrate the variety of different capacities that find expression even among what seem at first to be similar readings.

Presence

Readings gathered under the semantic node of presence approach Job 19:25–27 from a different angle. Instead of thinking of the end of Job's life, or even the end of the world, these readings consider 19:25–27 with the end of the book of Job in mind. In Job 38:1, YHWH emerges from a whirlwind, and the divinity briefly irrupts into Job's world. After the grandiloquent divine speeches, Job's second response (42:2–6) seems to mark a decisive turn. In 42:6, Job seems to say that his vision of God ("עיני ראתך"; cf. 19:27, "עיני ראו") has led him to relinquish his case.[150]

Job's words in 42:5–6 echo those in 19:25–27 ("ראו עיני//עיני ראתי" and "על-עפר"). Moreover, the threefold repetition of "sight" verbs in 19:26–27 parallels the pivotal thematic of sight in 42:6–7. It is not surprising, then, that many interpreters, even those in antiquity, construed 38:1–42:6 as the literary context in which to read 19:25–27. One example of this interpretive trajectory may be found in Hector Avalos's work in sensory criticism. Avalos notes what he calls the "visiocentricity" of the book of Job, or the "privileging of vision."[151] Avalos begins his with a particular reading of Job's utterance in 42:5 ("I had heard of you by the hearing of the ear, but now my eye sees you"), which Avalos interprets to mean that his seeing God "is an advance over, or culmination of, his previous experience with Yahweh."[152] And, in regard to Job 19:25–27, Avalos argues that "Job is quite adamant about hoping that he will see God regardless of his physical state."[153] In this reading the vision of God, and thus the sensation of the immediate presence of the divine, is Job's ultimate hope.[154]

In what follows, I can only gesture toward some of the interpretations that emanate from this semantic node of the text. If we return to the ancient world, we see that the Syriac Peshitta as well as early rabbinic midrash emphasize God's presence in 19:25–27 in strikingly different ways.

Syriac Peshitta: Revealing the Divine

Around the year 200 CE, readers from the Jewish community in the city of Edessa produced the Pesh, a Syriac translation of the biblical text.[155] The Pesh often woodenly replaces Hebrew words with Syriac cognates in the same syntactical order. Yet occasionally the Pesh is expansive or interpretive. In Job 19:25–27, the Syriac translators make sense of the Hebrew text by creative means, yet the text is still recognizable to those familiar with the MT or the LXX.

Pesh Job 19:25–27 reads as follows:

(25) w'n' yd' 'n' dprwqy ḥy hw wbswp' 'l 'r'' ntgl'
(26) w'l mšky hw 'tkrk hlyn w'l bry
(27) 'n tḥn' l'lh' 'yny ḥḥny nwhr' kwlyty msp hw gyr spt mn qymy

(25) I myself know that my redeemer lives,
and in the end he will be revealed upon the earth.
(26) But concerning my skin—
which these [things] have encircled—and upon my flesh:
(27) if my eye sees God, my heart will see the light.
But for now, my body has been consumed.

Several syntactical and semantic differences between the MT and Pesh Job are clear. Nevertheless it is possible that in this instance Pesh Job translated a *Vorlage* similar to the *Vorlage* of the MT, since most of the Syriac words in Pesh Job can be accounted for by the words present in the MT. The interpretive problems presented by the Hebrew text were solved by interpreting the passage as a theophany and translating connotations of words accordingly, dividing the verses differently than the MT, and rearranging the words in 19:27 to form a parallelistic structure.

In 19:25b, Pesh Job does not render Hebrew "קום" with the Syriac cognate "qym," though it does in every other instance.[156] Instead, Pesh Job has used the *ethpe'el* imperfect of the verb "gly," a cognate of Hebrew "גלה" with the identical gloss: "to uncover/reveal." In Pesh Job, Hebrew "גלה" is translated with Syriac "gly."[157] This substitution of one cognate for another is indicative of an interpretive decision, likely inspired by Pesh Job's translation of the troublesome word "אחרון" with the phrase "wbswp'" ("in the end"). Though the only other occurrence of "אחרון" in the Hebrew text of Job is translated in Pesh Job with its Syriac cognate, the Syriac word "swp" translates related words such as "אפס" (cf. Job 7:6).

The addition of the definite article and the preposition "in," both common in Pesh Job and generally acceptable in the translation of Hebrew poetry, allow for an otherwise grammatically unacceptable adverbial reading of "אחרון."[158] Taken this way, the notion of "rising" in "the end" likely connoted a theophany, and with the knowledge of the events of chapters 38–42, including YHWH's theophany (38:1), Pesh Job renders Hebrew "קום" with Syriac "gly." This interpretive move is underscored by the use of "'r''" instead of the cognate "'pr." While the translation of Hebrew עפר is inconsistent in Pesh Job, alternating between "'pr" (17:16) and "'r''" (20:11), the use of "'r''" ("ground, earth") more readily connotes the material world—as opposed to the heavens—as the location of the deity's theophanic manifestation. "Dust" does not clearly serve as an indicator of this trope.

Pesh Job reads both "אחר" and the "מן" from "מבשרי" as the Syriac preposition "'l," thus fashioning the parallel of skin//flesh with identical prepositions. As for the difficult Hebrew verb "נקפו," Pesh Job translates it as "נקף"-II, "to go around," as it is in Vulgate Job and OG Job. Pesh Job reads the difficult "זאת" as a substantive plural demonstrative, "these (things)," in order to find an adequate subject for the plural "נקפו." The final two words of Hebrew Job 19:26 have been combined with the first few words of 19:27.

We do not know whether Pesh Job read a text of Job 19:27 that varied significantly from the MT. But it is possible to reconstruct something akin to the Hebrew from the translation. Assuming that the *Vorlage* of Pesh Job is the same as that of the MT, several differences are striking: (1) the three verbs connoting sight have been reduced to two, the occurrence of "ראה" overlooked or combined with another verb of sight; (2) "ולא־זר" has morphed into "לאור" ("the light" with "ל" as a marker of the direct object), and (3) "my eyes" and "my kidneys" have been taken as the subjects of the sight verbs.

Pesh Job constructed grammatically and semantically parallel lines in its translation of verse 27, which might explain in part the difficult reading. The first two lines of the three-line verse, "tḥn' l'lh' 'yny" and "ḥḥny nwhr' kwlyty," share a verb-object-subject order, use the same initial verb, and both have body parts as the subject of the verb. It is likely that the translator noticed the multiplicity of words connoting sight and body parts and consequently constructed a parallelistic structure to sort out the syntax. The third line of the verse intensifies the usual Pesh Job translation of "כלה" (Syriac "swp"; cf. Job 4:9 and 7:6) and reads "חקי" metaphorically as "my position," the earlier repressed "qwm" here displacing another term. Either Pesh Job read a manuscript that differed from the MT and OG, or it translated difficult passages by rearranging words around a parallelistic structure, using the words left over—"בחקי" and "כלו"—to construct a third line. Since Kennicott and deRossi do not list any such witnesses to the MT and OG, the latter theory is more sound.[159]

Where the OG understood Job as speaking in the genre of a thanksgiving psalm, Pesh Job interprets Job's words as a prediction of the final theophany of the book. Like OG Job, Pesh Job understands Job's mention of his skin/flesh as metonymy for his great suffering. But, when Job sees God, his kidneys—namely, the things shot to pieces by God in Job 16:13—will "see the light." The translator uses a combination of two motifs—sight and light—which are used elsewhere in combination in the Pesh in the context of sharing a meal in the temple (Pesh Psalms 36:9), further suggesting the theophanic context. In short, Pesh Job construes this scene as a theophany. This reading depends on a particular construal of the verb "קום" in the context of the numerous sight verbs.[160]

Reading Presence: By Human Flesh, Seeing God

A large portion of the history of Jewish interpretation of Job 19:25–27 follows the theophanic trajectory also seen in the Syriac version. Not two centuries after the translation of the Pesh, we find a very similar reading in Genesis Rabba 48:1: "It is written, 'This, after my skin will have been peeled off, but from my flesh, I will see God' (Job 19:26). Abraham said, after I circumcised myself many converts came to cleave to this sign. 'But from my flesh, I will see God' [Job 19:26], for had I not done this [i.e., circumcised myself], on what account would the Holy Blessed One, have appeared to me? 'And the Lord appeared to him' [Gen 18:1]."[161] At this point in Genesis Rabba, the midrash is reading Genesis 18, wherein YHWH suddenly appears to Abraham "in the flesh" (1).[162] The events immediately preceding this encounter include the monumentally significant circumcision of Abraham and his family (17:1–27). As Daniel Boyarin explains, the midrash intuits that these two events are linked and then finds the perfect intertext to explain their precise relationship:

> Following its usual practices of interpretation, [the midrash] attributes a strong causal nexus to these events following on one another. Ostensibly, had Abraham not circumcised himself, God would not have appeared to him. This interpretation is confirmed by Job 19:26. . . . In this case, the verse of Job, which refers to the peeling off of

> skin, is taken by a brilliant appropriation to refer to the peeling off of the skin of circumcision, and the continuation of the verse that speaks of seeing God from one's flesh is taken as a reference to the theophany at Elon Mamre. . . . Circumcision of the flesh—i.e. peeling of the skin—provides the vision of God.[163]

Reading "נקפו" as a future anterior form of "נקף"-I ("will have been peeled off"), the midrash understands Job to be saying that one must have already been circumcised in order to see God. This explains Abraham's inability to see God before Genesis 17 as well as the sudden change in 18:1. And yet the midrash reads "נקפו" again, this time as "נקפו"-II: the converts "came to cleave to"—or "surround" (="הקף")—Abraham.[164] In this reading, two theophanies are linked: Job emphasizes his vision of God in 19:26–27, while Abraham receives God as a visitor in Genesis 18. As a result of these revelatory theophanies, many converts from nations have their own epiphany, namely, that the sign of Abraham reveals the divine.

Jewish mysticism soon appropriated this interpretation of Job 19:26 that read Job's cry under the rubric of divine presence. For the much later Zohar, "by means of circumcision one is opened up in such a way that God may be revealed; the physical opening engenders a space in which the theophany occurs."[165] The Zohar interprets Job 19:26 as such:

> He began another discourse and said, "But I would behold God from my flesh" (Job 19:26). Why [is it written] "from my flesh"? It should be rather "from myself"! It is, literally, "from my flesh." What is that [flesh]? As it is written, "The holy flesh will be removed from you" (Jer. 11:15), and it is written, "And my covenant will be in your flesh" (Gen. 17:13). It has been taught: he who is marked with the holy seal of that sign [of circumcision] sees the Holy One, blessed be He, from that very sign itself (I:94a).[166]

The Zohar begins by asking about the odd use of the word "בשר": why does Job see God with reference to his "flesh"? The answer, of course, is that Job was speaking about the power of the "holy seal" that allows one to see the divine "from that very sign itself"—that is, the specific point of the circumcised, absent flesh allows the divine presence to appear. This tension between presence and absence, the present deity and the absent flesh, constitutes an important element of Jewish mystical reading in general. As Elliot Wolfson notes, "The dynamic of circumcision. . . ., the play of closure/openness, . . . informs us about the nature of mystical hermeneutics as well: that which is hidden must be brought to light."[167]

Many other medieval Jewish interpreters agreed that this verse teaches that the human body is the locus of divine-human interaction, but they all proposed very different reasons why this is so. Samuel ben Nissim Masnut, for example, in his twelfth-century work *Ma'yan Ganim* interpreted Job 19:26 as follows: "'From my flesh I behold God,' is explained: 'From the formation of my limbs and from the arrangement of my body—contemplating them—I behold God.'"[168] Elsewhere, Masnut relates: "Abraham bar Hiyya closely follows Bahya in interpreting Job 19:26 to mean that 'from the formation of your body (literally, "flesh") and the arrangement of your limbs you can see and understand the wisdom of your Creator.'"[169] In this line of interpretation, the presence of the divine may be found through the very materiality of the human body. Here, the "מן" from "מבשרי" in 19:26 means that it is *by means of* my flesh that I see God. Whereas Genesis Rabba and the Zohar teach that a certain absence of flesh allowed for the presence of the divine, Masnut claims that the human body is the present sign that allows one to contemplate the absent deity. Still others took this call for bodily contemplation in a concrete sense, understanding it to sanction scientific study of human anatomy. Joseph ben Jehudah, the student of Maimonides, for example, cites Job 19:26 "as *locus probans* for the meritoriousness of studying medicine: 'From the wondrous formation of my body I recognize the wisdom of my Creator as manifold and wondrous.'"[170] These various interpretive strands have continued to diversify since the medieval period; in modern Jewish esoteric as well as philosophical discourses, the words of Job 19:26 still communicate a method of relating to the divine through the material of the human body.

Reading Presence: Seeing God in Human Flesh

Syriac-speaking Christians adopted the Jewish Pesh as their own translation of the Hebrew Bible, and as a result they inherited a textual tradition that, through the Syriac word *gly*, determined Job 19:25–27 as a statement concerning divine manifestation. Not surprisingly, Syriac Christians did not seem to think of this verse as fitting for funeral liturgies, and neither did they associate this passage with the resurrection.

In an eighth-century disputation, Sergius the Stylite offers the following argument to a Jewish interlocutor who claimed that God had not begotten a son: "Concerning the fact that for the sake of the salvation of humanity God came down from heaven, and put on a body, and was revealed on earth, Job said: I know that my savior lives, and at the last will be revealed on the earth."[171]

While Latin and Greek Christians generally understood Job to be speaking about the resurrection of the flesh, and for Jewish mystic readers the text taught that contemplation of various aspects of the human body would reveal aspects of the divine, Syriac Christians read this as a prophecy of the incarnation of Christ. For the Syriac Christian, Job's statement that his "redeemer" will be "revealed upon the earth" suggested that this redeemer could not, then, be an earthly creature. By specifying the earth as the locus of the revelation, Syriac Christians assumed that the redeemer must then not be on earth at the time of Job.

In Jacob of Serugh's (ca. 500 CE) fourth *memre* "Against the Jews," he also cites Job 19:25 to argue in favor of the Incarnation: "Job has said that he [i.e., the son of God] would be clearly revealed at the end, but he appeared on the earth in precisely the manner that he predicted."[172] Jacob here defends the use of Job 19:25 as a prediction of the Incarnation, presumably against criticisms that Jesus the Galilean did not seem to come with the clarity and force of a theophany. Yet Jacob responds: "Do not be blinded by the spirit of the Jewish sect, who, regarding him, do not see the son of God."[173] While Jacob's argument displays the characteristic churlish nature of Christian anti-Judaic discourses, his insults also play subtly on the text of Job 19:26–27. Job has promised that the redeemer will be clearly revealed on the earth, but the Syriac text also says "*if* my eye sees God" (19:27a), which implies that that problem may be with one's eyes ("Do not be blinded," "do not see the son of God") and not the manner of revelation.

Likewise, many later medieval Syriac theological treatises, such as those written by ninth-century Habib ibn Hidma, twelfth-century Dionysius bar Salibi, and thirteenth-century Bar Hebraeus, cite Job 19:26 as a proof text of the Incarnation.[174] Disputing the Incarnation with Muslims, bar Salibi while writes: "As a prophecy of incarnation, Job says: 'In the end he will be revealed to the ends of the earth—in the flesh.'[175] Here, Bar-Salibi's translation reduplicates the word "swp," giving it both a spatial ("ends of the earth") as well as temporal ("in the end") sense. While this claim advances the Christian argument for its universality, bar Salibi's final phrase, "in the flesh," creates significant tension: how could a particular human in a limited body extend his presence to the ends of the earth? Christians respond by gesturing to the paradox of the Incarnation itself: the universal divine became present to all of humanity through the particularity of one human.

Thus, the semantic node of presence, like that of survival, concerns itself with the nature of human flesh. Yet though these two groups of interpretations agree on much, their actual readings overlap in very few ways. It is as if these different groups of interpreters have constructed the *question* or *problem* posed by the text in different ways, and thus their responses by necessity propose very different solutions. As for the interpreters who understand Job 19:25–27 in terms of presence, they do not imagine that this text address the problem of the loss of human life, and thus they do not use this text to proclaim the recovery of fleshly health and abilities. Instead, these interpreters construe 19:25–27 as a solution to the problem of the separation between mundane flesh and transcendent divinity, seeing it as offering a particular way to restore the human-divine relationship. As for the specifics of this solution, readers vary considerably. For some, Job 19:25–27 teaches us that we may encounter the transcendent deity through contemplating human flesh, while others argue that Job 19:25–27 teaches us that the transcendent deity took the form of a mundane human body. In both scenarios, however, the originary problem is one of *absence:* humans are separated from the divinity but long for the divine presence. In very different ways, these Jewish and Christian readings all strain to overcome an ontological barrier between immanent and transcendent planes.

Justice

The interpretive trajectory of justice seeks to do justice to the text of the book of Job itself. Throughout the history of its reception, a surprising number of readers have managed to avoid the book of Job's probing questions and complex theological tensions. At times, however, careful readers with a tolerance for theological uncertainty have noticed that in the prologue the character of God creates quite an ethical mess. For example, in Job 2:3, God seems to casually admit that, though Job is an excellent person in every way, nevertheless God destroyed Job's life "for no reason." What sort of god, one might ask, would do this to a pious individual? For those inured to the language of Proverbs, this should come as quite a shock.

Here, the book of Job exposes a necessary tension between justice and law that sustains but simultaneously undermines both concepts.[176] While laws, including the legal system and the particular actions and decisions of judges and juries, are in theory particular instantiations of justice, each law or legal decision can only ever be a contingent, limited effort to render justice. Thus justice always exceeds any particular legal act, and as such any legal action must be scrutinized. Does it actually instantiate justice, or would justice be rendered more fully with an alternate law, legal system, or decision? Yet does justice exist without these particular instantiations? How would we know anything about justice if it we could not point to a court of law or a courageous defense of the rights of another person?

Israelite wisdom literature such as that found in the book of Proverbs generally claims that wisdom ultimately resides with the divine. Since God created and infused the heavens and the earth with wisdom, if sages devote themselves to its pursuit, they can catch glimpses of it (cf. Proverbs 3:19–20 and 8:22–36). In the Joban prologue, however, God admits to creating disharmony for no just cause (2:3). When Job recognizes that God's repeated assaults serve no purpose and indeed do not serve as a judgment—that is, are not *just*—Job simply concludes that God is unjust (9:22–24). Paradoxically, it is precisely at this point that Job decides to casts his interaction with God as a legal dispute, hoping beyond hope that justice itself transcends even God (cf. 23:5–7).[177]

Thus, the book of Job dramatizes a world in which divine justice should exist but tragically does not (cf. 12:6). God is the ultimate arbiter of justice but is unjust. God is the foundation and instantiation of the law but nevertheless is illegal or extralegal—beyond the touch of the law itself.

It is precisely here that Job gives voice to a hope for the possibility of legal vindication and ultimate justice even in a world where the foundation of justice is itself entirely unjust. Imaginatively, Job constructs a figure that personifies this justice beyond justice and dramatizes its forceful manifestation of the true law in God's presence (9:32–35, "מוכיח" ["arbiter"]; 16:18–22, "עד" ["witness"]; 19:25–27, "גאל" ["redeemer"]; 31:35–37, "לי שמע" ["one who hears me"]). Thus, the גאל of 19:25–27 embodies the excessive aspect of justice that has failed to inhere in the actions or principles of God, and Job calls for this excess to "rise up" on his behalf and force into being the coexistence of true justice and the law.

Generally, readings grouped in the semantic node of justice understand the word "גאל" in the sense of the "גֹּאֵל־הַדָּם," or "blood avenger." The figure of the avenger is provided for by the law (cf. Numbers 35:19) but operates outside of the legal system; this interstitial, extralegal (and yet lawful) mode of justice also points to the incongruity between justice and law. Job often laments God's lack of justice (Job 9:15–22); thus it is fitting that Job expresses his hope for a justice beyond God with the figure of the blood avenger. The blood avenger exists in the tension between justice and law. It is precisely this tension that drives Job's legal metaphor throughout the dialogues, and attentive readers throughout the ages have realized that the book provides no clear answers to these troubling problems.[178]

The twentieth-century Marxist Ernst Bloch, for example, sees the book of Job as a critical moment in the history of theological thought, since here Job "critiques theodicy as an ideology that is the opposite of faith[ful] protest and [the] hope for justice."[179] That is, Job dares to call God to task for failing to act in accordance with justice and thus for effectively abandoning those who suffer. Theodicy apologizes for God's failure to enact justice; Job realizes that these apologies distract one from the injustice that surrounds humanity.

According to Bloch, the whirlwind speeches, otherwise understood by the semantic node of presence as therapeutic theophany, underline the ultimate failure of theodicy to justify divine justice: "In fact, Yahweh's appearance and his words do everything to confirm Job's lack of faith in divine justice; far from being the theophany of the righteous God, they are like a divine atheism in regard to (or paying no attention to) the moral order. . . . [It is then] all the more certain that the would-be theodicy will turn out to be its opposite: the exodus of man from Yahweh, with the vision of a world that will rise above the dust (cf. 19:25)."[180] Bloch understands the God of the book of Job as a "divine atheist," one who does not believe in a principle of justice. As Bloch reads the text, Job courageously sets forth on an "exodus" from this false god who only serves to pacify those who are oppressed by suggesting either that they have earned their suffering or that *there is no justice* for which to fight. Yet in the figure of the גאל, which Bloch understands to refer not to God but rather to a blood avenger, the figure of the Exodus returns: "The Avenger-figure (19:25) is in fact closer to the Yahweh of Exodus, the Yahweh of 'Israel's courtship'—a spirit who has nothing at all in common with the present state of creation and world order."[181] Job thus rebels against the oppressive God of the book of Job while holding out hope for the return of the liberative power of the God of the Exodus, the God who has before fought against the unjust structure of power that exists in the world, symbolized by Pharaoh. This is the disruptive YHWH, who dismantles the unjust legal systems of those who oppress, who embodies the principle of justice beyond justice. Bloch is right that the divine speeches in the book of Job give no hint that God desires to upend the ethical and legal structure of the cosmos, even though were he to do so, it could result in a horrible breakdown of justice. Bloch seems to read Job's cry in a manner similar to Choon-Leong Seow, who understands Job's ironic reference to the גאל as a plea for God to once again claim the mantle of justice on behalf of those who suffer, effectively reclaiming the divine personality of the Exodus.[182]

Until the advent of critical biblical studies in the early modern era, the interpretive trajectory of justice seems to have been rather sparsely populated. Yet the potential for its manifestation was possible in the ancient world, as evidenced by the reading of Theodotion Job.[183] In the late Second Temple period, an anonymous Jewish translator's literal translation from the Hebrew text into Greek attempted to supplement or perhaps supplant the LXX.[184] The Theodotion translation of the book of Job survives only in fragments, but what remains of 19:25–27 reads as follows:

> (25) ὁ ἀγχιστεύς μου ζῇ καὶ ἔσχατον ἐπὶ χώματος ἀναστήσει
> (27) ἐξέλιπον οἱ νέφροι μου ἐν τῷ κόλπῳ μου[185]
>
> (25) My kinsman lives, and he will stand up last upon the earthen mound. . . .
> (27) My kidneys have become destitute in my chest.

Although Origen's sixth column of the Hexapla preserves little for the verses in question, it does appear that Theodotion Job allows for a reading quite different from either the theophanic Syriac or the lament-psalmic OG.

Theodotion Job's choice of "kinsman" ("ἀγχιστεύς") for "גאל" can be understood as a particularly wooden translation and thus of a piece with the overall translation profile associated with Theodotion Job.[186] For the only other use of the word "גאל" in MT Job (3:5), Theodotion Job supplies "ἀγχιστευσάτω," also a fairly wooden translation.[187]

While Theodotion Job does not force readers into a forensic interpretation of the text, it does offer the potential for reading "kinsman-redeemer," "legal vindicator" or "blood avenger" (and thus their forensic connotations) in a way that LXX Job and Pesh Job do not. Furthermore, in Theodotion Job this "kinsman" stands on "the earthen mound" ("χώματος"). This term, while vague, can potentially refer to Job's grave.

Within the existing literary context, it appears that readers of Theodotion Job could understand 19:25–27 to claim that Job's kinsman-redeemer will violently avenge Job's death or that Job's kinsman will continue to assert Job's legal complaint even after his death. The object of this vengeance would, in Theodotion Job's time, more likely be understood to be the friends and not God. Job has, in this same chapter, accused the friends of dismembering him (19:2), and in response to the friends' verbal attacks (19:28), he follows 19:25–27 with a warning that there will be "a punishment of the sword" that renders "a judgment" (19:29). Ancient readers could understand Job's angry complaints directed at God to culminate in this call for a "kinsman" to continue voicing his complaints.

The forensic potential available to the MT and some Greek versions did, in fact, manifest itself—albeit rarely—in the medieval period. Several prominent medieval Jewish interpreters seem to have understood Job's cry for a גאל to be a request for a גאל־הדם. Rashi stresses this element of Job's plea:

> "But I know that my Redeemer lives": You persecute me, but I know that my Redeemer lives to requite you, and He will endure and rise. "And the last on the earth, He will endure": After all earth dwellers will perish, He will endure last. "And after my skin, they have cut into this": Yet they do not pay heed to my Redeemer, but after the plague of my skin, they cut, strike, and pierce. This vexation and persecution that I mentioned, which is to me like one cutting into my skin.[188]

That is, Rashi sees God as Job's גאל־הדם, who is ready to wreak havoc on Job's friends for persecuting him. At issue is neither Job's physical restoration nor Job's interaction with God; rather, Rashi envisions a particular assertion of justice on behalf of Job.

Leopold Zunz, the nineteenth-century Jewish historian and founder of *Wissenschaft des Judentums,* provided perhaps the most compelling formulation of this semantic node. In 1845, Zunz published a history of Jewish culture, *Zur Geschichte und Literatur,* in which he analyzed the ways Jews commemorated their righteous dead, elaborating on the history of tombstones and epitaphs.[189] In a chapter titled "Remembrance of the Righteous," Zunz defended his seemingly antiquarian interests in vandalized tombstones and worn inscriptions. For Zunz, his work was not merely an escape into the past. His micro-histories helped the

Jewish community to reclaim the memory of their own past, to give honor to the righteous dead, and to protect and pass down their names.[190] In short, Zunz sought to redeem the repressed memories of the oppressed European Jews.

Dominant Christian construals of Jewish history had, for the most part, denigrated and marginalized Jews. For centuries the "histories" of the 1096 Christian massacre of Jews in the town of Worms had either recounted the story dispassionately or actively characterized the Jews as aggressors or thieves.[191] Yet Moses Mannheimer, following the work of Zunz, saw these events instead as a tragedy that cries out for justice. Mannheimer argued that those slain Jewish inhabitants of Worms did not deserve death, nor were they being tested: on the contrary, they were tragic martyrs for the Jewish cause. Mannheimer then encouraged Jewish scholars across Europe to restore and preserve Jewish tombstones, including the tombstone of twelve of the Jewish martyrs from Worms. Ludwig Lewysohn, a participant in this effort, wrote: "Soon 800 years will pass since these horrifying events took place. The memory of these immortal martyrs will be kept alive by their descendants. . . . This painful and extensive, anguished and glorious past may teach Israel the task for the present and its obligation to the future."[192] Like Zunz, Lewysohn sought to persuade Jewish historians to reread and thus redefine the past for the sake of those who have already perished.

Thus, Zunz saw his work as primarily redemptive in nature—restoring the memories of the dead if not the dead themselves. Noting that, quite often, the tombstones of medieval Jews were mutilated or reused, Zunz lamented that, though time had "extinguished the memory" of the deceased, they nevertheless continued to be "wounded" in death. Zunz triumphantly cited his own idiosyncratic translation of Job 19:25, which reads: "Aber es lebt ihnen ein Anwald, und wär' es der späteste, der auf dem Staube aufsteht!" (But there is a living advocate for them, and he will be the last to arise from the dust!).[193] For Zunz, the mantle of Job's גאל could be claimed by the historian. Writing history allows one to function as the advocate, the vindicator, the redeemer of the past, the one who restores justice by rereading and rewriting the dominant histories of the day. Zunz's translation of Job thus invokes an understanding of history in which the Jewish historian is called on to be the advocate of the Jewish dead.

Walter Benjamin, discussing the writing of history, agrees with Zunz that history can be used as a weapon to harm even the dead by destroying their memories but argues that by the same token, the historian can work against this enemy: "Only that historian will have the gift of fanning the spark of hope in the past who is firmly convinced that even the dead will not be safe from the enemy if he wins. And this enemy has not ceased to be victorious."[194] Though Zunz fought on behalf of the memories of a specific people, one may take a broader view of this project of historical redemption. In the face of historical injustices, the reception historian, like Leopold Zunz, can advocate for the inclusion of those interpretive voices whose memories have been all but extinguished.

Conclusion

Whatever Job says in 19:25–27, it stands in contrast to the extended lament uttered in 19:2–22. Job may wish that his cry be heard in a celestial court of law; he could hope for a theophanic encounter with the divine; or he may imagine a recovery of the various aspects of his life. All of these constructions of the text assume that Job here images something other than his current state. The tension between what is and what should (or will) be forms part of the contour of this text. Hope implies a difference between present and future, and thus Job implicitly asks readers to ponder the relationship between the actual situation and its virtual potentiality for change. Like the manifold readings of the text itself, Job's cry gestures toward the dynamic capacities of the process of life.

Each semantic node that I have articulated determines this tension between the actual and the virtual in a different manner. Each reading opens up different problematic fields to explore. The node of survival explores the complex relationship between life and death. The node of presence imagines different modes of associating—but not sublating—the material and the transcendental. Finally, the node of justice surveys the tension between the contingency of local manifestations of law and justice itself. All three of these interpretive nodes proffer a constellation of concepts that have no clear resolution. Rather, they create a space within which one may think. This space functions as an internal border that runs through the middle of the text as well as through each concept one may use to interpret it. Here is the truly natural, necessary borderline: it is the internal complicating folds that precede any external differentiation.

CONCLUSION

Nomadology and the Future of Biblical Studies

If there is an island of consensus amid the turbulent sea of biblical scholarship, it is this: wherever we encounter them, biblical texts are not quite at home. The biblical text has an uneasy relationship with modern contexts, to be sure—hence the very need for something like biblical scholarship. Yet even the oldest surviving fragments of biblical texts are displaced. Genesis cannot call Qumran "home," and neither can Numbers 6 point to Ketef Hinnom as its point of origin. Wherever there is a biblical text, the biblical scholar senses something unsettled about it. Biblical texts were displaced even within the hypothetical contexts that biblical scholars would claim were the "original" contexts. Moreover, the biblical text changes constantly through its long history. Thus it seems appropriate to describe the biblical text with vocabulary borrowed from the most prominent of biblical motifs, namely, the plight of displaced persons.

But there are different kinds of displacement. One might imagine the biblical text as an exile and thus as being forcibly removed from a beloved homeland and plunged into the chaos of a foreign context. Like Hebrews held in bondage in Egypt or Judaeans living in Babylonian captivity, biblical texts struggle with their decontextualized state, but always pine for their proper home, a place where they make sense. This is the idea of the text held by many so-called historical critical biblical scholars who work diligently to return these texts triumphantly to their native grounds. As we have seen, however, discerning the boundary between the homeland and exile seems impossible.

In contrast, one might conceive of the text as a migrant, one who decides to leave a homeland and strike out for other places that may hold brighter futures. The migrant person leaves because he or she is displaced within the homeland—perhaps for economic reasons, like, for example, the unemployed person who seeks work elsewhere, or cultural reasons, like the religious minority who seeks shelter in a more tolerant place. The migrant leaves an identifiable homeland and moves to another situated, sedentary, identifiable place in order to find a new home or something that will someday become a proper homeland, moves from one identity to another. One might think of Abraham and Sarah, who left their well-defined land and kin and set out for another particular place that had been promised.

Many biblical scholars unhappy with the exilic model of scholarship instead imagine the biblical text as a migrant. Redactional and canonical critics note the internal diversity, displacement, and growth signaled by the shape of the biblical texts themselves but nevertheless often name a single form of text to serve as the proper context or final form: the true homeland that the migrant reached at last. It seems as if many reception historians embrace this narrative as well. The text comes from a well-defined homeland, an original context and then heads to other well-defined locales to settle down and learn to be at home again. One also sees this impulse in the genealogical models that take inspiration from Michel Foucault, who is fascinated by the way ideas, bodies, and objects are molded into distinct forms with prescribed meanings in various contexts.[1] Yet the idea of the migrant text continues to presuppose the idea of a true homeland. Moreover, the very problems that disrupt any search for an original homeland or an original textual form also disrupt any search for an adopted homeland. Finding a home means stopping, settling down, becoming sedentary. And that is one thing these texts never seem to do.

In this book, I have offered a new model of the biblical text, one that draws on reception history's potential to conceive of texts as nomads instead of as refugees or migrants.[2] Nomads do not come from any fixed point, and neither are they headed toward any fixed point. Instead of yearning to return to one sedentary location the like exile or shifting between two sedentary locations like the migrant, the nomad is always moving between and beyond fixed points. For the nomad, there is no origin and no endpoint. Even for nomads who follow traditional routes, any point at which the he or she stops to rest is no more home than anywhere else. But neither is it less home than anywhere else. Home is a process—the road itself. Movement and change *is* the sedentary state.

Nomadology is the attempt to think about the nomad without conceiving of it in sedentary terms. It is the practice of studying processes without reducing them to a series of fixed points seen from a fixed perspective. The nomadologist would claim that biblical scholars confuse the momentary pauses of the nomadic text with its true home and mistake its fleeting expressions for its true essence. In order to study the nomad, one must follow the tracks through the steppe and watch for patterns of movement and action that always change over time and space. One must see how the nomad reacts to the ever-changing scenery. And one must keep an eye out for the nomad's multiple identities and shifting abilities and look at the scene from the many different perspectives opened up by the nomad's wandering steps.

In order to offer a perspective on my own meandering text, perhaps it would be best to retrace my own steps. I introduced this book with a brief meditation on borders, divides, and gaps. If reception history is a study of the text and its meanings that arise after its original context, then what, I asked, separates the original text from its receptions? Where does one draw the line?

I have concluded that the very notion of the original text of a biblical book is a paradox that obfuscates the processual dimension of all texts, especially those related to the traditions of a community—or, more precisely, many communities. The processual nature of biblical texts requires us to think in terms of time, and thus we must understand change—or difference—to be a fundamental part of the identity of biblical texts. That is, *internal difference* marks the identity of any biblical text. Furthermore, there is no natural or necessary hierarchy that emerges from the group of manuscripts, including translations, that function as the biblical text. One may organize these versions of the text in many different ways by means of many different criteria. Relative age is only one possibility, but there are others. I have offered a general means of drawing lines in order to differentiate texts (e.g., the book of Job from Testament of Job), but I have not found clear borderlines running between different forms of the same text. The OG version of Job, for example, is very different than the MT version of Job, but one cannot justify the idea that either of them stands as the "original" and thus clarifies the border between "the original book of Job" and "the reception of the book of Job."

I have also concluded that the very notion of the "original context" of a biblical book is a problematic concept. Biblical texts are, from the very moment of their initial inscription, already sedimented with various semantic, literary, and historical contexts. In addition, contexts themselves are not given, predetermined and predelineated units that automatically clarify the referential structure of texts. On the contrary, contexts initially provide the raw materials for an active determination (or construction) that then bears the title of "the context." Contexts are, from the very start, capable of signifying very different things to different people. While some construals are *wrong*, there is no particular construal of a context that is *right* in any universal sense. Contexts, like texts, can mean many things. There are no clear borderlines that differentiate even the "original context" of a text from "later contexts" in which one would find "receptions." Instead, borders separate a context from itself: that is, the many different potential determinations of a particular context show that the difference between original and reception resides within every context, even before it emerges in space and time.

As a result, I have concluded that reception history is *nothing* if it is understood as analyzing that which comes after the original. There is no such thing, since there was nothing entirely original in the first place. But by that same token, *everything* is then reception history if it is understood as analyzing how unoriginal texts manifest unoriginal meanings. I have therefore offered a different conception of reception history that does not found itself on a division between the original text, its original context, and later texts and contexts. Instead, one may understand the biblical text as a series of processes—text, reading, transmutations, and nonsemantic impact—whose nature it is to change over time. This change can manifest potentials proper to the text (e.g., different readings that account for the text in different but equally justifiable ways), or it can reorder the structure of the text from without (e.g., scribal redactions or translations), thus changing the constellation of potential readings that it may produce.

In order to think of both the local realizations of the text as well as its excess in relation to all of its local realizations, I turn to the thought of Gilles Deleuze. Three of Deleuze's concepts prove helpful for the task of reimagining biblical reception history. Approaching the biblical text in terms of its virtual and actual dimensions instead of thinking of it in terms of the possible and the actual accounts for the possibilities—or potentials—of a text that may not be present at hand but are nevertheless very real. For example, my own reading of Job 19:25–27 actualizes what was always a virtual potential of that text, even if it is a novel reading. One could certainly judge a particular reading as "not real," or not a part of a text's virtual capacities, but one could not claim that a potential reading should not be actualized. This shift may help biblical scholars to allow for the multiplicity of a given text's potential significations while nevertheless retaining the capacity for critical judgments.

Deleuze's emphasis on thinking in terms of problematic structures instead of in terms of problems in search of the correct solution is likewise constructive. In some aspects of life, the latter is doubtless more helpful, but for the criticism of literature, the former helps a reader to see far more of a text's capacities. Deleuze also offers biblical scholars a means of adjudicating between "good" and "bad" readings through the metaphor of topology. In topology, forms are considered homeomorphic if they can be stretched into each other without ripping or suturing. In the same way, two readings of a text may be considered virtual semantic potentials of that text if they can account for the text and its literary context without deforming the text to the point of collapse.

A nomadic reception history tells the story of the text's development by portraying the text as the protagonist. In order to achieve this goal, the reception historian must seek a viewpoint—or, more precisely, a series of different viewpoints—that reveals the text's own variation over time. With a mass of viewpoints in hand, the reception historian can then attempt to sort through them by means of nomadic distribution, which is Deleuze's term for an organization of material via internal, not external, criteria. In practice, this method asks reception historians to group readings by the contours of the readings themselves rather than the nationality, or religion, or gender, or temporal horizon of the given readers. I have suggested that reception historians may find it helpful to posit semantic nodes from which to gather diverse readings into manageable groups that are different yet nevertheless comparable. These semantic nodes are heuristic devices that aid in the sorting of materials, but they also should reflect general determinations of a given text's problematic structure.

Finally, offering the example of Job 19:25–27, I have shown that the original text and context harbor within themselves an array of potential determinations. These virtual multiplicities are brimming with semantic capacities that can be actualized in very different ways. I have gathered together diverse readings under three semantic nodes: survival, presence, and justice.

In short, this entire work has concerned itself with borderlines, or that which creates space between two separate entities. Repeatedly, I have found that this spacing exists not between different manuscripts or different contexts but rather as an internal differentiation within each text that simultaneously creates the conditions that allow for that text and its significance to change over time and limits any particular manifestation of a text or its significance from achieving dominance over the others since it, too, is but one of many potentials. In other words, everything is both its own original and its own reception—simultaneously source text and translation. The thing itself is its own boundary, and the natural lines are the internal ones.

As a result, I suggest that the time is ripe to reconceive the task of the biblical scholar. Though we should not ignore the putatively original contexts or the earliest recoverable forms of the text—surely they are just as important as any other contexts or forms—we must realize that any one determination of a text, context, or meaning is a limited and impoverished viewpoint on the given objectile. A single determination of a text reveals merely a fraction of that text's contour.

Within the field of biblical studies, we too often shut out the voices and memories of those who have actively participated in the production, redaction, preservation, and ongoing development of the text by constructing a line where none exists and imposing a hierarchy of text and meaning, subordinating some and glorifying others. The great divide does not run through any historical era, nor does it run between particular ethnic or religious groups; it does not divide texts into claimants and pretenders, nor does it bless one meaning as the real meaning of a text, relegating the others to the status of phantasms. It does not authorize, and it does not pathologize. It does not discern the true descendants from the bastard children. Rather, the true great divide—the divide between virtual potential and actual expression—runs through the middle of every text, asking, "What can this text do?"

NOTES

Introduction

1. On the distinction between reception history and traditional methods that produce proper biblical criticism, see Barton, *The Nature of Biblical Criticism*, 86.

2. See Seow, *Job 1–21*, for an extensive study of the prehistory of the book of Job.

3. I treat both of these scenarios as part of reception history merely for the sake of convenience. They overlap, at minimum, in their attention to the function of texts in various contexts, especially those contexts removed from the text's authors or editors. I use the phrase "reception history" only because it is widely known. Jacques Derrida and Henri Ronse's discussion of paleonymy broaches the subject of the metaphysical baggage that may accompany a term such as "reception history"; see *Positions*, 71.

4. Barr, *The Concept of Biblical Theology*, 447. See also Barton, *Oracles of God*, x.

5. Collins, *A Short Introduction to the Hebrew Bible*, 13.

6. Gunn, *"Judges" through the Centuries*, iv.

7. Some members of the BBC editorial board have employed this assumption in other settings. For example, John Sawyer writes that "what people believe the Bible means has often been more significant that what it originally meant. . . . It can also be fascinating and valuable to reconstruct what the world was like in the ancient Near East, and how teachings and prophecies of the Bible were originally understood by their earliest listeners or readers. . . . The study of postbiblical readings and artistic representations is known as reception history, or *Wirkungsgeschichte*" (*A Concise Dictionary of the Bible and Its Reception*, ix). Other editors have expressed other opinions, and individual volumes in the series manage this boundary in different ways.

8. Klauck et al., introduction, ix.

9. Seow, "Reflections on the History of Consequences," 563.

10. Sherwood, *A Biblical Text and Its Afterlives*, 9–10.

11. See Benjamin, "The Task of the Translator," Derrida, "Des tours de Babel," and Detweiler, "Overliving."

12. Tod Linafelt's work explores how texts such as Isaiah 40–66 and *Targum Lamentations* function as "survivals" of Lamentations 1–2. Though Linafelt does not offer a thorough discussion of the border between *vie* and *sur-vie*, his work, like Sherwood's, serves as a model for creative and careful reading. See *Surviving Lamentations*.

13. Gunn, *Judges through the Centuries*, 18.

14. See Newsom, "Genesis 2–3 and 1 Enoch 6–16."

15. Johnson, "Literary Criticism of Luke–Acts," 159.

16. Ricoeur, *Interpretation Theory*, 87–94.

17. Eagleton, *Literary Theory,* 64.

18. It is also important to note that Stanley Fish, the most famous of the reader-response critics, is persuasive only up to the point that he remains ambivalent about borders: Fish defers questions about the borders between interpretive communities and the different factions within a single interpretive community (e.g., questions concerning the boundary between reader and text: "What is that act an interpretation of? I cannot answer that question, but neither, I would claim, can anyone else"). See *Is There a Text in This Class?,* 165. One can sense infinite regress: how could an interpretive community understand the communal rules of interpretation of a text without already being able to decipher discourse, since the interpretive rules must be learned by means of discourse? In other words, interpretations are texts too: how do we read those enough to learn the rules that guide them? Perhaps more problematic is the Hegelian rejoinder: how do you know about that boundary between the interpretation and whatever that interpretation is an interpretation of if you do not already know that there is a text on the other side of that border?

19. See the essays in Knoppers and Levinson, *The Pentateuch as Torah;* see also Choi, *Traditions at Odds,* 3–5.

20. Choi, *Traditions at Odds,* 3–4.

21. Choi, *Traditions at Odds,* 2–3.

22. Kugel, *How to Read the Bible,* 7–8.

23. See Bernstein, "'Rewritten Bible.'"

24. Rowland, "A Pragmatic Approach to Wirkungsgeschichte."

25. Martindale, introduction, 9.

26. Nicholls, *Walking on the Water,* 27.

27. For example, see Gadamer, *Truth and Method,* 267–382.

28. Gadamer, *Truth and Method,* 366.

29. See, for example, Fish, *Is There a Text in This Class?,* 303–21.

30. See Gadamer, *Truth and Method,* 285.

31. For example, Gadamer claims that, in reading, the horizon of the object is "projected" by the interpreter in order to maintain the tension implied (and thus separation and difference, hence a strong border) in the act of understanding; this projected horizon is then "fused" in a "regulated way" through the "historically effected consciousness." This dialogue presupposes "otherness" and "a historical horizon that is different from the horizon of the present," yet Gadamer's insistence on continuity can be seen in his discussion of tradition and historically effected consciousness (see 305); his distaste for locating the true meaning in merely what has come from the past is also evident (see 366).

32. Gadamer, *Truth and Method,* 302.

33. Gadamer, *Truth and Method,* 298.

34. Gadamer, *Truth and Method,* 305–306.

35. Gadamer, *Truth and Method,* 295.

36. Gadamer, *Truth and Method,* 397, 396. Reconstructing the original author and audience is impossible if conceived of as a determinant judgment that can be proven, but it can also be conceived of as a judgment using a concept of reason, in which case the judgment can be disputed but not proven.

37. Gadamer, *Truth and Method,* 305, 457.

38. Gadamer, *Truth and Method,* 390.

39. Gadamer, *Truth and Method,* 460. Notice the singularity of the term "meaning" throughout Gadamer's discussion of texts.

40. Gadamer, *Truth and Method,* 303.

41. Gadamer, *Truth and Method,* 305.

42. Jauss, "The Identity of the Poetic Text in the Changing Horizon of Understanding," 7–8.

43. Jauss, *Toward an Aesthetic of Reception,* 29, 22.

44. In the memorable words of George Spencer-Brown, "We cannot make an indication without drawing a distinction" (*Laws of Form,* 1).

45. Peirce, *Collected Papers,* 98.

46. See, for example, Trotter, *Reading Hosea in Achaemenid Yehud,* 37–50.

1. The Miltonesque Concept of the Original Text

1. Emanuel Tov claims, for example, that "literary developments subsequent to the edition of M [the Masoretic text] are excluded from discussion. This pertains to presumed midrashic developments in the books of Kings, Esther, and Daniel reflected in G [the Greek version]" (*Textual Criticism of the Hebrew Bible,* 316).

2. See Martin's fascinating *Multiple Originals,* 9–61, which surveys the concept of the original text in several cognate fields. This chapter dovetails with Martin's book, as both examine the fluidity of text and meaning. My work focuses on the line between the original and its reception, since it seeks theoretical grounding for reception history. As such, I focus more on the particular ideas of particular biblical textual critics.

3. Barton, *The Nature of Biblical Criticism,* 41–43, for example, lays out objections to the phrase "original text."

4. Barton, *The Nature of Biblical Criticism,* 71.

5. See Tov, *Textual Criticism of the Hebrew Bible,* 177.

6. Tov, *Textual Criticism of the Hebrew Bible,* 168.

7. Epp, "The Multivalence of the Term 'Original Text' in New Testament Textual Criticism," 253.

8. Kenney, "Textual Criticism," 191; Hendel, "The Oxford Hebrew Bible," 329.

9. Hendel, "The Oxford Hebrew Bible," 332.

10. A new edition of Tov's introduction was published during the editing process of this book. While there are many new conversations and different points of view represented in Tov's updated work, it retains the qualified definition of original text and many of the quotations cited in this book remain.

11. Tov has at times hedged his more static (but still very influential) model of the original text. See his "The Status of the Masoretic Text in Modern Text Editions of the Hebrew Bible." See also Lemmelijn, "What Are We Looking for in Doing Old Testament Text-Critical Research?"

12. Some scholars even argued in favor of textual pluriformity before the discoveries; see Kahle, "Unterschungen zur Geschichte des Pentateuchtextes."

13. For example, the MT exhibits reworking of the books of Jeremiah and 1–2 Samuel in comparison to the OG. The OG, Tov argues, represents a post-MT expanded Hebrew *Vorlage* for OG 3 Kingdoms (=1 Kings), Esther, and Daniel. See Tov, "The Many Forms of Scripture."

14. Tov, *Textual Criticism of the Hebrew Bible,* 107, 114. Tov calls the Second Temple–era orthography "Qumran practice," while Ulrich ("The Dead Sea Scrolls and the Hebrew Scriptural Texts") argues that these scrolls reflect a wider phenomenon throughout Palestine and thus should not be labeled as a sectarian style. Evidence of early forms of biblical books that were later edited by the Samaritans is found in 4QpaleoExod[m]; see Sanderson, *An Exodus Scroll from Qumran.*

15. See Tov, *Textual Criticism of the Hebrew Bible,* 116, for a list of various Qumran manuscripts that contain unaligned readings; most important are texts that show significant variations, such as 4QJosh[a] 4QJudg[a] and 4QSam[a]. Tov estimates that "nonaligned" texts comprise a full 35 percent of Qumran scrolls.

16. As attested by, for example, 4QJer[b,d]; see Tov, "The Literary History of the Book of Jeremiah in the Light of Its Textual History."

17. See Tov, *Textual Criticism of the Hebrew Bible,* 177–79.

18. Tov, *Textual Criticism of the Hebrew Bible,* 1.

19. Tov, *Textual Criticism of the Hebrew Bible,* 183.

20. Tov, *Textual Criticism of the Hebrew Bible,* 177.

21. Tov, *Textual Criticism of the Hebrew Bible,* 195.

22. See Ulrich, *The Dead Sea Scrolls and the Origins of the Bible,* 93, and Tov's admission of the same in *Textual Criticism of the Hebrew Bible,* 93n34.

23. Lange, "'They Confirmed the Reading' (*y. Ta'an* 4.68a)," 51, 77.

24. Tov, *Textual Criticism of the Hebrew Bible,* 179.

25. Tov, *Textual Criticism of the Hebrew Bible,* 178.

26. For an overview of the problem posed by the Qumran variants, see Bogaert, "De Baruch à Jérémie."

27. Tov, *Textual Criticism of the Hebrew Bible,* 179.

28. Tov seems to follow Christian Ginsburg, who argues that "the words of the text, especially of the Pentateuch, were now finally settled, and passed over from the Soferim or redactors to the safe keeping of the Massorites. Henceforth the Massorites became the authoritative custodians of the traditionally transmitted text. Their functions were entirely different from their predecessors the Soferim" (*Introduction to the Massoretico-Critical Edition of the Hebrew Bible,* 421). See Van Seters, *The Edited Bible,* 60–112, for a detailed examination of this very question.

29. Ulrich, *The Dead Sea Scrolls and the Origins of the Bible,* 11.

30. Ulrich, *The Dead Sea Scrolls and the Origins of the Bible,* 39; see also Sanderson, *An Exodus Scroll from Qumran.*

31. 4QReworked Pentateuch is attested to by five fragmentary manuscripts, two of which, 4Q364 and 4Q365, contain significant text. The Song of Miriam occurs in 4Q365=4QRP[c].

32. Ulrich, *The Dead Sea Scrolls and the Origins of the Bible,* 115–20; Flint, *The Dead Sea Psalms Scrolls and the Book of Psalms,* 202–27. See also Segal, "4QReworked Pentateuch Or 4QPentateuch?," and Tov, *Textual Criticism of the Hebrew Bible,* 27.

33. See Tigay, "Conflation as a Redactional Technique."

34. As Julius Wellhausen notes, "The border between the text and gloss [is] so fluid that one does not know whether the removal of a verse that interrupts the context, belongs to the task of the textual or to that of literary criticism" (qtd. in Saebø, *On the Way to Canon,* 43). Sæbø also notes his own work with Zachariah, in which he saw that "the transmission of the text turned out to be productive, not only reproductive" (*On the Way to Canon,* 44).

35. See Tov, *Textual Criticism of the Hebrew Bible,* 319–27, for an overview of the textual problems in Jeremiah.

36. See Tov, *Textual Criticism of the Hebrew Bible,* 325–27, for the texts of the different versions.

37. Tov, *Textual Criticism of the Hebrew Bible,* 326.

38. One might analyze how the paradoxical "final/original" functions as a "transcendental signifier," or an anchor that organizes a conceptual system only by virtue of its ability to play several contradictory roles. See Bennington and Derrida, *Jacques Derrida,* 61.

39. Tov, *Textual Criticism of the Hebrew Bible,* 189.

40. For Greek corrections toward the MT, see Barthélemy, *Les devanciers d'Aquila;* for a brief discussion of nonaligned texts see Tov, *Hebrew Bible, Greek Bible, and Qumran,* 148–49.

41. See Cross, "The Ammonite Oppression of the Tribes of Gad and Reuben." For a brief overview of the issue, see Tov, *Textual Criticism of the Hebrew Bible,* 342–44.

42. Rofé, "The Acts of Nahash according to 4QSam[a]"; Tov, *Textual Criticism of the Hebrew Bible,* 343–44.

43. Tov, *Textual Criticism of the Hebrew Bible,* 191.

44. Tov, *Textual Criticism of the Hebrew Bible,* 189.

45. de Lagarde, *Anmerkungen zur griechischen Übersetzung der Proverbien,* 1–2.

46. See *b. Ketub* 106a, the reference to a "corrected scroll" in *b. Pesah* 112a, the "uncorrected scroll" in *b. Ketub* 19b, the three differing scrolls in the temple and the procedure used to adjudicate variants in *y. Ta'an.* 4.68a, and the exhortation to accuracy in *b. Sot* 20a (Tov, *Textual Criticism of the Hebrew Bible,* 32–33).

47. See Tov, *Textual Criticism of the Hebrew Bible,* 28–29.

48. See Tov, *Textual Criticism of the Hebrew Bible,* 28–29.

49. Tov, *Hebrew Bible, Greek Bible, and Qumran,* 177.

50. For a detailed overview, see Van Seters, *The Edited Bible,* 60–79.

51. See Albrektson, "Reflections on the Emergence of a Standard Text of the Hebrew Bible," 57.

52. See Levy, *Fixing God's Torah,* 7, and Ulrich, *The Dead Sea Scrolls and the Origins of the Bible,* 9. For a discussion of *y. Tal'an* 4.68a, see Van Seters, *The Edited Bible,* 65–79.

53. For an argument that the proto-MT scrolls were not given pride of place in the temple, see Lange, "'They Confirmed the Reading' (*y. Ta'an* 4.68a)," 29–80.

54. See Van Seters, *The Edited Bible,* 72.

55. Tov, *Hebrew Bible, Greek Bible, and Qumran,* 181.

56. See Tov, *Hebrew Bible, Greek Bible, and Qumran,* 181–88.

57. Ulrich, *The Dead Sea Scrolls and the Origins of the Bible,* 32.

58. Tov draws "qualitative and quantitative" distinctions between "authors-editors" who worked before the moment of the authoritative text and "copyists" who worked afterward (*Textual Criticism of the Hebrew Bible,* 190).

59. See Ulrich, *The Dead Sea Scrolls and the Origins of the Bible,* 1–50, and Saebø, *On the Way to Canon,* 36–46, for textual pluriformity at Qumran.

60. Tov, *Textual Criticism of the Hebrew Bible,* 189; see 258–85 for various types of intentional scribal alterations in proto-Masoretic and Masoretic texts.

61. See Tov, *Textual Criticism of the Hebrew Bible,* 282–83, 333–34.

62. See Tov, *Textual Criticism of the Hebrew Bible,* 270.

63. Tov, *Textual Criticism of the Hebrew Bible,* 283.

64. Tov, *Textual Criticism of the Hebrew Bible,* 85.

65. Tov, *Textual Criticism of the Hebrew Bible,* 178.

66. Tov, *Textual Criticism of the Hebrew Bible,* 28–29.

67. Tov, *Textual Criticism of the Hebrew Bible,* 39–67.

68. See Bennington and Derrida, *Jacques Derrida,* 241–58.

69. Hendel, "The Oxford Hebrew Bible," 324–51. For a critical review, see Williamson, "Do We Need a New Bible?"

70. Hendel, "The Oxford Hebrew Bible," 334.

71. Hendel, "The Oxford Hebrew Bible," 326.

72. Hendel, "The Oxford Hebrew Bible," 329–33.

73. Hendel, "The Oxford Hebrew Bible," 333; see also Tov, *Textual Criticism of the Hebrew Bible,* 177–79.

74. Hendel, "The Oxford Hebrew Bible," 333.

75. Hendel, "The Oxford Hebrew Bible," 331.

76. Hendel, "The Oxford Hebrew Bible," 332.

77. Hendel, "The Oxford Hebrew Bible," 335.

78. Hendel, "The Oxford Hebrew Bible," 331.

79. Hendel, "The Oxford Hebrew Bible," 327.

80. Hendel, "The Oxford Hebrew Bible," 327.

81. Hendel, "The Oxford Hebrew Bible," 333.

82. Hendel argues that the "point" at which composition transforms into transmission corresponds to a shift from "major to minor textual intervention" ("The Oxford Hebrew Bible," 332).

83. See Wills, *The Jew in the Court of the Foreign King,* 87–121.

84. See Collins, *Daniel,* 220; see also 2–38.

85. For example, in OG Daniel 4:43a, ms. 88 and Syro-Hexaplar read "whoever are caught saying anything," as opposed to Papyrus 967, which reads "whoever shall say anything." One might quickly dismiss ms. 88 and Syro-Hexaplar's reading as a later interpretive addition, but what besides sheer volume of changes differentiates this later alteration to the OG from the original OG alterations to the now-lost *Vorlage*? See Collins, *Daniel,* 213.

86. Hendel, "The Oxford Hebrew Bible," 334.

87. Hendel, "The Oxford Hebrew Bible," 350.

88. Goshen-Gottstein, "The History of the Bible-Text and Comparative Semitics," 198; Talmon, "Textual Criticism," 152.

89. Tov, *Textual Criticism of the Hebrew Bible,* 174, qtd. in Hendel, "The Oxford Hebrew Bible," 341.

90. Hendel, "The Oxford Hebrew Bible," 341.

91. Hendel, "The Oxford Hebrew Bible," 333–34; Tov, *Textual Criticism of the Hebrew Bible,* 177; Van Der Kooij, "The Textual Criticism of the Hebrew Bible Before and After the Qumran Discoveries," 174.

92. See Ulrich, "The Bible in the Making."

93. 4Q242, known as 4QPrayer of Nabonidus, is very similar to an episode in Dan 4:22–37, and "it provides a clear example of pre-Danielic tradition" (Stuckenbruck, "The Formation and Re-Formation of Daniel in the Dead Sea Scrolls," 103). 4Q243–44 and 245, known respectively as 4QPseudo-Daniel[b] and 4QPseudo-Daniel[c], and 4Q552–53, known as 4QFour Kingdoms, seem to develop the Daniel story (Stuckenbruck, "The Formation and Re-Formation of Daniel in the Dead Sea Scrolls," 113–20). 1QM "integrates the angelology of Daniel into a more explicitly dualistic scheme" (Stuckenbruck, "The Formation and Re-Formation of Daniel in the Dead Sea Scrolls," 128–30).

94. Collins does treat the story of Susanna and Bel and the Dragon in an appendix but does not treat the prayer in Daniel 3. On Daniel 1 and 7–12 as clear additions to the book of Daniel, see Collins, *Daniel,* 26–29.

95. See Collins, *Daniel,* 420–39.

96. See Collins, *Daniel,* 3.

97. Collins, *Daniel,* 3.

98. Collins, *Daniel,* 3.

99. See Koenig, *L'herméneutique analogique du judaïsme antique d'après les témoins textuels d'Isaïe,* for an argument that the small additions to 1QIs[a] form a coherent group of redactions that function by means of an analogical principle, much like the rabbinic *gezerah shavah.* See also Tov, *Textual Criticism of the Hebrew Bible,* 236–81, for a plethora of examples of variants in 1QIs[a].

100. Hendel, "The Oxford Hebrew Bible," 334.

101. On "strategies of containment" used for the simultaneous desire for and repression of a totality, see Jameson, *The Political Unconscious,* 52–53.

102. See Fox, "Editing Proverbs."

103. See Fox, *Proverbs 10–31,* 499–503; see also 753–65.

104. As Hendel writes, citing Borbone, "A critical text is actually the opposite of eclectic, since it attempts to reverse the eclectic agglomeration—from diverse times, places, and scribal hands—of secondary readings in the existing manuscripts" ("The Oxford Hebrew Bible," 334).

105. Fox, "Editing Proverbs," 6.

106. Fox, "Editing Proverbs," 7.

107. Fox, "Editing Proverbs," 13.

108. Fox, "Editing Proverbs," 7.

109. Fox, "Editing Proverbs," 5.

110. Fox, "Editing Proverbs," 8.

111. Fox, "Editing Proverbs," 9.

112. Fox, "Editing Proverbs," 9.

113. Fox, *Proverbs 1–9,* 418.

114. Fox, "Editing Proverbs," 6.

115. See Fox, *Proverbs 10–31,* 776–78.

116. Fox, *Proverbs 10–31,* 499–508.

117. Fox, "Editing Proverbs," 13.

118. Fox, "Editing Proverbs," 13.

119. Hendel, "The Oxford Hebrew Bible," 324.

120. Hendel, "The Oxford Hebrew Bible," 328.

121. Borges, "The Homeric Versions," 69.

122. See Goshen-Gottstein, *The Hebrew University Bible Project,* Rabin, Talmon, and Tov, *The Hebrew University Bible,* and Talmon and Goshen-Gottstein, *The Hebrew University Bible.*

123. Goshen-Gottstein, *The Book of Isaiah,* 7.

124. The typology of the nature of this divide is outlined in Lange, "'They Confirmed the Reading' (*y. Ta'an* 4.68a)," 31–45. Goshen-Gottstein and Talmon agree with the Hebrew Old Testament Text Project in this case, as does Tov. See Barthélemy, "Text, Hebrew, History of," and Sanders, "Hermeneutics of Text Criticism," 7n9.

125. Goshen-Gottstein, "The Development of the Hebrew Text of the Bible," 206.

126. Goshen-Gottstein, "The Textual Criticism of the Old Testament," 373.

127. Goshen-Gottstein, *The Book of Isaiah,* 17.

128. As Tov writes, "Those who claim that a certain reading is preferable to another actually presuppose one original text" (*Textual Criticism of the Hebrew Bible,* 168).

129. Goshen-Gottstein, *The Book of Isaiah,* 18; see also Goshen-Gottstein, "The Aleppo Codex and the Rise of the Massoretic Bible Text."

130. See Goshen-Gottstein, "Editions of the Hebrew Bible—Past and Future," for an overview of this process.

131. Goshen-Gottstein, *The Book of Isaiah,* 18.

132. Goshen-Gottstein, *The Book of Isaiah,* 20.

133. For a more detailed argument, see Goshen-Gottstein, "The Authenticity of the Aleppo Codex."

134. Goshen-Gottstein, "The Aleppo Codex and the Rise of the Massoretic Bible Text," 150.

135. Goshen-Gottstein, "The Aleppo Codex and the Rise of the Massoretic Bible Text," 149. See also Goshen-Gottstein, "Editions of the Hebrew Bible—Past and Future."

136. For the textual problems in MT 1–2 Samuel, see Tov's discussion of 1 Samuel 16–18 in *Textual Criticism of the Hebrew Bible,* 334–36, and Trebolle Barrera, "The Story of David and Goliath (1 Sam 17–18)."

137. That is, Maimonides has a good excuse to describe the LXX as deviant, because it deviates from his received tradition.

138. Goshen-Gottstein, *The Book of Isaiah,* 15.

139. Talmon, "Textual Criticism," 152.

140. Talmon, "Textual Criticism," 147.

141. Talmon, "Textual Criticism," 157.

142. See, for example, Tov's account of the use of the Greek text in Jewish communities of the Roman and Byzantine period (*Hebrew Bible, Greek Bible, and Qumran,* 184–88).

143. For a discussion of textual differences within the MT, see, for example, the evaluation and examples supplied by Orlinsky, "Prolegomenon," xx–xxiii.

144. On scribal interventions, see Tov, *Textual Criticism of the Hebrew Bible,* 50–76.

145. See, for example, Risinger et al.'s fascinating study "The Daubert/Kumho Implications of Observer Effects in Forensic Science."

146. This variation was clear even to twelfth-century CE Mishael ben Uzziel, who systematically compared the ben Asher and ben Naphtali systems. See Lipschütz, *Kitāb al-khilāf, the Book of Hillufim.*

147. Talmon, "Textual Criticism," 153.

148. See Ulrich, *The Qumran Text of Samuel and Josephus,* for example.

149. Martin, *Multiple Originals,* 50–56.

150. See *b. Shabbat* 55b. See also Leiman, "Masorah and Halakhah," 292 as well as the compendium of rabbinic disagreements with the MT in Aptowitzer, *Das Schriftwort in der rabbinischen Literatur.*

151. Note *b. Baba Batra* 14b and the order of *BHS;* see Leiman, "Masorah and Halakhah," 292, for a list of Jewish halakhah that endorse the Talmud over against the MT, with no opposing voices represented in the rabbinic tradition.

152. Talmon, "Textual Criticism," 157.

153. Talmud not only occasionally disagrees with the MT; it develops it. See *b. Baba Batra* 15a–b for development of the story of Job.

154. Talmon, "Textual Criticism," 164.

155. Talmon, "Textual Criticism," 163. The Samaritan text form and the OG/LXX text form, especially in translation, certainly continue to be in use even to this day.

156. Talmon, "Textual Criticism," 141–42.

157. Talmon, "Textual Criticism," 147.

158. Talmon, "Textual Criticism," 147.

159. See Ulrich, *The Dead Sea Scrolls and the Origins of the Bible,* 13.

160. See, for example, Talmon, "Textual Criticism," 48–49.

161. See Ulrich, *The Dead Sea Scrolls and the Origins of the Bible,* 8. One may point to the various ANE backgrounds to certain stories, such as the flood narratives of Mesopotamia and Genesis 6–9 (see Frymer-Kensky, "The Atrahasis Epic and Its Significance for Our Understanding of Genesis 1–9"), and one may also note the geographic, theological, and literary variations that signify different contexts of production for the various family cycles in Genesis 12–50 (see Rendtorff, *Das überlieferungsgeschichtliche Problem des Pentateuch,* 29).

162. Ulrich gives further examples: "Similarly, the editions of Joshua can be traced through the witness of 4QJosh[a] (corroborated by Josephus), the somewhat fuller LXX-Joshua, and the yet fuller MT-Joshua. Some further examples are the LXX-Jeremiah en-

larged into the MT-Jeremiah, the MT-Daniel enlarged into the LXX-Daniel, and the MT-Psalter enlarged into the 11QPs[a–b]-Psalter (11Q5–6)" ("The Dead Sea Scrolls and the Hebrew Scriptural Texts," 96).

163. Ulrich, *The Dead Sea Scrolls and the Origins of the Bible,* 11.

164. Ulrich, *The Dead Sea Scrolls and the Origins of the Bible,* 11.

165. Ulrich, *The Dead Sea Scrolls and the Origins of the Bible,* 11.

166. Ulrich, *The Dead Sea Scrolls and the Origins of the Bible,* 12.

167. Ulrich, *The Dead Sea Scrolls and the Origins of the Bible,* 14.

168. Ulrich, "The Dead Sea Scrolls and the Hebrew Scriptural Texts," 99.

169. Note, for example, the debate between Julius Africanus and Origen concerning the validity of Susanna and other clear interpolations to the book of Daniel; Julius argues that there is no known Hebrew *Vorlage* for Susanna and thus that it should not be considered part of the book of Daniel. But Origen replies that the Christian tradition has adopted the Septuagint and with it the "additions," admonishing Julius not to "remove the ancient boundary marks set up by your fathers" (Proverbs 22:28); see Origen, *PG* 11:41–85.

170. Ulrich, *The Dead Sea Scrolls and the Origins of the Bible,* 15.

171. See also Hayman, "The Original Text: A Scholarly Illusion?" Hayman argues that the final form is a historical accident and that the idea of an original text is an unhelpful construct. Yet Hayman, too, draws a line at the Second Temple period (understood as the original context of production), since the "circumstances under which the texts were created" determine how they can be analyzed.

172. Bowley and Reeves, "Rethinking the Concept of 'Bible,'" 4.

173. Bowley and Reeves, "Rethinking the Concept of 'Bible,'" 5.

174. Bowley and Reeves, "Rethinking the Concept of 'Bible,'" 6.

175. Bowley and Reeves, "Rethinking the Concept of 'Bible,'" 10.

176. Bowley and Reeves, "Rethinking the Concept of 'Bible,'" 17.

177. Bowley and Reeves, "Rethinking the Concept of 'Bible,'" 5–6.

178. Bowley and Reeves, "Rethinking the Concept of 'Bible,'" 13n46.

179. Thus, for example, the subtitle of P. Kyle McCarter's text-critical handbook: "Recovering the Text of the Hebrew Bible."

180. One may notice the similarities between the narrative underlying modern text criticism and the basic theological narrative of Christianity, namely that of pristine origin, a fall and its pathological consequences, and eventual salvation. For an example, see Bowley and Reeves, "Rethinking the Concept of 'Bible,'" 11–13, which follows this outline rather closely.

2. Living in Pottersville

1. See Nieder, "Seeing More Than Meets the Eye."

2. For an invigorating discussion of this problem, see Bennington, "Foundations."

3. Ulrich, *The Dead Sea Scrolls and the Origins of the Bible,* 71.

4. Astruc, *Conjectures sur les mémoires originaux dont il paraît que Moïse s'est servi pour composer le livre de la Genèse,* 10, 13.

5. See Noth, *The Deuteronomistic History,* and Van Seters, *Prologue to History.*

6. See, for example, Tov, *Textual Criticism of the Hebrew Bible,* chap. 7. For an incisive critique of the distinction between literary and textual criticism, see Stipp, "Das Verhältnis von Textkritik und Literaturkritik in neueren alttestamentlichen Veröffentlichungen."

7. Marx, *Capital,* 163.

8. The arguments in this paragraph derive from Žižek, *The Parallax View,* 351.

9. Barr, *Holy Scripture,* 85.

10. Tov, *Textual Criticism of the Hebrew Bible,* 1.

11. Tov, *Textual Criticism of the Hebrew Bible,* 118.

12. As Jacques Derrida notes, "The strange structure of the supplement appears here: by delayed reaction, a possibility produces that to which it is said to be added on" (*Speech and Phenomena,* 89).

13. For a different application of nominalism and realism to textual criticism, see Hendel, "Assessing the Text-Critical Theories of the Hebrew Bible after Qumran."

14. Though Platonic metaphysics posits abstract objects (in which the abstract object is nonspatiotemporal) and realism posits the existence of universals (in which universals are instantiated by different particulars), for the purposes of this general overview the two positions I briefly conflate them.

15. Tov, *Textual Criticism of the Hebrew Bible,* 134.

16. See Fox, "Editing Proverbs."

17. Fox, "Editing Proverbs," 8.

18. Fox, "Editing Proverbs," 8.

19. Fox, "Editing Proverbs," 8.

20. Thus, a specter is haunting textual criticism: the specter of the manuscript. See the discussion of "hauntology" in Derrida, *Specters of Marx.*

21. McCarter, *Textual Criticism,* 12. Hendel, as well, writes in favor of the substance and accidents distinction with respect to a copy text; see "The Oxford Hebrew Bible," 344.

22. See Fox, "Editing Proverbs," 8.

23. Fox, "Editing Proverbs," 18.

24. Clines, "Pyramid and the Net," 147.

25. Note, for instance, the inverted *nunim* in the MT, which likely signal some scribal lack of comprehension, and the *puncta extraordinaria,* which seem to predate the Masoretes, who nevertheless copied them without passing down any reason for doing so.

26. McGann, *The Textual Condition,* 60.

27. See Ulrich, *The Dead Sea Scrolls and the Origins of the Bible,* 20, for an example of how bibliographic codes may influence scholarly study of linguistic codes.

28. Schäfer, "Research Into Rabbinic Literature."

29. Schäfer, "Research Into Rabbinic Literature," 151.

30. Schäfer, "Research Into Rabbinic Literature," 152.

31. Saussure, *Course in General Linguistics,* 112.

32. Clines stresses the priority of the copy: "It is a postmodern perception that the distinction between original and copy is problematic." The copy occupies an odd ontological

space: something in between, but not merely a compromise between, the poles of alterity and identity ("Pyramid and the Net," 147).

33. Zumthor, *Essai de poétique médiévale;* Cerquiglini, *In Praise of the Variant.*

34. Cerquiglini, *In Praise of the Variant,* 38.

35. Cerquiglini, *In Praise of the Variant,* 39.

36. Cerquiglini, *In Praise of the Variant,* 3, 68.

37. On the structure of processes, see DeLanda, *Intensive Science and Virtual Philosophy,* 9–55.

38. Derrida, *Of Grammatology,* 41–2. Compare to the story of the priest muttering "mumpismus" in McCarter, *Textual Criticism,* 11.

39. Zeller, "A New Approach to the Critical Constitution of Literary Texts," 240–41.

40. Zeller, "A New Approach to the Critical Constitution of Literary Texts," 241.

41. See Fox, "Editing Proverbs," 10–12.

42. For the general source of the content of the following presentation, see Bennington and Derrida, *Jacques Derrida,* 23–41, Bennington, "Saussure and Derrida," and Saussure, *Course in General Linguistics.*

43. Saussure, *Course in General Linguistics,* 65–70. For his part, C. S. Peirce argues that the sign has three elements rather than two: the sign, the object, and the interpretant. The last grants a role to interpretive context and its ramifications, thus complicating the Saussurian dyad, but the argument concerning the identity of the "material" signifier/sign applies to both semiotic systems. See *The Essential Peirce,* 13–17.

44. Bennington and Derrida, *Jacques Derrida,* 32.

45. Saussure, *Course in General Linguistics,* 120.

46. Saussure, *Course in General Linguistics,* 117–18.

47. See Sanders, "Hermeneutics of Text Criticism," 4.

48. E.g., the characterization Nebuchadnezzar in Daniel 4 is different from that in chapters 1–3, and so readers may change their view of him, the different characterizations of kingship may alter perceptions of the rulers in chapters 5–12, and so forth.

49. Bowley and Reeves, "Rethinking the Concept of 'Bible,'" 4.

50. On the Hegelian concept of the concrete universal, see Stern, *Hegelian Metaphysics,* 143–76. On its Deleuzian interpretation, which I am referencing here, see Deleuze, *Desert Islands and Other Texts,* 43–44, and Williams, *Gilles Deleuze's Logic of Sense,* 96.

51. Derrida, "Living On/Border Lines," 69.

3. Anchor or Spandrel

1. Barton, *The Nature of Biblical Criticism,* 187.

2. Dobbs-Allsopp, "Rethinking Historical Criticism," 261.

3. Consider, for example, Barr's metaphor of containment when he claims that readers must respect "the historical situatedness of the text" (*The Concept of Biblical Theology,* 587) and Levenson's remark that historical-critical scholars assume that "the Bible can never be altogether disengaged from the culture of its authors" (*The Hebrew Bible, the Old Testament, and Historical Criticism,* 123).

4. Barton, *People of the Book?,* 41. Note also the nautically themed "historical moorings" in Barton, *The Nature of Biblical Criticism,* 80.

5. K. M. Newton's description of hermeneutics, frequently deployed by Jacob Neusner, recapitulates this arrangement: "The central concern of hermeneutics as it relates to the study of literature is the problem created by the fact that texts written in the past continue to exist and to be read while their authors and the historical context which produced them have passed away in time" (*Interpreting the Text*, 40–41).

6. "Biblical criticism has always taken for granted that the meaning a text has is connected with its origins in a particular historical and cultural setting—what some would call its "original" sense. . . . This is most obvious at the level of language" (Barton, *The Nature of Biblical Criticism*, 80).

7. Collins, *A Short Introduction to the Hebrew Bible*, 13.

8. See Jacks, "*Restauratio* and Reuse."

9. See Gould and Lewontin, "The Spandrels of San Marco and the Panglossian Paradigm," Gould, "The Exaptive Excellence of Spandrels as a Term and Prototype," and Gould, "Exaptation."

10. For example, the small bones in human middle ears are "now used for hearing, [but] two of these bones (the malleus and incus) were originally part of the lower jaw of our reptilian ancestors, who used them for chewing" (Ramachandran and Blakeslee, *Phantoms in the Brain*, 210).

11. This had all happened long before San Marco; the acceptance of domed basilicas as the style of Byzantine churches likewise derives from contingent circumstances. Early Eastern Roman Christian churches simply inherited a particular architecture and then later developed artistic motifs that used the space effectively. The number four carries particular significance since there are four canonical gospels, and so the four pendentives in Byzantine domes tend to be adorned with images of the four evangelists. See Lowden, *Early Christian and Byzantine Art*, 227–70.

12. Gould and Lewontin, "The Spandrels of San Marco," 581–83. Technically, these spaces are pendentives, but they could also be considered a type of spandrel. See Gould, "The Exaptive Excellence of Spandrels as a Term and Prototype," 10750.

13. Fish lungs, which were later repurposed as gas bladders, provide another example. See Farmer, "Did Lungs and the Intracardiac Shunt Evolve to Oxygenate the Heart in Vertebrates?"

14. See, for example, Simondon, "The Genesis of the Individual."

15. As Dale Martin has concluded in his research concerning the pedagogy of biblical studies in American theological institutions, historical criticism, or the theory that "the primary meaning of the text [is] what its meaning would have been in its original ancient context," is "still the dominant one" (*Pedagogy of the Bible*, 3.)

16. See Saussure, *Course in General Linguistics*, 11–24.

17. See Jakobson's "Langue and Parole: Code and Message" for a discussion of this substitution.

18. Collins, *A Short Introduction to the Hebrew Bible*, 13–14.

19. Barr, *The Semantics of Biblical Language*, 100–106.

20. Saussure, *Course in General Linguistics*, 101.

21. Saussure, *Course in General Linguistics*, 31. Saussure's example is the invention of the name "Lefébure."

22. Barr, *Holy Scripture,* 85.

23. Barr, *Holy Scripture,* 85.

24. Barr, *History and Ideology in the Old Testament,* 43.

25. Barton, *The Nature of Biblical Criticism,* 68, 71.

26. Barton, "Historical-Critical Approaches," 17–18.

27. Collins, *Encounters with Biblical Theology,* 2.

28. This is the logic set forth in Barr, *Concept of Biblical Theology,* and Collins, "Is a Critical Biblical Theology Possible?"

29. Barton, *The Nature of Biblical Criticism,* 80.

30. Sanders, *Canon and Community,* 22. For an overview of the anthological school and their use of the concept *relecture,* see Cook, "*Relecture,* Hermeneutics, and Christ's Passion in the Psalms."

31. Sawyer's second chapter on context provides a background for my comments in this chapter. As Sawyer argues, "The original *Sitz im Leben* of biblical language, however fascinating and academically rewarding a subject for research, is not the only situational context in which it has meaning. . . . [N]o biblical semantics would be complete without taking into account this wider notion of contextualization" (*Semantics in Biblical Research,* 7).

32. Sawyer, *Semantics in Biblical Research,* 5. Also see Jeremias, *The Book of Amos,* 145, for "היכל" as "palace" and Mays, *Amos,* 141, for "היכל" as "temple."

33. See the detailed discussion of this quotation and others in prophetic texts in Schultz, *The Search for Quotation,* 240–329.

34. For an example that highlights the interplay of diachrony and synchrony in semantic terms, see the discussion of "שגיות" in Psalm 19:13 and "כראי" in Nahum 3:6 and Psalm 22:17 in Flusser, *Judaism of the Second Temple Period,* 162–171. Tov, *Textual Criticism of the Hebrew Bible,* 41–43, also supplies examples, which include Deuteronomy 12:5 and Josh 21.

35. See Borges, "Pierre Menard, Author of Don Quixote," 36–45.

36. Barton, *The Nature of Biblical Criticism,* 83.

37. Borges, "Pierre Menard, Author of Don Quixote," 39.

38. Borges, "Pierre Menard, Author of Don Quixote," 40.

39. Take Psalm 20, for instance, which seems to have been adapted into a Hebrew poem. Is it possible for the Judahite scribe to function as the speaker of this utterance as if he wrote it in its entirety? See Nims and Steiner, "A Paganized Version of Psalm 20," Steiner, "The Aramaic Text in Demotic Script," and Zevit, "The Common Origin of the Aramaicized Prayer to Horus and of Psalm 20."

40. Collins, *The Bible after Babel,* 14.

41. Barton, *The Nature of Biblical Criticism,* 5. Barton also declares that all methods in biblical criticism share a concern for genre; see *Reading the Old Testament,* 199.

42. Barton relies J. A. Burrow's claim that "at the level of whole utterances—which is where the question of genre chiefly arises—speakers and writers construct utterances which can be recognized and construed by readers and listeners as utterances of a certain kind" (*Medieval Writers and Their Work,* 56, qtd. in Barton, *The Nature of Biblical Criticism,* 110).

43. Newsom, "Spying Out the Land," 445. See also Newsom, "Pairing Research Questions and Theories of Genre."

44. Gunkel and Begrich, *Introduction to Psalms,* 16.

45. Gunkel and Begrich, *Introduction to Psalms,* 20.

46. Gunkel and Begrich, *Introduction to Psalms,* 19–20.

47. For an explanation of texts shifting between genres, see Nasuti, *Defining the Sacred Songs.*

48. See, for example, Gerstenberger, *Psalms, Part 1,* 133.

49. See, for example, Mays, "The Question of Context in Psalm Interpretation," 17.

50. Gunkel and Begrich, *Introduction to Psalms,* 8.

51. Barton, *Reading the Old Testament,* 18.

52. Barton, *The Nature of Biblical Criticism,* 63–64.

53. See Gunkel and Begrich, *Introduction to Psalms,* 16.

54. See Sanders, *The Psalms Scroll of Qumran Cave 11 (11QPsa);* see also Ulrich, "From Literature to Scripture," 11. Note also 4QPsalms Pesher[a], which interprets Psalm 37 as if it were an oracle addressed to the Qumran community itself.

55. Wilson, "The Shape of the Book of Psalms," 138; cf. Whybray, *Reading the Psalms as a Book,* 36–87.

56. See the various arguments for Second Temple cultic use of psalms throughout Human and Vos, eds., *Psalms and Liturgy.*

57. Among various other examples, one could also gesture to the development of the genre of law code from its Mesopotamian context to its literary context within the Hebrew Bible. See Westbrook, "The Laws of Biblical Israel."

58. Collins, *A Short Introduction to the Hebrew Bible,* 13–14. Note the phrase "the time." As biblical texts are layer cakes, there are always at least several times and histories to which the text relates.

59. On this methodological question, see Strawn, "Comparative Approaches."

60. Van der Toorn, *Scribal Culture and the Making of the Hebrew Bible,* 28–39.

61. See, for example, Sasson, "On Choosing Models for Recreating Israelite Pre-Monarchic History."

62. An example of datable real referent is domesticated camels; camels were not domesticated in Bronze-age Palestine, so text that refers to domesticated camels in Genesis must have been written at a later time. An example of a datable displaced referent is the promise of the land, which is used as evidence for the claim that the Pentateuch must have been compiled and this motif written into the text during a time when the need for land was great, such as the time of the exile.

63. Hervey, "Context, the Ghost in the Machine," 68.

64. Miller, *Interpreting the Psalms,* 52–54.

65. The question is an important one, not easily dismissed by pragmatic approaches to biblical criticism. As Bronislaw Malinowski, the linguist and anthropologist who coined the phrase "context of situation," remarkes, "Utterance and situation are bound up inextricably with each other and the context of situation is indispensible for the understanding of the words. . . . [A] word without linguistic context is a mere figment and stands for nothing by itself, so in the reality of a spoken living tongue, the utterance has

no meaning except in its context of situation" (Malinowski, "The Problem of Meaning in Primitive Languages," 150). If Malinowski is correct, then determining which elements determine the context is an important and quite real problem.

66. Hervey sums up this difficult situation: "If every object of description needs to be externally contextualized in order to be interpreted, then every context used in explaining some other object is, itself, an object that needs to be contextualized . . . and so on ad infinitum. The upshot of this argument is that the requirement for external contextualization leads to infinite regression. On the other hand, if every object of description needs only to be internally contextualized, relative to other objects in the same closed system, then objects of description and interpretation merely explain one another mutually and reciprocally. The conclusion from this argument is that a requirement for internal contextualization leads to inherent descriptive circularity" ("Context, the Ghost in the Machine," 70).

67. Jameson, *The Ideologies of Theory,* 141.

68. Barr, *Concept of Biblical Theology,* 4.

69. Barr, *Concept of Biblical Theology,* 4.

70. Barr, *Concept of Biblical Theology,* 447.

71. Barr, *Concept of Biblical Theology,* 4.

72. For a variety of interpretations of *pesharim,* see De Troyer and Lange, eds., *Reading the Present in the Qumran Library.*

73. See Collins, *Daniel,* 38.

74. Grabbe, *Judaic Religion in the Second Temple Period,* 210–31, 271–91, provides a helpful overview of Second Temple conceptions of monotheism, resurrection and messianism.

75. See, for example, the way biblical texts find new contexts and radically new interpretations throghout Kalimi, *Early Jewish Exegesis and Theological Controversy.*

76. Collins, *Daniel,* 85.

77. See Levenson, *Resurrection and the Restoration of Israel,* 181–200.

78. Schegloff, "In Another Context," 223fn4.

4. On Tigers and Cages

1. Fox, "Job 38 and God's Rhetoric," 53.

2. See Derrida, *Limited Inc,* 7–8.

3. Derrida, *Limited Inc,* 12.

4. Bennington, "Derrida's 'Eighteenth Century,'" 392.

5. See Römer, *The So-Called Deuteronomistic History,* 128–32.

6. Benveniste, *Problems in General Linguistics,* 218.

7. Benveniste, *Problems in General Linguistics,* 220.

8. Fetzer, *Recontextualizing Context,* 3. For an historical overview of the concept of context as it applies to the practice of interpreting texts, see Dilley, "The Problem of Context in Social and Cultural Anthropology," and Burke, "Context in Context."

9. Burke, "Context in Context," 153.

10. One may find this as a staple of hermeneutical thought from Schliermacher through Dilthey to Gadamer and Ricouer. See Grondin, *Introduction to Philosophical Hermeneutics,* 91–120.

11. See Cook, *Applied Linguistics*, 49–59.

12. Eco notes the difference between *intentio auctoris* and *intentio operis*, the intentions of a historical author or of the "text itself" (*Interpretation and Overinterpretation*, 25).

13. See Nissinen, "Reflections on the 'Historical-Critical' Method," for an overview of these concerns.

14. As Spencer-Brown comments, "We cannot make an indication without drawing a distinction" (*Laws of Form*, 1). Luhmann and Spencer-Brown helpfully point out the radical contingency of distinctions and their incommensurability when compared. See Luhmann, "Kultur als historischer Begriff," 40–47.

15. Eilberg-Schwartz, *The Savage in Judaism*, 95.

16. Overdetermination, on the other hand, occurs when there are multiple, overlapping contextual causes for a particular identifiable event. See Boyd, "The Current Status of Scientific Realism," 41–42. Deleuze prefers to speak of "determinable" yet undetermined multiplicities; see *The Logic of Sense*, 100–101.

17. See DeLanda, *Intensive Science and Virtual Philosophy*, 9–41. DeLanda gives a thorough analysis of the problem of manifolds.

18. Deleuze also offers the helpful example of a battle, always "actualized in diverse manners at once," since different participants and observers will "grasp it at a different level of actualization within its variable present." That is, the battle is completely different for the general and the private, the hiding child and the stray dog, and yet it is the same thing ("the battle"), even though there is no point from which to see the "real" battle or to sum the battle up in perfect objectivity (*The Logic of Sense*, 100–101). James Williams contemplates Deleuze's use of a battle for his example: "This is not controversial if it is taken as the common view that many different perspectives exist on any given battle, but this is not Deleuze's lesson. He is not giving us a theory of interpretation where different standpoints cannot be reduced to one another and where a complete interpretation faces the challenge of bringing together an open-ended set of incommensurable perspectives without reducing them to one another. Instead, Deleuze asks himself . . . [w]hat does this condition imply for the perspectives, for the battle and for all other conditioned actual things? We do not have a number of perspectives on an actual battle, but rather a virtual battle as sense and event rendered through those perspectives and the illusion of the one true actual conflict in the battlefield" (*Gilles Deleuze's Logic of Sense*, 96–97). I explore Deleuze's concept of the virtual in chapter 5.

19. See Deleuze and Guattari, *A Thousand Plateaus*, 7–8.

20. Recent historiographical theorists have noted that historians must make determinations and thus "emplot" relations. But "emplotment" is not limited to historians: the historical actors themselves must emplot their own world, since the world does not present readymade plots. See Newsom, "Rhyme and Reason," and Weitzman, "Plotting Antiochus's Persecution."

21. Also note the Testament of Moses, the book of Judith, *pesher* Habakkuk, and possibly other Qumranic texts, such as 4QHistorical Text (= 4Q248), 4QpapPesudo–Ezekiel[e] (=4Q391), 4Q246, and possibly *pesher* Nahum. See Dimant and Strugnell, *Qumran Cave 4*, 55–57, 112–16, 208–12, 228–32, Berrin, *The Pesher Nahum Scroll from Qumran*, 100, Eshel, *The Dead Sea Scrolls and the Hasmonean State*, 13–29, and Harrington, *The Maccabean Revolt*.

22. Josephus's account is in *Ant.* 12.237–64; for text and translation of Diodorus's account, see Stern, *Greek and Latin Authors on Jews and Judaism*, 181–85.

23. For overviews of scholarly positions concerning Antiochus IV's persecution, see Gruen, "Hellenism and Persecution: Antiochus IV and the Jews," Schwartz, "Antiochus IV Epiphanes in Jerusalem," and Weitzman, "Plotting Antiochus's Persecution," 219–22. For varying attempts to reconstruct the Seleucid perspective, see Gruen, "Seleucid Royal Ideology," 24–53, Bevan, *The House of Seleucus*, 153, and Bringmann, *Hellenistische Reform und Religionsverfolgung in Judäa*, 111–40. For reconstructions of various Jewish perspectives, see Bickerman, *The God of the Maccabees*, 61–62, 76–92, Tcherikover, *Hellenistic Civilization and the Jews*, 186–203, and Schwartz, "Israel and the Nations Roundabout."

24. One may disagree with Bickermann's particular reconstructions of these perspectives (*God of the Maccabees*, 9–19), but it seems beyond question that several factions understood this event in mutually incompatible ways.

25. Collins, *Daniel*, 65. For an overview of the rhetorical approaches of these texts, see Gafni, "Josephus and 1 Maccabees," and Doran, *Temple Propaganda*.

26. Bickermann suggests that the rededication of a temple to Zeus Olympios could be seen as a Greek synchronistic practice (*God of the Maccabees*, 90–96). For non-Hellenistic and likely some pro-Hellenistic Jews, this act was understood to be and signify something quite different.

27. On the concept of symbolic worlds, see Newsom, *The Self as Symbolic Space*, 1–22, 92–95. See also the helpful Holland et al., *Identity and Agency in Cultural Worlds*, which Newsom cites.

28. I am not claiming that Antiochus and the Maccabees are "both right"; rather, I am suggesting that the means of adjudicating between them does not lie outside them but only within them. With some reservations, I prefer to see the conflict from the perspective of the Maccabees. But I realize that this is determination closes certain historical and ethical doors, even as it opens others. See Niklas Luhmann, *Theories of Distinction*, 11–18.

29. Newsom, "Bakhtin, the Bible, and Dialogic Truth," 294; Bakhtin, *Problems of Dostoevsky's Poetics*, 93.

30. Derrida, *Limited Inc*, 12.

31. Schwartz, "Antiochus IV Epiphanes in Jerusalem," 57.

32. Foucault, "Return to History," 429.

33. As Deleuze remarks, "It is not at all a question of different points of view on one story supposedly the same; for points of view would still be submitted to a rule of convergence. It is rather a question of different and divergent stories, as if an absolutely distinct landscape corresponded to each point of view" (*The Logic of Sense*, 260). Also, the "point of view is opened onto a divergence which it affirms: another town corresponds to each point of view, each point of view is another town, the towns are linked only by their distance and resonate only through the divergence of their series, their houses and their streets. There is always another town within the town" (*The Logic of Sense*, 174).

34. Voloshinov, *Marxism and the Philosophy of Language*, 80.

35. See Bennington and Derrida, *Jacques Derrida*, 15–83, for the background to these arguments.

36. Epictetus, *The Discourses as Reported by Arrian*, 143.

37. See the discussion in Schäfer, *Judeophobia*, 66–81.

38. See Gruen, "Hellenism and Persecution," 238, 256, 264. Some historians have sought to render the persecution interpretable by comparing it to a previous persecution of the Bacchanalian cult in Rome, which Antiochus had witnessed firsthand. This explanation, too, requires prior events to determine the event. All historical explanations follow this same pattern of recognition.

39. Harlan, "Intellectual History and the Return of Literature," 595.

40. See, for example, Keohane and Hoffmann, conclusion, 384.

41. See Derrida, "Différance."

42. See Fink, *The Lacanian Subject*, 64.

43. See Benjamin, "Theses on the Philosophy of History."

44. This statement, expounded in Luhmann, *Theories of Distinction*, 11–18, may be demonstrated formally by means of set theory, as Alain Badiou shows; see *Being and Event*, 23–27. Also see Badiou, *Logics of Worlds*, 109–13.

45. Bakhtin, *The Dialogic Imagination*, 294.

46. For this very reason, the spoken signifier is an ideal sound pattern, not an actual sound. See Saussure, *Course in General Linguistics*, 12–15.

47. See, for example, Derrida, *Of Grammatology*, 33.

48. See Derrida, *Limited Inc*, 7–10.

49. See Derrida, *Limited Inc*, 47–51, for a discussion of the grocery list.

50. "The supposedly simple and present origin itself has an origin in something else, and that something else, the origin's origin, is not an origin in the normal sense at all, because it cannot be simple or simply present" (Bennington, "Foundations," 234).

51. Miller, *Interpreting the Psalms*, 18–28.

52. Miller, *Interpreting the Psalms*, 23.

53. Miller, *Israelite Religion and Biblical Theology*, 248.

54. Barr, *The Concept of Biblical Theology*, 5.

55. As suggested by Fox's remark, quoted at the opening of this chapter, that "main concern in approaching a text is essentially . . . to ascertain the meaning of the text, which is to say, the authorial intention." See also the discussion of Fox and intentionality in chapter 1.

56. Barr, *Concept of Biblical Theology*, 4.

57. Hirsch, *The Aims of Interpretation*, 8. This perspective finds its most convincing form in Husserl's concept of "intentional objects." See his "Intentional Objects." But Husserl's theory of meaning, as well as Hirsch's, relies on a problematic theory of "prelinguistic" intention.

58. See Mele, "Against a Belief/Desire Analysis of Intention."

59. Van der Toorn, *Scribal Culture and the Making of the Hebrew Bible*, 40–48.

60. Foucault, "What Is an Author?"

61. Foucault, "What Is an Author?," 111.

62. Foucault, "What Is an Author?," 118–19.

63. Noegel argues that ancient Near Eastern modes of divination "evidences the existence of a scribal perception in which the written word or "sign" has the potential to be a great deal more than what it signifies" (*Nocturnal Ciphers*, 37).

64. Noegel, *Nocturnal Ciphers,* 123.

65. James Barr offers very helpful critiques of these arguments concerning the "power of words" in ancient Israel in "The Symbolism of Names in the Old Testament." Thiselton extends Barr's critique, arguing that even curses and blessings are simply "performatives," following the work of J. L. Austin; see his *Thiselton on Hermeneutics: Collected Works with New Essays,* 293. While Thiselton attempt to curb excessive speculations of "word-magic" proponents is justifiable, material cultural remains have shown that apotropaic and incantational uses of images and words was persistent. See, for example, Smoak, "Amuletic Inscriptions and the Background of YHWH as Guardian and Protector in Psalm 12."

66. See Person, "The Ancient Israelite Scribe as Performer," 602.

67. von Rad, *Old Testament Theology,* 83.

68. von Rad, *Old Testament Theology,* 85. For more examples, including many overstatements, see Thiselton, *Thiselton on Hermeneutics,* 283–85. For more thoughtful and contemporary comparative support for this argument, see Bahrani, *The Graven Image,* 127. Bharani claims that Mesopotamian words could inhabit the same "ontological register" as any "real" referent. See also Noegel, "'Sign, Sign, Everywhere a Sign,'" 143–45, and Frahm, "Reading the Tablet, the Exta, and the Body," 93–100.

69. See Bottéro, *Mesopotamia,* 85–93. For "generative" script, see Noegel, "'Sign, Sign, Everywhere a Sign,'" 146.

70. Note the use of this idiom for "nonlinguistic" referents in Psalms 7:16 and Joel 3:4.

71. Noegel, *Nocturnal Ciphers,* 7. As Frahm argues, "One of the main goals of commentaries employing etymology and etymography was to produce the illusion of an esoteric inner coherence of the texts they dealt with" ("Reading the Tablet, the Exta, and the Body," 96).

72. Noegel, "'Sign, Sign, Everywhere a Sign,'" 147. Divination was a common practice throughout the ancient Near East, including Israel and Judah, as noted in, for example, Genesis 30:27 and 44:15. See Noegel, *Nocturnal Ciphers,* 114.

73. See Noegel's discussion of Genesis 41:13 in *Nocturnal Ciphers,* 176–77.

74. See Jokiranta, "Pesharim," and Schiffman, "Contemporizing Halakic Exegesis in the Dead Sea Scrolls."

75. See Van der Horst, "*Sortes,*" 146–47.

76. Lange, "Literary Prophecy and Oracle Collection," 258.

77. Lange, "Literary Prophecy and Oracle Collection," 273.

78. See Clements, "The Prophet as Author," 100–101.

79. Nissinen, "The Historical Dilemma of Biblical Prophetic Studies," 110.

80. One may also look to the Psalms as an example of texts that were decontextualized during the period of their production for the precise purpose of separating them from any historical author or referent. See Kugel, "Topics in the History of the Spirituality of the Psalms," 133, 142, and Tigay, "On Some Aspects of Prayer in the Bible."

81. As shown by Hershel Parker, the invocation of the "text itself" takes for granted the work of textual critics and editors who assemble and construct the text itself. Text criticism that takes an author's intentions as a guide inevitably recapitulates the ideology of the New Critics. See his "'The Text Itself'" and *Flawed Texts and Verbal Icons.*

82. Parker, "Lost Authority," 769.

83. Parker, "Lost Authority," 772. See also Martin, *Multiple Originals,* 133.

84. Eco, *The Limits of Interpretation,* 44–63.

85. See the canonical reading proposed in, for example, Brueggemann, "Bounded by Obedience and Praise."

86. See Tov, *Textual Criticism of the Hebrew Bible,* 303, for more information.

87. Barton, *The Nature of Biblical Criticism,* 86. According to Hirsch, "Meaning is that which is represented by a text; it is what the author meant by his use of a particular sign sequence; it is what the signs represent. Significance, on the other hand, names a relationship between that meaning and a person, or a conception, or a situation or indeed anything imaginable" (*Validity in Interpretation,* 13).

88. Derrida, *Limited Inc,* 18, 56.

89. Derrida, *Limited Inc,* 7–9.

90. See Derrida, *Dissemination,* 152.

91. This is not to be confused with Barton's convenient straw man of the "completely free-floating" and contextless text (*The Nature of Biblical Criticism,* 79). As Derrida argues, "There are only contexts"; "nothing exists outside context" but at the same time "the limit of the frame or border of this context always entails a clause of non-closure" (*Limited Inc,* 152).

92. Rabinowitz proposes a four-fold typology of audience; see "Truth in Fiction." Rabinowitz distinguishes between "actual audience," "authorial audience," "narrative audience" and "ideal narrative audience."

93. Barton seems to assume such an addressee in referring to "that which must have existed in the minds of Amos' audience," as if it were a unity of interpretation (*The Old Testament,* 282).

94. Note Barr's statement that the "best material" comes from authors who "concentrate on what the writers/redactors/readers/audience thought" as opposed to "dogmatic arguments" that derive from later readers. For Barr, this division is a "boundary point" in biblical scholarship (*Concept of Biblical Theology,* 58).

95. See Barton, *The Nature of Biblical Criticism,* 179.

96. Barr, *Concept of Biblical Theology,* 57.

97. As Bennington comments, "Usually people work with a loose enough concept of context to suppose that there is a vague contemporaneity of writing and reading, but any rigorous concept must recognize that writing is from the start breaking with its context of 'production' and with every determined context of reception" (Bennington and Derrida, *Jacques Derrida,* 86).

98. Derrida discusses the addressee in *Limited Inc,* 7–9.

99. Bennington and Derrida, *Jacques Derrida,* 91.

100. One may include within this list of examples any recontextualizations of foreign motifs, characters, sayings, and so on, such as the "context" of the recontextualized Instruction of Amenemope, or the recontextualization of ancient Near Eastern law within the Pentateuch, or the recontextualization of Neo-Assyrian motifs in the Deuteronomistic history, or inner-biblical recontextualizations such as the book of Chronicles. See Fox, *Proverbs 10–31,* 753–69.

101. See Bennington and Derrida, *Jacques Derrida*, 51–52.

102. As Derrida explains, "Polysemy always puts out its multiplicities and variations with the horizon, at least, of some integral reading. . . . It forgets that its horizon is framed." Derrida contrasts polysemy to "dissemination," which does not foreclose on possible future readings (*Dissemination*, 350–51). Though this may sound paradoxical (a text cannot mean just anything, but at the same time its meanings cannot be numbered), it is not. There can be an uncountable number of justifiable meanings and also uncountable unjustifiable meanings. See Kanamori, "The Mathematical Development of Set Theory from Cantor to Cohen." In other words, let us dispense with the canard that absolute infinity is the only alternative to either univocity or limited polysemy.

103. There is not enough space even for a cursory attempt at categorizing answers to this question. Introductory textbooks such as Lycan, *Philosophy of Language*, and Lyons, *Semantics*, offer instructive overviews. For an analysis of meaning that roughly agrees with the presentation I offer here, see Bennington and Derrida, *Jacques Derrida*, 15–83.

104. See Scanlin, "The Study of Semantics in General Linguistics," 127.

105. Silva, *Biblical Words and Their Meaning*, 139.

106. See, for example, Wittgenstein, *Philosophical Investigations*, 60, and Ayer, *Language, Truth, and Logic*.

107. I happen to find Saussure's and Derrida's discussion of meaning to be convincing and particularly enlightening when it comes to biblical texts, whose internal relationships of inner-biblical rewriting thus find a new relevance. Yet my conclusions in this section also follow from Wittgenstein's theory of meaning, which claims that "if we had to name anything which is the life of the sign, we should have to say that it was its *use*" (*The Brown and Blue Books*, 4). In Wittgenstein's argument, investigating meaning does not require abstraction or generalization but rather a simple description of the diversity of ways in which the sign has been put use. If we extend this definition of meaning to include texts, then, scholars cannot not "give the meaning" of a text but rather, like good reception historians, should instead show the diversity of ways in which the text has been put to use. As Wittgenstein himself remarks, "Don't think but look!" (*Philosophical Investigations*, 27). For a pragmatist theory of meaning that covers some of the same ground, see Stout, "What is the Meaning of a Text?" Moreover, Quine's theory of meaning in light of his argument for the structural indeterminacy of translation supports many of these same conclusions. See *Word and Object*.

108. Saussure, *Course in General Linguistics*, 67.

109. Saussure, *Course in General Linguistics*, 167.

110. Wittgenstein, *Philosophical Investigations*, 126.

111. See Bennington, *Other Analyses: Reading Philosophy*, 225–26. This position is at odds with that of Hans-Georg Gadamer, for whom meaning is translation but a translation of a preexistent, prelinguistic substantial *Sache* that is itself unchanging. See *Truth and Method*, 389–99.

112. Meaning is thus secondary, supplementary to the text, something produced by an encounter with a text. See Derrida, "Living on/Border Lines," 62.

113. But Bennington adds the important qualification that the fact that "there is no signified does not imply that we place all the signifiers on the same level—we must respect

the effects of signifieds, of what gives itself out as a signified" (Bennington and Derrida, *Jacques Derrida*, 96–97). In other words, I must realize that, no matter how masterfully I account for the elements of the text, it continues to function beyond my reading.

5. Mapping the Garden of Forking Paths

1. Nietzsche, *On the Genealogy of Morality*, 51.

2. Deleuze, *The Fold*, 20–22.

3. As Deleuze argues, this logic can be applied to anything at all: "A body can be anything; it can be an animal, a body of sounds, a mind or an idea; it can be a linguistic corpus" (*Spinoza*, 127).

4. Spinoza, *A Spinoza Reader*, 155.

5. Deleuze, *The Logic of Sense*, 6.

6. Deleuze, *The Fold*, 60.

7. For example, the Basque language did not, until recently, differentiate between blue, green, and gray. See Trask, *The History of Basque*, 267–68.

8. For a brief overview of the science of color perception, see Hardin, *Color for Philosophers*, 1–40. See also Noë, *Action in Perception*, 123–61.

9. For this reason, the debate between universalists (e.g., Berlin and Kay, *Basic Color Terms*) and relativists (e.g., Saunders, "Revisiting Basic Color Terms") matters little here.

10. This simplified presentation ignores Mie scattering. A more detailed presentation, along with a historical resumé of the search for the coloring power of the sky, may be found in Pesic, *Sky in a Bottle*.

11. See Fish, "Interpreting the Variorum," 148, and Foucault, *The Archaeology of Knowledge*, 38, 191.

12. See Fox, *Proverbs 1–9*, 286–87.

13. Lenzi, "Proverbs 8:22–31," 706.

14. See Sawyer, *Semantics in Biblical Research*, 5–7.

15. Deleuze, *Difference and Repetition*, 212, 239, 245.

16. Deleuze, *Difference and Repetition*, 185–86.

17. Deleuze, *Difference and Repetition*, 193.

18. See Shaviro, *Without Criteria*, 34.

19. Shaviro, *Without Criteria*, 179–82. For a basic introduction to this concept, see May, *Gilles Deleuze*, 83–86.

20. See, for example, Hendel, "The Oxford Hebrew Bible," 330.

21. Deleuze, *The Logic of Sense*, 122.

22. Deleuze, *Difference and Repetition*, 211.

23. See the aptly titled Van der Horst, Key, and Hellingworth, "Photosensing in Chemotrophic, Non-Phototrophic Bacteria."

24. Deleuze, *Difference and Repetition*, 192.

25. There is often significant cultural resistance to restatements of the problem: consider the introduction of the front crawl stroke to British competitive swimming, which occurred in 1844. In London, two Ojibway Native Americans named Flying Gull and Tobacco exhibited the speed produced by their radical front crawl stroke, yet observers called the motions "totally un-European," saying "they lash the water violently with their

arms, like the sails of a windmill, and beat downwards with their feet, blowing with force, and forming grotesque antics." For the next thirty years, English swimmers kept to the breast stroke and avoided the front crawl stroke, even though it yielded impressive results (Littel, *Littel's Living Age,* 217).

26. Deleuze, *The Logic of Sense,* 114.

27. See DeLanda, *Intensive Science and Virtual Philosophy,* 15–16.

28. DeLanda, *Intensive Science and Virtual Philosophy,* 14.

29. Virtual multiplicities (or virtual ideas) coexist in a state of "perplication" and shade into one another. See Deleuze, *Difference and Repetition,* 236, 351.

30. Deleuze, *The Logic of Sense,* 150.

31. To be clear about my appropriation of topology, as well as evolutionary biology: the mathematical and scientific metaphors that I have been cultivating throughout this chapter are not meant to directly explain the process of textual development and reading. Yet biblical studies has long been dominated by particular metaphors, including hylomorphic metaphors, that emphasize stasis and final products. In order to develop a more process-oriented view of the biblical text, I have found it helpful to look at discourses familiar with process.

32. For an introductory overview of topology, see Huggett, *Everywhere and Everywhen,* 31–41, 64–88.

33. Bryant, *Difference and Givenness,* 68–69.

34. See Kline, *Mathematics for the Nonmathematician,* 452–77.

35. Huggett, *Everywhere and Everywhen,* 38.

36. See Peterson, *The Mathematical Tourist,* 59.

37. See, for example, the essays collected in Linafelt, ed., *Strange Fire.*

38. See Barton, *The Nature of Biblical Criticism,* 117–36.

39. On the concept of dynamic coemergence see Thompson, *Mind of Life,* 60–61.

40. See Collins, "The Exodus and Biblical Theology," and Levenson, "Exodus and Liberation."

41. This problem shares affinities with the paradox of infinite proliferation, as the translation becomes the text itself; it is both, yet never both at once, and becomes something quite different when it is seen from either perspective. See Deleuze, *The Logic of Sense,* 28–31.

42. See Collins, *Daniel,* 2–38.

43. See Yoder, *Proverbs,* xxi–xxxiii.

44. Jakobson, "On Linguistic Aspects of Translation." Derrida discusses Jakobson's text in "Des tours des Babel."

45. See the variety of material surveyed in Vicchio, *The Image of the Biblical Job.*

46. For an overview of Job's relationship to medieval music, see Denis, "Saint Job, patron des musiciens."

47. See Terrien, *The Iconography of Job through the Centuries,* 107.

48. For examples, see Meyer, "St. Job as a Patron of Music," 21–31, or Terrien, *The Iconography of Job,* 107.

49. See Fenlon, *The Renaissance,* 372; Denis, "Saint Job, patron des musiciens," 253–98.

50. See Henze, *Biblical Interpretation at Qumran,* 169. On the general use of psalms as amulets, see Collart, "Psaumes et amulettes."

51. See Cohn, *Tangled up in Text*, 121–201.

52. For example, the otherwise excellent treatment of Jonah in Yvonne Sherwood's *Survival of Jonah* surprisingly does not consider the formation and history of the text of Jonah but rather focuses on the readings of "the text."

53. Note the editorial dispute concerning this point in Van der Ploeg and Van der Woude, *Le Targum de Job de la grotte XI de Qumrân*, 87. It is very possible that the Qumran Targum included up to verse 17, but in any event there are known alternate endings to the book of Job, as is found in LXX Job 42:17, which claims to have received this longer ending from the "Syriac book" (likely an Aramaic Targum of some sort).

54. See Gentry, *The Asterisked Materials in the Greek Job*.

55. Deleuze, *Logic of Sense*, 114; Borges, "The Garden of the Forking Paths."

56. Borges, "The Garden of Forking Paths," 98.

57. Even the selection of two paths at once, for example, the selection of an ambiguous reading of Proverbs 8:30 that relies on a dual—or triple—resonance of "אמון," is itself a selection as well as a rejection of other readings.

58. Deleuze, *Difference and Repetition*, 234–39.

59. Williams, *The Transversal Thought of Gilles Deleuze*, 49.

60. Deleuze, *The Logic of Sense*, 150.

61. As Bonta and Protevi explain, "Actualization . . . is the construction of exclusive disjunctions, the selection of a series of singularities whose actualization precludes the simultaneous actualization of others, which would then have the modal status of the (virtual) 'road not taken'" (*Deleuze and Geophilosophy*, 27).

62. Deleuze, *Difference and Repetition*, 252.

63. For Deleuze and Guattari's discussion of mapping and for the image of the rhizome, see *A Thousand Plateaus*, 12–20.

64. See DeLanda, *Intensive Science and Virtual Philosophy*, 13–15.

65. See Deleuze, *Difference and Repetition*, 36–37. For an overview, see Parr, ed., *The Deleuze Dictionary*, 181–86.

66. See Deleuze, *The Logic of Sense*, 59–61.

67. See Deleuze, *Cinema*, 12–28.

68. Deleuze, *The Fold*, 23.

6. Justice, Survival, Presence

1. See Deleuze, *Essays Critical and Clinical*, xxii.

2. On attempts to date the book of Job, see Seow, *Job 1–21*, 54–62.

3. See the helpful review of the history of compositional theories in Newsom, *The Book of Job*, 3–31.

4. See Newsom, *The Book of Job*, 1–11.

5. See Newsom, "Narrative, Ethics, Character, and the Prose Tale of Job," 124, and Gordis, *The Book of Job*, 573–75.

6. For scholars who date Elihu to the Hellenistic period, see Mende, *Durch Leiden zur Vollendung*, 419–27, and Wahl, *Der gerechte Schöpfer*, 182–87.

7. See Spiegel, "Noah, Danel, and Job."

8. Greenstein, "The Language of Job and Its Poetic Function."

9. See Hankins, "Job and the Limits of Wisdom," Newsom, *The Book of Job,* and Habel, *The Book of Job.*

10. See Kraeling, *Book of the Ways of God,* 89, who argues that Job 19:25 echoes the Ba'al cycle.

11. See Habel, *The Book of Job,* 273.

12. Gunkel and Begrich, *Introduction to Psalms,* 148.

13. Berlin, *Lamentations,* 89–94.

14. Levenson, *Resurrection and the Restoration of Israel,* 38.

15. On the topic of Job's appropriation of genres, see Newsom, *The Book of Job,* 130–68.

16. See Clines, *Job 1–20,* 457–66, and Habel, *The Book of Job,* 302–309. For another view of the legal metaphor, see Newsom, *The Book of Job,* 150–66, 201–11.

17. "The point is not at all to claim the liberty to read out of context, which would be meaningless (one always reads in one or several contexts), but to interrogate the coherence of the concept of context deployed in this way" (Bennington and Derrida, *Jacques Derrida,* 85).

18. My arguments concerning the Greek and Syriac texts may be found in the following chapter.

19. This taxonomy is my own construction, and it does not aim to contain or explain every single reading throughout history. The data can be divided up in a number of ways, and future readings in unexpected contexts will doubtless require a reconceptualization of this schema.

20. This is the activity that Deleuze defines as "nomadic distribution." Dividing up the marbles by their color or size, regardless of their placement on the floor, would, in Deleuze's terminology, be defined as a "sedentary distribution." See Parr, ed. *The Deleuze Dictionary,* 181–86.

21. For a thoroughgoing forensic reading, the New English Bible is a classic example: "But in my heart I know that my vindicator lives, and that he will rise last to speak in court; and I shall discern my witness standing at my side and see my defending counsel, even God himself, whom I shall see with my own eyes, I myself and no other. My heart failed when you said."

22. Clines, *Job 1–20,* 468.

23. See Driver, "Problems of the Hebrew Text and Language," and Clines, *Job 1–20,* 460.

24. This, however, is no reason to discount it as a reading, though it is quite interesting to note that many readers who criticize others for "inventing" meanings for ancient words see no problem in stretching other ancient words to suit their interpretive case. For this reading of "אחרון," see Dhorme, *A Commentary on the Book of Job,* 283: "It is clear that . . . אחרון is God. . . . He who will have the last word . . . [as] a witness in a court of justice."

25. Habel, *The Book of Job,* 273.

26. Ibid.

27. For "זכר" as "signifying the resumption of relations between God" and humanity, see Schottroff, *Gedenken im alten Orient und im Alten Testament,* which Clines cites (*Job 1–20,* 331).

28. Habel, *The Book of Job,* 306.

29. Clines, "Belief, Desire, and Wish in Job 19, 23–27," 367.

30. Clines, "Belief, Desire, and Wish in Job 19, 23–27," 370.

31. On the various defensible ways to interpret this text, see Newsom, "The Book of Job," 629.

32. See Clines, "Belief, Desire, and Wish," 363–69, and Clines, *Job 1–20,* 437–38, 457–70.

33. See Clines, *Job 1–20,* 461–62, 479.

34. See Clines, "Belief, Desire, and Wish in Job 19, 23–27," 366.

35. Interestingly, Clines and Habel seem driven by a need for consistency when it comes to the identity of Job's imagined גאל: Clines quotes Ringgren, who points out that "since the lawsuit here stands in the context of a dispute with God, it seems unlikely that God himself would appear as vindicator and legal attorney against himself," adding "nor is it a heavenly being." See "Belief, Desire, and Wish in Job 19,23–27," 365.

36. Though Clines does admit an irony to these words: they do, in fact, come true, but not at all in the way that Clines's Job imagines. See "Belief, Desire, and Wish in Job 19,23–27," 369.

37. On the many fascinating nuances of legal metaphors in Job, see Newsom, *The Book of Job,* 150–61.

38. See Levenson, *Resurrection and the Restoration of Israel,* 39.

39. Concerning "living": the use of "חי" does not ordinarily function as a verb meaning "to give life," as it does in other recovery-of-life tropes, but its mere presence in the midst of a lament introduces the motif of life. YHWH is at times called "the living God" (cf. Deuteronomy 5:23 and Joshua 3:10) even in the context of lament or thanksgiving psalms (cf. Psalms 42:3 and 84:3). On the use of "חיה" in recovery-of-life tropes, note Isaiah 38:16: "Restore me to health and make me live!" ("תחלימני והחיני"). The *pi'el* of "חיה" is often used to connote YHWH's preserving of life, rescuing and healing those in need of aid, those who are captured by the power of death. Kraus has argued that this text reveals that YHWH as a giver of life is one of the ideas behind the conception of YHWH as the living God. Thus the mention of YHWH as cosmic life source in Nehemiah 9:6, in which "חיה" is in the *pi'el,* intersects with the individual reviving acts of YHWH in the Psalms (30:3, 71:20, 80:18, 85:6, 119:25). This is probably the understanding behind the saying "YHWH kills and makes alive" (Deuteronomy 32:39, 1 Samuel 2:6, 2 Kings 5:7, 4 Maccabees 18:18–19, "Hades" in Tobias 13:2, and Wisdom 16:13). See Kraus, *Theology of the Psalms,* 146. Concerning "redeemer": the very same psalmist who proclaims that "you have maintained my just cause!" also recounts a prior experience of salvation with a spatial metaphor: "You are the one who lifts me from the gates of death" (9:13). Likewise, the author of Psalm 119 writes, "Plead my cause [ריבי ריבה] and redeem me [גאלי]; give me life [חיהי] according to your promise" (154). In these poems, forensic words function as reviving metaphors. As with psalms that focus on protection from enemies or recovery from illness, the *Sitz im Leben* of these forensic situations are unrecoverable, and thus they function as general terms for affliction that result in a diminished experience of life. Concerning "rise up": again, "קום" functions differently here than it does in many other recovery-of-life tropes. Yet the appearance of "קום" is tantalizing: in the Psalms, the author can

conceive of restoration to life spatially, as in Psalm 30:3: "YHWH, you brought my life up from Sheol." This type of restoration is characterized by verbs and prepositions that connote upward movement, such as "עלה" (Psalms 30:4 and 40:2), or "קום" (in a negative sense, in Psalms 36:13, 41:8, 88:10, 140:10, and Job 14:12; in a positive sense in Psalms 40:3, 41:10, and 113:7, Job 24:22, 1 Samuel 2:8, 2 Kings 13:21, Isaiah 26:14 and 26:19, Hosea 6:2, and Micah 7:8). This upward motion is metaphorical, unless it corresponds to the healing of an individual, who can then stand upright.

40. Seow, "Job's *Go'el*, Again," 706. As Gunkel has noted, many of the individual lament and thanksgiving psalms seem to have a connection with the temple cult. It appears that in cultic ritual, life can be preserved or restored (as in Psalm 17, wherein the psalmist asks YHWH to "deliver my life" [13] and then describes what he expects his experience of salvation will amount to: "As for me, I shall behold [חזה] your face in righteousness" [15]). Another psalmist frets that his life is in danger, because the wicked lurk in darkness ready to shoot him to death (11:2), but the response comes that "YHWH is in his holy temple" (11:4) and that "the upright shall behold [חזה] his face" (11:7). In Psalm 63, the psalmist, once in mortal danger (9), has "looked upon [חזה] you in the sanctuary" (2), and it is the enemies that will "descend to the depths of the earth" instead of the psalmist (9). While this sentiment constitutes a largely cultic understanding of salvation, such language was easily appropriated by later authors.

41. This is broadly true of ancient Near Eastern lamentations and sufferer texts. In the Akkadian poem "A Sufferer's Salvation," the metaphors of both upward movement and recovery of the wasted body occur together. Also, in "Ludlul Bel Nemeqi" ("I Will Praise the Lord of Wisdom"), an Akkadian thanksgiving hymn to Marduk, both spatial and healing metaphors describe the recovery of the individual. See Hallo and Younger, eds. *The Context of Scripture* 1.152, 43–44; 1.153, 486–92.

42. Barré has argued for a different reading, presupposing YHWH as the גאל: since the word "חי" occurs in close proximity to "קום" in 19:25, Barré sees this as an artfully muted use of the "fixed formulaic pair" "קום/חיה," which usually signals "revivification" and healing (cf. 2 Kings 12:20–21 and Isaiah 26:14 and 26:19). See his "New Light on the Interpretation of Hosea VI 2" and "A Note on Job XIX 25."

43. Barré, "A Note on Job xix 25," 108–109.

44. Kraeling, *Book of the Ways of God,* 89.

45. Zuckerman, *Job the Silent,* 114–15.

46. Other examples include Samuel Terrien's reading that Job wishes that, after his death, he would witness his own vindication in front of the deity; since, as a shade, he could not participate in such proceedings, Job "would recieve new flesh for the specific purpose of the divine-human interview" after death. Terrien emphasizes that this is not resurrection but a temporary resuscitation that would allow Job "to plead his defense before God," to again "be made fully alive" ("The Book of Job," 1055). Also see Janzen, *Job,* 134–35. Janzen develops a surprisingly traditional reading that discusses "resurrection."

47. Suriano, "Death, Disinheritance, and Job's Kinsman-Redeemer," 66.

48. Suriano, "Death, Disinheritance, and Job's Kinsman-Redeemer," 65.

49. Suriano, "Death, Disinheritance, and Job's Kinsman-Redeemer," 65.

50. See Unterman, "The Socio-Legal Origin for the Image of God as Redeemer of Israel."

51. For a discussion of the divine speeches, see Newsom, *The Book of Job*, 234–58.

52. Seow, "Job's *Go'el*, Again," 706.

53. Ewald, *Das Buch Ijob*, 200. "I shall nevertheless behold—God, shall then still feel the joy of the appearance and immediate presence of God also as the judge and defender of my innocence, which I cannot enjoy before the death of the body! and then, as follows of itself, with spiritual eyes, not with my present ones, and yet as certainly and as clearly and sensibly as possible. Whoever beholds God becomes conscious of the pure light, the clear truth, and the eternal life, feeling no separation and no disagreement at all between himself and God, accordingly no alarm, no fear nor punishment: of being able to do this in this bodily life Job has long ago completely despaired, but he now knows that he can and certainly will do it spiritually after physical death." For permutations of this view, also see Dillmann, *Hiob*, 182–90, Kissane, *The Book of Job*, 120–21, and Weiser, *Das Buch Hiob*, 152–53.

54. Duhm, *Das Buch Hiob*, 103. "'Without my body'—that is, although I am dead. The body indeed remains under the earth, Job himself will, rather like Samuel [in] I Samuel 28 . . . , rise up from the ground as a spirit and even as a spirit will see God himself. חזה is well known to be used as a description of ecstatic visions."

55. Ewald, *Das Buch Ijob*, 202. "But the view of perhaps nearly all modern scholars, that Job expresses here an earthly hope and does not at all speak of the time after death, is much worse, and, indeed, totally false. This view is opposed to the words themselves, it is opposed to the connection of the thoughts, it sins against the meaning of the whole book and against the plain advance from 14:13–15 to 16:18 ff., and finally to this passage."

56. Psalm 143 contains the metaphor of the poet's suffering and impending doom as existence in Sheol (3, 7), along with revivification language (11), and forensic language (2).

7. Trajectories of Job 19:25–27

1. As Lyotard writes, "The word survivor implies that an entity that is dead or ought to be is still alive" ("The Survivor," 151).

2. For "literature of survival," see Linafelt, *Surviving Lamentations*, 31.

3. Linafelt, *Surviving Lamentations*, 31.

4. See Jacques Derrida, *Learning to Live Finally*, 33.

5. Wiesel and Beal, "Matters of Survival," 2.

6. Linafelt, *Surviving Lamentations*, 30; Lamentations is both a "survival of literature" and a "literature of survival."

7. Linafelt, *Surviving Lamentations*, 33.

8. It is possible, but not likely, that Aramaic targums, such as 11Q Targum Job, were prepared earlier than the Old Greek translation. See Shepherd, *Targum and Translation*, for a discussion.

9. OG Job challenges the interlinear paradigm of the LXX translation, because it occasionally imports verses from other biblical books (e.g., OG Job 34:13=Psalm 24:1). On the literary quality of Job: for example, in Job 1:5, instead of translating "ויהי" with "καὶ

ἐγένετο" as it is translated usually in the LXX, OG Job translates it with "καὶ ὡς," representing a more standard Greek style. See Hatch, *Essays in Biblical Greek*, 215–45. On the translation style, see Fernández Marcos, "The Septuagint Reading of the Book of Job," esp. 252–55.

10. See Driver and Gray, *A Critical and Exegetical Commentary on the Book of Job*, xlix–l, lxxv–lxxvi, and Dhorme, *Book of Job*, ccii–cciii. On the possibilty of a different *Vorlage*, see Jeffrey, "The Masoretic Text and the Septuagint Compared, with Special Reference to the Book of Job."

11. See Seow, *Job 1–21*, 7.

12. Fernández Marcos, "The Septuagint Reading of the Book of Job," 257.

13. Ziegler, *Iob*. Note the later textual variation, especially in "ἀέναος" in verse 25 and τὸ δέρμα μου in verse 26. Unfortunately I do not have the space to examine the textual history of Job 19:25–27, but this chapter gestures toward the fruitful history of the OG/LXX. Its textual changes both derive from particular readings from the text and generate semantic possibilities for new readings.

14. Adapted from Cox, "Iob," 681. Note the subsitution of "unloose" for "undo" in verse 25.

15. Driver and Gray, *A Critical and Exegetical Commentary on the Book of Job*, 128; Dhorme, *A Commentary on the Book of Job*, 284.

16. This has been observed in other Jewish writings from the Hellenistic era; see Katz, "Septuagintal Studies in the Mid-Century," 122, cited in Tremblay, *Job 19, 25–27 dans la Septante et chez les pères grecs*, 202.

17. Pace Driver and Gray, *A Critical and Exegetical Commentary on the Book of Job*, 128.

18. This modification also allows the translator to replicate the words while achieving better Greek style by creating subordinate clauses using participles.

19. Driver and Gray, *A Critical and Exegetical Commentary on the Book of Job*, 128.

20. See Seow, "Job's *Go'el*, Again," 692, where he suggests this reading for the Hebrew text. It is a live possibility that this reading is supported by OG Job.

21. The Hebrew text of Job could be read as Janus parallelism with a defective spelling of "אלה," thus representing both "these (terrible things)" and God with the same word. This confusion of deity and sufferings seems fittingly Joban and thus a tantalizing option, and it reminds the reader that an ironic tinge may well be present in Job's call for a redeemer.

22. See Dhorme, *A Commentary on the Book of Job*, 285, and Driver and Gray, *A Critical and Exegetical Commentary on the Book of Job*, 128.

23. "The translator inserted the verb συντέλεω there, though it is not found in the Hebrew" (Tremblay, *Job 19, 25–27 dans la Septante et chez les pères grecs*, 202).

24. Seow, "Job's Go'el, Again," 697.

25. By the time of OG Job, *waw-yodh* confusion was common; thus "my kidneys" could be read as a Hiphil imperfect of "כלה" with a first-person object suffix.

26. See Tremblay, *Job 19, 25–27 dans la Septante et chez les pères grecs*, 191–92, for a discussion of the possible senses of "ἐκλύω."

27. Tremblay argues for a reading of this passage as an argument for the resurrection, especially in light of OG Job's translation of Job 14. See *Job 19, 25–27 dans la Septante et chez les pères grecs*, 161–219.

28. Pietersma and Wright, *A New English Translation of the Septuagint*, 681.

29. Pietersma and Wright, *A New English Translation of the Septuagint*, xv.

30. Pietersma and Wright, *A New English Translation of the Septuagint*, xv.

31. Benjamin, "Task of the Translator," 73. As Derrida writes, "The *sur*, 'on,' 'super-,' and so forth . . . also designates the figure of a passage by *trans*-lation, the *trans*- of an *Übersetzung*," "the simultaneous transgression and reappropriation of a language" ("Living on/Border Lines," 71).

32. See Tremblay, *Job 19, 25–27 dans la Septanteet chez les pères grecs*, 122, and Dieu, "Le Texte de Job du Codex Alexandrinus et ses principaux temoins."

33. The OG colophon is not present in the Sahidic and in Oxyrrhynchus Papyri, no. 3522. Asterisked in Syro-Hex, it probably derives from Theodotion. See Fernández Marcos, "The Septuagint Reading of the Book of Job," 264.

34. See Schnocks, "The Hope for Resurrection in the Book of Job," 297.

35. Vernon Robbins ("The Crucifixion and the Speech of Jesus," 38–39) has also argued that, in the New Testament, John 19:30 alludes to Job 19:25–27. In the four Gospels, all of the speech Jesus utters while on the cross seems to reference the Septuagint, and the word "τετέλεσται" ("it is finished") in John 19:30 finds its strongest Septuagintal resonance in Job 19:26–27, which repeats "συντετέλεω" twice. In this reading, Jesus suggests that his body's act of "enduring these sufferings" will allow for certain "things" to "be accomplished" ("συντελέσθη") and "fulfilled" ("συντετέλεσται"). While this reading may or may not discern the intent of the author of the gospel, for a community intent on finding connections between Jesus's death and the Hebrew scriptures, this connection would not seem far fetched at all.

36. See Levenson, *Resurrection and the Restoration of Israel*, 35–66.

37. This section relies on the work of Tremblay, who in *Job 19, 25–27 dans la Septante chez les pères grecs* traces the reception of this text in early Christian theologians. See especially 281–380.

38. See Hagner, *The Use of the Old and New Testaments in Clement of Rome*, 174.

39. Clement of Rome, *PG* 1, 265. Translation from Ehrman, *The Apostolic Fathers*, 83. For similar agrarian imagery for the resurrection in Jewish literature, see *b. Kethuboth* 111b and *b. Sanhedrin* 91a–91b.

40. On the *testimonia* theory, see, for example, Tremblay, *Job 19, 25–27 dans la Septante chez les pères grecs*, 288–93. For an argument that this altered citation comes from memory, see Hagner, *The Use of the Old and New Testaments in Clement of Rome*, 100–101.

41. See Boliek, *The Resurrection of the Flesh*, 21–22.

42. Boliek, *The Resurrection of the Flesh*, 22.

43. See Bakke, *"Concord and Peace,"* 167.

44. Clement of Rome, *PG* 1, 265. Translation from Ehrman, *The Apostolic Fathers*, 45.

45. As Clines writes, "Against any view of bodily resurrection it need only be noted that it contradicts everything the book has said previously about the finality of death (7:9; 10:21; 14:10, 12)" (*Job 1–20*, 464).

46. See, for example, Balentine, *Job*, 299.

47. Jerome, letter 108, *NPNFSS* 6, 221.

48. See the remarks in Bynum, "Images of the Resurrection Body in the Theology of Late Antiquity."

49. See Bynum, *The Resurrection of the Body in Western Christianity, 200–1336,* 24n8.

50. Keller, "The Last Laugh," 389.

51. For example, note the description given by the medieval poet Bonvesin de la Riva: people will still eat bread, but it will be "of the whitest white, . . . precious and sweet," and people will recover their own bodies, but "no one is rotten inside . . . nor does their breath smell bad" (Bynum, "Images of the Resurrection," 594–95).

52. On Origen, see Benz and Klostermann, eds., *Origines Werke X,* 668. For the Greek text of Julian the Arian's discussion of Job 19:25–27, see Hagedorn, *Der Hiobkommentar des Arianers Julian,* 123. For Cyril of Jerusalem, see *PG* 33, 1033–36. For Epiphanius of Salamis, see Holl, *Epiphanius 1,* 119–20. For Hesychius of Jerusalem, see his *Homeliés sur Job, version arménienne,* 563–65. Note also Didymus the Blind's use of Job 19:26 to bolster Origen's argument that God in Genesis 3 did not create clothes for Adam and Eve but rather created corporeal bodies for them in Genesis 3:21. See Layton, *Didymus the Blind and His Circle in Late-Antique Alexandria,* 106.

53. For an overview of Origen's conception of the resurrection, see Bynum, *The Resurrection of the Body,* 63–71, and Crouzel, "La doctrine origeniennne du corps réssuscité."

54. Origen, *Commentary on Matthew* 17.26; The Greek text of Origen's citation of Job 19:25–26 can be found in Benz and Klostermann, *Origines Werke X,* 668. Origen cites this passage in his commentary on Matt 22:23–33, in which the Sadducees deny the resurrection.

55. "It is clear that Origen does not argue here against heretics but rather against those who did not accept his conception of the resurrection of the dead, which was itself considered heretical. To make it clear that his views approximated those of the majority of the Church, he ends this digression by testifying that he, too, believes in the words . . . of Job" (Roukema, "La résurrection des morts dans l'interprétation origénienne de 1 Corinthiens 15," 166).

56. It is likely that Augustine and perhaps Ambrose's interpretations derive from this source. A manuscript of the Itala version reads as follows: "Scio enim quia aeternus est qui me resoluturus est, super terram resurget cutis mea, quae haec patitur: a Domino enim mihi haec contigerunt, quorum ego mihi conscius sum, quae oculus meus vidit et non alius, et omnia mihi consummata sunt in sinu." See Duvivier and Sabatier, *Bibliorum sacrorum Latinae versiones antiquae, seu Vetus Italica, et caeterae quaecunque in codicibus mss. et antiquorum libris reperiri potuerunt,* 866.

57. Severus of Antioch, *A Collection of Letters from Numerous Syriac Manuscripts,* lxix.

58. The translation of the text of Job 19:25–27, especially the use of the word "revealed," is striking, since it constitutes an odd mixture of the LXX and the Peshitta. Though Severus wrote in Greek and read the LXX, he found enormous popularity among Syriac-speaking Christians who preserved and translated his texts. Here, the Syriac translator has emended Severus's quotation of the LXX with a few words from the Peshitta. We will see that the Syriac tradition follows another interpretive trajectory altogether that derives from the Syriac translation, but the existence of Severus in Syriac reminds us that no interpretive trajectory, nor any interpretive community, may seal themselves off

and retain strict boundaries of identity. There is always the "other" already within those bounds.

59. John Chrysostom, *Lettres à Olympias,* 192.

60. John Chrysostom, *Commentaire sur Job,* 47. It might be possible to translate Chrysostom's words as follows: "I think so, and even about the resurrection of the body, at least that the resurrection, of which they speak, is the deliverance of the corrupt who held fast." Yet the translation given in the body of the text seems more consistent with the immediate literary context.

61. See, for example, Zink, "Impatient Job," 147.

62. See Lange, "Literary Prophecy and Oracle Collection."

63. Jerome had already translated this passage from LXX Job, and he stayed fairly close to his translation of that passage in the Vulgate.

64. The Vulgate text itself constitutes a textual process that remained in considerable flux for many centuries. As a result, there are many textual variants that constitute the Vulgate text of Job 19:25–27. Space prohibits an exploration of this text's development here, but the textual apparatus of the *Biblia sacra* provides an overview of the early centuries of this process. Owing to the common use of the Vulgate in liturgy, inscriptions and images, there is even more considerable textual variety in the Latin tradition. I have here represented the critical edition that aims at Jerome's edition, simply because Jerome's reading is in question here. See Gasquet, ed., *Biblia sacra iuxta latinam Vulgatam versionem ad codicum fidem edita, libri Hester et Job,* 143.

65. Notably, Jerome also reads "אחרון" temporally ("in novissimo"), adding to the text's eschatological flavor. He also interprets "נקפו" as a passive of "נקף"-I, meaning "enveloped in" ("rursum circumdabor").

66. For an early version of this argument, see Mombert, "On Job xix 25–27," 29. For a more recent version, see Hester, *Job,* 58.

67. Driver and Gray, *A Critical and Exegetical Commentary on the Book of Job,* 173.

68. Jerome had translated the LXX into Latin to replace the difficult Vetus Latina (Itala) text; at that time, he translated this text as: "Scio enim quia aeternus est qui me resoluturus est super terram resurget cutis mea quae haec patitur a domino enim mihi haec contigerunt, quorum ego mihi conscius sum, quae oculus meus vidit, et non alius: et omnia mihi consummata sunt in sinu." In 19:25, Jerome interprets "יקום" a causative ("יקים"). Between his translation of the LXX to the Vulgate, Jerome transitions from interpreting Job 19:25–27 as a return from Sheol conceit to reading it in light of the doctrine of Resurrection, the final return to life.

69. Jerome, letter 53, *PG* 22, 545.

70. The resurrection of the flesh "became a key element in the fight against Docetism . . . and Gnosticism. . . . The statements of belief for catechumens that appeared around 200 and soon after gave rise to various local creeds (one of which, the old Roman, became the so-called Apostle's Creed) required assent to the doctrine of *resurrectio carnis*" (Bynum, *The Resurrection of the Body,* 26). See also Kelly, *Early Christian Creeds.*

71. Bynum, "Death and Resurrection in the Middle Ages," 595.

72. Jerome's letter became quite influential in later medieval theology as a robust defense of the resurrection of the flesh; see Bynum, *The Resurrection of the Body,* 86–89.

73. Jerome, *Against John of Jerusalem,* 30 (=*PL* 23, 375–82).

74. Jerome even rejects the seed metaphor from 1 Corinthians 15, because it seems to him to downplay the continuity of the flesh. See *Against John of Jerusalem,* 23–26 (=*PL* 23, 390–95).

75. Bynum, "Death and Resurrection in the Middle Ages," 595.

76. See also Augustine, *City of God* 22.29 for a less full-throated endorsement of the importance of the flesh in Job 19:25–27.

77. Ceillier, *Histoire générale des auteurs sacrés et ecclésiastiques,* 819.

78. For an overview of Gregory's *Moralia* and a justification of its identity as an exegesis of the book of Job, see Schreiner, *Where Shall Wisdom Be Found?,* 22–54.

79. For example, the *Glossa ordinaria,* a supremely important group of Bibles with marginal and interlinear commentary, almost exclusively carried Gregory's words throughout the book of Job, so much so that "the story of the *Glossa ordinaria* to the book of Job is a story of Gregory the Great. . . . Certainly the compiler of the *Glossa ordinaria* to Job had a complete text of Gregory's *Moralia* before him" (Matter, "The Church Fathers and the *Glossa Ordinaria,*" 92). See also Gibson, "The Twelfth-Century Glossed Bible."

80. Note also, in different circumstances, Didymus the Blind's use of Job 19:26 to discuss Adam and Eve's enfleshment in Genesis 3; see Layton, *Didymus the Blind and His Circle in Late-Antique Alexandria,* 106.

81. Adriaen, ed., *Sancti Gregorii magni moralia in Job, libri XI–XXII,* 743–45. An English translation may be found in Gregory the Great, *Morals on the Book of Job,* 164.

82. The complete text of the *Moralia* may be found in *PL* 75–76. For the quoted passage, see Adriaen, *Sancti Gregorii magni moralia in Job, libri XI–XXII,* 743–45, and Gregory the Great, *Morals on the Book of Job,* 164, for the English translation.

83. Gregory the Great, *Morals on the Book of Job,* 165–66.

84. Gregory the Great, *Morals on the Book of Job,* 169.

85. Brueggemann, *The Psalms and the Life of Faith,* 212.

86. Note also the appearance of Job 19:25–27 in early homilies and catechetical practices, which could also come under the rubric of performance. See, for example, Hesychius, *Homliés sur Job, version arménienne,* 563–65.

87. See Paxton, *Christianizing Death,* 24.

88. Jacques Derrida, "Rams," 140.

89. Note the stress on the collective context of the funeral service in McLaughlin, "Consorting with Saints," 35.

90. McCall, *Do This,* 136.

91. See Vogel, *Medieval Liturgy,* 135–224.

92. Andrieu, *Les Ordines romani du haut moyen âge,* 523–30; Frank, "Der älteste erhaltene Ordo defunctorum der römischen Liturgie und sein Fortleben in Totenagenden des frühen Mittelalters"; Sicard, *La liturgie de la mort dans l'Eglise latine des origines à la réforme carolingienne,* 1–257.

93. Paxton, *Christianizing Death,* 38.

94. Sicard, *La liturgie de la mort dans l'Eglise latine des origines à la réforme carolingienne,* 2–33.

95. "Mox ut eum viderint et exitum appropinquare communicandus est de sacrificio sancto etiamsi comedisset ipsa die qui communio erit ei defensor et adiutor in resurrectione iustorum. Ipsa eum resuscitabit" (Sicard, *La liturgie de la mort dans l'Eglise latine des origines à la réforme carolingienne,* 35–39).

96. Paxton, *Christianizing Death,* 38.

97. Andrieu, *Les Ordines romani du haut moyen âge,* 529; Sicard, *La liturgie de la mort dans l'Eglise latine des origines à la réforme carolingienne,* 141; Ntedika, *L'évocation de l'au-delà dans la prière pour les morts,* 242.

98. See Ntedika, *L'évocation de l'au-delà dans la prière pour les morts,* 242, 119–22.

99. Ntedika, *L'évocation de l'au-delà dans la prière pour les morts,* 242.

100. Ntedika, *L'évocation de l'au-delà dans la prière pour les morts,* 242.

101. Paxton, *Christianizing Death,* 42.

102. Seow, "Job's *Go'el,* Again," 700–701.

103. Pérez de Urbel and Gonzáles y Ruiz-Zorilla, eds., *Liber comicus,* 550. See also Andrieu, *Les Ordines romani du haut moyen âge,* 529.

104. Ntedika, *L'évocation de l'au-delà dans la prière pour les morts,* 239–40.

105. Ntedika, *L'évocation de l'au-delà dans la prière pour les morts,* 239n63.

106. Férotin, *Le liber ordinum en usage dans l'Église wisigothique et mozarabe d'Espagne du V au XI siècles,* 121.

107. Durand, *Recherches sur l'iconographie de Job des origines de l'art chrétien jusqu'au XIIIe siècle,* 55.

108. See Seow, "Job's *Go'el,* Again," 705.

109. See Clines, *Job 1–20,* 457–58.

110. Of course, one could construe Job's claim to "know" to be just that—a profession of surety, especially since the verb "ידע" most often functions in this manner. Seow ("Job's Go'el, Again," 705) does not endorse this interpretation but also does not rule it out.

111. See Binski, *Medieval Death,* 54.

112. The most famous of these Renaissance musical settings are Orlando di Lasso's two *lectiones: Sacrae lectiones ex propheta Iob* (1560) and *Lectiones sacrae novem, ex libris Hiob excerptae* (1582). The use of Job 19:25–27 in these settings doubtless led to its inclusion in the libretto for Handel's *Messiah.*

113. Ottosen, *The Responsories and Versicles of the Latin Office of the Dead,* 44.

114. See Wieck, *Time Sanctified,* 166–67.

115. See Renevey, "Looking for a Context."

116. The lessons are as follows: (1) Job 7:16–21, (2) Job 10:1–7, (3) Job 10:8–12, (4) Job 13:22–28, (5) Job 14:1–6, (6) Job 14:13–16, (7) Job 17:1–3, 11–25, (8) Job 19:20–27, and (9) Job 10:18–22. This is surprising because Christian readings of Job tend to minimize the dialogues. Note, for example, how Jacobus de Voragine treats chapters 3–38 of the book of Job: "Then after that Job and they talked and spake together of his sorrow and misery, of which S. Gregory hath made a great book called: 'The Morals of S. Gregory,' which is a noble book and a great work. But I pass over all the matters and return unto the end" (*The Golden Legend,* 55–56).

117. Ottosen, *The Responsories and Versicles of the Latin Office of the Dead,* 59. Note Ottosen's theory of the creation of tension between these differing versions of 19:25–27 in note 16. In one response (R 14), the text begins with "Credo quod redemptor meus vivit"

("I believe that my redeemer lives"), but in the lesson it begins with "scio" ("I know"), thus representing multiple interpretations of Job's proclamation within one liturgical practice (44).

118. See Wieck, *Time Sanctified*, 166–67, for the full biblical citations in the Office of the Dead.

119. Wieck, *Painted Prayers*, 118.

120. Ottosen, *The Responsories and Versicles of the Latin Office of the Dead*, 44.

121. Derrida, *Limited Inc*, 6–9.

122. Bennington and Derrida, *Jacques Derrida*, 45.

123. For a powerful reading of this ambiguity, see Seow, "Job's *Go'el*, Again," 695.

124. Bynum, *The Resurrection of the Body in Western Christianity*, 200–336, 342.

125. For example, the following from Sardinia, Olmedo, dating to the sixth century: "hic situs Silibus eccle|siae sanctae minister | expectat Christi ope | ursus sua vivere carne | et gaudia lucis nobae | ipso dominante videre" (*CIL* X 7972; *CLE* 786; *ILCV* 3445). Another such inscription that dates from the sixth century was found in Catania, Sicily; see Gasperini, "Su un epitafio catinense con ripresa scritturistica." Many others dating from 650–850 CE have been discovered in the Cathedral of St. Erasmus in Formia and elsewhere in Italy; see Gasperini, "Le scoperte epigrafiche sotto S. Erasmo a Formia," and Felle, *Biblia epigraphica*, 298–300, 556.

126. *ILCV* 2399; Felle, *Biblia epigraphica*, 366.

127. *ILCV* 1053; *CIL* V 6728; *CLE* 709; Felle, *Biblia epigraphica*, 276–78.

128. Ricci and Tagliamonte, "Iscrizioni cristiane nelle Collezioni comunali," 180.

129. Note also the astounding survival of a funerary inscription of Job 19:25–27 in the recycled stone that the belltower of the church in Pomposa, Italy, is composed of. See Russo, "Un'epigrafe con citazione biblica (lob, XIX, 25–27) nel campanile di Pomposa."

130. Lomatrine and Segagni, "San Felice, tomba della badessa Ariperga," 248; Treffort, "Appels à la prière et oraisons de pierre dans les inscriptions funéraires des VIIIe-XIe siècles," 278–79.

131. Strafella, "Una sepoltura dipinta nell'abbazia di San Benedetto di Leno."

132. Treffort, "Appels à la prière et oraisons de pierre dans les inscriptions funéraires des VIIIe-XIe siècles," 278–79.

133. Strafella, "Una sepoltura dipinta nell'abbazia di San Benedetto di Leno," 169–70.

134. Lomatrine and Segagni, "San Felice, tomba della badessa Ariperga," 248.

135. Wirth, "Die Nachrichten über Begräbnis und Grab Bischof Bernwards von Hildesheim in Thangmars Vita Bernwardi"; Treffort, "Appels à la prière et oraisons de pierre dans les inscriptions funéraires des VIIIe-XIe siècles," 278.

136. While some scholars have suggested that parts of this vita, including this pericope, are later fabrications, note the defense in Collins, *Reforming Saints*, 149–50n40. See also Wirth, "Die Nachrichten über Begräbnis und Grab Bischof Bernwards von Hildesheim in Thangmars Vita Bernwardi," 310, who seems ambivalent.

137. The inscription reads: "+ SCIO ENIM QVOD REDEMPT[OR] MEV[S VI]VIT ET IN NOV[I]SSIMO / DIE DE / TERRA SVRRECTVRVS SVM · [E]T RVRSVM CIRCVMDABOR PELLE MEA / ET IN CAR/NE MEA VI/DEBO D(EV)M SALVATOREM MEVM · QVEM VISVRVS SVM EGO IPSE ET / OCVLI / MEI CONSPECTVRI SVNT

ET NON ALIVS · REPOSITA EST HEC SPES MEA IN SINV MEO" (Wirth, "Die Nachrichten über Begräbnis und Grab Bischof Bernwards von Hildesheim in Thangmars Vita Bernwardi," 310–11).

138. Wirth, "Die Nachrichten über Begräbnis und Grab Bischof Bernwards von Hildesheim in Thangmars Vita Bernwardi," 310–11.

139. Tschan, *Saint Bernward of Hildesheim*, 89, 103, 200–202.

140. Cassuto, "Nuove iscrizioni ebraiche di Venosa."

141. See Roemer, "Turning Defeat into Victory."

142. Zunz, *Zur Geschichte und Literatur*, 421.

143. Cassuto, "Nuove iscrizioni Ebraiche di Venosa," 9; Starr, *The Jews in the Byzantine Empire, 641–1204*, 113.

144. See Noy, *Jewish Inscriptions of Western Europe*, 73, 237. See also the attempted but problematic rebuttal in Park, *Conceptions of Afterlife in Jewish Inscriptions*.

145. See especially the tombstones from Venosa described in Noy, *Jewish Inscriptions of Western Europe*, 61–150.

146. For example, see the discussion of Oniyahu and Uriyahu in Suriano, "Death, Disinheritance, and Job's Kinsman-Redeemer," 55.

147. Goodman notes the firmly material nature of Saadiah's notion of salvation: "The concept of extramundial salvation is simply not central to Saadiah's thinking, as it is not to the Hebrew Bible in general. The world is not thought of as a place from which one needs to be saved—although, or because, one can be saved in it or through it" (*The Book of Theodicy*, 292n10).

148. Al-Fayyumi, *The Book of Theodicy*, 289.

149. Al-Fayyumi, *The Book of Theodicy*, 289.

150. On the various ways of interpreting 42:6, see Newsom, *The Book of Job*, 28–30.

151. Avalos, "Introducing Sensory Criticism in Biblical Studies," 55.

152. Avalos, "Introducing Sensory Criticism in Biblical Studies," 55.

153. Avalos, "Introducing Sensory Criticism in Biblical Studies," 56.

154. The author Frederick Buechner offers a classic, popular example of this sort of reading: "All his life he had heard about God. . . . But now it was no longer a matter of hearing descriptions of God because finally he had heard and seen him for himself. . . . [As for Job's children and possessions], he never got an explanation about them because he never asked for one, and the reason he never asked for one was that he knew that even if God gave him one that made splendid sense out of all the pain and suffering that had ever been since the world began, it was no longer splendid sense that he needed because with his own eyes he had beheld, and not as a stranger, the one who in the end clothed all things, no matter how small or confused or in pain, with his own splendor. And that was more than sufficient" (*Peculiar Treasures: A Biblical Who's Who*, 68).

155. For a text of Pesh Job, see Rignell, ed., *Job*.

156. Cf. Job 1:20, 4:4, 7:4, 8:15, 11:17, 14:12, 15:29, 16:8, 16:12, 19:18, and 20:27 (note "קום" in parallel with "גלה"). See especially 31:14, in which God is the subject of the verb, the action almost certainly to be understood as God's manifestation; this is also rendered with "qym" in Pesh Job.

157. Cf. Job 12:22, 20:27, 20:28, 30:16, 36:10, 36:15, and 38:17.

158. The adverbial use is exclusively with the feminine "אחרון." See Seow, "Job's *Go'el*, Again," 695.

159. See Kennicott, *Vetus Testamentum hebraicum cum variis lectionibus*, 478–524, and de Rossi, *Variae lectiones Veteris Testamenti ex immensa mss.*, 105–38.

160. Weitzman, *The Syriac Version of the Old Testament*, 234, also argues, albeit briefly, that "in P the expectation is eschatalogical."

161. Qtd. in Wolfson, "Circumcision, Vision of God, and Textual Interpretation," 192.

162. Wolfson, "Circumcision, Vision of God, and Textual Interpretation," 207–15. Wolfson claims that this is the earliest known connection between circumcision and theophany.

163. Boyarin, "'This We Know to be the Carnal Israel,'" 492.

164. See Freedman and Simon, eds., *Midrash Rabbah*, 1:406n.4.

165. Wolfson, "Circumcision, Vision of God, and Textual Interpretation," 205–6.

166. Qtd. in Wolfson, "Circumcision, Vision of God, and Textual Interpretation," 206.

167. Wolfson, "Circumcision, Vision of God, and Textual Interpretation," 207.

168. Altmann, *Von der mittelalterlichen zur modernen Aufklärung*, 15.

169. Altmann, *Von der mittelalterlichen zur modernen Aufklärung*, 20.

170. Altmann, *Studies in Religious Philosophy and Mysticism*, 25.

171. Hayman, *The Disputation of Sergius the Stylite against a Jew*, 1. Sergius begins by citing the Syriac version of the creed; see the East and West Syriac recensions in Ferguson, *Recent Studies in Early Christianity*, 289.

172. Jacob Serugh, *Homélies contre les Juifs*, 129.

173. Serugh, *Homélies contre les Juifs*, 129.

174. Graf, *Die schriften des Jakobiten Habib ibn Hidma, Abu Ra'ita*, 120; Bar Hebraeus, *Le candélabre du sanctuaire de Grégoire Abou'lfaradj dit Barhebraeus*, 17.

175. Amar, *Dionysius bar Salibi*, 67.

176. See Derrida, "Force of Law."

177. For an extended analysis of the points laid out here, see Hankins, "Job and the Limits of Wisdom."

178. See Newsom, *The Book of Job*, 150–65.

179. Pinnock, *Beyond Theodicy*, 72.

180. Bloch, *Atheism in Christianity*, 103–4.

181. Bloch, *Atheism in Christianity*, 101.

182. Seow, "Job's *Go'el*, Again," 705.

183. For a discussion of Theodotion Job, see Gentry, *The Asterisked Materials in the Greek Job*, 406–10.

184. See Tov, *Textual Criticism of the Hebrew Bible*, 145.

185. For the fragmentary text of Theodotion Job 19:25 and 19:27, see Frederick Field, *Origenis Hexaplorum quae supersunt*, 2:36.

186. See Gentry, "The Place of Theodotion–Job," 229.

187. Field, *Origenis Hexaplorum*, 2:9.

188. See Shoshanna, ed., *Sefer Iyyov be-veit midrasho shel Rashi* [*The Book of Job in the School of Rashi*], 116–17.

189. Zunz, *Zur Geschichte und Literatur*, 121–310.

190. Roemer, *Jewish Scholarship and Culture in Nineteenth-Century Germany,* 68. See also Roemer, "Turning Defeat into Victory," 65–80.

191. Roemer, "Turning Defeat into Victory," 69–70.

192. Qtd. in Roemer, *Jewish Scholarship and Culture in Nineteenth-Century Germany,* 69.

193. Zunz, *Zur Geschichte und Literatur,* 421.

194. Benjamin, "Theses on the Philosophy of History," 255.

Conclusion

1. In "Nietzsche, Genealogy, History," for example, Foucault remarks that "the body is the inscribed surface of events. . . . Genealogy, as an analysis of descent, is thus situated within the articulation of the body and history. Its task is to expose a body totally imprinted by history" (147).

2. On the nomad and nomadology, see Deleuze and Guattari, *A Thousand Plateaus,* 387–467.

BIBILOGRAPHY

Adriaen, Marc. *Sancti Gregorii magni moralia in Job, libri XI–XXII.* Corpus christianorum, series latina 143A. Turnhout: Brepols, 1979.

Albrektson, Bertil. "Reflections on the Emergence of a Standard Text of the Hebrew Bible." In *Congress Volume: Göttingen 1977.* VTS 29. Edited by John Emerton, 49–65. Leiden: Brill, 1978.

Al-Fayyumi, Saadiah Ben Joseph. *The Book of Theodicy: Commentary on the Book of Job.* Edited and translated by Lenn Evan Goodman. New Haven, CT: Yale University Press, 1988.

Altmann, Alexander. *Studies in Religious Philosophy and Mysticism.* Vol. 2. Ithaca, NY: Cornell University Press, 1969.

———. *Von der mittelalterlichen zur modernen Aufklärung.* Tübingen: Mohr Siebeck, 1987.

Amar, Joseph P. *Dionysius bar Salibi: A Response to the Arabs.* CSCO 614–15. Louvain: Peeters, 2005.

Andrieu, Michel. *Les Ordines romani du haut moyen âge.* Vol. 4. Spicilegium sacrum lovaniense 28. Louvain: Spicilegium, 1956.

Aptowitzer, Victor. *Das Schriftwort in der rabbinischen Literatur.* 4 vols. 1906–15. Reprint. New York: Ktav, 1970.

Astruc, Jean. *Conjectures sur les mémoires originaux dont il paraît que Moïse s'est servi pour composer le livre de la Genèse, avec des remarques qui appuient ou qui éclaircissent ces conjectures.* Bruxelles: Chez Friex, 1753.

Attridge, Harold, et al. *Qumran Cave 4.VIII: Parabiblical Texts.* Pt. 1. DJD 13. Oxford, UK: Clarendon, 1994.

Austin, J. L. *How to Do Things with Words.* Cambridge, MA: Harvard University Press, 1962.

Avalos, Hector. "Introducing Sensory Criticism in Biblical Studies: Audiocentricity and Visiocentricity." In *This Abled Body: Rethinking Disabilities in Biblical Studies.* Edited by Hector Avalos, Sarah Melcher, and Jeremy Schipper, 47–60. Atlanta, GA: Society of Biblical Literature, 2007.

Ayer, A. J. *Language, Truth, and Logic.* Mineola, NY: Dover, 1952.

Badiou, Alain. *Being and Event.* Translated by Oliver Feltham. London: Continuum, 2005.

———. *Logics of Worlds.* Translated by Alberto Toscano. London: Continuum, 2009.

Bahrani, Zainab. *The Graven Image: Representation in Babylonia and Assyria.* Philadelphia: University of Pennsylvania Press, 2003.

Bakhtin, Mikhail. M. *The Dialogic Imagination: Four Essays.* Edited by Michael Holquist. Translated by Caryl Emerson and Michael Holquist. Austin: University of Texas Press, 1981.

———. *Problems of Dostoevsky's Poetics.* Translated by Caryl Emerson. Minneapolis: University of Minnesota Press, 1984.

Bakke, Odd M. *"Concord and Peace": A Rhetorical Analysis of the First Letter of Clement with an Emphasis on the Language of Unity and Sedition.* Tübingen: Mohr Siebeck, 2001.

Balentine, Samuel. *Job.* Smyth and Helwys Commentary. Macon, GA: Smyth and Helwys, 2006.

Ball, Charles J. *The Book of Job: A Revised Text and Version.* Rev. ed. Oxford, UK: Clarendon, 1922.

Bar Hebraeus. *Le candélabre du sanctuaire de Grégoire Abou'lfaradj dit Barhebraeus: Quatrime base, de l'incarnation.* PO 31:1. Paris: Firmin-Didot, 1964.

Barr, James. *The Concept of Biblical Theology: An Old Testament Perspective.* Minneapolis, MN: Fortress, 1999.

———. *History and Ideology in the Old Testament: Biblical Studies at the End of a Millennium.* Oxford: Oxford University Press, 2000.

———. *Holy Scripture: Canon, Authority, Criticism.* Oxford: Oxford University Press, 1983.

———. *The Semantics of Biblical Language.* Oxford: Oxford University Press, 1961.

———. "The Symbolism of Names in the Old Testament." *Bulletin of the John Rylands Library* 52.1 (1969): 11–29.

Barré, Michael L. "New Light on the Interpretation of Hosea VI 2." *Vetus Testamentum* 28.2 (1978): 129–41.

———. "A Note on Job xix 25." *Vetus Testamentum* 29.1 (1979): 107–9.

Barthélemy, Dominique. *Les devanciers d'Aquila.* VTS 10. Leiden: Brill, 1963.

———. "Text, Hebrew, History of." In *The Interpreter's Dictionary of the Bible.* Supp. vol. Edited by Kieth Crim, 878–81. Nashville, TN: Abingdon, 1976.

Barthes, Roland. "The Death of the Author." In *Image, Music, Text,* 142–48. Translated by Stephen Heath. New York: Hill and Wang, 1977.

Barton, John. "Historical-Critical Approaches." In *The Cambridge Companion to Biblical Interpretation,* 9–20. Edited by John Barton. Cambridge: Cambridge University Press, 1998.

———. *The Nature of Biblical Criticism.* Louisville, KY: Westminster John Knox, 2007.

———. *The Old Testament: Canon, Literature and Theology.* Aldershot, UK: Ashgate, 2007.

———. *People of the Book? The Authority of the Bible in Christianity.* Louisville, KY: Westminster John Knox, 1989.

———. *Reading the Old Testament: Method in Biblical Study.* 2nd ed. Louisville, KY: Westminster John Knox, 1996.

Beardsley, Monroe, and William K. Wimsatt. *The Verbal Icon: Studies in the Meaning of Poetry.* Lexington: University of Kentucky Press, 1954.

Beaucamp, Evode. "Le goël de Jb 19,25." *Laval théologique et philosophique* 33.3 (1977): 309–10.

Benjamin, Walter. "Task of the Translator: An Introduction to the Translation of Baudelaire's 'Tableaux Parisiens.'" In *Illuminations: Essays and Reflections*, 69–82. Edited by Hannah Arendt. Translated by Harry Zohn. New York: Schocken, 1968.

———. "Theses on the Philosophy of History." In *Illuminations: Essays and Reflections*, 253–64. Edited by Hannah Arendt. Translated by Harry Zohn. New York: Schocken, 1968.

Bennington, Geoffrey. "Derrida's 'Eighteenth Century.'" *Eighteenth-Century Studies* 40.3 (2007): 381–93.

———. "Foundations." *Textual Practice* 21.2 (2007): 231–49.

———. *Other Analyses: Reading Philosophy*. CreateSpace, 2004.

———. "Saussure and Derrida." In *The Companion to Saussure*. Edited by Carol Sanders, 186–204. Cambridge: Cambridge University Press, 2005.

Bennington, Geoffrey, and Jacques Derrida. *Jacques Derrida*. Translated by Geoffrey Bennington. Chicago: University of Chicago Press, 1993.

Benveniste, Émile. *Problems in General Linguistics*. Translated by Mary Elizabeth Meek. Coral Gables, FL: University of Miami Press, 1971.

Benz, Ernst, and Erich Klostermann, eds. *Origenes Werke X: Commentarius in Matthaeum I*. GCS 40. Leipzig: Hinrichs, 1935.

Berlin, Adele. *Lamentations*. Interpretation. Louisville, KY: Westminster John Knox, 2002.

Berlin, Brent, and Paul Kay. *Basic Color Terms: Their Universality and Evolution*. Berkeley: University of California Press, 1969.

Bernstein, Moshe J. "'Rewritten Bible': A Generic Category Which Has Outlived Its Usefulness?" *Textus* 22 (2005): 169–96.

Berrin, Shani L. *The Pesher Nahum Scroll from Qumran: An Exegetical Study of 4Q169*. STDJ 53. Leiden: Brill, 2004.

Bevan, Edwyn. *The House of Seleucus*. 2 vols. London: Edward Arnold, 1902.

Bickerman, Elias J. *The God of the Maccabees: Studies on the Meaning and Origin of the Maccabean Revolt*. Studies in Judaism and Late Antiquity 32. Translated by Horst R. Moehring. Leiden: Brill, 1979.

Binski, Paul. *Medieval Death*. Ithaca, NY: Cornell University Press, 1996.

Bizos, Marcel. *Syntaxe grecque*. Paris: Librairie Vuibert, 1947.

Blanchot, Maurice. "Translating." *Sulfur* 26 (1990): 82–86.

Bloch, Ernst. *Atheism in Christianity: The Religion of the Exodus and the Kingdom*. Translated by J. T. Swann. New ed. London: Verso, 2009.

Bogaert, P. M. "De Baruch à Jérémie: Les deux rédactions conservées du livre de Jérémie." In *Le livre de Jérémie*. BETL 54. Edited by Pierre-Maurice Bogaert, 168–73. Leuven: Leuven University Press, 1981.

Bonta, Mark, and John Protevi. *Deleuze and Geophilosophy: A Guide and Glossary*. Edinburgh: Edinburgh University Press, 2004.

Borges, Jorge Luis. "The Garden of the Forking Paths." In *Ficciones*, 89–101. Edited by Anthony Kerrigan. New York: Grove, 1962.

———. "The Homeric Versions." In *Selected Non-Fictions,* 69–74. Edited by Eliot Weinberger. Translated by Esther Allen, Suzanne Jill Levine, and Eliot Weinberger. New York: Viking, 1999.

———. "Pierre Menard, Author of Don Quixote." In *Labyrinths: Selected Stories and Other Writings,* 36–44. New York: New Directions, 1962.

———. *The Total Library: Non-fiction, 1922–1986.* Edited by Eliot Weinberger. Translated by Ester Allen, Suzanne Jill Levine, and Eliot Weinberger. London: Penguin, 1999.

Bottéro, Jean. *Mesopotamia: Writing, Reasoning, and the Gods.* Translated by Zainab Bahrani and Marc Van De Mieroop. Chicago: University of Chicago Press, 1995.

Bowley, James E., and John C. Reeves. "Rethinking the Concept of 'Bible': Some Theses and Proposals." *Henoch* 25.1 (2003): 3–18.

Boyarin, Daniel. "'This We Know to Be the Carnal Israel': Circumcision and the Erotic Life of God and Israel." *Critical Inquiry* 18 (1992): 474–505.

Boyd, Richard N. "The Current Status of Scientific Realism." In *The Current Status of Scientific Realism.* Edited by Jarrett Leplin, 41–83. Berkeley: University of California Press, 1984.

Bringmann, Klaus. *Hellenistische Reform und Religionsverfolgung in Judäa: Eine Untersuchung zur jüdisch-hellenistichen Geschichte (175–163 v. Chr.).* Göttingen: Vandenhoeck und Ruprecht, 1983.

Brueggemann, Walter. "Bounded by Obedience and Praise: The Psalms as Canon." *Journal for the Study of the Old Testament* 16.50 (1991): 63–92.

———. *The Message of the Psalms: A Theological Commentary.* Minneapolis, MN: Fortress, 1984.

———. *The Psalms and the Life of Faith.* Edited by Patrick Miller. Minneapolis, MN: Fortress, 1995.

———. "Response to James L. Mays, 'The Question of Context.'" In *The Shape and Shaping of the Psalter.* Edited by J. Clinton McCann, 29–41. JSOTSup 159. Sheffield, UK: JSOT Press, 1993.

Bryant, Levi. *Difference and Givenness: Deleuze's Transcendental Empiricism and the Ontology of Immanence.* Evanston, IL: Northwestern University Press, 2008.

Budde, Karl. *Das Buch Hiob, übersetzt und erklärt.* Göttingen: Vandenhoeck und Ruprecht, 1896.

Buechner, Frederick. *Peculiar Treasures: A Biblical Who's Who.* New York: HarperCollins, 1979.

Burke, Peter. "Context in Context." *Common Knowledge* 8.1 (2002): 152–77.

Burnett, Stephen. "Later Christian Hebraists." In *Hebrew Bible/Old Testament: The History of its Interpretation, from the Renaissance to the Enlightenment.* Edited by Magne Saebø and Michael Fishbane, 785–801. Gottingen: Vandenhoeck und Ruprecht, 2008.

Burrow, J. A. *Medieval Writers and Their Work: Middle English Literature, 1100–1500.* Oxford: Oxford University Press, 1982.

Buss, Martin J. *Biblical Form Criticism in Its Context.* JSOTSup 274. Sheffield, UK: Sheffield Academic Press, 1999.

Bynum, Caroline Walker. "Death and Resurrection in the Middle Ages: Some Modern Implications." *Proceedings of the American Philosophical Society* 142.4 (1998): 589–96.

———. "Images of the Resurrection Body in the Theology of Late Antiquity." *Catholic Historical Review* 80.2 (1994): 215–37.

———. *The Resurrection of the Body in Western Christianity, 200–1336*. New York: Columbia University Press, 1995.

Camille, Michael. "Seeing and Reading: Some Visual Implications of Medieval Literacy and Illiteracy." *Art History* 8.1 (1985): 26–49.

Cassuto, Umberto. "Nuove iscrizioni ebraiche di Venosa." *Archivio storico per la Calabria e la Luciana* 4 (1934): 1–9.

Ceillier, Remi. *Histoire générale des auteurs sacrés et ecclésiastiques*. Vol. 14. 2nd ed. Paris: Vivès, 1863.

Cerquiglini, Bernard. *Éloge de la variante: Histoire critique de la philologie*. Paris: Seuil, 1989.

———. *In Praise of the Variant: A Critical History of Philology*. Parallax: Re-visions of Culture and Society. Translated by Betsy Wing. Baltimore, MD: Johns Hopkins University Press, 1999.

Childs, Brevard. *Introduction to the Old Testament as Scripture*. Philadelphia: Fortress, 1979.

Choi, John H. *Traditions at Odds: The Reception of the Pentateuch in Biblical and Second Temple Period Literature*. Library of Hebrew Bible/Old Testament Studies 518. London: Clark, 2010.

Clements, Ronald E. "The Prophet as Author: The Case of the Isaiah Memoir." In *Writings and Speech in Israelite and Ancient Near Eastern Prophecy*. SBLS 10. Edited by Ehud Ben Zvi and Michael H. Floyd, 89–101. Atlanta, GA: Society of Biblical Literature, 2000.

Clines, David J. A. "Belief, Desire, and Wish in Job 19,23–27: Clues for the Identity of Job's 'Redeemer.'" In *"Wünschet Jerusalem Frieden": Collected Communications to the XIIth Congress of the International Organization for the Study of the Old Testament, Jerusalem 1986*. Edited by Matthias Augustin and Klaus-Dietrich Schunck, 363–70. Frankfurt am Main: Peter Lang, 1988.

———. *Job 1–20*. WBC 17. Dallas, TX: Word, 1989.

———. *Job 21–37*. WBC 18A. Nashville, TN: Nelson, 2006.

———. "Pyramid and the Net: The Postmodern Adventure in Biblical Studies." In vol. 1 of *On the Way to the Postmodern: Old Testament Essays, 1967–1998*, 138–57. JSOTSupp 292. Sheffield, UK: JSOT Press, 1998.

Cohn, Yehudah. *Tangled up in Text: Tefillin and the Ancient World*. Atlanta, GA: Society of Biblical Literature, 2008.

Collins, David J. *Reforming Saints: Saint's Lives and their Authors in Germany, 1470–1530*. Oxford: Oxford University Press, 2008.

Collins, John J. *The Bible after Babel: Historical Criticism in a Postmodern Age*. Grand Rapids, MI: Eerdmans, 2005.

———. *Daniel: A Commentary on the Book of Daniel*. Hermeneia. Edited by Frank Moore Cross. Minneapolis, MN: Fortress, 1993.

———. *Encounters with Biblical Theology*. Minneapolis, MN: Fortress, 2005.

———. "The Exodus and Biblical Theology." *Biblical Theology Bulletin* 25.4 (1995): 152–60.

———. "Is a Critical Biblical Theology Possible?" In *The Hebrew Bible and Its Interpreters*. Edited by Doulgas A. Knight and Gene M. Tucker, 1–17. Atlanta, GA: Scholars Press, 1990.

———. *A Short Introduction to the Hebrew Bible*. Minneapolis, MN: Fortress, 2007.

Cook, Guy. *Applied Linguistics*. Oxford: Oxford University Press, 2003.

Cook, Stephen L. "*Relecture*, Hermeneutics, and Christ's Passion in the Psalms." In *The Whirlwind: Essays on Job, Hermeneutics and Theology in Memory of Jane Morse*. Edited by Stephen Cook, Corinne L. Patton, and James W. Watts, 181–205. Sheffield, UK: Sheffield Academic Press, 2001.

Cooper, Alan. "Reading and Misreading the Prologue to Job." *Journal for the Study of the Old Testament* 15.46 (1990): 67–79.

Croatto, J. Severino. *Exodus: A Hermeneutics of Freedom*. Maryknoll, NY: Orbis, 1981.

Cross, Frank Moore. "The Ammonite Oppression of the Tribes of Gad and Reuben: Missing Verses from 1 Samuel 11 Found in 4QSamuel[a]." In *Studies in Biblical and Cuneiform Literatures History, Historiography and Interpretation*. Edited by Hayim Tadmor and Moshe Weinfeld, 148–58. Jerusalem: Humanities Press, 1983.

———. "The History of the Biblical Text in the Light of Discoveries in the Judaean Desert." *The Harvard Theological Review* 57.4 (1964): 281–99.

Cross, Frank Moore, and Shemaryahu Talmon. *Qumran and the History of the Biblical Text*. Cambridge, MA: Harvard University Press, 1978.

Crouzel, Henri. "La doctrine origénienne du corps réssuscité." *Bulletin de littérature ecclésiastique* 81 (1980): 175–200, 241–66.

DeGrood, David H. *Philosophies of Essence: An Examination of the Category of Essence*. Amsterdam: John Benjamins, 1976.

de Lagarde, Paul. *Anmerkungen zur griechischen Übersetzung der Proverbien*. Leipzig: F. A. Brockhaus, 1863.

DeLanda, Manuel. "Deleuze, Diagrams and the Open-Ended Becoming of the World." In *Becomings: Explorations in Time, Memory and Futures*. Edited by Elizabeth Grosz, 29–41. Ithaca, NY: Cornell University Press, 1999.

———. "Immanence and Transcendence in the Genesis of Form." In *A Deleuzian Century?* Edited by Ian Buchanan, 499–514. Durham, NC: Duke University Press, 1999.

———. *Intensive Science and Virtual Philosophy*. London: Continuum, 2002.

Deleuze, Gilles. *Cinema I: The Movement-Image*. Minneapolis: University of Minnesota Press, 1986.

———. *Difference and Repetition*. Translated by Paul Patton. New York: Columbia University, Press, 1994.

———. *Desert Islands and Other Texts*. Translated by Michael Taormina. New York: Semiotext(e), 2003.

———. *Essays Critical and Clinical*. Edited by D. W. Smith. Translated by Michael A. Greco and Daniel W. Smith. Minneapolis: University of Minnesota Press, 1997.

———. *Expressionism in Philosophy: Spinoza*. Translated by Martin Joughin. Cambridge, MA: MIT Press, 1990.

———. *The Fold: Leibniz and the Baroque*. Translated by Tom Conley. Minneapolis: University of Minnesota Press, 1993.

———. *The Logic of Sense*. Edited by Constantin V. Boundas. Translated by Mark Lester and Charles Stivale. New York: Columbia University Press, 1990.

———. *Proust and Signs: The Complete Text*. Translated by Richard Howard. Minneapolis: University of Minnesota Press, 2003.

———. *Spinoza: Practical Philosophy*. Translated by Robert Hurley. San Francisco: City Lights, 1988.

Deleuze, Gilles, and Felix Guattari. *A Thousand Plateaus: Capitalism and Schizophrenia*. Translated by Brian Massumi. Minneapolis: University of Minnesota Press, 1987.

Deleuze, Gilles, and Claire Parnet. *Dialogues II*. New York: Columbia University Press, 2007.

Denis, Valentin. "Saint Job, patron des musiciens." *Revue belge d'archéologie et d'histoire de l'art* 21.4 (1952): 253–98.

de Rossi, Giovanni. *Variae lectiones Veteris Testamenti ex immensa mss*. Vol. 4. Parmae: Ex regio typographeo, 1788.

Derrida, Jacques. "Des tours des Babel." In *Psyche: Inventions of the Other*. Vol. 1, 191–225. Edited by Peggy Kamuf and Elizabeth Rottenburg. Stanford, CA: Stanford University Press, 2007.

———. "Différence." In *Margins of Philosophy*, 1–27. Translated by Alan Bass. Chicago: University of Chicago Press, 1982.

———. *Dissemination*. Translated by Barbara Johnson. Chicago: University of Chicago Press, 1981.

———. "Force of Law: The Mystical Foundation of Authority." *Cardozo Law Review* 11.5–6 (1990): 919–1045.

———. *Learning to Live Finally: An Interview with Jean Birbaum*. Edited by Pascale-Anne Brault and Michael Nass. Hoboken, NJ: Melville House, 2007.

———. *Limited Inc*. Translated by Samuel Weber. Evanston: Northwestern University Press, 1988.

———. "Living On/Border Lines." In *Deconstruction and Criticism*. Edited by Harold Bloom, 75–176. New York: Continuum, 1979.

———. *Of Grammatology*. Translated by Gayatri Spivak. Corrected ed. Baltimore, MD: Johns Hopkins University Press, 1998.

———. "Rams: Uninterrupted Dialogue—Between Two Infinities, the Poem." In *Sovereignties in Question: The Poetics of Paul Celan*, 135–63. Edited by Thomas Dutoit and Outi Pasanen. New York: Fordham University Press, 2005.

———. *Specters of Marx: The State of the Debt, The Work of Mourning and the New International.* Translated by Peggy Kamuf. New York: Routledge, 1994.

———. *Speech and Phenomena and Other Essays on Husserl's Theory of Signs.* Translated by David Allison. Evanston, IL: Northwestern University Press, 1973.

———. *Without Alibi.* Translated by Peggy Kamuf. Stanford, CA: Stanford University Press, 2002.

Derrida, Jacques, and Henri Ronse. *Positions.* Translated by Alan Bass. Chicago: University of Chicago Press, 1981.

De Troyer, Kristin, and Armin Lange, eds. *Reading the Present in the Qumran Library: The Perception of the Contemporary by Means of Scriptural Interpretations.* Atlanta, GA: Society of Biblical Literature, 2005.

Detweiler, Robert "Overliving." *Semeia* 54 (1991): 239–55.

Dhorme, Édouard. *A Commentary on the Book of Job.* Translated by Harold Knight. Nashville, TN: Nelson, 1984.

Dieu, Léon. "Le texte de Job du Codex Alexandrinus et ses principaux temoins." *Muséon* 13 (1912): 223–74.

Dilley, Roy. M. "The Problem of Context in Social and Cultural Anthropology." *Language and Communication* 22.4 (2002): 437–56.

Dillmann, August. *Hiob.* Leipzig: Hirzel, 1891.

Dimant, Devorah, and John Strugnell. *Qumran Cave 4: Parabiblical Texts, Pseudo-Prophetic Texts.* DJD 30. Oxford, UK: Clarendon, 2001.

Dobbs-Allsopp, F. W. "Rethinking Historical Criticism." *Biblical Interpretation* 7.3 (1999): 235–71.

Doran, Robert. *Temple Propaganda: The Purpose and Character of 2 Maccabees.* Catholic Biblical Quarterly Monograph Series 12. Washington, DC: Catholic Biblical Association of America, 1981.

Driver, Samuel R., and George B. Gray. *A Critical and Exegetical Commentary on the Book of Job.* Edinburgh: Clark, 1921.

Driver, Godfrey R. "Problems of the Hebrew Text and Language." In *Alttestamentiliche Studien, Friedrich Nötscher zum 60: Geburtstag gewidmet.* Edited by Hubert Junker and Johannes Botterweck, 46–61. Bonn: Hanstein, 1950.

Duhm, Bernard. *Das Buch Hiob: Erklärt.* Freiburg im Breisgau: Mohr, 1897.

Durand, Jannic. *Recherches sur l'iconographie de Job des origines de l'art chrétien jusqu'au XIIIe siècle.* Paris: L'école des Chartres, 1981.

Duvivier, Jean, and Pierre Sabatier. *Bibliorum sacrorum latinae versiones antiquae, seu Vetus Italica, et caeterae quaecunque in codicibus mss. et antiquorum libris reperiri potuerunt.* Paris: Didot, 1751.

Eagleton, Terry. *Literary Theory: An Introduction.* 2nd ed. Malden, MA: Blackwell, 1996.

Eco, Umberto. *Interpretation and Overinterpretation.* Translated by Stefan Collini. Cambridge: Cambridge University Press, 1992.

———. *The Limits of Interpretation.* Bloomington: Indiana University Press, 1990.

Ehrman, Bart. *The Apostolic Fathers: I Clement, II Clement, Ignatius, Polycarp, Didache.* Cambridge, MA: Harvard University Press, 2003.

Eidevall, Göran. *Prophecy and Propaganda: Images of Enemies in the Book of Isaiah*. Winona Lake, IN: Eisenbrauns, 2009.

Eilberg-Schwartz, Howard. *The Savage in Judaism: An Anthropology of Israelite Religion and Ancient Judaism*. Bloomington: Indiana University Press, 1990.

Epictetus. *The Discourses as Reported by Arrian: The Manual, and Fragments*. Vol. 1. Trans. William Abbott Oldfather. Cambridge, MA: Harvard University Press, 1966.

Epp, Eldon J. "The Multivalence of the Term 'Original Text' in New Testament Textual Criticism." *Harvard Theological Review* 92.3 (1999): 245–81.

Eshel, Ḥanan. *The Dead Sea Scrolls and the Hasmonean State*. Grand Rapids, MI: Eerdmans, 2008.

Ewald, Heinrich. *Das Buch Ijob*. Göttingen: Vandenhoeck und Ruprecht, 1854.

Farmer, Colleen. "Did Lungs and the Intracardiac Shunt Evolve to Oxygenate the Heart in Vertebrates?" *Paleobiology* 23.3 (1997): 358–72.

Felle, Antonio. *Biblia epigraphica: La sacra scrittura nella documentazione epigrafica dell'orbis christianus antiquus (III–VIII secolo)*. Inscriptiones christianae italiae, subsidia 5. Bari: Epiduglia, 2006.

Fenlon, Iain. *The Renaissance: From the 1470s to the End of the 16th Century*. Upper Saddle River, NJ: Prentice Hall, 1989.

Ferguson, Everett. *Recent Studies in Early Christianity: A Collection of Scholarly Essays*. New York: Garland, 1999.

Fernández Marcos, Natalio. "The Septuagint Reading of the Book of Job." In *The Book of Job*. BETL 114. Edited by Willem A. M. Beuken, 251–66. Leuven: University of Leuven Press, 1994.

Fernández Marcos, Natalio, eds. *The Septuagint in Context: Introduction to the Greek Version of the Bible*. Translated by Wilfred G. E. Watson. Leiden: Brill, 2000.

Férotin, Marius. *Le liber ordinum en usage dans l'Église wisigothique et mozarabe d'Espagne du V au XI siècles*. Monumenta ecclesiae liturgica 5. Paris: Firmin-Didot, 1904.

Fetzer, Anita. *Recontextualizing Context: Grammaticality Meets Appropriateness*. Philadelphia: John Benjamins, 2004.

Field, Frederick. *Origenis Hexaplorum quae supersunt: Sive, Veterum interpretum graecorum in totum Vetus Testamentum fragmenta*. 2 vols. Oxford: Oxford University Press, 1871.

Fink, Bruce. *The Lacanian Subject: Between Language and Jouissance*. Princeton, NJ: Princeton University Press, 1997.

Fish, Stanley. *Is There a Text in This Class? The Authority of Interpretive Communities*. Cambridge, MA: Harvard University Press, 1980.

Flint, Peter W. *The Dead Sea Psalms Scrolls and the Book of Psalms*. STDJ 17. Leiden: Brill, 1997.

Flint, Peter W., and Patrick D. Miller. *The Book of Psalms: Composition and Reception*. VTS 99. Leiden: Brill, 2005.

Flusser, David. *Judaism of the Second Temple Period: The Jewish Sages and Their Literature*. Vol. 2. Translated by Azzin Yadin. Grand Rapids, MI: Eerdmans, 2009.

Fohrer, Georg. *Das Buch Hiob*. Gutersloh: Gerd Mohn, 1963.

Foucault, Michel. *The Archaeology of Knowledge.* Translated by Rupert Swyer. London: Tavistock, 1986.

———. "Nietzsche, Genealogy, History." In *Language, Counter-Memory, Practice: Selected Essays and Interviews,* 139–65. Translated by Donald Bouchard and Sherry Simon. Edited by Donald Bouchard. Ithaca, NY: Cornell University Press, 1977.

———. "Return to History." In vol. 2 of *Aesthetics, Method, and Epistemology: The Essential Works of Michel Foucault,* 419–31. Edited by James D. Fabion. New York: New Press, 1998.

———. "What Is an Author?" In *Language, Counter-Memory, Practice: Selected Essays and Interviews,* 113–38. Edited by Donald Bouchard. Translated by Donald Bouchard and Sherry Simon. Ithaca, NY: Cornell University Press, 1977.

Fox, Michael V. "Amon Again." *Journal of Biblical Literature* 115.4 (1996): 699–702.

———. "Editing Proverbs: The Challenge of the Oxford Hebrew Bible." *Journal of Northwest Semitic Languages* 32.1 (2006): 1–22.

———. "Job 38 and God's Rhetoric." *Semeia* 19 (1981): 53–61.

———. *Proverbs 1–9: A New Translation with Introduction and Commentary.* AB 18A. New York: Doubleday, 2000.

———. *Proverbs 10–31: A New Translation with Introduction and Commentary.* AB 18B. New Haven, CT: Yale University Press, 2009.

Frahm, Eckart. "Reading the Tablet, the Exta, and the Body: The Hermeneutics of Cuneiform Signs in Babylonian and Assyrian Text Commentaries and Divinatory Texts." In *Divination and Interpretation of Signs in the Ancient World.* Edited by Amar Annus, 93–142. Chicago: University of Chicago Press, 2010.

Frank, Hieronymus. "Der älteste erhaltene Ordo defunctorum der römischen Liturgie und sein Fortleben in Totenagenden des frühen Mittelalters." *Archiv für Liturgiewissenschaft* 7.2 (1962): 360–415.

Freedman, Harry, and Maurice Simon, eds. *Midrash Rabbah.* Vols. 1–2. London: Soncino Press, 1939.

Frymer-Kensky, Tikva. "The Atrahasis Epic and Its Significance for Our Understanding of Genesis 1–9." *Biblical Archaeologist* 40.4 (1977): 147–55.

Gabler, Hans W. "The Synchrony and Diachrony of Texts: Practice and Theory of the Critical Edition of James Joyce's *Ulysses.*" *Textus* 1 (1981): 305–26.

Gadamer, Hans-Georg. *Truth and Method.* Translated by Joel Weinsheimer and Donald G. Marshall. 2nd rev. ed. New York: Continuum, 2004.

Gasperini, Lidio. "Su un epitafio catinense con ripresa scritturistica." *Civiltà classica e cristiana* 13.1 (1992): 63–69.

Gasquet, Francis., ed. *Biblia sacra iuxta latinam Vulgatam versionem ad codicum fidem edita, libri Hester et Job.* Rome: Typis polyglottis vaticanis, 1951.

Gentry, Peter John. *The Asterisked Materials in the Greek Job.* Atlanta, GA: Society of Biblical Literature, 1995.

Gerstenberger, Erhard. *Psalms, Part 1: With an Introduction to Cultic Poetry.* Forms of the Old Testament Literature. Grand Rapids, MI: Eerdmans, 1988.

Gibson, Margaret T. "The Twelfth-Century Glossed Bible." *Studia Patristica* 23 (1989): 232–44.

Ginsburg, Christian D. *Introduction to the Massoretico-Critical Edition of the Hebrew Bible.* London: Trinitarian Bible Society, 1897.

Gordis, Robert. *The Book of God and Man: A Study of Job.* Chicago: University of Chicago Press, 1965.

———. *The Book of Job: Commentary, New Translation, and Special Studies.* New York: Jewish Theological Seminary of America, 1978.

Goshen-Gottstein, Moshe H. "The Aleppo Codex and the Rise of the Massoretic Bible Text." *Biblical Archaeologist* 42.3 (1979): 145–63.

———. "The Authenticity of the Aleppo Codex." *Textus* 1 (1960): 17–58.

———. "The Development of the Hebrew Text of the Bible: Theories and Practice of Textual Criticism." *Vetus Testamentum* 42.2 (1992): 204–13.

———. "Editions of the Hebrew Bible—Past and Future." In *Sha'arei Talmon: Studies in the Bible, Qumran, and the Ancient Near East Presented to Shemaryahu Talmon.* Edited by Shemaryahu Talmon, Michael A. Fishbane, Emanuel Tov, and Weston W. Fields, 221–42. Winona Lake, IN: Eisenbrauns, 1992.

———. *The Hebrew University Bible Project: The Book of Isaiah.* Jerusalem: Magnes, 1965.

———. "The History of the Bible-Text and Comparative Semitics: A Methodological Problem." *Vetus Testamentum* 7.2 (1957): 195–201.

———. "The Rise of the Tiberian Bible Text." In *Biblical and Other Studies.* Edited by Alexander Altmann, 79–122. Cambridge, MA: Harvard University Press, 1963.

———. "The Textual Criticism of the Old Testament: Rise, Decline, Rebirth." *Journal of Biblical Literature* 102.3 (1983): 365–99.

Gould, Stephen J. "Exaptation: A Crucial Tool for an Evolutionary Psychology." *Journal of Social Issues* 47.3 (1991): 43–65.

———. "The Exaptive Excellence of Spandrels as a Term and Prototype." *Proceedings of the National Academy of Sciences* 94.20 (1997): 10750–55.

Gould, Stephen J., and Richard C. Lewontin. "The Spandrels of San Marco and the Panglossian Paradigm: A Critique of the Adaptationist Programme." *Proceedings of the Royal Society of London* B 205.1161 (1979): 581–98.

Grabbe, Lester L. *Judaic Religion in the Second Temple Period: Belief and Practice from the Exile to Yavneh.* London: Routledge, 2000.

Graf, Georg. *Die Schriften des Jakobiten Habib ibn Hidma, Abu Ra'ita.* CSCO 131. Louvain: Durbecq, 1951.

Gray, John. "The Massoretic Text of the Book of Job, the Targum and the Septuagint Version in Light of the Qumran Targum (11Qtarg Job)." *Zeitschrift für die alttestamentliche Wissenschaft* 28.3 (1974): 331–50.

Greenstein, Edward L. "The Language of Job and Its Poetic Function." *Journal of Biblical Literature* 122.4 (2003): 651–66.

Gregory the Great. *Morals on the Book of Job.* Vol. 2. Edited and translated by James Bliss. Oxford, UK: John Henry Parker, 1845.

Grelot, Pierre. "La Septante de Daniel IV et son substrat sémitique." *Revue biblique* 81.1 (1974): 45–66.

Grondin, Jean. *Introduction to Philosophical Hermeneutics*. Translated by Joel Weinsheimer. New Haven, CT: Yale University Press, 1997.

Gruen, Erich. "Seleucid Royal Ideology." *Society of Biblical Literature Seminar Papers* 38 (1999): 24–53.

Gunkel, Herman and Joachim Begrich. *Introduction to Psalms: The Genres of the Religious Lyric of Israel*. Mercer Library of Biblical Studies. Macon, GA: Mercer University Press, 1998.

Gunn, David M. *"Judges" through the Centuries*. BBC. Malden, MA: Blackwell, 2005.

Habel, Norman. *The Book of Job*. OTL. Philadelphia: Westminster, 1985.

Hagedorn, Dieter. *Der Hiobkommentar des Arianers Julian*. Berlin: Walter de Gruyter, 1973.

Hagner, Donald A. *The Use of the Old and New Testaments in Clement of Rome*. Leiden: Brill, 1973.

Hallo, William W., and K. Lawson Younger, eds. *The Context of Scripture*. 3 vols. Leiden: Brill, 1996.

Hankins, C. Davis. "Job and the Limits of Wisdom." Emory University, PhD diss., 2011.

Hardin, C. L. *Color for Philosophers: Unweaving the Rainbow*. Indianapolis, IN: Hackett, 1988.

Harlan, David. "Intellectual History and the Return of Literature." *American Historical Review* 94.3 (1989): 581–609.

Harper, John. *The Forms and Orders of Western Liturgy from the Tenth to the Eighteenth Century: A Historical Introduction and Guide for Students and Musicians*. Oxford: Oxford University Press, 1991.

Harrington, Daniel J. *The Maccabean Revolt: Anatomy of a Biblical Revolution*. Wilmington, DE: Michael Glazier, 1988.

Hartley, John E. *The Book of Job*. Grand Rapids, MI: Eerdmans, 1988.

Hatch, Edwin. *Essays in Biblical Greek*. Oxford: Clarendon, 1889.

Hayman, A. P. "The Original Text: A Scholarly Illusion?" In *Words Remembered, Texts Renewed: Essays in Honour of John F. A. Sawyer*. Edited by Jon Davies, Wilfred G. E. Watson, and Graham Harvey, 434–49. Sheffield, UK: Sheffield Academic Press, 1995.

Hendel, Ronald. "Assessing the Text-Critical Theories of the Hebrew Bible after Qumran." In *The Oxford Handbook of the Dead Sea Scrolls*. Edited by Timothy H. Lim and John J. Collins, 281–302. Oxford: Oxford University Press, 2010.

———. "The Oxford Hebrew Bible: Prologue to a New Critical Edition." *Vetus Testamentum* 58.3 (2008): 324–51.

———. "Qumran and a New Edition of the Hebrew Bible." In vol. 1 of *The Bible and the Dead Sea Scrolls: Scripture and the Scrolls*. Edited by James H. Charlesworth, 149–65. Waco, TX: Baylor University Press, 2006.

Henze, Matthias. *Biblical Interpretation at Qumran*. Grand Rapids, MI: Eerdmans, 2005.

Hervey, Sándor G. "Context, the Ghost in the Machine." In *The Problem of Context*. Edited by Roy Dilley, 61–72. New York: Berghahn, 1999.

Hesychius of Jerusalem. *Homeliés sur Job, version arménienne*. PO 42:1–2. Edited and translated by Charles Renoux and Charles Mercier. Turnhout: Brepols, 1983.

Hirsch, E. D. *The Aims of Interpretation*. Chicago: University of Chicago Press, 1976.

———. "Objective Interpretation." *PMLA* 75.4 (1960): 463–79.

———. *Validity in Interpretation*. New Haven, CT: Yale University Press, 1973.

Hoeppe, Götz. *Why the Sky Is Blue: Discovering the Color of Life*. Princeton, NJ: Princeton University Press, 2007.

Holl, Karl. *Epiphanius 1: Ancoratus und Panarion Haer, 1–33*. GCS 25. Leipzig: Hinrichs, 1915.

Holland, Dorothy, et al. *Identity and Agency in Cultural Worlds*. Cambridge, MA: Harvard University Press, 2001.

Holman, Jan. "Does My Redeemer Live or Is My Redeemer the Living God? Some Reflections on the Translation of Job 19, 25." In *The Book of Job*. BETL 114. Edited by Willem Beuken, 377–81. Leuven: University of Leuven Press, 1994.

Hölscher, Gustav. "Hiob 19,25–27 und Jubil 23,30–31." *Zeitschrift für die alttestamentliche Wissenschaft* 53.1 (1935): 277–83.

Hug, J. Leonhard. *Hug's Introduction to the New Testament*. Edited by Moses Stuart. Translated by David Fosdick. Andover, MA: Gould and Newman, 1836.

Huggett, Nick. *Everywhere and Everywhen: Adventures in Physics and Philosophy*. New York: Oxford University Press, 2010.

Human, Dirk, and Cas J. A. Vos. *Psalms and Liturgy*. JSOTSup 410. London: Clark, 2004.

Husserl, Edmund. "Intentional Objects." In *Early Writings in the Philosophy of Logic and Mathematics*, 345–87. Translated by Dallas Willard. Dordrecht: Kluwer, 1993.

Irwin, William A. "Job's Redeemer." *Journal of Biblical Literature* 81.3 (1962): 217–29.

Jacks, Philip. "*Restauratio* and Reuse: The Afterlife of Roman Ruins." *Places* 20.1 (2008): 10–20.

Jacob Serugh. *Homélies contre les Juifs*. PO 38:1. Edited by M Albert. Turnhout: Brepols, 1976.

Jakobson, Roman. "Langue and Parole: Code and Message." In *On Language*, 80–109. Cambridge, MA: Harvard University Press, 1990.

———. "On Linguistic Aspects of Translation." In *On Translation*. Edited by A. Reuben Brower, 232–39. Cambridge, MA: Harvard University Press, 1959.

Jameson, Frederic. *The Ideologies of Theory: Essays, 1971–1986*. Vol. 1. London: Routledge, 1988.

———. *The Political Unconscious: Narrative as a Socially Symbolic Act*. Ithaca, NY: Cornell University Press, 1981.

Janzen, J. Gerald. *Job*. Interpretation. Atlanta, GA: John Knox, 1985.

Jauss, Hans-Robert. "The Identity of the Poetic Text in the Changing Horizon of Understanding." In *Reception Study: From Literary Theory to Cultural Studies*. Edited by James L. Machor and Philip Goldstein, 7–27. New York: Routledge, 2001.

———. *Toward an Aesthetic of Reception*. Translated by Timothy Bahti. Minneapolis: University of Minnesota Press, 1982.

Jeffrey, James. "The Masoretic Text and the Septuagint Compared, with Special Reference to the Book of Job." *Expository Times* 36 (1924–25): 70–73.

Jeremias, Jorg. *The Book of Amos: A Commentary*. OTL. Louisville, KY: Westminster John Knox, 1998.

John Chrysostom. *Commentaire sur Job*. Vol. 2. SC 348. Edited by Henri Sorlin and Louis Neyrand. Paris: Cerf, 1988.

———. *Lettres à Olympias*. SC 13. Edited by Anne-Marie Malingrey. Paris: Cerf, 1947.

Johnson, Luke Timothy. "Literary Criticism of Luke-Acts: Is Reception-History Pertinent?" *Journal for the Study of the New Testament* 28.2 (2005): 159–62.

Jokiranta, Jutta. "Pesharim: A Mirror of Self-Understanding." In *Reading the Present in the Qumran Library: The Perception of the Contemporary by Means of Scriptural Interpretations*. Edited by Kristin De Troyer and Armin Lange, 23–35. Atlanta, GA: Society of Biblical Literature, 2005.

Jong, Matthijs J. de. *Isaiah among the Ancient Near Eastern Prophets: A Comparative Study of the Earliest Stages of the Isaiah Tradition and the Neo-Assyrian Prophecies*. Leiden: Brill, 2007.

Kahle, Paul. "Unterschungen zur Geschichte des Pentateuchtextes." In *Opera minora*, 3–37. Leiden: Brill, 1956.

Kalimi, Isaac. *Early Jewish Exegesis and Theological Controversy: Studies in Scriptures in the Shadow of Internal and External Controversies*. Leiden: Brill, 2002.

Kamesar, Adam. *Jerome, Greek Scholarship, and the Hebrew Bible*. Oxford: Oxford University Press, 1993.

Kanamori, Akihiro. "The Mathematical Development of Set Theory from Cantor to Cohen." *Bulletin of Symbolic Logic* 2.1 (1996): 1–71.

Katz, Peter. "Septuagintal Studies in the Mid-Century: Their Links with the Past and their Present Tendencies." In *The Background of the New Testament and Its Eschatology: Studies in Honor of C. H. Dodd*. Edited by William K. Davies and David Daube, 176–208. Cambridge: Cambridge University Press, 1954.

Keller, Catherine. "The Last Laugh: A Counter-Apocalyptic Meditation on Moltmann's The Coming of God." *Theology Today* 54.3 (1997): 381–91.

Kelly, J. N. D. *Early Christian Creeds*. 3rd ed. New York: David McKay, 1972.

Kennicott, Benjamin. *Vetus Testamentum hebraicum cum variis lectionibus*. Vol. 1. Oxford, UK: Clarendon, 1776.

Kenney, E. J. "Textual Criticism." In vol. 18 of *Encyclopedia Britannica*, 189–95. 15th ed. New York: Encyclopedia Britannica, 1974–75.

Keohane, Robert and Stanley Hoffmann. Conclusion. In *After the Cold War: International Institutions and State Strategies in Europe, 1989–1991*. Edited by Robert Keohane, Joseph Nye, and Stanley Hoffmann, 381–404. Center for International Affairs Series. Cambridge, MA: Harvard University Press, 1993.

Kissane, E. J. *The Book of Job: Translated from a Critically Revised Hebrew Text with Commentary*. Dublin: Browne and Nolan, 1939.

Klauck, Hans-Josef et al., eds. Introduction. *Encyclopedia of the Bible and Its Reception.* Vol. 1, 00–00. Berlin: Walter de Gruyter, 2009.

Kline, Morris. *Mathematics for the Nonmathematician.* Mineola, NY: Dover, 1985.

Knoppers, Gary, and Bernard Levinson. *The Pentateuch as Torah: New Models for Understanding its Promulgation and Acceptance.* Winona Lake, IN: Eisenbrauns, 2007.

Koenig, Jean. *L'herméneutique analogique du judaïsme antique d'après les témoins textuels d'Isaïe.* VTS 33. Leiden: Brill, 1982.

Kooij, Arie van der. "The Textual Criticism of the Hebrew Bible before and After the Qumran Discoveries." In *The Bible as Book: The Hebrew Bible and the Judaean Desert Discoveries.* Edited by Emanuel Tov and Edward D. Herbert, 167–77. London: British Library, 2002.

Kraeling, Emil. *Book of the Ways of God.* New York: Scribner, 1939.

Kraus, Hans-Joachim. *Theology of the Psalms.* Translated by Keith Crim. Minneapolis, MN: Fortress, 1992.

Kugel, James. *How to Read the Bible: A Guide to Scripture, Then and Now.* New York: Free Press, 2007.

———. "Topics in the History of the Spirituality of the Psalms." In vol. 1 of *Jewish Spirituality.* Edited by Arthur Green, 113–44. London: Routledge, 1986.

Lange, Armin. "Literary Prophecy and Oracle Collection." In *Prophets, Prophecy and Prophetic Texts in Second Temple Judaism.* Edited by Michael Floyd and Robert D. Haak, 248–75. London: Clark, 2006.

———. "'They Confirmed the Reading' (*y. Ta'an* 4.68a): The Textual Standardization of Jewish Scriptures in the Second Temple Period." In *From Qumran to Aleppo: A Discussion with Emanuel Tov about the Textual History of Jewish Scriptures in Honor of His 65th Birthday.* Edited by Armin Lange, Matthias Weigold, and József Zsengeller, 29–80. Göttingen: Vandenhoeck und Ruprecht, 2009.

Langston, Scott. *Exodus Through the Centuries.* BBC. Malden, MA: Blackwell, 2006.

Layton, Richard. *Didymus the Blind and His Circle in Late-Antique Alexandria: Virtue and Narrative in Biblical Scholarship.* Urbana-Champaign: University of Illinois Press, 2004.

Leiman, Sid Z. "Masorah and Halakhah: A Study in Conflict." In *Tehilla le-Moshe: Biblical and Judaic Studies in Honor of Moshe Greenberg.* Edited by Mordechai Cogan, Barry L. Eichler, and Jeffrey H. Tigay, 291–306. Winona Lake, IN: Eisenbrauns, 1997.

Lemmelijn, Bénédicte. "What Are We Looking for in Doing Old Testament Text-Critical Research?" *Journal of Northwest Semitic Languages* 23.2 (1997): 69–80.

Lenzi, Alan. "Proverbs 8: 22–31: Three Perspectives on Its Composition." *Journal of Biblical Literature* 125.4 (2006): 687–714.

Levene, Nancy K. *Spinoza's Revelation: Religion, Democracy, and Reason.* Cambridge: Cambridge University Press, 2004.

Levenson, Jon D. "Exodus and Liberation." *Horizons in Biblical Theology* 13.2 (1991): 134–74.

———. *The Hebrew Bible, the Old Testament, and Historical Criticism: Jews and Christians in Biblical Studies*. Louisville, KY: Westminster John Knox, 1993.

———. *Resurrection and the Restoration of Israel: The Ultimate Victory of the God of Life*. New Haven, CT: Yale University Press, 2006.

Levy, B. Barry. *Fixing God's Torah: The Accuracy of the Hebrew Bible Text in Jewish Law*. Oxford: Oxford University Press, 2001.

Lewysohn, Ludwig. *Nafshot Zadikim: Sechzig Epitaphien von Grabstein des israelitischen Friedhofs zu Worms*. Frankfurt: Naer, 1855.

Lieberman, Saul. *Hellenism in Jewish Palestine: Studies in the Literary Transmission, Beliefs and Manners of Palestine in the I Century bce–IV Century ce*. 2nd ed. New York: Jewish Theological Seminary, 1962.

Linafelt, Tod, ed. *Strange Fire: Reading the Bible after the Holocaust*. Sheffield, UK: Sheffield Academic Press, 2000.

———. *Surviving Lamentations: Catastrophe, Lament, and Protest in the Afterlife of a Biblical Book*. Chicago: University of Chicago Press, 2000.

Lipschütz, Lazar. *Kitāb al-khilāf, the Book of Hillufim*. Jerusalem: Magnes, 1965.

Littel, Eliakim. *Littel's Living Age*. Vol. 1. London: T. H. Carter, 1844.

Lomartire, Saverio, and Anna Segagni. "Tomba della badessa Ariperga." In *Il futuro dei Longobardi: Catalogo della mostra*. Edited by Carlo Bertelli, 248–49. Milan: Broglio, 2000.

Lowden, John. *Early Christian and Byzantine Art*. London: Phaidon, 1997.

Luhmann, Niklas. "Kultur als historischer Begriff." In *Gesellschaftsstruktur und Semantik: Studien zur Wissenssoziologie der modernen Gesellschaft*, 31–54. Frankfurt am Main: Suhrkamp, 1995.

———. *Theories of Distinction: Redescribing the Descriptions of Modernity*. Edited by William Rasch. Translated by Joseph O'Neill, Elliott Schreiber, Kerstin Behnke, and William Whobrey. Stanford, CA: Stanford University Press, 2002.

Lust, Johan. "The Story of David and Goliath in Hebrew and in Greek." *Ephemerides theologicae lovanienses* 59.1 (1983): 5–25.

Luz, Ulrich. *Matthew in History: Interpretation, Influence, and Effects*. Minneapolis, MN: Fortress, 1994.

Lycan, William G. *Philosophy of Language: A Contemporary Introduction*. London: Routledge, 2008.

Lyons, John. *Semantics*. Vol. 1. Cambridge: Cambridge University Press, 1977.

Lyotard, Jean-François. "The Survivor." In *Toward the Postmodern*, 144–63. Edited by Robert Harvey. Highlands, NJ: Humanities Press, 1993.

Maas, Paul. *Textual Criticism*. Translated by Barbara Flower. Oxford, UK: Clarendon, 1958.

Mackenzie, Adrian. *Transductions: Bodies and Machines at Speed*. London: Continuum, 2006.

Malinowski, Bronislaw. "The Problem of Meaning in Primitive Languages." In *The Problem of Meaning in Primitive Languages*. Edited by C. K. Ogden, I. A. Richards,

Bronislaw Malinowski, and F. G. Crookshank, 146–52. London: Harcourt, Brace, 1946.

Martin, Dale. *Pedagogy of the Bible: An Analysis and Proposal*. Louisville, KY: Westminster John Knox, 2008.

Martin, Gary D. *Multiple Originals: New Approaches to Hebrew Bible Textual Criticism*. Atlanta, GA: Society of Biblical Literature, 2010.

Masnut, Samuel Ben Nissim. *Ma'yan Ganim*. Edited by Salomon Buber. Berlin: 1889.

Matter, E. Ann. "The Church Fathers and the *Glossa Ordinaria*." In vol. 1 of *The Reception of the Church Fathers in the West: From the Carolingians to the Maurists*. Edited by Irena D. Backus, 83–111. Leiden: Brill, 1996.

May, Todd. *Gilles Deleuze: An Introduction*. Cambridge: Cambridge University Press, 2005.

Mays, James L. *Amos: A Commentary*. OTL. Louisville, KY: Westminster John Knox, 1969.

———. "The Question of Context in Psalm Interpretation." In *The Shape and Shaping of the Psalter*. Edited by J. Clinton McCann, 1–14. JSOTSup 159. Sheffield, UK: JSOT Press, 1993.

Martindale, Charles. Introduction. *Classics and the Uses of Reception*. Edited by Charles Martindale and Richard F. Thomas, 1–13. Malden, MA: Blackwell, 2006.

Marx, Karl. *Capital*. Vol. 1. Translated by Ben Fowkes. London: Penguin, 1992.

McCall, Richard D. *Do This: Liturgy as Performance*. Notre Dame, IN: University of Notre Dame Press, 2007.

McCarter, P. Kyle. *Textual Criticism: Recovering the Text of the Hebrew Bible*. Minneapolis, MN: Fortress, 1986.

McDonald, Lee Martin, and James A. Sanders, eds. *The Canon Debate*. Peabody, MA: Hendrickson, 2002.

McGann, Jerome J. *A Critique of Modern Textual Criticism*. Chicago: University of Chicago Press, 1983.

———. *The Textual Condition*. Princeton, NJ: Princeton University Press, 1991.

McLaughlin, Megan. *Consorting with Saints: Prayer for the Dead in Early Medieval France*. Ithaca, NY: Cornell University Press, 1994.

Meek, T. J. "Job XIX 25–27." *Vetus Testamentum* 6.1–4 (1956): 100–103.

Mele, Alfred R. "Against a Belief/Desire Analysis of Intention." *Philosophia* 18.2–3 (1988): 239–42.

Mende, Theresia. *Durch Leiden zur Vollendung*. Trier: Paulinus, 1990.

Meyer, Kathi. "St. Job as a Patron of Music." *Art Bulletin* 36.1 (1954): 21–31.

Michel, Walter L. "Confidence and Despair: Job 19, 25–27 in the Light of Northwest Semitic Studies." In *The Book of Job*. Edited by Willem A. M. Beuken, 157–77. BETL 114. Leuven: University of Leuven Press, 1994.

Miller, Patrick D. *Interpreting the Psalms*. Philadelphia: Fortress, 1986.

———. *Israelite Religion and Biblical Theology*. Sheffield, UK: Sheffield Academic Press, 2000.

Mombert, J. I. "On Job xix 25–27." *Journal of the Society of Biblical Literature and Exegesis* 2.1 (1882): 27–39.

Mowinckel, Sigmund. "Hiobs go'el und Zeuge im Himmel." *Beiheft zur Zeitschrift für alttestamentliche Wissenschaft* 41 (1925): 207–12.

Muilenburg, James. "Form Criticism and Beyond." *Journal of Biblical Literature* 88.1 (1969): 1–18.

Nasuti, Harry. *Defining the Sacred Songs: Genre, Tradition and the Post-Critical Interpretation of the Psalms.* JSOTSup 218. Sheffield, UK: Sheffield Academic Press, 1999.

Newsom, Carol A. "Bakhtin, the Bible, and Dialogic Truth." *Journal of Religion* 76.2 (1996): 290–306.

———. "The Book of Job." In *The New Interpreter's Bible.* Vol. 4, 317–637. Nashville, TN: Abingdon, 1996.

———. *The Book of Job: A Contest of Moral Imaginations.* Oxford: Oxford University Press, 2003.

———. "Genesis 2–3 and 1 Enoch 6–16: Two Myths of Origin and Their Ethical Implications." In *Shaking Heaven and Earth: Essays in Honor of Walter Brueggemann and Charles B. Cousar.* Edited by Christine Roy Yoder, Kathleen M. O'Connor, E. Elizabeth Johnson, and Stanley P. Saunders, 7–23. Louisville, KY: Westminster John Knox, 2005.

———. "Narrative, Ethics, Character, and the Prose Tale of Job." In *Character and Scripture: Moral Formation, Community, and Biblical Interpretation.* Edited by William P. Brown, 121–34. Winona Lake, IN: Eerdmans, 2002.

———. "Pairing Research Questions and Theories of Genre: A Case Study of the Hodayot." *Dead Sea Discoveries* 17.3 (2010): 270–88.

———. "Rhyme and Reason: The Historical Resumé in Israelite and Early Jewish Thought." In *Israel's Prophets and Israel's Past: Essays on the Relationship of Prophetic Texts and Israelite History in Honor of John H. Hayes.* Edited by Brad E. Kelle and Megan B. Moore, 215–33. London: Clark, 2006.

———. *The Self as Symbolic Space: Constructing Identity and Community at Qumran.* Leiden: Brill, 2004.

———. "Spying out the Land: A Report from Genology." In *Seeking out the Wisdom of the Ancients: Essays Offered to Honor Michael V. Fox on the Occasion of His Sixty-Fifth Birthday.* Edited by Ronald L. Troxel, Kelvin G. Friebel, and Dennis R. Magary, 437–50. Winona Lake, IN: Eisenbrauns, 2005.

Newton, K. M. *Interpreting the Text: A Critical Introduction to the Theory and Practice of Literary Interpretation.* New York: Harvester/Wheatsheaf, 1990.

Nicholls, Rachel. *Walking on the Water: Reading Mt. 14: 22–33 in the Light of Its Wirkungsgeschichte.* Leiden: Brill, 2008.

Nieder, Andreas. "Seeing More Than Meets the Eye: Processing of Illusory Contours in Animals." *Journal of Comparative Physiology* A 188.4 (2002): 249–60.

Nietzsche, Friedrich. *Basic Writings of Nietzsche.* Edited and translated by Walter Kaufmann. New York: Random House, 2000.

———. *On the Genealogy of Morality*. Edited by Keith Ansell-Pearson. Translated by Carol Diethe. Cambridge: Cambridge University Press, 1994.

Nims, Charles F., and Richard C. Steiner. "A Paganized Version of Psalm 20: 2–6 from the Aramaic Text in Demotic Script." *Journal of the American Oriental Society* 103.1 (1983): 261–74.

Nissinen, Martti. "The Historical Dilemma of Biblical Prophetic Studies." In *Prophecy in the Book of Jeremiah*. Edited by Hans M. Barstad and Reinhard G. Kratz, 103–20. Berlin: Walter de Gruyter, 2009.

———. "Reflections on the 'Historical-Critical' Method: Historical Criticism and Critical Historicism." In *Method Matters: Essays on the Interpretation of the Hebrew Bible in Honor of David L. Petersen*. Edited by Joel M. LeMon and Kent H. Richards, 479–504. Atlanta, GA: Society of Biblical Literature, 2009.

Noë, Alva. *Action in Perception*. Cambridge, MA: MIT Press, 2004.

Noegel, Scott. *Nocturnal Ciphers: The Allusive Language of Dreams in the Ancient Near East*. Chicago: American Oriental Society, 2007.

———. "'Sign, Sign, Everywhere a Sign': Script, Power, and Interpretation in the Ancient Near East." In *Divination and Interpretation of Signs in the Ancient World*. Edited by Amar Annus, 143–62. Chicago: University of Chicago Press, 2010.

Noth, Martin. *The Deuteronomistic History*. JSOTSup 15. Sheffield, UK: JSOT Press, 1981.

Noy, David. *Jewish Inscriptions of Western Europe*. Vol. 1: *Italy (Excluding the City of Rome), Spain and Gaul*. Cambridge: Cambridge University Press, 1993.

Ntedika, Joseph. *L'évocation de l'au-delà dans la prière pour les morts: Étude de patristique et de liturgie latines, IVe–VIIIe siècles*. Louvain: Nauwelaerts, 1971.

Orlinsky, Harry M. "Prolegomenon: The Masoretic Text, a Critical Evaluation." In *Introduction to the Massoretico-Critical Edition of the Hebrew Bible*. Edited by Christian D. Ginsburg, i–xlv. New York: Ktav, 1966.

Ottosen, Knud. *The Responsories and Versicles of the Latin Office of the Dead*. Aarhus: Aarhus University Press, 2008.

Park, Joseph S. *Conceptions of Afterlife in Jewish Inscriptions: With Special Reference to Pauline Literature*. Tübingen: Mohr Siebeck, 2000.

Parker, Hershel. *Flawed Texts and Verbal Icons: Literary Authority in American Fiction*. Evanston, IL: Northwestern University Press, 1984.

———. "Lost Authority: Non-Sense, Skewed Meanings, and Intentionless Meanings." *Critical Inquiry* 9.4 (1983): 767–74.

———. "'The Text Itself': Whatever That Is." *Textus* 3 (1987): 47–54.

Parr, Adrian, ed. *The Deleuze Dictionary*. New York: Columbia University Press, 2005.

Patton, Paul. *Deleuze and the Political*. London: Routledge, 2000.

Paxton, Frederick S. *Christianizing Death: The Creation of a Ritual Process in Early Medieval Europe*. Ithaca, NY: Cornell University Press, 1996.

Peirce, Charles S. *Collected Papers*. Vol. 4. Edited by Charles Hartshorne and Paul Weiss. Cambridge, MA: Harvard University Press, 1933.

———. *The Essential Peirce: Selected Philosophical Writings*. Edited by Nathan Houser and Christian J. W. Kloesel. Bloomington: Indiana University Press, 1992.

Pérez de Urbel, Justo, and Atilano Gonzáles y Ruiz-Zorilla, eds. *Liber comicus: Edition critica*. Serie liturgica 2–3. Madrid: Monumenta hispaniae sacra, 1950.

Perraymond, Myla. *La figura di Giobbe nella cultura paleocristiana tra esegesi patristica e manifestazioni iconografiche*. Vatican City: Pontificio istituto di archeologia cristiana, 2002.

Person, Raymond, Jr. "The Ancient Israelite Scribe as Performer." *Journal of Biblical Literature* 117.4 (1998): 601–9.

Pesic, Peter. *Sky in a Bottle*. Cambridge, MA: MIT Press, 2005.

Peterson, Ivars. *The Mathematical Tourist: New and Updated Snapshots of Modern Mathematics*. New York: Owl Books, 1998.

Pietersma, Albert, and Benjamin G. Wright, eds. *A New English Translation of the Septuagint*. Oxford: Oxford University Press, 2007.

Pinnock, Sarah K. *Beyond Theodicy: Jewish and Christian Continental Thinkers Respond to the Holocaust*. Albany: State University Press of New York, 2002.

Pope, Marvin. *Job*. AB 15. 3rd ed. Garden City, NY: Doubleday, 1973.

Porter, Stanley E., and Christopher D. Stanley. *As It Is Written: Studying Paul's Use of Scripture*. Society of Biblical Literature Symposium Series 50. Atlanta, GA: Society of Biblical Literature, 2008.

Quine, W. V. O. *Word and Object*. Cambridge, MA: MIT Press, 1960.

Rabin, Chaim Shemaryahu Talmon, and Emanuel Tov. *The Hebrew University Bible: The Book of Jeremiah*. Jerusalem: Magnes, 1997.

Rabinowitz, Peter J. "Truth in Fiction: A Reexamination of Audiences." *Critical Inquiry* 4.1 (1977): 121–41.

Ramachandran, V. S., and Sandra Blakeslee. *Phantoms in the Brain: Probing the Mysteries of the Human Mind*. New York: William Morrow, 1998.

Rendsburg, Gary. *Redaction of Genesis*. Winona Lake, IN: Eisenbrauns, 1986.

Rendtorff, Rolf. *Das überlieferungsgeschichtliche Problem des Pentateuch*. Berlin: Walter de Gruyter, 1977.

Renevey, Denis. "Looking for a Context: Rolle, Anchoritic Culture and the Office of the Dead." In *Medieval Texts in Context* Edited by Graham D. Cale and Denis Renevey, 192–210. New York: Routledge, 2008.

Ricci, Cecilia, and Gianluca Tagliamonte. "Iscrizioni cristiane nelle Collezioni comunali: Inedite e revisioni." *Bullettino della Commissione archaeologia comunale di Roma* 96 (1994): 179–94.

Ricoeur, Paul. *Interpretation Theory: Discourse and the Surplus of Meaning*. Fort Worth, TX: Texas Christian University Press, 1976.

Rignell, Lars G., ed. *Job: The Old Testament in Syriac according to the Peshitta Version*. Leiden: Brill, 1993.

Risinger, D. Michael, et al. "The Daubert/Kumho Implications of Observer Effects in Forensic Science: Hidden Problems of Expectation and Suggestion." *California Law Review* 90.1 (2002): 1–56.

Robbins, Vernon K. "The Crucifixion and the Speech of Jesus." *Forum* 4.1 (1988): 33–46.

Roemer, Nils. *Jewish Scholarship and Culture in Nineteenth-Century Germany: Between History and Faith*. Madison: University of Wisconsin Press, 2005.

———. "Turning Defeat into Victory: *Wissenschaft des Judentums* and the Martyrs of 1096." *Jewish History* 13.2 (1999): 65–80.

Rofé, Alexander. "The Acts of Nahash according to 4QSam[a]." *Israel Exploration Journal* 32.2–3 (1982): 129–33.

Römer, Thomas. *The So-Called Deuteronomistic History: A Sociological, Historical and Literary Introduction*. London: Clark, 2005.

Roukema, Reimar. "La résurrection des morts dans l'interprétation origénienne de 1 Corinthiens 15." In *La résurrection chez les Pères*. Cahiers de Biblia Patristica 7. Edited by Jean-Marc Prieur, 161–77. Strasbourg: Université Marc Bloch, 2003.

Rowland, Chris. "A Pragmatic Approach to *Wirkungsgeschichte:* Reflections on the Blackwell Bible Commentary Series and on the Writing of Its Commentary on the Apocalypse." Paper presented at Evangelisch-Katholischer Kommentar Biannual Meeting, Germany, March 21–23, 2004.

Russo, Eugenio. "Un'epigrafe con citazione biblica (Iob, XIX, 25–27) nel campanile di Pomposa." *Vetera christianorum* 30.1 (1993): 109–22.

Saebø, Magne. *On the Way to Canon: Creative Tradition History in the Old Testament*. Sheffield, UK: Sheffield Academic Press, 1998.

Sanders, James A. *Canon and Community: A Guide to Canonical Criticism*. Minneapolis, MN: Fortress, 1984.

———. "Hermeneutics of Text Criticism." *Textus* 18 (1995): 1–26.

———. *The Psalms Scroll of Qumran Cave 11 (11QPsa)*. DJD 4. Oxford, UK: Clarendon Press, 1965.

Sanderson, Judith E. *An Exodus Scroll from Qumran: 4QpaleoExodm and the Samaritan Tradition*. Atlanta, GA: Scholars Press, 1986.

Sasson, Jack. "On Choosing Models for Recreating Israelite Pre-Monarchic History." *Journal for the Study of the Old Testament* 6.21 (1981): 3–24.

Saunders, Barbara. "Revisiting Basic Color Terms." *Journal of the Royal Anthropological Institute* 6.1 (2000): 81–99.

Saussure, Ferdinand de. *Course in General Linguistics*. Edited by Charles Bally and Albert Schehaye. Translated by Roy Harris. Chicago: Open Court Publishing, 1983.

Sawyer, John F. A. *A Concise Dictionary of the Bible and Its Reception*. Louisville, KY: Westminster John Knox, 2009.

———. *Sacred Languages and Sacred Texts*. London: Routledge, 1999.

———. *Semantics in Biblical Research: New Methods of Defining Hebrew Words for Salvation*. Naperville, IL: Allenson, 1972.

Scanlin, Harold P. "The Study of Semantics in General Linguistics." In *Linguistics and Biblical Hebrew*. Edited by Walter R. Bodine, 125–36. Winona Lake, IN: Eisenbrauns, 1988.

Schäfer, Paul. *Judeophobia: Attitudes towards the Jews in the Ancient World*. Cambridge, MA: Harvard University Press, 1997.

———. "Research into Rabbinic Literature: An Attempt to Define the *Status Quaestionis*." *Journal of Jewish Studies* 37.2 (1986): 139–52.

Schegloff, Emanuel A. "In Another Context." In *Rethinking Context: Language as an Interactive Phenomenon*. Edited by Alessandro Duranti and Charles Goodwin, 191–227. Cambridge: Cambridge University Press, 1992.

Schiffman, Lawrence. "Contemporizing Halakic Exegesis in the Dead Sea Scrolls." In *Reading the Present in the Qumran Library: The Perception of the Contemporary by Means of Scriptural Interpretations*. Edited by Kristin De Troyer and Armin Lange, 35–41. Atlanta, GA: Society of Biblical Literature, 2005.

Schniedewind, William. *Society and the Promise to David: The Reception History of 2 Samuel 7: 1–17*. Oxford: Oxford University Press, 1999.

Schnocks, Johannes. "The Hope for Resurrection in the Book of Job." In *The Septuagint and Messianism*. Edited by Michael A. Knibb, 291–99. Journées bibliques de Louvain 53. Leuven: Leuven University Press, 2006.

Schottroff, Willy. *Gedenken im alten Orient und im Alten Testament: Die Wurzel zakar im semitischen Sprachkreis*. Wissenschaftliche Monographien zum Alten und Neuen Testament 15. Neukirchen-Vluyn: Neukirchener, 1967.

Schreiner, Susan. *Where Shall Wisdom Be Found? Calvin's Exegesis of Job from Medieval and Modern Perspectives*. Chicago: University of Chicago Press, 1994.

Schultz, Richard. *The Search for Quotation: Verbal Parallels in the Prophets*. JSOTSup 180. Sheffield, UK: Sheffield Academic Press, 1999.

Schwartz, Daniel R. "Antiochus IV Epiphanes in Jerusalem." In *Historical Perspectives, from the Hasmoneans to Bar Kokhba in Light of the Dead Sea Scrolls: Proceedings of the Fourth International Symposium of the Orion Center, 27–31 January 1999*. Edited by David Goodblatt, Avital Pinnick, and Daniel R. Schwartz, 45–56. Leiden: Brill, 2001.

Schwartz, Seth. "Hebrew and Imperialism in Jewish Palestine." In *Ancient Judaism in its Hellenistic Context*. Edited by Carol Bakhos, 53–84. Leiden: Brill, 2005.

———. "Israel and the Nations Roundabout: I Maccabees and the Hasmonean Expansion." *Journal of Jewish Studies* 42.1 (1991): 16–38.

Searle, J. R. *Speech Acts: An Essay in the Philosophy of Language*. Cambridge: Cambridge University Press, 1970.

Segal, Michael. "4QReworked Pentateuch or 4QPentateuch?" In *The Dead Sea Scrolls Fifty Years after Their Discovery: Proceedings of the Jerusalem Congress, July 20–25, 1997*. Edited by Lawrence H. Schiffman, 391–99. Jerusalem: Israel Exploration Society, 2000.

Seow, Choon-Leong. "Job's *Go'el*, Again." In *Gott und Mensch im Dialog: Festschrift für Otto Kaiser zum 80. Geburtstag*. Edited by Markus Witte, 689–709. Beihefte zur Zeitschrift für die alttestamentliche Wissenschaft 345/II. Berlin: Walter de Gruyter, 2004.

———. *Job 1–21*. Illuminations. Grand Rapids, MI: Eerdmans, 2013.

———. "Reflections on the History of Consequences: The Case of Job." In *Method Matters: Essays on the Interpretation of the Hebrew Bible in Honor of David L. Petersen*. Edited by Joel M. LeMon and Kent H. Richards, 561–86. Atlanta, GA: Society of Biblical Literature, 2009.

Sergius the Stylite. *The Disputation of Sergius the Stylite against a Jew.* Edited by Allison Peter Hayman. CSCO 339. Louvain: Secrétariat du corpus scriptorum christianorum orientalium, 1973.

Severus of Antioch. *A Collection of Letters from Numerous Syriac Manuscripts.* Edited and translated by Ernest W. Brooks. Paris: Graffin, 1915.

Shaviro, Stephen. *Without Criteria: Kant, Whitehead, Deleuze, and Aesthetics.* Cambridge, MA: MIT Press, 2009.

Shepherd, David. *Targum and Translation: A Reconsideration of the Qumran Aramaic Version of Job.* Leiden: Brill, 2004.

Sherwood, Yvonne. *A Biblical Text and Its Afterlives: The Survival of Jonah in Western Culture.* Cambridge: Cambridge University Press, 2000.

Shoshanna, Avraham, ed. *Sefer Iyyov be-veit midrasho shel Rashi* [*The Book of Job in the School of Rashi*]. Jerusalem: Makhon Ofeq, 2000.

Sicard, Damien. *La liturgie de la mort dans l'Eglise latine des origines à la réforme carolingienne.* LQF 63. Münster: Aschendorff, 1978.

Silva, Moises. *Biblical Words and Their Meaning: An Introduction to Lexical Semantics.* Rev. ed. Grand Rapids, MI: Zondervan, 1994.

Simon, Richard. *Histoire critique du vieux testament.* Edited by Pierre Gibert. Montrouge: Bayard, 2008.

Simondon, Gilbert. "The Genesis of the Individual." In *Incorporations.* Edited by Jonathan Crary and Sanford Kwinter, 297–319. New York: Zone Books, 1992.

Smoak, Jeremy D. "Amuletic Inscriptions and the Background of YHWH as Guardian and Protector in Psalm 12." *Vetus Testamentum* 60.3 (2010): 421–32.

Spencer-Brown, George. *Laws of Form.* London: George Allen and Unwin, 1969.

Spinoza, Baruch. *A Spinoza Reader: The Ethics and Other Works.* Edited by Edwin Curley. Princeton, NJ: Princeton University Press, 1994.

Starr, Joshua. *The Jews in the Byzantine Empire, 641–1204.* Ann Arbor: University of Michigan Press, 1939.

Steiner, Richard C. "The Aramaic Text in Demotic Script: The Liturgy of a New Year's Festival Imported from Bethel to Syene by Exiles from Rash." *Journal of the American Oriental Society* 111.2 (1991): 362–63.

Stern, Robert. *Hegelian Metaphysics.* Oxford: Oxford University Press, 2009.

Stipp, Hermann-Josef. "Das Verhältnis von Textkritik und Literarkritik in neueren alttestamentlichen Veröffentlichungen." *Biblische Zeitschrift* 34.1 (1990): 16–37.

Strafella, Serena. "Una sepoltura dipinta nell'abbazia di San Benedetto di Leno." *Brixia Sacra* 3.2 (2006): 159–86.

Strawn, Brent. "Comparative Approaches: History, Theory, and the Image of God." In *Method Matters: Essays on the Interpretation of the Hebrew Bible in Honor of David L. Petersen.* Edited by Joel M. LeMon and Kent H. Richards, 117–42. Atlanta, GA: Society of Biblical Literature, 2009.

Stout, Jeffrey. "What is the Meaning of a Text?" *New Literary History* 14.1 (1982): 1–12.

Stuckenbruck, Loren. "The Formation and Re-Formation of Daniel in the Dead Sea Scrolls." In vol. 1 of *The Bible and the Dead Sea Scrolls: Scripture and the Scrolls*. Edited by James H. Charlesworth, 110–30. Waco, TX: Baylor University Press, 2006.

Suriano, Matthew J. "Death, Disinheritance, and Job's Kinsman-Redeemer." *Journal of Biblical Literature* 129.1 (2010): 49–66.

Talmon, Shemaryahu. "Textual Criticism: The Ancient Versions." In *Text in Context: Essays by Members of the Society for Old Testament Study*. Edited by A. D. H. Mayes, 141–70. Oxford: Oxford University Press, 2000.

———. "The Three Scrolls of the Law that Were Found in the Temple Court." *Textus* 2 (1962): 14–27.

Talmon, Shemaryahu, and Moshe Goshen-Gottstein. *The Hebrew University Bible: The Book of Ezekiel*. Jerusalem: Magnes, 2004.

Tanselle, G. Thomas. "The Editorial Problem of Final Authorial Intention." *Studies in Bibliography* 29 (1976): 167–211.

———. *A Rationale of Textual Criticism*. Philadelphia: University of Pennsylvania Press, 1989.

———. "Textual Criticism." In *The New Princeton Encyclopedia of Poetry and Poetics*. Edited by Alex Preminger, Terry V. F. Brogan, and Frank J. Warnke, 1273–76. Princeton, NJ: Princeton University Press, 1993.

Tcherikover, Victor. *Hellenistic Civilization and the Jews*. Translated by E. Simon Applebaum. Philadelphia: Jewish Publication Society, 1961.

Terrien, Samuel. L. "The Book of Job: Introduction and Exegesis." In *The New Interpreter's Bible*, 877–1198. Nashville, TN: Abingdon, 1954.

———. *The Iconography of Job through the Centuries: Artists as Biblical Interpreters*. University Park: Pennsylvania State University Press, 1996.

Thiselton, Anthony. *Thiselton on Hermeneutics: Collected Works with New Essays*. Grand Rapids, MI: Eerdmans, 2006.

Thompson, Evan. *Mind of Life: Biology, Phenomenology, and the Sciences of Mind*. Cambridge, MA: Belknap, 2007.

Tigay, Jeffrey H. "Conflation as a Redactional Technique." In *Empirical Models for Biblical Criticism*. Edited by Jeffrey H. Tigay, 53–96. Philadelphia: University of Pennsylvania Press, 1985.

———. "On Some Aspects of Prayer in the Bible." *AJS Review* 1 (1976): 363–79.

Tompkins, Jane P. "An Introduction to Reader-Response Criticism." In *Reader-Response Criticism: From Formalism to Post-Structuralism*. Edited by Jane Thompkins, ix–xxvi. Baltimore, MD: John Hopkins University Press, 1980.

Tov, Emanuel. *Hebrew Bible, Greek Bible, and Qumran*. Tübingen: Mohr Siebeck, 2008.

———. "The Literary History of the Book of Jeremiah in the Light of Its Textual History." In *Empirical Models for Biblical Criticism*. Edited by Jeffrey H. Tigay, 211–37. Philadelphia: University of Pennsylvania Press, 1985.

———. "The Many Forms of Scripture: Reflections in Light of the LXX and 4QReworked Pentateuch." In *From Qumran to Aleppo: A Discussion with Emanuel Tov about the Textual History of Jewish Scriptures in Honor of His 65th Birthday*. Edited by Armin

Lange, Mattias Weigold, and József Zsengellér, 11–28. Göttingen: Vandenhoeck und Ruprecht, 2009.

———. "The Status of the Masoretic Text in Modern Text Editions of the Hebrew Bible: The Relevance of Canon." In. *The Canon Debate* Edited by Lee Martin McDonald and James A. Sanders, 234–51. Peabody, MA: Hendrickson, 2002.

———. *Textual Criticism of the Hebrew Bible.* 2nd rev. ed. Minneapolis, MN: Fortress, 2001.

Trask, R. L. *The History of Basque.* London: Routledge, 1997.

Trebolle Barrera, Julio. "The Story of David and Goliath (1 Sam 17–18): Textual Variants and Literary Composition." *Bulletin of the International Organization for Septuagint and Cognate Studies* 23 (1990): 16–30.

Treffort, Cécile. "Appels à la prière et oraisons de pierre dans les inscriptions funéraires des VIIIe–XIe siècles." In *Appels à la prière et oraisons de pierre dans les inscriptions funéraires des VIIIe–XIe siècles.* Edited by Jean-François Cottier, 273–90. Turnhout: Brepols, 2006.

Tremblay, Hervé. *Job 19, 25–27 dans la Septante et chez les pères grecs: Unanimité d'une tradition.* Paris: Gabalda, 2002.

Trotter, James. *Reading Hosea in Achaemenid Yehud.* JSOTSup 328. Sheffield, UK: Sheffield Academic Press, 2001.

Tschan, Francis. J. *Saint Bernward of Hildesheim.* Vol. 3. South Bend, IN: University of Notre Dame Press, 1942.

Tur-Sinai, Naphtali Hirsch. *The Book of Job: A New Commentary.* Jerusalem: Kiryath Sepher, 1957.

Ulrich, Eugene. "The Bible in the Making: The Scriptures Found at Qumran." In *The Bible at Qumran: Text, Shape, and Interpretation.* Edited by Peter Flint and Tae Hun Kim, 51–66. Grand Rapids, MI: Eerdmans, 2001.

———. "The Dead Sea Scrolls and the Hebrew Scriptural Texts." In vol. 1 of *The Bible and the Dead Sea Scrolls: The Second Princeton Symposium on Judaism and Christian Origins.* Edited by James H. Charlesworth, 77–100. Waco, TX: Baylor University Press, 2006.

———. *The Dead Sea Scrolls and the Origins of the Bible.* Studies in the Dead Sea Scrolls and Related Literature. Grand Rapids, MI: Eerdmans, 1999.

———. "From Literature to Scripture: Reflections on the Growth of a Text's Authoritativeness." *Dead Sea Discoveries* 10.1 (2003): 3–25.

———. *The Qumran Text of Samuel and Josephus.* Atlanta, GA: Scholars Press, 1978.

Unterman, Jeremiah. "The Socio-Legal Origin for the Image of God as Redeemer of Israel." In *Pomegranates and Golden Bells: Studies in Biblical, Jewish, and Near Eastern Ritual, Law and Literature in Honor of Jacob Milgrom.* Edited by David P. Wright, David N. Freedman, and Avi Hurvitz, 399–405. Winona Lake, IN: Eisenbrauns, 1995.

van der Horst, Pieter. "*Sortes:* Sacred Books as Instant Oracles in Late Antiquity." In *Sortes: Sacred Books as Instant Oracles in Late Antiquity.* Edited by Pieter Willem van der Hoorst, 143–74. Leuven: Peeters, 1998.

van der Horst, Michael A., Jason Key, and Klaas Hellingworth. "Photosensing in Chemotrophic, Non-Phototrophic Bacteria: Let There be Light Sensing Too." *Trends in Microbiology* 15.12 (2007): 554–62.

van der Ploeg, J. P. M., and Adam S. van der Woude. *Le Targum de Job de la grotte XI de Qumrân*. Leiden: Brill, 1971.

van der Toorn, Karel. *Scribal Culture and the Making of the Hebrew Bible*. Cambridge, MA: Harvard University Press, 2007.

van der Woude, Adam S. "Pluriformity and Uniformity: Reflections on the Transmission of the Old Testament." In *Sacred History and Sacred Texts in Early Judaism: A Symposium in Honour of Adam S. van der Woude*. Edited by Florentino Garcia Martínez and Jan Bremmer, 151–69. Kampen: Kok Pharos, 1998.

Van Seters, John. *The Edited Bible: The Curious History of the "Editor" in Biblical Criticism*. Winona Lake, IN: Eisenbrauns, 2006.

———. *Prologue to History: The Yahwist as Historian in Genesis*. Louisville, KY: Westminster John Knox, 1992.

Vicchio, Stephen J. *The Image of the Biblical Job*. 3 vols. Eugene, OR: Wipf and Stock, 2006.

Vogel, Cyrille. *Medieval Liturgy: An Introduction to the Sources*. Edited by William G. Storey and Niels Krogh Rasmussen. Washington, DC: Pastoral Press, 1986.

Voloshinov, Valentin N. *Marxism and the Philosophy of Language*. Translated by Ladislav Matejka and I. R. Titunik. Cambridge, MA: Harvard University Press, 1986.

von Rad, Gerhard. *Old Testament Theology*. 2 vols. Translated by David M. G. Stalker. London: Oliver and Boyd, 1962–65.

Voragine, Jacob de. *The Golden Legend; or, Lives of the Saints*. Vol. 2. Edited and translated by William Caxton. London: Dent, 1900.

Wahl, Harald-Martin. *Der gerechte Schöpfer: Eine redaktions- und theologiegeschichtliche Untersuchung der Elihureden, Hiob 32–37*. Berlin: Walter de Gruyter, 1993.

Waltke, Bruce, and Michael P. O'Connor. *An Introduction to Biblical Hebrew Syntax*. Winona Lake, IN: Eisenbrauns, 1990.

Watts, James W., ed. *Persia and Torah: The Theory of Imperial Authorization of the Pentateuch*. SBLS 17. Atlanta, GA: Scholars Press, 2001.

Weis, Richard D. "*Biblia Hebraica Quinta* and the Making of Critical Editions of the Hebrew Bible." *TC: A Journal of Biblical Textual Criticism* 7 (2002).

Weiser, Artur. *Das Buch Hiob*. Göttingen: Vandenhoeck und Ruprecht, 1951.

Weitzman, Michael P. *The Syriac Version of the Old Testament*. Cambridge: Cambridge University Press, 1999.

Weitzman, Steven. "Plotting Antiochus's Persecution." *Journal of Biblical Literature* 123.2 (2004): 219–34.

Wellhausen, Julius. *Der Text der Bücher Samuelis untersucht*. Göttingen: Vanderhoeck und Ruprecht, 1871.

Westbrook, Raymond. "The Laws of Biblical Israel." In *The Hebrew Bible: New Insights and Scholarship*. Edited by Frederick E. Greenspahn, 99–119. New York: New York University Press, 2008.

White, Hayden. *Tropics of Discourse: Essays in Cultural Criticism*. Baltimore, MD: Johns Hopkins University Press, 1978.

Whybray, Norman. *Reading the Psalms as a Book*. JSOTSup 222. Sheffield, UK: Sheffield Academic Press, 1996.

Wieck, Roger. *Painted Prayers: The Book of Hours in Medieval and Renaissance Art*. New York: George Braziller, 1997.

———. *Time Sanctified: The Book of Hours in Medieval Art and Life*. New York: George Braziller, 1988.

Wiesel, Elie, and Timothy K. Beal. "Matters of Survival: A Conversation." In *Strange Fire: Reading the Bible after the Holocaust*. Edited by Tod Linafelt, 22–35. Sheffield, UK: Sheffield Academic Press, 2000.

Williams, James. *Gilles Deleuze's "Difference and Repetition": A Critical Introduction and Guide*. Edinburgh: Edinburgh University Press, 2003.

———. *Gilles Deleuze's "Logic of Sense": A Critical Introduction and Guide*. Edinburgh: Edinburgh University Press, 2008.

———. *The Transversal Thought of Gilles Deleuze: Encounters and Influences*. Manchester, UK: Clinamen, 2005.

Williamson, H. G. M. "Do We Need a New Bible? Reflections on the Proposed Oxford Hebrew Bible." *Biblica* 90.2 (2009): 153–75.

Wills, Lawrence M. *The Jew in the Court of the Foreign King: Ancient Jewish Court Legends*. Minneapolis, MN: Fortress, 1990.

Wilson, Gerald. *The Editing of the Hebrew Psalter*. Society of Biblical Literature Dissertation Series 76. Chico, CA: Scholars Press, 1985.

———. "The Shape of the Book of Psalms." *Interpretation* 46.2 (1992): 129–42.

Wilton, Patrick. "More Cases of *Waw Explicativum*." *Vetus Testamentum* 44.1 (1994): 125–28.

Wirth, Karl-August. "Die Nachrichten über Begräbnis und Grab Bischof Bernwards von Hildesheim in Thangmars Vita Bernwardi." *Zeitschrift für Kunstgeschichte* 22.4 (1959): 305–23.

Wittgenstein, Ludwig. *The Brown and Blue Books*. Oxford, UK: Blackwell, 1958.

———. *Philosophical Grammar*. Edited by Rush Rhees. Translated by Antony Kenny. Oxford, UK: Blackwell, 1974.

———. *Philosophical Investigations*. Translated by G. E. M. Anscombe. New York: Macmillan, 1953.

Wolfson, Elliott R. "Circumcision, Vision of God, and Textual Interpretation: From Midrashic Trope to Mystical Symbol." *History of Religions* 27.2 (1987): 189–215.

Yoder, Christine Roy. *Proverbs*. Abingdon Old Testament Commentaries. Nashville, TN: Abingdon, 2009.

Zeller, Hans. "A New Approach to the Critical Constitution of Literary Texts." *Studies in Bibliography* 28 (1975): 231–64.

Zevit, Ziony. "The Common Origin of the Aramaicized Prayer to Horus and of Psalm 20." *Journal of the American Oriental Society* 110.2 (1990): 213–28.

Ziegler, Joseph. *Iob*. Septuaginta: Vetus Testamentum graecum. Auctoritate academiea scientiarum gottingensis editum XI/4. Göttingen: Vandenhoeck und Ruprecht, 1982.

Zink, James K. "Impatient Job: An Interpretation of Job 19: 25–27." *Journal of Biblical Literature* 84.2 (1965): 147–52.

Žižek, Slavoj. *The Parallax View*. Cambridge, MA: MIT Press, 2006.

Zuckerman, Bruce. *Job the Silent: A Study in Historical Counterpoint*. Oxford: Oxford University Press, 1991.

Zumthor, Paul. *Essai de poétique médiévale*. Paris: Seuil, 1972.

Zunz, Leopold. *Zur Geschichte und Literatur*. Berlin: Veit und Comp, 1845.

SUBJECT INDEX

There are several different collections and translations of the Hebrew Bible used in this text which are indicated as follows:

LXX	Septuagint Bible
MT	Masoretic Text Bible
OG	Old Greek Bible
Pesh	Peshitta, the Palestinian Syriac translation
Proto-MT	before Masoretic Text translation
Proto-OG	before Old Greek translation
Q	Qumran manuscript
Rabba	collective text from classical rabbinic literature
Theodotion	Greek translation by Theodotion
Vulgate	Latin translation

Abraham, 192–93; and Sarah, 202–203
Abraham bar Hiyya, 194
adaptationist theories of evolutionary development, 77–78
"Against the Jews" (Jacob of Serugh), 195
Aleppo codex: as base text of the HUB, 45–46; comparing Job (Leningrad codex) to the, 149; as essence of the Masoretic tradition, 40–41; historic textual development role of the, 43
American flag context, 96–97
Amos: ascertaining meaning through historical context, 81; internal recontexualization problem and dividing meaning of, 82–83; multiple meanings found in, 83; Sawyer's reconstruction of Amos 8:3, 90; semantic possibilities revealed in copy by Masoretes, 84
anchoring: genre as providing text, 85–87; identifying historical context of text for, 78, 79–80, 88–92; problem of internal recontextualization for, 82–85; spandrels instead of, 78; three ways that biblical critics' approach text, 79–80
Antiochus IV, 97, 98, 99, 102, 176, 224n28
apocalypse of Weeks, 97
archetype concept: Fox's move to hyparchetype from, 33–34; Hendel's conception of original text as, 28, 29; OHB project's aim to present text as universally valid, 34–35, 36; OHB's evidence of textual pluriformity reflecting different, 56; of original text of the book of Daniel, 31–32; of story of Susanna in book of Daniel, 32–33
architectural recontextualization, 77
Ariperga's funerary inscription, 186
Aristotle, 58
ben Asher, Aaron, 40, 42, 46
ben Asher school, 40, 41–42
Astruc, Jean, 53–54
audience: meaning as productions of texts, contexts, and, 118–19; original, 110; Rabinowitz's four-fold typology of, 227n92; as receiver of the text, 109–110; reconstructing the original author and, 208n36
Augustan Forum (Rome), 185–86
Augustine, 5
Austin, J. L., 111
authorial intention: as the basis for editorial choice, 35–37; Fox on importance of ascertaining, 93; reconstructing Proverbs' collective, 35; significances of, 107–109; texts on artifac-

tural manuscripts as incarnations of, 59–60
authority: Hendel's argument on primary text and, 31; as originalizing textual supplements, 57; telos and textual, 17–18, 109; Tov on how text is transformed and defined through, 23, 24–27, 31
authors: cultural differences in the concept of, 105; distinctions between copyists and "authors-editors," 212n58; of J document in the Pentateuch, 88; original meaning defined by the, 104–107; reconstructing the original audience and, 208n36; Samaritan Pentateuch (SamPent), 21; taking the audience into account, 109–11; traditionally anonymous scribes as, 88; two voices of in/and biblical contexts of, 105–107. *See also* copyists
Avalos, Hector, 189, 190

Bailey, George (*It's a Wonderful Life* character), 55
Bar Hebraeus, 195
Bar Salibi, Dionysius, 195
Barr, James: "back there and then" concept of, 90–92; on division of original audience and later audiences, 110; on genre as text at moment of enunciation, 86; on how the author defines the original meaning, 104; on importance of dividing original and later contexts, 89–90; on locating the range of text meaning, 81; on meaning of text within specific historical language context, 80–81; metaphor of containment used by, 218n3; on need to organize texts in hierarchy of originality, 52, 55, 57; on "power of words," 226n65; reception history as defined by, 90; on reception history as history of effects of writing, 3; regarding the necessity of original text, 57; *The Semantics of Biblical Language* by, 80
Barré, Michael L., 157
Barthélemy, Dominique, 44
Barton, John: on anchoring meaning to historical context, 75, 76; "literary competence" as defined by, 87; on locating the range of text meaning, 81; on variety of possible original texts, 15
BBC series, 8
Beal, Timothy, 164, 173
Bel and the Dragon story, 3, 213n94
Benjamin, Walter, 4, 163, 169, 200
Bennington, Geoffrey, 93, 94, 110, 112
Berlin, Adele, 145
Berlin Wall, 101
Bernward of Hildesheim, 186–87
BHQ (Biblia Hebraica Quinta), 144–45
Biblia hebraaica (Kittle), 40
Biblia hebraica stuttgartensia, 6
biblical reception history: Barr's definition of, 90; book of Job used to illustrate model of repeated textual experimentation, 142–62; borders of the original context and the reader's context, 2, 4–5, 9–13; Choi's definition of, 7; comparing original text used in traditional versus, 15–16; considering reception history as story of text capacities, 140–41; framework for a processual, 119–31; "history of consequences" approach to, 4; importance of discerning contours of constitutional boundary of, 3; nomadic reception history model of, 131–41; reader horizon and historical horizon considered in, 9–10, 208n31; "scrapbook of effects" of many studies of, 8; traditional statement beginning study of, 3–4; typical disinterest in theories of reception in, 7–8; where to begin with a study of, 1–2, 13–14. *See also* history; reception-historical studies
biblical scholars: how authoritative text is treated by, 23–27, 31; interested in reconstructing the historical context of text, 74; reconceiving their task as mapping of the process of text development, 68–74; text critic and historicist literary critic roles played by, 14

biblical text: Collins on the inherent ambiguity of all, 84–85; comparing alternative historic perspectives of, 4–5; comparing critical text to eclectic, 213n104; considered as processes and not essences, 65–74; considering reception history as story of capacities of, 140–41; constructions of legitimate textual filiation of, 27, 31; defining the relationship between historical context and, 76; dialogic, 98–99; displaced migrant metaphor of, 202–203; divide between virtual potential and actual expression in every, 206; drift as essential characteristic of, 109; durability characteristic of, 93–94; examining how ontology determines how to approach the, 58–74; as exemplars of contextual mobility, 102–104; "finalization" of, 90–91; Hendel's eclectic theory to manage diversity of, 27–33; meaning as productions of readers, contexts, and, 118–19; network of signs that comprise a, 68–69; nomadic distributions to categorize, 141, 205–206; nonsemantic impact of, 136; as objectiles (object-projectiles), 116–17, 139–140, 222n66; "postdivide" period of, 44–45; reading process of, 138–140, 232n21; shift from "written prophecy" to "literary prophecy," 106–107; "social production" concept of, 63–64; telos and authority of, 17–18, 109; three ways of contextualizing, 79–80; Tov on how authority defines and transforms, 23–27; transmutation process of, 133–36; tripartite schema model's approach to meaning of, 5; "the trope of death" used in, 145–47, 155, 168; where to begin a study of reception history of, 1–2, 13–14. *See also* borders/boundaries; original text

Biblical Text and Its Afterlives, A (Sherwood), 4

biblical text composition: Astruc's multiple-sources argument on Genesis, 53–54; ending of the developmental process of, 48; the great divide impact on, 42–44, 48–50; loss of pluriformity of, 48–50; process of textual formation, 137; "social production" concept of, 63–64; Talmon on the four main stages of development of, 45; text as process conception of, 65–74; Ulrich on development and, 46–49

biblical text development: how translation impacts, 169–170; intertwined with reading process, 133; process of textual formation, 132–33, 137

biblical text identity: author's intentions and, 59–60; Cerquiglini on pluriformity as part of, 66; considering text as a process to define, 65–74; as defined by multiple and different versions, 67; determined by future events and contexts, 101–102; how categorizations can rely on preconceived notions of, 141, 205–206; nominalism approach to define, 61–65, 67, 73; problem of the "Bibles" versus "Bible," 72–73; realism approach to define true, 58–61, 67, 73; repeatability of signs contributing to, 69–71; semiotic codes contributing to, 64–65; thought of as means of difference, 71

biblical textual criticism: Barton on identifying generic expectations of culture as essence of, 85; of biblical text within boundaries of original context, 4; comparing original text used in traditional versus reception history, 15–16; considering reception history as story of text capacities, 140–41; Eagleton's periodizing history of modern literary theory approach to, 5–6; "eisegesis" practice of, 6; ethics inherent in the practice of, 69; examining borderline of original text from receptions to reframe, 2, 4–5, 9–13; external conditions and procedures of text's transmission described by, 18; Gadamer's impact of reader horizons and historical horizons approach to, 9–10, 208n31; Hendel's editorial theory of, 27–33; how the ontology of text determines approaches to, 58–74; illusion of borders in, 52–55; making and remaking border distinctions, 12–13; Miltonesque narrative and modern task of, 50–51; moving beyond essentialism, 117; New Critics approach to, 5, 107, 226n81; nominalism approach to, 61–65, 67, 73; realism approach to, 58–61, 67, 73; relationship between problems and solutions driving, 124–27, 205; rethinking from perspective of pluriform text, 46–50; Ricoeur's tripartite schema model's approach to, 5, 6; role of historical context in, 79–80; semiotic codes providing insights into signifying structure of, 64–65; similarities between narratives of Christianity and modern, 216n180; spandrels instead of anchors for, 78; task of determining historical context to determine meaning, 76–77; text as a process approach to, 65–74; textual recontextualization concept used in, 78; Tov's definition of, 55; urtext theory of, 17, 18, 28–29, 38–39, 42, 44–45; zookeeping metaphor for, 93–95

biblical textual multiplicity: Deleuze on dramatization of potentials of virtual, 138–39; the great divide and, 42–44; Hendel's eclectic approach used in the OHB project, 27–33; multiplicity in historical context contributing to, 97–100; radical revisions of Qumran manuscripts and, 31–32, 47; Tov on authoritative changes resulting in, 23, 24–27, 31; Ulrich's research on biblical text composition and, 46–49; "virtual multiplicity" notion of, 121–22, 128–29. *See also* pluriformity

"biblical theology" movement, 89–90

Bickermann, Elias, 97, 98

bildad, 147

binding *tefillin* practice, 138

Blackfoot Confederacy borders, 11–12, 13

Blackwell Bible Commentary series, 3

Bloch, Ernst, 197–98

"blood avenger" figure, 197–98, 199

Borbone, Pier Giorgio, 28

borders/boundaries: of "the Americas," 12; as being nonexistent, 11; fluidity of text and gloss, 211n34; historical events creating the Blackfoot Confederacy, 11–12, 13; how pluriformity complicates any, 75–76; the illusion of biblical text, 52–55; as internal differentiation that allows for changing meaning, 206; mapping book of Job to discover constitutive, 143–62; between original and reception contexts, 2, 4–5, 9–13; original audience and later audiences, 110; original context used to local original and reception, 75; scholarship remaking of distinctions of, 12–13; separate or clarification function of, 11; Stanley Fish's work on, 208n18; as transient and open to change, 12. *See also* biblical text

Borges, Jorge Luis: "The Garden of the Forking Paths" on Ts'ui Pên by, 116, 138–39; "Pierre Menard: Author of the Quixote" by, 83–84; quote by, 15; on translations of Homeric epics, 37

Bowley, James, 48–50, 72

Boyarin, Daniel, 192–93

Bryant, Levi, 129

Buechner, Frederick, 243n154

Bynum, Caroline Walker, 177, 184

Byzantine architecture, 77, 219n11

Byzantine Jewish graveyard (Venosa, Italy), 187–88

Calvin, John, 90

Cassuto, Umberto, 187–88

categorization: nomadic distribution for, 141, 205–206; sedentary distribution for, 141, 232n20

Celan, Paul, 180

Cerquiglini, Bernard, 65–66, 69

Cervantes, Miguel de, 83–84

chess game, 127–28

Choi, John, 7
Christian community: death liturgies practiced by, 179–83; debate over resurrection within the, 171–79, 239n70; funeral monuments of the, 183–89; Jewish Pesh adopted by Syriac-specking, 192–95
Christianity: early liturgies of, 180; funerary monuments and epitaphs, 184–89; similarities between narratives of modern text criticism and, 216n180; tracing the history of Bible reception in, 4. *See also* resurrection
circumcision, 192–93
Clines, David: critique of the Platonic structure of text criticism by, 62–63; on Job's "belief that God is his enemy," 182; on semantic node of justice in book of Job, 152–54
Collins, John J.: on the ambiguity of text, 84–85; comparing proto-OG Daniel and proto-MT Daniel, 29; on locating the range of text meaning, 81; on placing the Bible in its historical context, 76, 88; on role of historical context in text criticism, 79–80; on structure of the text of Exodus, 131; on synchronic contextualization in historical-critical methodology, 81
community: acceptance of text because of alterations made, 56; court system providing legal traditions of, 148; death liturgies practiced by, 179–83; debate over resurrection in Christian, 171–79; funerary monuments inscribing survival of the, 183–89; God's destruction of Job's, 148, 156; Job's faith that God will restore his, 156; Qumran, 42, 90; religious identity created through reception of text by, 34–38, 42–47; Saadiah Gaon on survival and essential role of, 188–89; Samaritan, 17, 20; "systems of intelligibility" of, 119; text constructed the interpretative, 8, 119; Tov on authority to change text held by the, 23, 24–27, 31. *See also* Jewish community
Community of the Renewed Covenant, 42. *See also* Qumran manuscripts
context: authorship in/and biblical, 105–107; coexistence of inside and outside, 100–102; as creating meaning, 111, 113–14; determined or determinable nature of, 95–104; determining American flag, 96–97; dialogic text, 98–99; examples of historiographical problem of, 97–98; iterability of signs in multiple, 109; meaning as productions of readers, texts, and, 118–19; meaning determined by future events and, 101–102; as open and not closed, 96–100; recontextualizations of foreign, 227n100; texts as exemplars of mobility of, 102–104; various meanings and ways to use term of, 95. *See also* historical context; original context
copying: phantasms (poor copies), 59; Plato's realism approach on poor versus authentic, 58–59; postmodern perception of problematic original distinction from, 217n32; as source of both text survival and corruption, 61
copyists: adding the story of Susanne to Daniel, 32–33, 63; considering mistakes made by, 56; distinctions between "authors-editors" and, 212n58; *maggihim* (professional Talmud correctors), 23; meaning of original Don Quixote and that added by, 83–84; Samaritan Pentateuch (SamPent), 21; scribal alterations made by, 26, 43; Tov's distinguishing between authors-editors and, 20–22. *See also* authors
Cox, Claude, 168
cultural objects: action of sky bluing example of, 117–18; Nietzsche's process-oriented study of, 116. *See also* objectiles (object-projectiles)
culture: book of Jeremiah functioning as part of larger system of, 65; conception of author determined by, 105; Levenson on the Bible read in context of, 218n3; multiple ways to con-

strue interactions within, 96; resistance to restatements of the problem due to, 229n25; textual criticism task of identifying generic expectations of, 85
Cyril of Jerusalem, 174

Daniel, book of: Aramaic court stories (chapters 2–6), 53; Bel and the Dragon story in, 3, 213n94; characterization of Nebuchadnezzar in, 218n48; comparing OG and MT, 72, 73; comparing OG and Syro-Hexaplar, 212n85; comparing proto-OG and proto-MT, 29–30, 53; examining Hendel's archetypes in the, 29–31; 1QM, 31; formation and re-formation in the Dead Sea Scrolls of, 213n93; 4Q242 and 4Q530, 31; 4Q243–45 and 4Q552–53, 31; historiographical problems of context in, 97–98; Maccabean-era chapters (chapters 7–12), 53; Qumran manuscripts showing multiplicity of, 31–32, 47; story of Susanna in, 32–33, 63, 213n94, 216n169; textual "finalization" of, 91
Darwin's theory, 77
David's Compositions (11Q5 27.2–11), 86–87
de Lagarde, Paul, 18, 23, 24, 46, 71
Dead Sea Scrolls Publication Project, 17
death: "death after life" (Luke 23:46), 185; 1 Clement use of sleep as metaphor for, 171; funerary monuments commemorating, 183–89, 199; Job 19:25–27 as rejection of, 164; "the trope of death," 145–47, 155, 168. *See also* resurrection
death liturgies, 179–83
Deleuze, Gilles: alluding to nature of context, 93; on biblical texts studied as objectiles, 116–17; on determining a point of view, 141, 205–206, 224n33; on different perspectives of a battle, 223n18; on "disjunctive synthesis" of history, 99; on distinction between virtual and actual, 119–24, 154, 205; on dramatization during reading process, 138–39; reimagining biblical reception history using concepts of, 205–206; rethinking relationship between problems and solutions, 124–27, 205; on sedentary distribution to categorize, 141, 232n20; on thinking in terms of topology, 127–31, 205; "virtual multiplicity" notion of, 121–22, 128–29
Derrida, Jacques: death liturgy during wake of Gadamer spoken by, 180; on iterability of signs, 109; "Nachleben" notion of, 4; on open nature of context, 98; on polysemy as dissemination, 228n102; text as part of differential network, 73; textual supplement created through attempts to change meaning, 112–13
Deuteronomy, book of: contextual openness of reading evidenced in, 94; reliance on deictics or indicators, 94–95
Dhorme, Édouard, 166
dialogic text, 98–99
Dionysius bar Salibi, 195
Dobbs-Allsopp, F. W., 76
"dog" linguistic sign, 69–70, 71
domesticated camels, 221n62
Don Quixote (Cervantes), 83–84
dramatization, 138–39
drift (text), 109
Driver, Samuel, 166, 177
Duhm, Bernard, 160

Eagleton, Terry, 5
"Early Christian and Jewish Interpreters" (Gunn), 4
eclectic theory of text criticism: OHB project's application of Hendel's, 27–33; Provers as possible goals of Hendel's "reverse," 33
Eco, Umberto, 108
Egyptian hieroglyphs, 136
Eilberg-Schwartz, Howard, 96
"eisegesis" practice, 6
Elihu, 165
Eliphaz, 147
Encyclopedia of the Bible and Its Reception (EBR), 3–4

Enochic Animal Apocalypse, 97
Epictetus, 100
Epiphanius of Salamis, 174
"escaping" text, 93–95
essentialism, 117
Euclidean view of triangle, 129, 130, 131
Eutychius, bishop of Constantinople, 178
Ewald, Heinrich, 159–160
Exodus, book of: Greek Septuagint version of the, 132; history of readings revealing tendencies of, 140–41; liberatory capacity of, 119, 140; producing divergent meaning in various reading settings, 131; the Yahweh of, 198
Ezekiel, book of, 143

fall of Berlin Wall, 101
"finalization" of text, 90–91
1 Samuel: 4QSam, 22, 24; Masoretic preservation of so-called corrupt text of, 41
Fish, Stanley, 119, 208n18
Flavian of Vercelli, Bishop, 185
Flint, 21
form criticism: contributions to the study of ancient text by, 85–87; on genre as providing anchor to text to its context, 85
Foucault, Michel, 99, 105, 119, 203
4Q242 (4QPrayer of Nabonidus), 213n93
4QpaleoExod, 20–21
4QReworked Pentateuch (reclassified as 4QPentateuch), 20–21
4QSam, 22, 24
Fox, Michael: concerns over textual nihilism, 69; on discerning the correct readings within possible readings, 121; on history of textual development of Proverbs, 33–38; on importance of ascertaining authorial intention, 93; moving from Hendel's archetype to hyparchetype, 33–34; nominalism argument of, 61; on Platonic distinction between ideal text and manuscripts, 59–60; on relativistic acceptance of every text-form as valid, 36–37; on three possible meanings of a Hebrew word in Proverbs, 120
French Resolution, 101
Freud, Sigmund, 101
funerary monuments: inscribing survival in the book of Job, 183–89; literature of survival as form of, 184; *Wissenchaft des Judentums practice for,* 187–88, 199

Gadamer, Hans-Georg, 8–9, 180
"Garden of the Forking Paths, The" (Borges), 138
Genesis, book of: ANE backgrounds to certain stories in the, 215n161; Astruc's multiple-sources argument on composition of, 53–54; comparing ancient Israelites and Augustine's understanding of, 5; concept of authorship taken out of context in, 104; historical context of, 82
genre of text: as context, 85–87; Israelite cultic song genres, 86–87; as key to original meaning, 86
God. *See* YHWH (God)
Goshen-Gottstein, Moshe: communal commitments signaled by, 40; natural priority of the MT assumed by, 44; original text as defined by, 16; practical reformulation of textual criticism approach by, 45; review of history of text criticism by, 43–44; on "strict philological evidence" of different readings, 30; textual criticism as study of extant texts by, 38–42
Gossa ordinaira, 240n79
Gould, Stephen Jay, 77
Gray, George, 166
great divide: description and significance for textual history, 42–44; as divide between virtual potential and actual expression, 206; implications for original context by, 50; loss of pluriformity during, 48–50
Greenstein, Edward, 143
Gregory the Great, 178–79
Gunkel, Hermann, 85–86, 145
Gunn, David, 4

Habakkuk in Pesher Habakkuk, 7
Habel, Norman, 142, 144, 145, 151, 152, 153–54
Habib ibn Hidma, 195
Hankins, Davis, 144
Hebrew Bible: BHQ (Biblia Hebraica Quinta) version of, 144–45; *Biblia hebraica stuttgartensia* critical edition of the, 6; definitions of proto-MT, proto-OG, and proto-Samaritan Pentateuch editions of, 19; focus on history of interpretation within Jewish or Christian contexts of, 7; Gossa ordinaira, 240n79; Jubilees seen as attempt to rewrite the, 49; NJB (New Jerusalem Bible) of, 149; NRSV (New Revised Standard Version) of, 149; Oxford Hebrew Bible (OHB) project, 27–33, 56; Pesh (Syriac translation), 190–95; placed in its historical context by restoring text anchors, 76–78; recovery-of-life trope metaphors found in, 155–56; return-to-life trope metaphors found in, 155, 176; significant textual diversity before the common era by, 17; Theodotion translation of, 73, 184, 198–99; Tov's distinguishing between authors-editors and copyists of the, 20–22; Vulgate translation of, 176–77, 239nn64, 68. *See also* LXX (Septuagint); Samaritan Pentateuch (SamPent); individual books
Hebrew Bible (MT): Aleppo's original status as first production of the entire, 41; comparing proto-OG Jeremiah and, 21–22, 41; continuous changes made to, 26; differences between OG and, 17, 210n13; pluriform text of the, 47; relationship between OG version of Daniel and, 72, 73; similarities between modern textual critics and the, 43; stabilization during late Second Temple period, 29; textual divergence between OG and, 35–36; textual stabilization of the proto-MT, 18–19; Tov on text developments later than the, 19–20; variance found even within the, 67; variants found within the, 43–44, 47
Hebrew Bible (OG): Armenian and Coptic daughter translations of, 59; differences between MT and, 17, 210n13; Göttingen edition of, 165–66; priest Josephus' claim on using text derived from, 24; relationship between MT version of Daniel and, 72, 73; story of Susanna (book of Daniel) from, 32–33; textual divergence between MT and, 35–36; Tov on suitability for text criticism of, 59; Tov on variant edition of Jeremiah in, 19. *See also* Job (OG)
Hebrew Bible (proto-MT): as the "Bible," 37; comparing proto-OG Daniel 4–5 and, 29–30, 53; development and similarities of the, 24; examining the authority of originality for, 23–27; hyparchetype of Proverbs, 34; Oxford Hebrew Bible (OHB) project representation of, 28, 56
Hebrew Bible (proto-OG): comparing MT Jeremiah and, 21–22, 41; comparing proto-MT Daniel 4–5 and, 29–30, 53; Fox on hyparchetype of Proverbs, 34; Oxford Hebrew Bible (OHB) project representation of, 28, 56; as the "reception of the Bible," 37
Hebrew University Bible (HUB): Aleppo codex of base text of the, 40–41, 43, 45–46; practical textual pluriformity with recovery of true text, 38–46; Tov's service editor of the, 17
Hendel, Ronald: archetype concept of original text by, 28, 29, 31–33; on "definitive text" concept, 37–38; eclectic theory of textual criticism developed by, 27–33; on Goshen-Gottstein's egalitarian textual ontology, 39; original text as defined by, 16; on "primary readings" versus "secondary readings," 28–29; Proverbs as possible goal of "reverse eclecticism" of, 33; so-called epistemological problem of, 30–31
hermeneutics, 219n5

Hervey, Sándor, 88–89
Hesychius of Jerusalem, 174
Hexapla (Origen), 48, 137, 198
hierarchy. *See* original text hierarchy
Hirsch, E. D., 104, 105, 108, 113
historical context: anchoring meaning to, 78, 79–80, 88–92; Barr on meaning of text within specific, 80–81; considering the problematic character of, 126; defining the relationship between a text and, 76, 219n15; domesticated camels used as datable real referent, 221n62; hermeneutics concern with, 219n5; multiplicity of, 97–100; task of reconstructing text's, 74. *See also* context; original context
historical horizon of reading, 9–10
historical-critical scholarship: argument supporting genre as context, 85–87; Barr's "back there and then" concept for, 90–92; biblical criticism role of, 79–80; determining meaning by determining the historical context, 76–77, 219n15; limitations of "contextualization" practice in, 92; meaning of Amos ascertained through historical context, 81, 82–83; problem of internal recontextualization for identifying context, 82–85; reconstructing the historical context of text task of, 74; synchronic contextualization notion of, 81–82. *See also* meaning
historiographical problem of context, 97–98
history: acting as advocate in act of writing, 200; as weapon to harm even the dead, 200–201; *Wirkungsgeschichte* (or "history of effects"), 8, 207n7. *See also* biblical reception history
Homeric epics translations, 37
Horace, 172
horizon of expectations, 10–11
human body: debate over the materiality resurrection of, 177–79; God's Incarnation of flesh, 194–96; as locus of divine-human interaction, 192–94; metaphors of recovery of the wasted, 234n40
hyparchetype concept: Fox's expansion from archetype to, 33–34; of proto-MT Proverbs, 34, 35

ideal text: approaching text as process to identify, 65–74; nominalism approach to identifying, 61–65, 67, 73; Platonic distinction between material text (manuscripts) and, 59–60; Platonic realism approach to identifying, 58–61, 67, 73; Proverbs conceived as differential, 71. *See also* original text
identity. *See* biblical text identity
Instructions of Amenemope, 132
intention. *See* authorial intention
interlingual transmutation, 133
internal recontextualization problem, 82–85
interpretive communities, 119
intersemioic transmutation, 133, 134
intralingual transmutation, 133
Irenaeus, 90–91
Iron Curtain, 101
Israelite cultic song genres, 86–87
It's a Wonderful Life (film), 55

J document, 88
Jacob of Serugh, 195
Jakobson, Roman, 133
Jameson, Frederic, 89
Jauss, Hans-Robert, 8, 10–11
Jehudah, Joseph ben, 194
Jeremiah, book of: comparing proto-OG and MT versions of, 21–22, 41; functioning as part of larger cultural system, 65; HUB edition of, 17; Masoretes' use of the proto-OG, 57; Tov on the proto-OG variant edition of, 19; two versions of a joke in MT and OG, 108
Jerome: support for resurrection of human body by, 177–78; Vulgate translation by, 176–77, 239n68
Jerusalem temple: acts of the Seleucids at the, 100; Amos 3:3 as reference to the, 121; rededication to

Zeus Olympios (167 BCE), 98. *See also* Second Temple period
Jewish community: Christian construals as denigrating and marginalizing, 200; Christian massacre of Worms (1096), 200; Qumran, 42, 90; Shoah (Holocaust) of, 130, 131; *Wissenchaft des Judentums* practice for funerary monuments, 187–88, 199. *See also* community
Jewish funerary epigraphy, 187–89
Jewish revolt (132 CE), 48
Job (OG): as challenging interlinear paradigm of the LXX translation, 235n9; Job's recovery of life in, 170–79, 234n46, 235n53; survival trajectory of, 165–89. *See also* Hebrew Bible (OG)
Job, book of: borderline separating Original text from receptions of, 2; comparing MT with Qumran versions, 143; differences between different manuscripts of the, 137; Janus parallelism in, 236n21; Job's courtroom fantasy, 148, 233n35; mapping Job 19:25–27, 142–62; Office of the Dead's readings from the, 183; relationship between problems and solutions in the, 124; shared imagery between Lamentations, Psalms, and, 146; "structural mutation" in some texts of, 130; Theodotion translation of, 198–99; three semiotic codes found in the, 149–61; trajectories of Job 19:25–27, 163–201; transmutation example of musicians' effect on Job's pain in, 135; "the trope of death" used in the, 145–47, 155, 168; "visiocentricity" or "privileging of vision" of the, 190; where to begin study of reception history of, 1–2
Job content mapping (19:25–27): determining literary contexts, 145–48; discovering constitutive boundary and potential meaning through, 162; initial context(s) of, 144–48; of justice, survival, presence semantic nodes, 149–61; overview of the, 142–43; question of the initial context, 143–44
Job's justice trajectory (19:25–27): on the blood avenger figure, 197–98, 199; exploring the tension between the actual and the virtual, 201; Job's courtroom fantasy, 148, 233n35; kinsman-redeemer of, 198–99; providing hope for possibility of ultimate justice, 197; question of character of God in, 196–201; on tension between law and justice, 196
Job's presence trajectory (19:25–27): circumcision allowing vision of God, 192–93; exploring the tension between the actual and the virtual, 201; God's Incarnation of flesh, 194–96; Jewish Pesh translation and interpretation of, 194–95; overview of, 189–190
Job's survival trajectory (19:25–27): death liturgies, 179–83; exploring the tension between the actual and the virtual, 201; funerary monuments inscribing survival, 183–89; Job's recovery of life, 170–79, 234n46, 235n53; John Chrystostom's opinion on Job's hope for resurrection, 175; LXX Job's immanence of resurrection, 170–79; Nicene Creed association with, 182; OG Job's recovery of life, 165–170; overview of, 163–65; Severus of Antioch's comments on, 174–76
John, the bishop of Jerusalem, 177
John Chrysostom, 175
Johnson, Luke Timothy, 5
Jonah, book of: Christian interpretation of, 4; examination of *Nachleben* (afterlife) of the, 4
Josephus, 43, 47, 91, 97
Josephus (priest), 24
Joshua, book of: comparing different versions of the, 215n162; Zionist context reading of, 119
Journal of Jewish Studies, 64
Jubilees, 49

Judaism: great divide period, 42–44, 48–50; Jerusalem temple, 98, 100, 121; lack of privileged text or canon within, 24, 48–49; *maggihim* (professional Talmud correctors) form used in, 23; tracing the history of Bible reception in, 4; *Wissenchaft des Judentums* practice for funerary monuments symbolic of resurrection, 187–88, 199. *See also* Qumran manuscripts; rabbinic literature; Second Temple period
Julian the Arian, 174
Justa from Cordoba tombstone, 185
justice: "blood avenger" figure of, 197–98, 199; Job 19:25–27 semiotic code on, 149–55; Job 19:25–27 trajectory on, 196–201; Job's courtroom fantasy, 148, 233n35

Kahle, Paul, 71
kaige-Theodotion (story of Susanna), 32
Kanizsa triangle, 52
Keller, Catherine, 173
Kenny, E. J., 16
Ketef Hinnom silver rolls, 57
ketib-qere (scribal alternations), 26, 43
King, Thomas, 1, 11–12
kinsman-redeemer, 198–99
Kissinger, Henry, 101
Kraeling, Emil, 157
Kugel, James, 7

Lamentations, 146
Lange, Armin, 19, 106
language: flexible enough to be adaptable, 102–103; repeatable and identifiable signs for functional, 102. *See also* linguistic system; utterances
Lefébure mispronunciation, 67
Leningrad codex: comparison of Aleppo codex and, 40–41, 149; modern shift to Aleppo codex from the, 43
Lenzi, Alan, 120, 121
Levenson, John, 131
Lewontin, Richard, 77
Lewysohn, Ludwig, 200
"life after death" (Job 19:25–26), 185
Linafelt, Tod, 163, 164
linguistic signs: biblical text identity through repeatability of, 69–71; as having three elements of sign, object, and interpretant, 218n43; indicating author intention or lack of intention, 107–109; iterability of, 109; nature of written, 103; signifier and signified relationship as definition of, 70–71, 111–12. *See also* signified; signifiers
linguistic system: Deuteronomy's reliance on deictics or indicators, 94–95; distinction of synchronic and diachronic aspects of, 80; "dog" sign, 69–70, 71; Saussure's individual speech acts (*parole*) and *langue*, 79; semantic nodes of the, 64–65, 149–61. *See also* language
"literacy prophecy," 107
"literature of survival" concept, 163
"live beyond," 164, 180, 183
"living over," 164
"living through," 164, 173
Luhmann, Niklas, 96
LXX (Septuagint): copying mistakes in the, 56; Greek and Latin translations of book of Job in, 174; how translation impacts the meaning of, 169–170; Job (OG) challenging interlinear paradigm of the Job in, 235n9; Job's immanence of resurrection, 170–79; NETS (New English Translation of the Septuagint), 169; pluriform text of, 47, 67; Proverbs 5:22a absence from the, 35; Proverbs 9:12, 166. *See also* Hebrew Bible

Maas, Paul, 33
Maccabean revolt, 126, 224n28
maggihim (professional Talmud correctors), 23
Maimonides: Aleppo codex relied upon by, 40; textual traditions of the, 41–42
Mannheimer, Moses, 200
manuscripts: functioning as part of larger cultural system, 65; measurable ef-

fects on the history of text by, 61; as phantasms, 60; Platonic distinction between ideal text and material text of, 59–60; semiotic codes and identity of specific, 64–65. *See also* Qumran manuscripts
Martin, Gary, 43
Martindale, Charles, 8
Marx, Karl, 54
Masnut, Samuel ben Nissim, 193–94
McCall, Richard, 180
McCarter, Kyle, 61, 73
McGann, Jerome, 63, 64
meaning: borders as internal differentiation allowing for changing, 206; context as creating, 111, 113–14; defined by the author, 104–107; determined by first determining historical context, 76–77; determined by future events and contexts, 101–102; determining American flag context and, 96–97; distinction between virtual and actual, 119–24, 154, 205; divide between reception history and original is also a divided, 74; of *Don Quixote* original and copies, 83–84; examining borderline of original text from receptions to reframe, 2, 4–5, 9–13; as function of relations, 111–13; genre of text as key to text's original, 86; historical context of Amos and, 81, 82–83; horizon of expectations impacting, 10–11; mapping book of Job to discover constitutive boundary and, 143–62; as productions of texts, contexts, and readers, 118–19; reading process producing, 138–140; significance compared to, 227n87; as substitution for signifiers, 112; tension between reader horizon and historical horizon for, 9–10, 208n31; textual supplement created through attempts to change, 112–13; of utterances by speakers, 220n42; Wittgenstein's theory of, 228n107. *See also* historical-critical scholarship; original meaning
medieval Jewish tombstones, 187–88
Meir, Rabbi, 43
Menard, Pierre, 83–84
Mesopotamian flood myth, 3
Mesopotamian hymnody, 86
migrant text metaphor, 202–203
Milikowski, Chaim, 64
Miller, Patrick, 103–104
Moralia in Job (Gregory of Great), 178
Mozarabic liturgy, 181–82
MT (Masoretic Text). *See* Hebrew Bible (MT)
multiplicity. *See* biblical textual multiplicity

Nachleben (afterlife) [book of Jonah], 4
"Nachträglichkeit" (after-the-fact restructuration), 102
Native Americans: the displacement, 11–12, 13; reading book of Joshua in context of, 119
Nehemiah, book of, 120
NETS (New English Translation of the Septuagint), 169
New Critics, 5, 107, 226n81
Newsom, Carol, 85, 144
Nicene Creed, 182
Nicholls, Rachel, 8
Nietzsche, Friedrich, 75, 116
nihilistic relativism, 61–62
"nine choirs of angels" image, 187
Nissinen, Martti, 107
NJB (New Jerusalem Bible), 149
Noah's flood story, 3
Noegel, Scott, 106
nomadic distributions: categorization of text using, 141, 205–206; Deleuze's "point of view" for using, 141, 205–206, 224n33; semantic nodes that exemplify procedure of, 149–61
nomadic reception history: advantages of the, 203–204; considering reception history as story of text's capacities, 140–41; introduction to, 131–32; nomadic distributions of reception, 141, 149–61; offered as new model of biblical text, 203–206; overview of the

four processes of, 132–33; process of nonsemantic impact, 132, 136; process of reading, 133, 138–140; process of textual formation, 132–33, 137; process of transmutation, 133–36
nominalism: Clines's less extreme, 62–63; counterarguments and debates over, 62–65; denial inherent in the, 67, 73; Fox's diachronic perspective of, 61; original text hierarchy rejected by, 65; universals rejected by, 61
nonsemantic impact process: introduction to the, 132–33; of the Rosetta Stone, 136; tracing the history of a text, 136
non-Tiberian MT text, 44
Noth, Martin, 54
Noy, David, 188
NRSV (New Revised Standard Version), 149
Ntedika, Joseph, 181
Numbers, book of, differences beteen Ketef Hinnom and MT texts of, 57

objectiles (object-projectiles): Deleuze on studying biblical text as, 116–17; reading process providing compelling study of, 139–140, 222n66. *See also* cultural objects
Office of the Dead (Roman Catholic Church), 182–83
officio defunctorum, 185
OG (Old Greek) text. *See* Hebrew Bible (OG)
Olympia, 175
"On the Genealogy of Morality" (Nietzsche), 116
Ordines romani, 180
Ordo defunctorum, 180–81
Origen, 1, 48, 137, 174, 198, 238n55
original audience, 110
original context: Barr on importance of dividing later contexts from, 89–90; definition of the, 13; "escape" of text from their, 93–95; examining the borders between reception and, 2, 4–5, 9–13; the great divide implications for, 50; historical context for anchoring the text to, 77, 78–80, 82–87, 88–92; Job 19:25–27 mapping exercise to discover initial and, 143–48; locating the boundary between original and reception by means of the, 75; pluriformity found in, 46–50; problematic concept of, 204–205; resignification principle of each new reading of, 47–48; schematizing definitions of original text by pointing to, 14; "social production" concept of, 63–64. *See also* context; historical context
original meaning: defined by the author, 104–107; divide between reception history and, 74; various definitions of, 75. *See also* meaning
original sin narrative, 5
original text: Barr on the necessity of, 57; Barr's concept of hierarchy of, 52, 55, 57; comparing traditional and reception history use of, 15–16; constructed under authority of legitimate textual filiation, 27, 31; definition of the, 13, 14; differentiated from later (corrupt or altered) versions, 14; distinguishing between secondary readings and primary or, 28–29, 57; examining the borders that impact the meaning of, 2, 4–5, 9–13; Hayman on illusion of, 216n171; imagining a world without an, 55–58; Oxford Hebrew Bible (OHB) project's archetype definition of, 28; paradoxical moment of final origin of, 18–23; postmodern perception of problematic copy distinction from, 217n32; schematized by pointing to original context, 14; so-called epistemological problem of identifying, 30–31; Tov's definition and discernment of, 15–16, 18, 29, 39; Ulrich on eight possibilities for meaning of, 46–47; ways of determining the identity of the secondary and, 13–14. *See also* biblical text; ideal text

original text hierarchy: Barr on need to organize texts on basis of, 52, 55, 57; labeling alterations as errors or corruptions, 65; nominalism's rejection of, 65; Platonic text criticism building a qualitative, 58–61
Orwell, George, 69
Ottosen, Knud, 183
Oxford Hebrew Bible (OHB) project: aim to present text as universally valid archetype, 34–35, 38; as effort to "restore" text to its earlier state, 28; as genuinely eclectic edition, 27–28; original text defined as archetype in the, 28, 29, 31–32; proto-MT and proto-OG represented in the, 28; textual pluriformity showed in the, 56

Parker, Herschel, 107–108
parole (individual speech acts), 79
Paul: authorship by, 104; resurrection description by, 170
Paxton, Frederick, 180–81
Pentateuch: boundary between composition and reception of the, 7; 4QReworked Pentateuch (reclassified as 4QPenateuch), 20–21; J document of, 88; surplus of variants and editions for the books of, 31
Persher Habakkuk, 7
Peshitta (Syriac translation of Hebrew Bible), 190–92
Peshitta Job, 177
Philo, 43, 91
"Pierre Menard: Author of the Quixote" (Borges), 83–84
Platonic text criticism: on good versus poor ("phantasms") copies, 58–59; nihilistic opposition to idealism of, 61–62; nominalism counterargument to, 61–65; realism approach of, 58–61, 67, 73
pluriformity: arguments on the loss of biblical text, 48–50; in biblical text contexts, 46–50; Cerquiglini on text identity existing through its, 66; the great divide impact on, 42–44; how it complicates any boundary of textual criticism, 75–76; HUB's goal of practical textual, 38–46; irreducible biblical text, 67; Oxford Hebrew Bible (OHB) project's evidence of, 56; Qumran manuscripts and synchronic, 17–18, 47, 54, 67. *See also* biblical textual multiplicity
"point of view": Deleuze on determining a, 141, 205–206, 224n33; Deleuze's example of different perspectives of a battle, 223n18
"Pragmatic Approach to *Wirkungsgeschichte*, A" (Rowland), 8
presence: Job 19:25–27 semiotic code on, 149–150, 159–61; Job 19:25–27 trajectory on, 189–96, 201; therapeutic theophany of, 197
primary text. *See* original text
problem-solution relationship, 124–27, 205
processual reception history framework: relationship between problems and solutions component of, 124–27, 205; on thinking in terms of topology, 127–31; on the virtual and the actual, 119–24, 154, 205
proto-MT (Masoretic Text) text. *See* Hebrew Bible (proto-MT)
proto-OG (Old Greek) text. *See* Hebrew Bible (proto-OG)
Proverbs, book of: analogy of children in textual criticism of, 37; as anthology of anthologies, 33; "author" of the collectivity that makes up, 35; authorial intention in the OG, 35; as both text and translation, 132–33; claiming that wisdom resides with the divine, 196; conceived as differential ideal, 71; concept of authorship taken out of context in, 104; difficulty of discerning core of identity of, 58; Fox's argument on history of textual development of, 33–38; Fox's three possible meanings on Hebrew word used in, 120; hyparchetype of proto-MT, 34, 35; Instructions of Amenemope source for verses in, 132; as

possible goal of Hendel's "reverse eclecticism," 33; realism approach to text criticism of, 58, 59–60; reception history of OG, 34; textual divergence between MT and OG in, 35–36
Psalms, book of: ancient audience of, 110; David's Compositions (11Q5 27.2–11), 86–87; decontextualization of, 103–104, 226n80; generic shifts evidenced in, 85–86; Israelite cultic song genres found in the, 86–87; mixed-genre nature of, 85; Psalm 91 functioning as apotropaic text, 136; recovery-of-life trope metaphors in the, 155; return-to-life trope metaphors in the, 155; Second Temple period understanding of, 87; shared imagery between Lamentations, Job, and, 146; thanksgiving psalms related to survival, 234n40
Pudd'nhead Wilson (Twain), 107–108

Quine, W. V. O., 15
Qumran community: loss of textual pluriform tradition of the, 42; rewriting of biblical texts by interpreters of the, 90
Qumran manuscripts, 31; "back there and then" application to, 90; borderline scrutiny of the, 7; comparing MT book of Job with versions among the, 143; 11Q11, 136; as evidence of biblical canon development, 63; evidence of copying versus intentionally insertion of new material, 20–21; 1QM (Daniel), 31; 4Q242 and 4Q530 (Daniel), 31; 4Q242 (4QPrayer of Nabonidus), 213n93; 4Q243–45 and 4Q552–53 (Daniel), 31; 4QpaleoExod, 20–21; 4QReworked Pentateuch (reclassified as 4QPenateuch), 20–21; 4QSam, 22, 24; "nonaligned" texts comprising the, 210n15; Qumran Targum (11QtgJob), 137; synchronic pluriformity discovered in the, 17–18, 47, 54, 67; textual multiplicity of, 31–32, 42, 54. *See also* Community of the Renewed Covenant; Judaism; manuscripts

rabbinic literature: ideological and theological interpretation incorporated by, 24; pluriform text of, 47; Rabbinic Targum, 177; semiotic codes providing insights into signifying structure of, 64–65; as undermining traditional text-critical ideology, 64; the Zohar, 193–94. *See also* Judaism
Ramses II (pharaoh), 120
Rashi, 199
"Rayleigh scattering," 118
reader horizon in reading, 9–10, 208n31
reading process: Buechner's example of the, 243n154; Deleuze on dramatization during the, 138–39; Deleuze on nomadic distribution to organize, 141, 205–206, 224n33; mapped over time to discern long-term tendencies of text, 140–41; meaning produced through the, 138–140; New English Bible example of forensic, 232n21; as providing more compelling objectile of study, 139–140, 222n66; textual development process interwined with, 133
realism approach: author's intention considered in, 59–60; denial inherent in the, 67; on measuring extant conflicting manuscripts, 73; Plato's ontology applied to text criticism, 58–59; recovering the ideal work using the, 59–61
reception-historical studies: Choi's definition of, 7; on the history of effects of writing rather than origins, 3; Nietzsche's process-oriented study of cultural objects applied to, 116; reader horizon and historical horizon considered in, 9–10, 208n31; traditional statement beginning, 3–4; where to begin with a, 1–2, 13–14; *Wirkungsgeschichte* (or "history of effects"), 8, 207n7. *See also* biblical reception history; history

recovery-of-life trope metaphors, 155–56
Reeves, John, 48–50, 72
Renaissance, 131
resignification principle, 47–48
resurrection: Christian doctrine of, 156; death liturgies and the, 179–83; debate over the materiality of human body in, 177–79, 239n70; funerary inscriptions expressing hope for bodily, 184–85; Jewish and Christian development of concept of, 170; Job 19:25–27 as proclaiming otherwordly, 164, 170–79, 184–85; John Chrysostom's opinion on Job's hope for the, 175; Origen's conception of the, 238n55; Origen's view of the, 174; Paul's description of the, 170; reviving metaphors to describe YHWH (God), 233n39; *Wissenchaft des Judentums* practice for funerary monuments symbolic of, 187–88. *See also* Christianity; death; survival
return-to-life trope metaphors, 155, 176
"rewritten Bible" debate, 7
"Rezeptionsgeschichte" (or "reception history"), 8
Ricoeur, Paul, 5
Ricoeur's tripartite schema model, 5, 6
Roman Catholic Church's Office of the Dead, 182–83
Romanticism (nineteenth century), 5
Rome's *centro storico,* 76–77
Rosetta Stone, 136
Roukema, Reimar, 174
Rowland, Christopher, 8
rubber ball topology, 129

Saadiah Gaon, 188–89, 243n147
Sadducces, 174
Samaritan Pentateuch (SamPent): authoritative claims of the, 25; copyists and authors of the, 21; origins of the, 17; pluriform text of the, 47, 67. *See also* Hebrew Bible
Sanders, J. A., 44, 47–48
Saussure, Ferdinand de: differential identity concept of, 72; on distinction between synchronic and dichronic study of linguistics, 80; on evolution through mispronunciation, 67; individual speech acts (*parole*) and linguist (*language*) concepts of, 79; model of the linguistic sign by, 70–71, 111–12; on semiotic codes and text identity, 64–65
Sawyer, John, 82–83, 90
Schäfer, Peter, 64
sebririn (scribal alternations), 43
2 Samuel, book of, 41
Second Temple period: authoritative text chosen during the, 18; authority to determine textual movement of originality from the, 23–27; BHQ (Biblia Hebraica Quinta) as close to text of the, 144–45; binding *tefillin* practice during the, 136; book of Psalms as understood during the, 87; distinction used to organize study of, 96; ending of the developmental process of biblical text composition during, 48–50; the great divide during the, 42–44; recognizing the historical supplements of the, 57; stabilization of the MT in the late, 29; textual traditions regarded as sacred during the, 25; Tov on moment of textual originality as soon after the, 18–19. *See also* Jerusalem temple; Judaism
secondary text: Barr on distinguishing primary and, 57; Tov on discerning between primary and, 39; ways of determining the identity of the original and, 13–14
Seleucids: acts at the Jerusalem Temple by, 100; Daniel 7–12 perspective by, 99; general religious tolerance position of the, 101
Semantics of Biblical Language, The (Barr), 80
semiotic codes: comparing different versions of book of Job, 149–61; description and function of, 64–65; of justice (book of Job), 149–55, 196–201; of presence (book of Job), 149–150, 159–

61, 189–96, 197; of survival (book of Job), 149–150, 155–59, 163–89; of survival (Saadiah Gaon), 188–89
Seow, Choon-Leong, 4, 145, 198
Septuagint. *See* LXX (Septuagint)
Severus of Antioch, 174–76, 238n58
Sherwood, Yvonne, 4
Shoah (Holocaust), 130, 131
Sicard, Damien, 180
signified: definition of, 70; ideality of "dog" and, 70–71; linguistic sign as relationship of signifiers and, 70, 111–12; respecting effects of, 228n113; significance compared to meaning, 227n87. *See also* linguistic signs
signifiers: definition of, 70; dictionary for producing network of, 112; ideality of "dog" and, 70–71; linguistic sign as relationship of signified and, 70, 111–12; meaning as substitution for, 112; semiotic codes composed of, 64–65, 149–61. *See also* linguistic signs
Silva, Moisés, 111
sky bluing action, 117–18
"social production" concept, 63–64
socioliterary conventions, 85
solution-problem relationship, 124–27, 205
Song of Miriam, 20
Song of Roland (medieval poem), 66
speech act theory, 111
Spencer-Brown, G., 96
Spinoza, Baruch, 117
"Spying out the Land: A Report from Genology" (Newsom), 85
Stuckenbruck, Loren, 31
Suriano, Matthew, 158
survival: book of Job's semiotic code on, 150, 155–59; "death after life" (Luke 23:46), 185; death liturgy practice of, 179–83; funerary monuments inscribing, 183–89; Job's survival trajectory (19:25–27), 163–89, 201; "life after death" (Job 19:25–26), 185; "literature of survival" concept, 163; "live beyond, living over, living through," 164, 173, 180, 183; reviving metaphors to describe YHWH (God), 233n39; Saadiah Gaon's semiotic code on, 188–89; thanksgiving psalms related to, 234n40. *See also* resurrection
Susanna story (book of Daniel), 32–33, 63, 213n94, 216n169
synchronic contextualization notion, 81–82
Syriac Christians, 192–95

Talmon, Shemaryahu: assumption of priority of the MT by, 44; communal commitments signaled by, 40; on four main stages of development of biblical text, 45; on one version of Scripture promulgated by the Sages, 44; on Qumran's textual multiformity refuting the urtext theory, 42; tolerance of textual pluriformity by, 30, 44
Talmud, 43
Tanselle, Thomas, 35
Tebtunis Papyri 49.6, 168
telos concept, 17–18, 109
text criticism. *See* biblical textual criticism
text development. *See* biblical text development
textual movement: authority as transforming and redefining, 23, 24–27, 31; relativistic acceptance of any text-form as, 36–37
textual recontextualization, 78
Thangmar, 186
Theododotion (Hebrew Bible translation), 73, 184, 198–99
therapeutic theophany, 197
Tiberian MT, 44
Tigay, Jeffrey, 21
tiqqunê soferim (scribal alterations), 26, 43
tombstone inscriptions. *See* funerary monuments
topology thinking: applied to reading, 130–31; chess game example of, 127–28; differential relations considered in, 127–28; shift from Euclidean view

of triangle to, 129, 130, 131; topological features of a rubber ball, 129
Torah qua Mosaic law, 7
Tov, Emanuel: assumption of priority of the MT by, 44; on authority of community to change text, 23, 24–27, 31; contributions to textual criticism by, 17; on discerning between primary and secondary text, 39; distinguishing between authors-editors and copyists, 20–22; on the Ketef Hinnom silver rolls, 57; on the moment of textual originality, 18–19; on OG as suited for textual criticism, 59; original text as defined by, 15–16, 18, 29; on reason as derived from religious identities, 34; on text's development occurring later than the MT, 19–20; on textual criticism used to describe external conditions and procedures, 18; on treatment of authoritative text, 23–27, 31; work on proto-OG and MT versions of Jeremiah, 21
translation: how biblical text development is impacted by, 169–170; Jerome's Vulgate, 176–77
transmutation process: book of Job example of, 135; comparing intralingual, interlingual, and intersemioic, 133–34; connecting communities, traditions, and discourses through, 135–36; how they emerge from text or readings, 134–35
Tremblay, Hervé, 167
triangle (Euclidean view), 129, 130, 131
tripartite schema model of biblical criticism, 5, 6
Trollope, Anthony, 82
trope system: evidence on OG Job and LXX readers' understanding of, 175–76; recovery-of-life trope metaphors, 155–56; return-to-life trope metaphors, 155, 176; "the trope of death," 145–47, 155, 168
Truth and Method (Gadamer), 8–9
Twain, Mark, 107–108

Ugaritic Ba'al cycle, 157
Ulrich, Eugene: on composition of biblical texts, 46–49; on differences between copying and intentionally inserting new material, 20, 21; on irreducible pluriformity of the biblical text, 67; on loss of pluriformity of the texts, 48; original text as defined by, 16; on pluriform text of the MT, 47; of Qumran texts as evidence of biblical canon development, 63
urtext theory of textual criticism: directed against the "postdivide" period, 44–45; Goshen-Gottstein's questioning attitude toward, 38–39; OHB's substitution of archetype concept for, 28–29; Talmon on Qumran's textual multiformity refuting, 42; Tov's argument favoring the, 17, 18
utterances: Barr concerning "power of words" and, 226n65; "context of situation" of, 221n65; of Jesus while on the cross, 237n35; understood by speakers and listeners, 220n42. *See also* language

van der Kooij, Arie, 31
Van Seters, John, 24, 54
vertification theories, 111
Vetus Latina text, 182
"virtual multiplicity": Deleuze's concept of, 121–22; finding distinction between two different, 128–29
Voloshinov, Valentin, 100
Voyager spacecraft, 109
vulgaretexte theory, 71
Vulgate text, 176–77, 239nn64, 68

Warfield, B. B., 16
Williams, James, 139
Wirkungsgeschichte (or "history of effects"), 8, 207n7
Wissenscaft des Judentums, 187–88, 199
Wittgenstein, Ludwig, 111, 113, 228n107
Wolfson, Elliot, 193
"world behind the text" schema, 5
"world in front of the text" schema, 5

"world in the text" schema, 5
writing history: acting as advocate in act of, 200; as weapon to harm even the dead, 200–201
"written prophecy," 106

YHWH (God): covenant between all living and, 94; creation of the world by, 21; circumcision as providing the vision of, 192–93; Job imagining restoration by, 156; Job's courtroom fantasy on, 148, 233n35; Job's justice semiotic code and trajectory on the character of, 149–55, 196–201; Job's presence semiotic code and trajectory on, 149–150, 159–61, 189–96, 201; on Job's suffering inflicted for no reason, 154–55; Job's survival semiotic code and trajectory on, 150, 155–59, 163–89, 201; Job's vision of, 189–190; resuscitation of the redeemer as mercy of, 157; reviving metaphors to describe, 233n39; the Yahweh of Exodus, 198

Zeller, Hans, 68, 69, 72
Zhou Enlai, 101
Zohar, the, 193–94
zookeeping metaphor, 93–95
Zophar, 147
Zuckermann, Bruce, 157
Zumthor, Paul, 65
Zunz, Leopold, 199–201
Zur Geschichte und Literatur (Zunz), 199

SCRIPTURE INDEX

There are several different collections and translations of the Hebrew Bible used in this text which are indicated as follows:

LXX	Septuagint Bible
MT	Masoretic Text Bible
OG	Old Greek Bible
Pesh	Peshitta, the Palestinian Syriac translation
Proto-OG	before Old Greek translation
Q	Qumran manuscript
Rabba	collective text from classical rabbinic literature
Theodotion	Greek translation by Theodotion
Vulgate	Latin translation

Note that 1 Maccabees, 2 Maccabees, and Qohelet have been listed with the Hebrew Bible.

Hebrew Bible

Genesis
- 1–3, **5**
- 4:10, **148**
- cf. 15:2, **146**
- 27:34–37, **106**

Exodus
- 18:21, **156**
- 24, 11, **159**
- cf. 33:20, **159**

Numbers
- 5:16–31, **106**
- 6:24–26, **57**
- 6, **202**
- 11:26, **106**
- 24:4, **156**
- cf. 35:19, **197**

Deuteronomy
- 5:1–5, **94**
- 5:3, **94–95**

Deuteronomy (LXX) 20:3, **168**

Ezekiel
- 14:14, 14:20, **143**
- 37, **91**

Ezekiel (LXX) 7:15, **168**

1 Samuel
- NRSV 10:27, **22**
- MT 16–17, **22–23**
- 17:29, **168**
- 28, **160**

1 Samuel (4QSam) 22, **24**

2 Samuel (LXX)
- 16:2, **168**
- 17:29, **168**

1 Kings 2:2, **146**

2 Chronicles 7:11, **146**

Nehemiah 4:4, **106**

1 Maccabees, **97**, **98–99**, **102**
- 3:48, **106**
- 9:8, **168**

1 Maccabees (LXX)
- 3:17, **168**
- 9:8, **168**

2 Maccabees
- 8:23, **106**
- 97–98, **102**

Job
- 1–2, **143**
- 1:1–2:13, **143**, **160**
- 1:2, 4–5, **164**
- 1:5, **167**
- 1:18–19, **143**
- 2:3, **148**, **196**
- cf. 2:5–8, 12–13, **164**
- cf. 2:11–12, **143**
- cf. 2.3, **154**

3:1–42:6, **143**
4.17, **147**
5:20, **147**
cf. 9:3, **151**
9:15–16, **148**
9:15–22, **197**
9:22–24, **196**
cf. 9:22, **148**
9:32–35, **152**, **197**
9:32, **148**
9:33–34, **148**
9:33, **152**, **153**
9:35, **148**
9.2b, **147**
cf. 10:9, **181**
cf. 12.6, **196**
13–21, **158**
14:1–22, **147**
14:7–17, **151**
14:8, **151**
14:12, **151**
14:13, **151**
14:14, **151**
14:15–17, **151**
15–21, **145**
cf. 15:20–35, **145**, **147**
16–17, **145**, **147**
16:8, **148**, **151**
16:9–16, **148**
16:13, **146**
16:17, **148**
cf. 16:18–19, **154**
16:18–22, **152**, **197**
16:19–21, **151**
16:19, **151**, **152**
17:1, **146**
17:7, **146**
cf. 18:5–21, **145**, **147**
18:19, **147**
19:2–22, **201**
19:2, **148**
cf. 19:2, **186**
cf. vs. 19:3, 23, 29, **151**
19:6–12, **148**
19:7–20, **155**, **156**
19:7–22, **145**
19:10–12, **146**
19:13–19, **148**
19:13–22, **154**, **156**
19:23–24, **154**, **155**
19:23–27, **151**
19:23, **151**
19:24, **148**
19:25–27, **2**, **142–161**, **163–201**, **197**, **201**, **205**
19:25, **148**, **151**, **155**, **157**, **181**, **186**, **200**
19:26–27, **159**
19:26, **186**
19:26a, 19:26b, **154**
19:26b–27, **154**
19:26b–27a, **156**
19:26b, **156**, **160**
19:27, **159**
cf. 19:27b, **167**
19:27c, **154**
19:29, **151**
19:381–42:6, **189–190**
19, **145**, **146**, **147**
cf. 20:5–29, **145**
20:5–29, **147**
20:26, **147**
21, **145**, **147**
23:3, **160**
cf. 23:4, **151**
cf. 23:5–7, **196**
26–27, **156**
26:5–7, **160**
31:35–37, **197**
34:32, **156**
38:1–42:6, **159**
38:1–42.6, **189–190**
38:1, **189**
42:2–6, **189**
42:5, **152**, **190**
cf. 42:7–9, **143**
42:7–17, **143**
42:10–12, **152**
42:11, **137**

Job Qumran Targum (11QtgJob), **137**

Job (LXX)
19:25, **174**
19:26, **169–170**
30:1, **168**
42:17a, **172**

Job (MT)
3:5, **198**
15–21, **165**
19:26, **168**
Job (OG)
1:1–5, **179**
1:2–3, **173**
1:5, **167**
1:21, **183**
4:1, **176**
4:5, **170**
cf. 5:27, **166**
7:1–10, **181**
10:22, **183**
14:12, **170**, **175**
14:14, **167**
cf. 16:18, **172**
cf. 17:13–16, **172**
19:2–22, **172**
19:25–27, **174**
19:25, **168**, **182**
19:26–27, **179**
19:26, **167–168**, **168**, **171**, **172**, **175**, **179**
19:26b, **167**, **168**
19:27, **168**, **173**, **178**
19:27a, **167**
cf. 19:27b, **167**
19:27c, **167**
19:30:2, **167**
21:13, **167**
cf. 21:13, **167**
42:7–17, **172**, **179**
cf. 42:13, **173**
42:17, **170**
Job (Pesh)
4:9, **192**
7:6, **192**
16:13, **192**
17:16, **191**
19:25–27, **190**, **192**, **195**
19:25, **195**
19:25b, **191**
19:26–27, **193**
19:26, **191**, **192**, **193–194**, **195**
19:27, **191–192**
19:27a, **195**
20:11, **191**
38–42, **191**
38:1, **191**
Job (Theodotion)
19:2, **199**
19:25–27, **198**, **199**
19:28, **199**
19:29, **199**
Job (Vulgate)
19:25–27, **176–177**
19:25b, **176**
19:26, **187**
Psalm (OG) 40:9–11, **168**
Psalm (11Q5) 27.2–11, **86–87**
Psalms
1, 73, 119, **87**
9:4, **155**
9, **161**
11:4, **155**
11:7, **155**, **167**
16:9–10, **156**
17:2, **167**
17:15, **156**
17:20, **155**
18:44, **155**
20, **220n39**
27:12, **151**
cf. 29:5–9, **160**
30:3, **155**, **156**
30:4, **155**
30:6, **185**
30, **85–86**
31:20, **155**
39:14, **146**
40:2, **155**
40.3, **155**
41:10, **155**
48, **111**
56:14, **156**
71:13, **161**
71:20, **161**
73:9, **105**
80:18, **155**
85:6, **155**
86:13, **156**
88:10, 15, **146**
88:17–19, **146**
91, **136**
92:11, **156**
109:17–18, **105**

113, **181**
114, **181**
119:25, **155**
119:154, **151**, **155**
119, **85**
137:3, **110**
143:2, **161**
143:3, 7, **161**
147:15, **105**
Psalms (LXX)
3:6, **171**
3, **171**
12:4, **171**
27:1, 7–9, **171**
27:7, **171**
87:6, **171**
Psalms (MT)
31:6, **185**
41:9–11, **168**
48:3, **110**
Psalm (Vulgate), 30:6, **185**
Proverbs
1–9, **36**
cf. 3:19–20, **196**
5:22a, **35**
cf. 8:22–36, **196**
8:30, **120**, **121**
9:12, **35**, **166**
18:7, **105**
18:20–21, **105**
22:17–23:11, **132**
25–29, **36**
25:1, **36**, **132**
31:10–31, **36**
Proverbs (LXX)
3:11, **168**
9:12, **166**
Qohelet 12:12 (Dead Sea Scrolls), **142**
Song 6:13, **156**
Isaiah
1:1, **156**, **167**
52:13–53:12, **91**
55:10–11, **105**
Jeremiah
1:9–10, **105**
1:11–12, **106**
9–10, **21**
Jeremiah (LXX) 14:12, **168**
Jeremiah (MT)
10:1–5, **21**
10:6–8, 10, **21**
10:11, **21**
23:33, **108**
Jeremiah (OG) 23:33, **108**
Jeremiah (proto-OG)
10:1–5, **21**
10:1–5a, 9, 5b, 11–12, **21**
Lamentations
2:15, **110**
3:2, **146**
3:5a, **146**
3:58, **161**
Amos
1:1, **167**
8:1–2, **106**
8:3, **82–83**, **90**, **121**

New Testament

Matthew 22:23, **174**
Luke 23:46, **185**
John 20:27, **173**
1 Corinthians
15:39–40, **170**
15:50, **170**
Revelation
1:20, **187**
cf. 7:7, **187**

Other Scriptures & References

1 Clement
24–27, **172**
24:2, **172**
24:3, **173**
24:4–5, **172**
26:1–3, **170–171**, **172**
CTU 1.6.III.8–9, **157**
1 Enoch, **49**
Genesis Rabba
17:1–27, **192**
17, **193**
18:1, **192**, **193**
48:1, **192**
Testament of Levi 5:4, **168**

Classical Greek References

Odyssey 10.286, **168**
Phaedrus 67d, **168**
Theogonis 1339, **168**

BRENNAN W. BREED is an assistant professor of the Old Testament at Columbia Theological Seminary. In 2012, he earned a PhD in religious studies from Emory University. He lives in Decatur, Georgia, with his wife, Catherine, and his two children, Frederick and Margaret Ann.

www.ingramcontent.com/pod-product-compliance
Lightning Source LLC
LaVergne TN
LVHW050148080826
844660LV00002B/122

* 9 7 8 0 2 5 3 0 1 2 5 2 4 *